HTML, XHTML & CSS

Sixth Edition

VISUAL QUICKSTART GUIDE

 Peachpit Press

by Elizabeth Castro

**HTML, XHTML, and CSS, Sixth Edition:
Visual QuickStart Guide**
by Elizabeth Castro

Peachpit Press

1249 Eighth Street
Berkeley, CA 94710
(510) 524-2178
(510) 524-2221 (fax)

Find us on the Web at: *www.peachpit.com*
Or check out Liz's Web site at *www.cookwood.com*

To report errors, send a note to *errata@peachpit.com*

Peachpit Press is a division of Pearson Education

ISBN: 0-321-43084-0

0 9 8 7 6 5

Printed in the United States of America

For my parents
(all four of them!)
who didn't always agree,
but who supported me anyway.

Special thanks to:

Nancy Davis, at Peachpit Press, who has given me the most perfect combination of encouragement, editing, and friendship.

Andrei Pasternak and **Mimi Heft**, and all the other folks at Peachpit Press, for all their help getting this book out.

Kate Reber and **Nolan Hester**, both formerly of Peachpit Press, for their help with earlier editions of this book.

The Web is an incredible resource. Not only do people share their knowledge freely on their Web sites, but they are also incredibly generous with their time, helpfully answering my questions, no matter how arcane. In particular, I'd like to thank **Larry Ullman**, whose *PHP for the World Wide Web: Visual QuickStart Guide, Second edition* is an excellent way to begin with PHP, and who kindly helped me polish up my first scripts *(http://www.dmcinsights.com/phpmysql/)*, **Richard Ishida**, whose tutorials at the W3C *(http://www.w3.org/International/)* on creating Multilingual Web sites are invaluable; **Patrick Woolsey**, at Barebones Software *(http://www.barebones.com)*, for very helpful and timely answers to all my encoding and BBEdit questions, **Alan Wood**, whose Unicode Resources Web site *(http://www.alanwood.net/unicode/)* was a major source of information for the Symbols and Non-English Characters chapter, **Jeffrey Zeldman**, whose online magazine, *A List Apart* *(http://www.alistapart.com)*, is an essential resource for Web designers, and **Paul Boutin**, **Douglas Bowman**, **Dan Cederholm**, **Patrick Griffiths**, **Ian Hickson**, **Molly Holzschlag**, **Steve Krug**, **Drew McLellan**, **Eric Meyer**, **John Oxton**, **Dave Shea**, **Geoff Stearns**, and **Danny Sullivan**, whose books, blogs, Web sites, and generosity I have found most inspiring.

Andreu, for his feedback, for his great Photoshop tips, and for sharing his life with me; and **my sweet kids** to whom I can finally reply, "Yes, I can play with you now."

Llumi and **Xixo**, for chasing cherry tomatoes and each other around my office and for helping me think up examples of (X)HTML documents; and the new generation of **Sky**, **Night**, and **Sir Edmund**, who we still hope might come back.

And all the readers of earlier versions of this book, who took the time to write me with accolades, questions, and suggestions.

Table of Contents

INTRODUCTION

The World Wide Web is the Gutenberg press of our time. Just about anyone can create their own Web site and then present it to the Internet public. Some Web pages belong to businesses with services to sell, others to individuals with information to share. You get to decide what your page will be like.

All Web pages are written with some form of HTML. HTML lets you format text, add graphics, sound, and video, and save it all in a text file that any computer can read.

HTML is not hard to learn or to master. It is much more an exercise in careful typing and consistency than in mind-blowingly complicated procedures. You can have a simple HTML page up and running in just a few minutes. And while there are many software programs that will create HTML code for you, writing HTML yourself means you won't have to study new software nor be limited by its features.

In this book, you'll find clear, easy-to-follow instructions that will take you through the process of creating Web pages step by step. It is ideal for the beginner, with no knowledge of HTML, who wants to begin to create Web pages.

If you're already familiar with HTML, this book is a perfect reference guide. You can look up topics in the hefty index and consult just those subjects about which you need more information.

The Internet, the Web, and HTML

Sure, you've heard of the Internet, but what is it exactly? Simply put, the Internet is a collection of computers that are all connected to each other. Many people have 24-hour, high-speed broadband connections—through DSL, cable, or satellite—while others use a modem to link their home computers during a certain amount of time each day. Regardless of the type of connection, once you're on, you and your computer become a part of the Internet and are linked to every other computer that's also connected at that moment.

The World Wide Web, for its part, is much more ethereal. It is an ever-changing, kaleidoscopic collection of hundreds of millions of documents, all of which reside someplace on the Internet and are written in some form of HTML.

HTML, or *HyperText Markup Language*, has two essential features—hypertext and universality. Hypertext means you can create a link in a Web page that leads the visitor to any other Web page or to practically anything else on the Internet. It means that the information on the Web can be accessed from many different directions. Tim Berners-Lee, the creator of the Web, wanted it to work more like a person's brain and less like a static source of data, such as a book.

Universality means that because HTML documents are saved as Text Only files, virtually any computer can read a Web page. It doesn't matter if your visitors have Macintosh or Windows machines, or whether they're on a Unix box or even a handheld device like a Palm. The Web is open to all.

Open but Not Equal

However, while HTML is available to all, that doesn't mean that everyone experiences it the same way. It's something like Central Park in New York City. You and I can both go take a walk there. However, if you live in a penthouse apartment on Fifth Avenue and I sleep on a bench, our view of the park will be quite different.

So it is with HTML. While practically any computer can display Web pages, what those pages actually look like depends on the type of computer, the monitor, the speed of the Internet connection, and lastly, the software used to view the page: the *browser*. The most popular browsers today are Internet Explorer, Firefox, Opera, and Safari with handhelds and PDAs gaining momentum every day. Unfortunately, none of these displays a Web page exactly like the next. So it turns out it's not enough to design a beautiful park, you've also got to worry about your visitor's accommodations.

But as you worry, remember that your control is limited. While the New York City Tourist Board would like to ensure that everyone has a good time in their town, they're not handing out free vouchers for rooms at the Park Plaza Hotel, and some people wouldn't accept them even if they did, preferring instead a bed and breakfast or their sister's house. You get the idea. The moral is this: People will be viewing your pages with vastly different setups. Create your pages accordingly—so that the largest number of visitors can view your page as close to the way you want them to as is possible. This book will show you how.

The Browser Wars

Now imagine what would happen if each hotel and apartment building on Fifth Avenue staked out a bit of Central Park and put a fence around it, limiting access to its own residents. It's bad enough that those of us on park benches can only glimpse in to "exclusive" areas. But, there's also the problem that folks from one hotel can't get to the piece of park that belongs to the other hotel. Instead of a rich, public resource, teeming with rollerbladers, hot dog carts, and strolling elders, the park is divided into small, sterile, isolated lots.

In 1994, Netscape Communications put up the first fences on the Web in the so-called *browser wars*. In order to attract users, they threw universality to the wind and created a set of extensions to HTML that only Netscape could handle. For example, Web surfers using Netscape could view pages with colored text, photographs, and other improvements. Surfers with any other browser would get errors and funny-looking results. Or nothing at all.

But people liked those extensions so much that they flocked to Netscape's "hotel". By 1996, it had become the most popular computer program in the world. Microsoft started fencing in its own chunk of the Web. Again, to attract users they added non-standard extensions that only Internet Explorer, Microsoft's browser, could recognize.

According to The Web Standards Project *(www.webstandards.org)*, founded by a coalition of top-flight designers disgusted with the increasing fragmentation of the Web, at the height of the browser wars, Web designers were wasting an incredible 25% of their time devising workarounds for proprietary tags, writing multiple versions of pages to satisfy each browser, and simply educating their clients about the impossibility of creating certain effects for all browsers. It was a mess.

The Push for Standards

The Web's United Nations is an organization called the World Wide Web Consortium *(www.w3.org)*, often abbreviated as W3C, and directed by the Web's inventor, Tim Berners-Lee. Its aim is to convince the Web community of the importance of universality while attempting to satisfy its thirst for beautiful looking pages. Their work is to remove existing fences and guard against new ones.

The W3C's membership list *(http://www.w3.org/Consortium/Member/List)* reads like a *Who's Who* of movers and shakers on the Web and includes such longtime players as Apple (of iTunes and iPod fame, among others), Adobe (maker of important Web design tools like Photoshop), America Online (which absorbed Netscape Communications as it imploded in 1998), Opera (makers of the Opera browsers for desktop computers and handhelds), and Microsoft (whose Internet Explorer browser took over the #1 spot from Netscape and hasn't looked back), and more modern companies like Google (the ultra-popular search engine and more), and Mozilla Corporation (makers of the popular open source Firefox browser that is the first competition Explorer has had in years). The idea is that these companies come together and agree on the standards and then try to differentiate their products with speed, ease of use, price, or other features that don't turn the Web back into the tower of Babel.

HTML 3.2: Standardization begins

The W3C's first answer to the Web's balkanization was to standardize the proprietary extensions, including some in the official specifications and removing others altogether. At the same time, they encouraged browser manufacturers to support the official HTML specifications as closely as possible, so that a Web page written to standards would behave the same way across browsers.

Attacks on the Ivory Tower

Lately (mid 2006), there has been a crescendo of rising voices complaining about the W3C's slow pace, overemphasis of the abstract, and lack of concrete results. Many Web designers, including those who led the charge for standardization, feel ignored by the W3C and its corporate backers.

Almost seven years after HTML 4.01 and XHTML became *Official Recommendations*, there is no consensus from the W3C on where we go from here. Almost eight years after CSS2 became an Official Recommendation, there is not a single browser that fully supports it, despite the fact that every major browser was developed by a member of the W3C. CSS3 is still in *Working Draft* stage, and perhaps years from completion, let alone implementation.

Some designers have taken matters into their own hands, creating extensible standards-based solutions *(http://microformats.org/)*. For more, see Jeffrey Zeldman's article "An Angry Fix" *(http://www.zeldman.com/2006/07/17/an-angry-fix/)* and John Oxton's *"No I am not bloody sorry" (http://joshuaink.com/blog/753/no-i-am-not-bloody-sorry)*.

What should you do meanwhile? For the time being, I recommend what I've always recommended: moderation. Follow the standards but don't be a slave to them. Even Ivory Soap is only 99.4% pure.

HTML 4 and CSS

The W3C's next move was much more bold. The old version of HTML joined content, structure, and formatting instructions in a single document, which was simple but not very powerful. The W3C envisioned a new system in which formatting instructions could be saved separately from the content and structure and thus could be applied not just to a single paragraph or Web page but to an entire site, if so desired. So, in the new HTML version 4, the W3C marked most of the formatting elements for future removal from the specifications. These elements would henceforth be *deprecated*, and their use discouraged. At the same time, they created the new system for formatting instructions— called *Cascading Style Sheets*, or *CSS*—to fill the gap.

The original specifications for Cascading Style Sheets mostly limited themselves to recreating HTML effects. CSS Level 2, published in 1998 and lightly updated to Level 2.1 in 2006, however, brought new capabilities, in particular the ability to position elements on a Web page with great precision. CSS could now not only recreate HTML's formatting, it could make professional looking layouts.

However, between proprietary extensions and just plain sloppy code, HTML pages themselves were still a mess. Most browsers bent over backward to accommodate them, always in slightly different ways, which just made the whole situation worse. And there was still no standard system for adding new features. HTML was simply not a sturdy enough platform upon which to build. The W3C decided that we all needed a bit of structure. Their answer was XML, or *Extensible Markup Language*.

XML and XHTML

From the outside, XML looks a lot like HTML, complete with tags, attributes, and values. But rather than serving as a language just for creating Web pages, XML is a language for *creating other languages*. You can use XML to design your own custom markup language which you can then use to format your documents. Your custom markup language will contain tags that actually describe the data that they contain.

And herein lies XML's power: If a tag identifies data, that data becomes available for other tasks. A software program can be designed to extract just the information that it needs, perhaps join it with data from another source, and finally output the resulting combination in another form for another purpose. Instead of being lost on an HTML-based Web page, labeled information can be reused as often as necessary.

But, as always, power comes with a price. XML is not nearly as lenient as HTML. To make it easy for XML *parsers*—software that reads and interprets XML data—XML demands careful attention to upper- and lowercase letters, quotation marks, closing tags, and other minutiae. In addition, there are billions of Web pages already written in HTML and millions of servers and browsers that already know how to read them.

The solution was quite clever. The W3C rewrote HTML *in* XML. This new language had all of the features of HTML and thus could be understood by every browser on the planet. And since its entire lexicon came from HTML, people who already knew HTML only had to learn a few basic syntax rules before they were off and running. And at the same time, since it used XML's syntax, it gained all of XML's power and flexibility and was a perfect foundation for CSS. It was to be the best of both worlds. It's name? XHTML.

The Push for Standards

CSS and Browser Support

While XHTML and CSS are a powerful combination, there is one small wrench that has continued to plague Web designers: browser support. While it didn't seem to be much of a problem to add extensions willy-nilly, when it comes down to serious, full support of the specifications, no browser has yet been up to the task. However, it's important to note that they've come a long way.

Netscape 6, completely reformed from its extension-madness days, now boasts good CSS support. Too bad its user base is down to less than 1 percent. Firefox 1.5, the Open Source dynamo which rose from the ashes of Netscape's demise (and was even called Phoenix and Firebird early in its history), has excellent CSS support as does Opera 9, whose user base is expanding by leaps and bounds particularly in the handheld and mobile telephone markets. And Internet Explorer, currently the most used browser, has steadily improved its CSS support, although it still has a number of glaring bugs and what sometimes seem like arrogant and obstinate omissions.

All in all, most users use browsers that support CSS either well, or very well. While the number of users on legacy browsers a few years ago might have given folks pause before contemplating a switch to CSS, that number has dwindled below 5% (some say below 2%) and continues to fall. And even many of these are on Internet Explorer 5.5 whose support, though not stellar, was really not that bad.

In short, there's never been a better time to move confidently over to CSS.

XHTML vs. HTML: What Should You Use?

And now an admission. I liked HTML. I thought it was great that you didn't have to obsess over punctuation. Maybe I'm just lazy, but I honestly believe that the Web's popularity is due in part to the fact that browsers cut us all some slack. It made it easy to write Web pages, and so all of us did. Now, a couple of billion pages later, perhaps it's time to change our ways. Or perhaps not.

There are a lot of people out there that will tell you that HTML is evil and XHTML is the *only* solution. I think that's silly. XHTML is a great improvement over HTML. It's stronger, more flexible, more powerful, more likely to be supported in the future, and can be expanded to fit any need. But I'll tell you something. Sometimes you don't need to fill every need. Sometimes, you just want to publish a simple page without stressing over every last quotation mark.

Luckily there is a lot of middle ground. There are actually three standard flavors of both HTML and XHTML. The first, called *transitional*, allows the use of the deprecated tags. The second, called *strict*, prohibits the use of any of the deprecated tags. The third flavor, *frameset*, allows both the use of deprecated tags and the use of frames, which have fallen into such disfavor that I've moved the chapter that describes them out of the book and onto my Web site *(see page 25)*. You can combine each of these flavors in varying degrees with CSS. Which combination you choose may depend on several factors. (Keep reading.)

Deciding between HTML, XHTML, and CSS:

While I don't recommend using proprietary extensions—since they leave out part of your audience—there are a lot of other options. Here are some guidelines.

- The bigger the site, the more important it is that you use CSS and XHTML. The former makes it easy to apply, edit, and update formatting across the entire site; the latter gives your page the structure it needs to make sure it lasts into the future.

- Many companies and government agencies, including the U.S. government, require that your Web page fulfill specific *accessibility* requirements in order to make their sites available to people with disabilities. In these cases, you should adhere as closely as possible to XHTML strict, with CSS for formatting. And be sure to check the company's or agency's pertinent guidelines for details in your particular case.

- Large commercial sites that want to reach the widest audience may opt for transitional XHTML, taking advantage of some deprecated tags' practically universal support, while banking on XHTML's rock-solid stability. These kinds of sites will very likely shift to the more powerful CSS as their comfort level with it grows.

- Small or personal sites may want to take advantage of HTML's easy-going syntax along with CSS's powerful formatting and an occasional deprecated tag where necessary.

- My personal choice is to use XHTML and CSS and a bare minimum of deprecated tags.

XHTML considered dangerous?

There are some who question the move to XHTML. The problem stems from the fact that in order for XHTML to be backwards compatible and work in older browsers, one small concession had to be made: it had to be sent from the server in a way that browsers already understood: labeled as *html*. The idea was that as browsers evolved, they would eventually be able to understand XHTML pages served as *xhtml*.

Unfortunately, that just hasn't happened. As of mid 2006, Internet Explorer 7, which will most likely assume the #1 browser mantle from IE 6 once it comes out of beta, still cannot understand XHTML files served as xhtml. That means that designers can still not take advantage of XML's strength and even worse, according to Ian Hickson, in *http://hixie.ch/advocacy/xhtml*, that pages written in XHTML and served as html can be more of a hindrance to the push toward standards then a help. He suggests that we should stick with HTML until browsers can serve xhtml.

But then, of course, we're stuck with the snake who devours her own tail. Personally, I favor moving towards XHTML and its promise of standardization and power rather than sticking with HTML until some mythical future when browsers will lead the way toward standards. If we all write in XHTML now, it will be in the browser manufacturers' interest to support XHTML. And then we will all reap the benefits that it promises.

```
<fieldset id="personal">

<label>Name:</label><input type="text"
name="name" size="30" /> <br />

<label>Address:</label><input type="text"
name="address" size="30" /> <br />

<label>Town/City:</label><input type="text"
name="city" size="30" /> <br />

<label>State:</label><input type="text"
name="state" size="2" maxlength="2" /><br />

<label>Zipcode:</label><input type="text"
name="zip" size="5" maxlength="5" /> <br />

<label>Customer ID:</label><input
type="password" name="code" size="8" />

</fieldset>
```

Figure i.1 *On many pages, you'll find a snippet of XHTML code, with the pertinent sections highlighted in blue.*

```
#personal label {position:absolute; left: 20px; font-
size: 90%; padding-top: .2em;}

input {margin-left: 9em; margin-bottom:.2em;
line-height: 1.4em; }
```

Figure i.2 *If the CSS code is relevant to the example, it is shown in its own box, again with the pertinent sections highlighted in blue.*

Figure i.3 *The XHTML and CSS are then displayed in one or more browsers so you can see how it looks in real life. (This example is from page 264.)*

How This Book Works

If you've ever been to a different part of your country than where you're from, you've probably noticed how the folks there talk, well, a little funny. They use different words or they say them with a different accent. And yet, you understand them just fine even if you chuckle about it in the car afterwards. That's the way it is with HTML and XHTML. In their case, they share *precisely* the same vocabulary (to the letter) but have a slightly different syntax.

Since they are so similar, I'll teach you HTML and XHTML at the same time. I'll start by explaining the syntax differences that distinguish them. And then throughout the book I will explain the vocabulary that they share. In those explanations, I use the stricter XHTML syntax **(Figure i.1)**. You can either use it as is (to write XHTML), or opt for the looser HTML syntax (to write HTML). It's up to you.

It would be tiresome to have to refer to *HTML and XHTML* all the time, so I have chosen to use the abbreviated *(X)HTML* to refer to both at once. In the few instances I use one of the individual names, you'll know that the information pertains to that language only and not to the other.

CSS is incorporated into the descriptions of (X)HTML—again, that means, *both* HTML and XHTML—as a natural extension and yet a separate tool. While the information about CSS is concentrated in Chapters 7–14, you'll find bits and pieces throughout the book, next to the part of (X)HTML to which it is most applicable **(Figure i.2)**.

In this book, I have included illustrations from the major browsers on both Windows and Mac **(Figure i.3)**. While you may stick with one browser, there's no telling what your visitors will use. I recommend getting used to how other browsers show (X)HTML.

How This Book Works

What's Changed in the Sixth Edition

The first edition of this book, published in 1996, had 11 chapters, 2 appendices, and just 176 pages. The sixth edition in your hands has 25 chapters, 6 appendices and more than 450 pages. This book has expanded and adapted as (X)HTML and CSS have grown and changed.

What's new

The curious thing this time around is that (X)HTML and CSS have not changed considerably since the last edition. That does not mean, however that the book is just a rehashing of that earlier edition, because indeed the Web itself has changed dramatically. In the three short years since the Fifth Edition, we have seen a maturing of CSS layout techniques, which we'll explore with brand new code examples in particular in Chapter 11 but throughout the CSS chapters in general, a surge in Web pages being rewritten with CSS in order to be viewed in handhelds and mobile telephones (Chapter 13), the move away from Perl/CGI in favor of PHP along with CSS formatting of form elements (Chapter 17), a veritable explosion of audio and video, which I'll help you deal with in Chapter 18, and a move toward frequently updated blogs which has led to syndication, RSS feeds, and podcasting, which we'll tackle in Chapter 25.

And although many of the other chapters have the same titles, all have been completely updated to reflect the latest browsers, the most standard XHTML and CSS techniques, and the fact that the book is now printed in glorious full color!

Internet Explorer 7

Internet Explorer 7 was still in beta as this book went to press, and so the illustrations that show Internet Explorer 7 are actually Internet Explorer 7 *beta 2* and *beta 3*. It is possible, though unlikely, that the display of (X)HTML and CSS will change slightly when the final program is released.

What's gone

Finally, I also made the difficult decision to completely remove four chapters. These are the chapters from the Fifth Edition on frames, WML (which has been supplanted by XHTML+CSS), and the two Old Way chapters on deprecated and little used formatting tags, and deprecated and even less used layout tags.

Although most of the elements described in those chapters are still considered valid though deprecated (X)HTML, they have fallen so far out of favor that few self-respecting Web page creators would touch them. I suggest you avoid them as well. However, for historical reasons as well as for completeness (perhaps you'll meet them somewhere and need to know how they work), I will make those chapters available on my Web site for download as a PDF. You can find them at *http://www.cookwood.com/html6ed/oldway*. The user name is *oldway*, and the password is *di7nosaur*.

The HTML VQS Web Site

With the Web constantly changing, it seemed most appropriate to add a dynamic element to this book: the HTML VQS 6th edition Web site *(http://www.cookwood.com/html/)*.

On my site, you'll find the full source code for every one of the examples in this book, including the (X)HTML and the CSS *(http://www.cookwood.com/html6ed/examples/)*, a list of errata, updates, articles, reviews and comments, and even the full table of contents and index.

There are also several resources available on my site that I hope you'll enjoy, including color tables, symbol and character tables, hexadecimal tables, and complete lists of both (X)HTML elements and attributes and of CSS properties and values.

Next, as I was writing this book, I amassed a collection of lesser tips and tricks that simply didn't fit on the appropriate page. I've made them all available on the site.

Finally, you'll find a lively Question and Answer Forum *(www.cookwood.com/html/qanda)* where you can post your most vexing questions—and easy ones, too. While I hang out there and will do my best to answer, there is a dedicated team of Web designers who usually beat me to the punch. If you're so inclined, feel free to step in and answer questions yourself. Your help will be greatly appreciated.

See you on the Web!

WEB PAGE BUILDING BLOCKS

1

While Web pages have become increasingly complex, their underlying structure remains remarkably simple. A Web page is made up of three principal components: *text content,* the actual headers and paragraphs that appear on the page; occasional *references* to more complex content like links, images, and perhaps Flash animations; and *markup*— instructions that describe how the content and references should be displayed. It is important to note that each of these components is comprised exclusively of text. This essential feature means that Web pages can be saved in text-only format and viewed on practically any browser on any platform. It guarantees the universality of the Web.

Web pages also include information about the language or script in which the text was written *(the encoding)* as well as the kind of markup that describes it *(doctype).*

I will devote this chapter to explaining each of these important concepts.

Note: As I mentioned in the introduction, I use *(X)HTML* to refer to both HTML 4 and XHTML 1.0 in situations where they have identical properties, as in "*(X)HTML*'s `table` element". On the other hand, for those instances in which I'm highlighting special characteristics unique to one or the other, I will use their individual names: "*XHTML* requires quotation marks around attribute values." For more details, consult *How This Book Works* on page 23.

Markup: Elements, Attributes, and Values

(X)HTML is an ingenious system of including information about the content right in a text document. This information—called *markup*, accounting for the *m* in (X)HTML—can include formatting instructions as well as details about the relationships between parts of the document. However, because the markup itself is comprised chiefly of text, the document is practically universally accessible.

(X)HTML has three principal types of markup: *elements*, *attributes*, and *values*. Later on in the book we'll also talk about *declarations* *(see page 40)* and *entities (see page 336)*.

Elements

Elements are like little labels that identify and structure the different parts of a Web page: "This is a *header*, that thing over there is a *paragraph*, and that is *important* information." Some elements have one or more attributes, which further describe the purpose and content, if any, of the element.

Elements can contain text and/or other elements, or they can be empty. A non-empty element consists of an *opening tag* (the element's name and attributes, if any, enclosed in less than or greater than signs), the *content*, and a *closing tag* (a forward slash followed by the element's name, again enclosed in greater than and less than signs) **(Figure 1.1)**.

An *empty* element looks like a combination opening and closing tag, with an initial less than sign, the element's name followed by any attributes it may have, a space, a forward slash, and the final greater than sign **(Figure 1.2)**.

In XHTML, the closing tag is *always required* In HTML, it is sometimes optional. The corresponding section in this book for each element will provide the pertinent details.

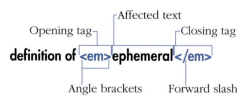

Figure 1.1 *Here is a typical (X)HTML element. The opening and closing tags surround the text that will be affected. In this case, the word "ephemeral" will be* emphasized, *which in most browsers means it will be set in italics.*

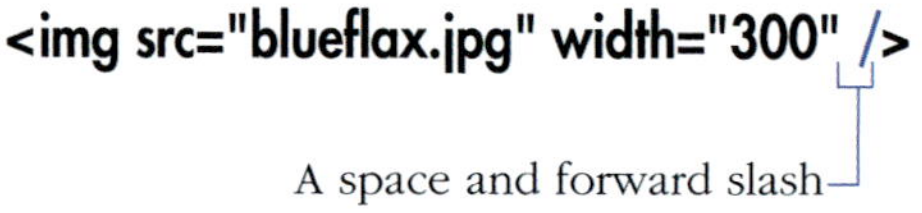

<img src="blueflax.jpg" width="300" />

A space and forward slash

Figure 1.2 *Empty elements, like* img *shown here, do not surround any text content. They have a single tag which serves both to open and close the element. In HTML the final slash is optional. In XHTML it is required.*

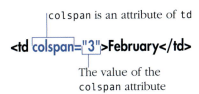

colspan is an attribute of td

<td colspan="3">February</td>

The value of the
colspan attribute

Figure 1.3 *Here is a td element (for a table cell) with a simple attribute-value pair. Attributes are always located inside an element's opening tag. Their values should always be enclosed in quotation marks.*

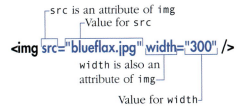

src is an attribute of img
Value for src

<img src="blueflax.jpg" width="300" />

width is also an
attribute of img

Value for width

Figure 1.4 *Some elements, like img shown here, can take one or more attributes, each with its own value. The order is not important. Separate each attribute-value pair from the next with a space.*

<link rel="stylesheet" type="text/css"
media="screen" href="blueflax.css" />

Predefined value

Figure 1.5 *Some attributes only accept specific values. For example, the media attribute in the link element can be set to screen, handheld, or print, among others, but you can't just make up a value for it.*

Attributes and Values

Attributes contain information *about* the data in the document, as opposed to being that data itself **(Figures 1.3** and **1.4)**. In XHTML, an attribute's value must always be enclosed in quotation marks. In HTML, quotes may sometimes be omitted *(see page 38)* though I recommend you always use them anyway.

While you'll find complete details about each attribute's acceptable values in this book, let me give you an idea of the kinds of values you'll run into.

Some attributes can accept any value at all, others are more limited. Perhaps the most common are those that accept *enumerated* or predefined values. In other words, you must select a value from a standard list of choices **(Figure 1.5)**. In XHTML, enumerated values are always written in all lowercase letters. (In HTML, the case doesn't matter.)

Many attributes require a number or percentage for their value, particularly those describing size and length. A numeric value never includes units. Where units are applicable, as in the height of text or the width of an image, they are understood to be pixels.

The attributes controlling color can contain values that are either a color name or a hexadecimal representation of the red, green, and blue content of the color. You can find a list of the sixteen predefined color names as well as a selection of hex colors on the inside back cover of this book. You can find instructions for creating your own hex colors on page 126. Note that (X)HTML does not support numeric or percentage values for color.

Some attributes reference other files and thus must contain values in the form of a URL, or *Uniform Resource Locator*, a file's unique address on the Web. We'll talk more about URLs beginning on page 35.

Markup: Elements, Attributes, and Values

Block vs Inline

An element can be *block-level* or *inline*. If it is block-level, it will always be displayed on a new line, like a new paragraph in a book. If it is inline, it will be displayed in the current line, like the next word in a paragraph.

Block-level elements are considered the bigger structural pieces of your Web page, and as such can usually contain other block-level elements, inline elements, and text. Inline elements, in contrast, can generally only contain other inline elements and text.

(Elements can also be *list-items*, which is considered distinct from block-level or inline, but it seems such a small category as to hardly warrant discussion outside of Chapter 15, *Lists.*)

```
<div><img src="blueflax.jpg" alt="Blue Flax (Linum lewisii)" width="300" height="175" />

<p>I am continually amazed at the beautiful, delicate Blue Flax that somehow took hold in my garden.

They are awash in color every morning, yet not a single flower remains by the afternoon.

They are the very definition of <em>ephemeral</em>.</p>

<p>&copy; 2002 by Blue Flax Society.</p>

</div>
```

Figure 1.6 *The block-level elements, shown here highlighted in bold, are* div *and* p. *The inline elements, highlighted but without bold, are* img *and* em.

Figure 1.7 *Each block-level element starts on a new line. The inline elements (in this case, the image and the italic text) continue the line begun by the block-level element in which they are contained.*

```
<div>
    <img src="blueflax.jpg" ... />
    <p>... of
        <em>ephemeral</em>
    </p>
    <p>... by Blue Flax Society</p>
</div>
```

Figure 1.8 *The* div *element is parent to the* img *and both* p *elements. Conversely, the* img *and* p *elements are children (and descendants) of the* div. *The first* p *element is parent to the* em *tag. The* em *is a child of the first* p *and also a descendant (but not a child) of the* div.

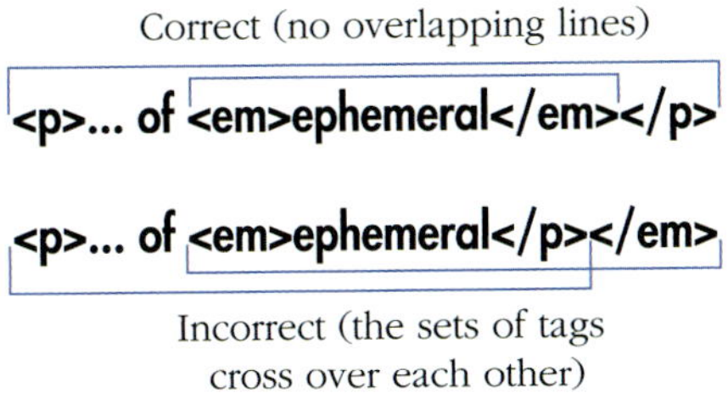

Correct (no overlapping lines)

`<p>... of <em>ephemeral</em></p>`

`<p>... of <em>ephemeral</p></em>`

Incorrect (the sets of tags
cross over each other)

Figure 1.9 *Elements must be properly nested. If you open* p *and then* em, *you must close* em *before you close* p.

Parents and Children

If one element contains another, it is considered to be the *parent* of the enclosed, or *child* element. Any elements contained in the child element are considered *descendants* of the outer, parent element **(Figure 1.8)**. You can actually create a family tree of a Web page, that both shows the hierarchical relationships between each element on the page and uniquely identifies each element.

This structure is a key feature of (X)HTML code and facilitates adding style to the elements (which we'll introduce in Chapter 7, *Style Sheet Building Blocks*) and applying JavaScript effects to them (briefly discussed in Chapter 20, *A Taste of JavaScript*).

It is important to note that when elements contain other elements, each element must be properly *nested*, that is fully contained within its parent. Whenever you use a closing tag, it should correspond to the last unclosed opening tag. In other words, first open A then open B, then close B and then close A **(Figure 1.9)**.

A Web Page's Text Content

The text contained within elements is perhaps a Web page's most basic ingredient. If you've ever used a word processor, you've typed some text. Text in an (X)HTML page, however, has some important differences.

First, (X)HTML collapses extra spaces or tabs into a single space and either converts returns and line feeds into a single space or ignores them altogether **(Figures 1.10 and 1.11)**.

Next, HTML used to be restricted to ASCII characters—basically the letters of the English language, numerals, and a few of the most common symbols. Accented characters (common to many languages of Western Europe) and many everyday symbols had to be created with special character references like **é** (for *é*) or **©** (for ©).

Nowadays, you have two options. Although you can still use character references, it's often easier to simply type most characters as they are and then encode your (X)HTML files in *Unicode* (and particularly with UTF-8). Because Unicode is a superset of ASCII—it's everything ASCII is, and a lot more—Unicode-encoded documents are compatible with existing browsers and editors. Browsers that don't understand Unicode will interpret the ASCII portion of the document properly, while browsers that do understand Unicode will display the non-ASCII portion as well. (For more details, see Chapter 21, *Symbols and Non-English Characters*.)

The only symbol that you *must* not type in directly is the **&**. Since it has special meaning in (X)HTML, namely to begin those character references, it *must always* be expressed as **&** when used as text, as in *AT&T*. For more details, consult *Adding Characters from Outside the Encoding* on page 336.

```
<div><img src="blueflax.jpg" alt="Blue Flax (Linum lewisii)" width="194" height="175" />

<p>I am continually amazed at the beautiful, delicate Blue Flax that somehow took hold in my garden.

They are awash in color every morning, yet not a single flower remains by the afternoon.

They are the very definition of <em>ephemeral</em>.</p>

<p>&copy; 2002 by Blue Flax Society.</p>

</div>
```

Figure 1.10 *The text content is basically anything outside of the markup. Note that each line happens to be separated with a carriage return. Also, I've used a special character reference* © *for the copyright symbol to ensure that it is properly displayed no matter how I save this document.*

Figure 1.11 *Note how the extra returns are ignored when the document is viewed with a Web browser and the character reference is replaced by the corresponding symbol (©).*

```
<div><img src="tigerlily.jpg" alt="Tiger Lily (Lilium
lancifolium)" width="133" height="130" />

<p>Tiger lilies are like their mammalian cousins,
hiding in the grass with their color jumping out at
you when you least expect it. </p>

<p>They are as omnipresent as the real tiger is
rare, found along so many roads and highways
that they are sometimes called <em>Ditch
Lilies</em>.</p>

<p>&copy; 2006 by Blue Flax Society.</p>

</div>
```

Figure 1.12 *In this (X)HTML document, there is a reference to a file called* tigerlily.jpg, *which the browser will access, open, and load when it loads the rest of the page.*

Figure 1.13 *Images, and other non-text content, are referenced from a Web page and the browser displays them together with the text.*

Links, Images, and Other Non-Text Content

Of course, what makes the Web so vibrant are the links from one page to another, the images, Flash animations, QuickTime movies, MP3 songs, and more. Instead of actually enclosing the external files in the (X)HTML file, these files are saved independently and are simply *referenced* from within the page. Since the reference is nothing more than text, the (X)HTML file remains universally accessible.

Most browsers can handle links and images without much trouble. They can't necessarily handle every other kind of file, however. If you reference a file that your visitor's browser doesn't understand, the browser will usually try to find a *plugin* or *helper application*—some appropriate program on the visitor's computer—that is capable of opening that kind of file. You can also give browsers extra information about how to download plugins for viewing particular files if the visitor doesn't already have one on their computer.

We'll cover images in Chapter 5, *Images,* and go over plugins and helper applications in Chapter 18, *Video, Audio, and other Multimedia.*

File Names

Like any other text document, a Web page has a file name that identifies itself to you, your visitors, and to your visitors' Web browser. There are a few tips to keep in mind when assigning file names to your Web pages that will help you organize your files, make it easier for your visitors to find and access your pages, and ensure that their browsers view the pages correctly.

Use lowercase file names

Since the file name you choose for your Web page determines what your visitors will have to type in order to get to your page, you can save your visitors from inadvertent typos (and headaches) by using only lowercase letters in your file names. It's also a big help when you go to create links between your pages yourself. If all your file names have only small letters, it's just one less thing you'll have to worry about.

Use the proper extension

The principal way a browser knows that it should read a text document as a Web page is by looking at its extension: .htm or .html. If the page has some other extension, like say ".txt", the browser will treat it as text, and show all your nice code to the visitor.

- Macintosh users—unless you're on a Mac server and *all* your visitors use Macs—this goes for you, too.

- Windows folks, be aware that Windows doesn't always reveal a document's real extension. Change your Folder Options, if necessary, so you can see extensions.

- Only people still on Windows 3.1 (all six of them) are limited to .htm. Practically everyone else can use either .htm or .html without problem. Just be consistent to avoid having to remember which one you used.

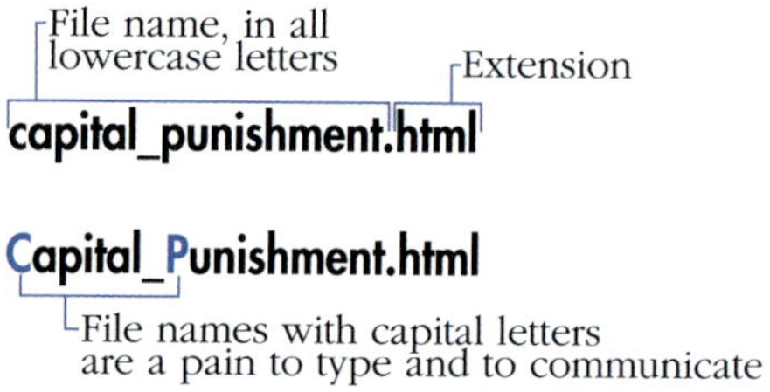

File name, in all lowercase letters ┌Extension

capital_punishment.html

Capital_Punishment.html
└File names with capital letters are a pain to type and to communicate

Figure 1.14 *Remember to use all lowercase letters for your file names and to consistently add either the .htm or .html extension. Mixing upper- and lowercase letters makes it harder for your visitors to type the proper address and find your page.*

http://www.yoursite.com/WebPages/ TORTURE/Capital_Punishment.html

Figure 1.15 *Use all lowercase letters for your directories and folders as well. The key is consistency. If you don't use uppercase letters, your visitors (and you) don't have to waste time wondering, "Now, was that a capital C or a small one?"*

Figure 1.16 *Your basic URL contains a scheme, server name, path, and file name.*

Figure 1.17 *A URL with a trailing forward slash and no file name points to the default file in the last directory named (in this case the* liz *directory). Some common default file names are* index.html *and* default.htm*.*

Figure 1.18 *When the user clicks this URL, the browser will begin an FTP transfer of the file* prog.exe*.*

Figure 1.19 *A URL for an email address includes the* mailto *scheme followed by a colon but no forward slashes, and then the email address itself.*

Figure 1.20 *To reference a file on a local Windows machine, use the* file *scheme. For Macintosh, use* file:///Harddisk/path/file-name*. No vertical bar is required. (This sometimes works for Windows as well.)*

URLs

Uniform Resource Locator, or *URL,* is a fancy name for *address.* It contains information about where a file is and what a browser should do with it. Each file on the Internet has a unique URL.

The first part of the URL is called the *scheme.* It tells the browser how to deal with the file that it is about to open. The most common scheme you will see is HTTP, or *Hypertext Transfer Protocol.* It is used to access Web pages **(Figure 1.16)**.

The second part of the URL is the name of the server where the file is located, followed by the path that leads to the file and the file's name itself. Sometimes, a URL ends in a trailing forward slash with no file name given **(Figure 1.17)**. In this case the URL refers to the default file in the last directory in the path (which generally corresponds to the home page), often called *index.html* or *default.htm.*

Other common schemes are HTTPS, for secure Web pages; FTP (File Transfer Protocol) for downloading files **(Figure 1.18)**; Mailto, for sending email **(Figure 1.19)**; and File, for accessing files on a local hard disk or local file sharing networks **(Figure 1.20)**.

A scheme is generally followed by a colon and two forward slashes. Mailto and News are exceptions; these take only a colon.

Notice that the File scheme uses three slashes. That's because the host, which in other schemes goes between the second and third slashes, is assumed to be the local computer. Always type schemes in lowercase letters.

URLs

Absolute URLs

URLs can be either absolute or relative. An *absolute URL* shows the entire path to the file, including the scheme, server name, the complete path, and the file name itself. An absolute URL is analogous to a complete street address, including name, street and number, city, state, zip code, and country. No matter where a letter is sent from, the post office will be able to find the recipient. In terms of URLs, this means that the location of the absolute URL itself has no bearing on the location of the actual file referenced—whether it is in a Web page on your server or on mine, an absolute URL will look exactly the same.

When you're referencing a file from someone else's server, you'll always use an absolute URL. You'll also need to use absolute URLs for FTP sites, or any kind of URL that doesn't use an HTTP protocol.

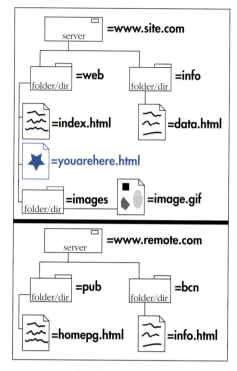

Figure 1.21 *The document that contains the URLs—*youarehere.html *in this case—is the reference point for relative URLs. In other words, relative URLs are relative to that file's location on the server. Absolute URLs don't care where they are located.*

File name	Absolute URL (can be used anywhere)	Relative URL (only works in *youarehere.html*)
index.html	www.site.com/web/index.html	index.html
image.gif	www.site.com/web/images/image.gif	images/image.gif
data.html	www.site.com/info/data.html	../info/data.html
homepg.html	www.remote.com/pub/homepg.html	*(none: use absolute)*
info.html	www.remote.com/bcn/info.html	*(none: use absolute)*

Absolute URLs vs. Relative URLs

URLs

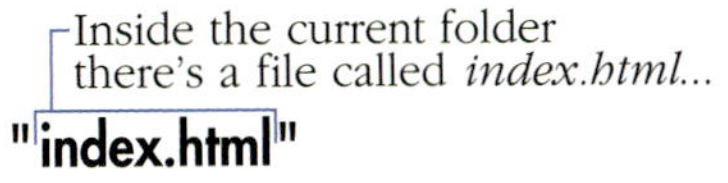

Inside the current folder
there's a file called *index.html*...

"index.html"

Figure 1.22 *The relative URL for a file in the same folder (see Figure 1.21) as the file that contains the link is just the file's name and extension.*

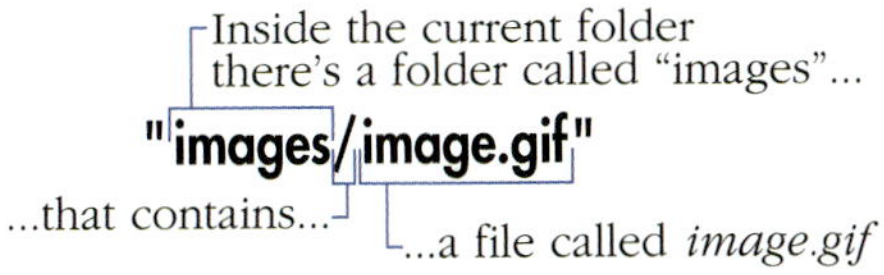

Inside the current folder
there's a folder called "images"...

"images/image.gif"

...that contains... ...a file called *image.gif*

Figure 1.23 *For a file that is within a folder inside the current folder (see Figure 1.21), add the folder's name and a forward slash in front of the file name.*

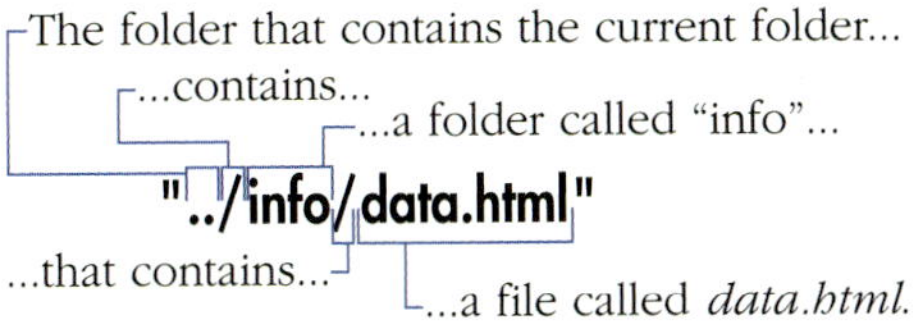

The folder that contains the current folder...
...contains...
...a folder called "info"...

"../info/data.html"

...that contains... ...a file called *data.html*.

Figure 1.24 *This file, as you can see in Figure 1.21, is in a folder that is inside the folder that contains the current folder (whew!). In that case, you use two periods and a slash to go up a level, and then note the subdirectory, followed by a forward slash, followed by the file name.*

Relative URLs

To give you directions to my neighbor's house, instead of giving her complete address, I might just say "it's three doors down on the right". This is a *relative* address—where it points to depends on where the information originates. With the same information in a different city, you'd never find my neighbor.

In the same way, a *relative URL* describes the location of the desired file with reference to the location of the file that contains the URL itself. So, you might have the URL say something like "show the xyz image that's in the same directory as this page".

The relative URL for a file that is in the same directory as the current page (that is, the one containing the URL in question) is simply the file name and extension **(Figure 1.22)**. You create the URL for a file in a subdirectory of the current directory by typing the name of the subdirectory followed by a forward slash and then the name and extension of the desired file **(Figure 1.23)**.

To reference a file in a directory at a *higher* level of the file hierarchy, use two periods and a forward slash **(Figure 1.24)**. You can combine and repeat the two periods and forward slash to reference any file on the same hard disk as the current file.

Generally, for files on the same server, you should always use relative URLs. They're much easier to type and they make it easy to move your pages from a local system to a server. As long as the relative position of each file remains constant, the links will work correctly.

One added advantage of relative URLs is that you don't have to type the scheme—as long as it's HTTP.

URLs

HTML vs. XHTML

I like to imagine HTML as a laid-back don't-sweat-the-details kind of person. Perhaps not quite as hard-working as XHTML, but much happier and at ease with herself. XHTML, on the other hand is downright uptight. Always vigilant, never taking a rest. Sure, she gets more done, but what a price!

Before I go off the deep end with my personification of Web page code types, let me tell you the specifics. For starters, know that HTML 4 and XHTML 1.0 use *precisely the same* elements, attributes, and values. The difference is in the syntax.

- Where HTML doesn't care if you use the `html`, `head` and `body` elements, and `DOCTYPE`, XHTML requires them.

- Where HTML lets you omit some closing tags, XHTML insists on them for every element, even empty ones. For the best compatibility with browsers, add a space and / to empty elements and include an independent closing tag for non-empty elements (**Figures 1.25–1.28**). Note that the slash is not strictly valid in empty elements in HTML, though all browsers I've seen simply ignore it.

- Where HTML lets you omit quotes around attribute values that contain just letters, numbers and four simple symbols (-, ., _, and :), XHTML gets nightmares (and generates errors) if you leave quotes out (**Figures 1.29** and **1.30**).

- Where HTML is flexible about case, XHTML is not, demanding that all elements, attributes, and predefined values be in lowercase (**Figures 1.31** and **1.32**).

- Where HTML allows you to omit values that have the same name as the attribute, XHTML insists that all values be stated explicitly (**Figures 1.33** and **1.34**).

```
<p>I am continually amazed at the beautiful,
delicate Blue Flax that somehow took hold in my
garden.

They are awash in color every morning, yet not a
single flower remains by the afternoon.

They are the very definition of <em>ephemeral
</em>.

<p>&copy; 2002 by Blue Flax Society.
```

Figure 1.25 *In HTML, some elements, like* p, *do not require a closing tag. Subsequent* p *tags implicitly close earlier ones.*

```
<p>I am continually amazed at the beautiful,
delicate Blue Flax that somehow took hold in my
garden.

They are awash in color every morning, yet not a
single flower remains by the afternoon.

They are the very definition of <em>ephemeral
</em>.</p>

<p>&copy; 2002 by Blue Flax Society.</p>
```

Figure 1.26 *In XHTML, all elements must have closing tags.*

```
<img src=blueflax.jpg alt="Blue Flax (Linum
lewisii)" width=300 height=175>
```

Figure 1.27 *In HTML, empty elements do not have a final slash, though browsers won't complain if they do.*

```
<img src="blueflax.jpg" alt="Blue Flax (Linum
lewisii)" width="300" height="175" />
```

Figure 1.28 *In XHTML, even empty elements must have a closing tag. While an independent closing tag for an empty element, like* </img>, *would be technically correct, adding a space and / to the single* img *tag ensures compatibility with non-XHTML-savvy browsers.*

```
<img src=blueflax.jpg alt="Blue Flax (Linum
lewisii)" width=300 height=175 align=left>
```

Figure 1.29 *In HTML, attribute values only need to be quoted when they contain spaces or other special characters (anything besides letters, numbers, hyphens, periods, underscores, or colons). So, in this example, only the* alt *attribute's value must be quoted (though it wouldn't hurt to quote all of them).*

```
<img src="blueflax.jpg" alt="Blue Flax (Linum
lewisii)" width="300" height="175" align="left" />
```

Figure 1.30 *In XHTML, all attribute values must always be enclosed in quotes.*

```
<IMG SRC=blueflax.jpg ALT="Blue Flax (Linum
lewisii)" width=300 height=175 align=LEFT>
```

Figure 1.31 *In HTML, it doesn't matter if you write element names, attribute names, or predefined values in upper- or lowercase.*

```
<img src="blueflax.jpg" alt="Blue Flax (Linum
lewisii)" width="300" height="175" align="left" />
```

Figure 1.32 *In XHTML, all element names, attribute names, and predefined values must be written in lowercase.*

```
<hr width=75% noshade>
```

Figure 1.33 *In HTML, some attributes, like* noshade *shown here, don't require any value.*

```
<hr width="75%" noshade="noshade" />
```

Figure 1.34 *In XHTML, attribute values must be stated explicitly. For those attributes that in HTML have no value, simply repeat the attribute's name as its value.*

What do you get for your troubles?

You might be wondering if it's worth it to worry about every last quotation mark. The answer is, it depends.

XHTML's rigidity affords a lot of advantages. Think of a clean workshop, with hammers and screwdrivers hanging in their places on the wall and all the nuts and bolts in labeled containers. It's so easy to find what you need that it makes projects a hundred times easier. Similarly, XHTML helps you keep your code consistent, well structured, and free of non-standard tags, which in turn makes it easier to update and edit, to format with CSS, to generate from or convert into a database, and to adapt for other systems, like handhelds.

In addition, XHTML is a logical step in the transition from HTML to XML, since it uses familiar HTML elements and attributes together with modern XML syntax. And since XHTML is the new standard, you can be sure that it will be used with other new and future technologies.

Perhaps one of XHTML's most important gifts is that its insistence on standards makes it more likely to be properly and consistently supported by current browsers, on all platforms—which makes good business sense. And since Web page accessibility is now required by U.S. law, and the laws of many other nations, it is something that should not be ignored. For more information on accessibility laws, visit the W3C Web Accessibility Initiative at *http://www.w3.org/WAI/.*

For more details about why standards matter, I recommend a trip to The Web Standards Project (*http://www.webstandards.org*), a consortium of designers turned diplomats determined to end the browser wars, and Jeffrey Zeldman's *A List Apart*, an excellent online magazine for Web designers (*http://www.alistapart.com*).

HTML vs. XHTML

Versions, Flavors, and DOCTYPE

There are three current flavors of both HTML 4 and XHTML 1.0: *strict, transitional,* and *frameset.* In an attempt to separate structure from formatting, the W3C has been earmarking some elements for eventual removal from the specifications. (X)HTML strict is characterized by its prohibition of these so-called *deprecated* tags. The only difference between transitional and frameset, both of which consider deprecated tags to be valid, is that the latter allows frames (which you can find out more about on my Web site).

Does it matter which version you use? The flip answer is "not to me". I think it's perfectly reasonable to use HTML and depend on its easy-going nature if you're writing a personal site. If you want your pages to follow strict standards, take advantage of XHTML's ability to connect to databases and the like, work well with styles, and be easily updated for future systems, use XHTML.

Likewise, if you use deprecated tags, you should use the transitional flavor of either HTML or XHTML. No deprecated tags? Use strict. If your site uses frames, use the frameset flavor. Note that there is no strict flavor that allows frames—which clues you in about what the W3C thinks of them.

You can state which version and flavor you're using in your document by using a DOCTYPE *declaration (see page 56).* Once that information is part of your Web page, you can use a validator to determine if the code used in your page actually corresponds to the code allowed for that version and flavor. Validators are a great way to check for typos and in general, to make sure your code is correct. For more details, see page 345.

Note that there are earlier versions of HTML (3.2 and earlier), but they are outdated and not particularly useful.

```
<!DOCTYPE html

    PUBLIC "-//W3C//DTD XHTML 1.0
Transitional//EN"

    "http://www.w3.org/TR/xhtml1/DTD/xhtml1-
transitional.dtd">
```

Figure 1.35 *Here is the official* DOCTYPE *for XHTML transitional documents. You can find a list of* DOCTYPE *declarations on my Web site. (They're rather a drag to type in manually.)*

Versions, Flavors, and DOCTYPE

```
body {background:url(bg_flax.jpg) bottom right no-
repeat}

p {font-family: "Trebuchet MS", "Helvetica", sans-
serif; font-weight: bold; color:3366cc; }

img {float:left;margin-right:10px}
```

Figure 1.36 *Some browsers, notably Internet Explorer, do not care if you leave out the initial hash sign (#) for a hexadecimal color. While you may think that's nice of them, it lets Web developers write bad code which then breaks on other browsers.*

Figure 1.37 *If you omit the* DOCTYPE, *Explorer continues to act in its non-standard, quirky way, and displays the text in blue. But it shouldn't!*

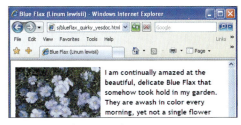

Figure 1.38 *If you use the* DOCTYPE, *IE assumes you want it to follow the standards, and so it disregards the faulty color value (and displays the text as black).*

Figure 1.39 *Once the CSS is corrected to include the missing # symbol, use of the DOCTYPE once again produces blue text (properly, in standards mode).*

The DOCTYPE and Standards vs. Quirks mode

In the old days, when each browser had its own way of interpreting HTML and CSS, Web designers often used workarounds or *hacks* that depended on a browser's quirky behavior in order to create a desired effect on a Web page.

In an effort to keep pages designed for these quirky browsers from breaking in newer browsers, later versions of Explorer and then other browsers (but not Opera) created two modes of operation: quirks and standards mode. When opening a Web page, such a browser first checks if there is a proper DOCTYPE declaration. If it finds one, it assumes the page has been designed using all the power of standards, and displays it accordingly in *standards* mode (or sometimes *strict* mode, though this is more confusing since it has nothing to do with strict (X)HTML). If there is no proper DOCTYPE declaration (or if it is omitted entirely), the browser assumes the page is old-fashioned and relies on obsolete browser bugs, and displays it in that way. This is called *quirks* mode.

This system was designed to let you write standards-based pages for the future without losing your quirks-based pages of the past. However, its very tolerance for bugs ensures that unorthodox code sticks around a lot longer. I recommend writing good, solid, standard code and not worrying about quirks mode at all.

I'll show you how to write appropriate DOCTYPE declarations on page 56.

The Default Display of (X)HTML

Every Web browser has a default system for displaying each kind of (X)HTML element. While the system may vary from browser to browser, they all maintain the basic structure that you set forth in the Web page.

So, for example, a level one header (h1) will always be set larger than a level two header (h2), which will always be larger than a level three header (h3). Similarly, an em element will always be set off from the surrounding text in order to emphasize it.

That doesn't mean that the h1 element will always be in say, 24pt Times, or that emphasis will always be achieved with italics. While the default display systems are very similar on all personal computer-based browsers—including Explorer, Firefox, and Opera on both Macs and PCs **(Figure 1.40)**, they are quite different on PDAs, cell phones, and of course, on aural browsers. And that's a good thing. The structure of the Web page is maintained but its display is adapted to fit the browser on which it appears. And that means your Web page is universally accessible and intelligible.

It doesn't mean, however, that your Web page is a work of art. A browser's default display system is typically quite generic. Luckily you can override that system by applying *styles* to your elements. We'll get to them beginning in Chapter 7, *Style Sheet Building Blocks*. First, we'll learn how to write some (X)HTML.

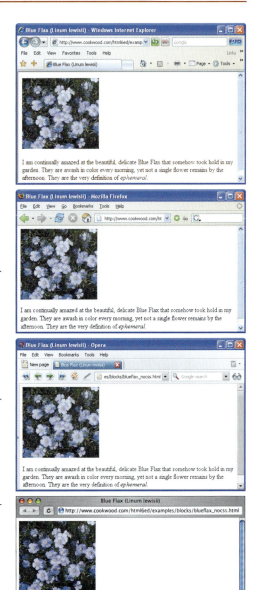

Figure 1.40 *With no styles applied, the text appears after the image, in its default font and color. Most current versions of major browsers (from the top down: IE 7, Firefox 1.5, Opera 8.54, Safari 1.3) have very similar defaults. Safari is slightly different because it's on a Mac, but it's very close to the Firefox and Opera browsers for Macintosh.*

WORKING WITH WEB PAGE FILES

2

Before you start writing (X)HTML elements and attributes, it's important to know how to create the files in which you'll use such code. In this chapter, you'll learn how to create, edit, and save Web page files. I'll also touch on some design and organizational considerations.

If you can't stand waiting any longer, and already know how to create the actual files, skip ahead to Chapter 3, *Basic (X)HTML Structure*, where I begin to explain the (X)HTML code itself.

Designing Your Site

Although you can just jump in and start writing Web pages right away, it's a good idea to first think about and design your site. That way, you'll give yourself direction and you'll need to reorganize less later.

To design your site:

1. Figure out why you're creating this site. What do you want to convey?

2. Think about your audience. How can you tailor your content to appeal to this audience? For example, should you add lots of graphics or is it more important that your page download quickly?

3. How many pages will you need? What sort of structure would you like it to have? Do you want visitors to go through your site in a particular direction, or do you want to make it easy for them to explore in any direction?

4. Sketch out your site on paper.

5. Devise a simple, consistent naming system for your pages, images, and other external files *(see page 34)*.

✔ Tips

■ Don't overdo the design phase of your site. At some point, you've got to dig in and start writing.

■ If you're not very familiar with the Web, do some surfing first to get an idea of the possibilities. You might start with Yahoo *(http://www.yahoo.com)*, Google's Web directory *(http://www.google.com/dirhp)* or even your competitors.

■ There are lots of good books on Web design. Some of the authors I recommend are Dan Cederholm, Jeffrey Zeldman, Dave Shea, and Steve Krug.

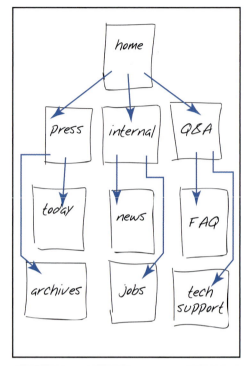

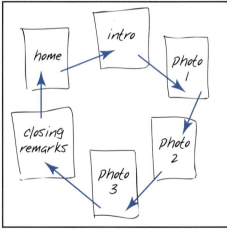

Figure 2.1 *Sketching out your site and thinking about what it might contain can help you decide what sort of structure it needs: a centralized, hierarchical model (top), a circular model that leads the visitor from one page to the next (above), or some other system.*

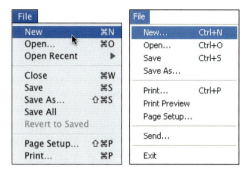

Figure 2.2 *Open your text editor or word processor and choose File > New. (Shown are TextEdit for Macintosh at left and WordPad for Windows on the right.)*

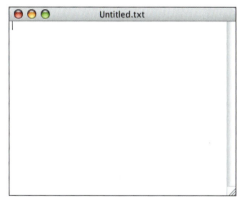

Figure 2.3 *On a Macintosh, you can use Text-Edit to write the (X)HTML code for your page.*

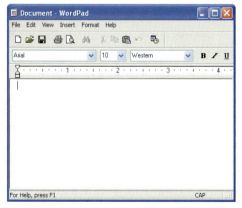

Figure 2.4 *This is WordPad, one of the programs Windows users can use to create (X)HTML pages.*

Creating a New Web Page

You don't need any special tools to create a Web page. You can use *any* word processor, even WordPad or TextEdit, which are included with the basic Windows and Macintosh system software.

To create a new Web page:

1. Open any text editor or word processor.

2. Choose File > New to create a new, blank document **(Figure 2.2)**.

3. Create the (X)HTML content as explained in the rest of this book, starting on page 55.

4. Be sure to save your file as directed on page 46.

✔ Tips

■ If you like Microsoft Word, you can use it for writing (X)HTML too. Just be sure to save the file correctly (as text-only and with the .htm or .html extension). For more details, see pages 46–48.

■ If you use Dreamweaver, or some other Web page editor to start your pages, you can still tweak the (X)HTML code by hand. Just choose File > Open from your text editor of choice and open the file. Then use the rest of this book to add your own (X)HTML tags and create the (X)HTML page *you* want.

■ You *can* use TextEdit or WordPad, but if you want to get fancy, try BBEdit for Mac or HTML-Kit for Windows. Both display (X)HTML tags in color, and have powerful search and replace functions, syntax checkers for debugging problematic pages, and assorted other helpful features. For more details, consult *(X)HTML Editors* on page 434.

Saving Your Web Page

Web pages are created with a text editor or word processor but are meant to be viewed with multiple browsers on multiple platforms. To be accessible to all of these different programs, Web pages are saved in a universal "text-only" format—without any proprietary formatting that a word processor might otherwise apply.

So that browsers (and servers) recognize Web pages and know to interpret the markup they contain, as well as distinguish them from plain text files that are not Web pages, Web page files also have the *.htm* or *.html* extension.

Because of that extension, a Web page's icon matches the system's default browser and not the word processor with which the file was written. Indeed, when you double-click a Web page file, it is opened in a browser, not a word processor. This is great for Web surfers, but it adds an extra step to editing Web pages *(see page 50)*.

In short, when you save your Web page, you must save it in text-only format with either the .htm or .html extension.

To save your Web page:

1. Once you've created your Web page, choose File > Save As from your word processor **(Figure 2.6)**.

2. In the dialog box that appears, choose Plain Text or Text Document (or however your program words it) for the format.

3. Give the document the .htm or .html extension. (This is very important!)

4. Choose the folder in which to save the Web page.

5. Click Save.

Figure 2.5 *An Excel worksheet has the .xlsx extension and is identified with the Excel icon (top). If you double-click it, it is displayed in Excel. A Web page file, no matter the word processor you create it with, has the .htm or .html extension but is identified with the default browser's icon. If you double-click it, it is displayed with your default browser (not the word processor).*

Figure 2.6 *Choose File > Save As from your word processor or text editor.*

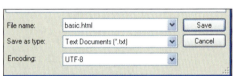

Figure 2.7 *In WordPad for Windows, give your file a name with the .htm or .html extension, choose Text Documents next to Save as type, and then click Save.*

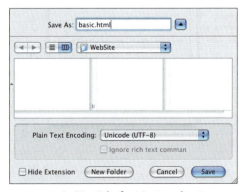

Figure 2.8 *In TextEdit for Macintosh, give your file a name, choose a location, and click Save.*

Figure 2.9 *On Windows computers, choose Tools > Folder Options to view this dialog box. Click the View tab and scroll down until you see Hide extensions for known file types. Make sure it is unchecked if you want to be able to see a file's extension (like .html) on the Desktop.*

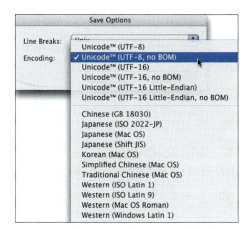

Figure 2.10 *Many word processors, like the excellent BBEdit shown, let you choose the encoding for your file, so that you can save symbols and characters from different languages in the same document. BBEdit, as of version 7, automatically saves your file with the same encoding as you will declare in your document a little later on (page 59, to be exact). It's a lovely feature!*

✔ Tips

■ It doesn't matter whether you use .htm or .html (unless you're still on Windows 3.1! In that case, use .htm.) However, consistency will make it easier to remember your URLs later.

■ Some word processors (like Microsoft Word and Corel WordPerfect to name a few) offer a "Save as HTML" or "Save as Web page" option. *Don't touch it!* That option is for folks who want to create a Web page from a word processing document without learning HTML and it completely messes up hand-written code *(see page 48)*.

■ Some text editors on Windows annoyingly add their default extension to your file name, even if you've already specified .htm or .html. Your file, now named *webpage.html.txt* won't be properly viewed in a browser. To make matters worse, Windows often hides extensions on the Desktop so that the problem is not completely obvious, especially to the uninitiated. There are two solutions. The first is to enclose your file name in double quotes when you save your document. This should keep the extra extension from being added. Next, you can display the extensions on the Desktop **(Figure 2.9)** and then select the offending extension and eliminate it. For details, see my Web site *(see page 26)*.

■ When you choose a text-only format, your file is usually saved with your system's default character encoding. If you want to create Web pages in another encoding (perhaps to include special symbols or text in other languages), you'll have to use a text editor that lets you choose the encoding **(Figure 2.10)**. For more details, see Chapter 21, *Symbols and Non-English Characters*.

Saving Your Web Page

About Microsoft Word and Web Pages

Word can automatically create Web pages from existing documents, often whether you want it to or not. Its commands are particularly confusing to Web page designers who create their own markup code—which is probably you if you're reading this book.

Word's "Web Page" file type (available in the Save dialog box and in older versions of Word as the Save as Web Page menu command) means "convert the present document into HTML, adding markup where there is formatting, and saving as text-only with the .htm extension". There are two problems with this command. First, it converts your (X)HTML tags into plain text, using special symbols. Second, Microsoft adds an incredible amount of proprietary code. If you're writing your own markup with this book, you don't want to use this option.

Instead, choose File > Save As, choose Plain Text (*.txt) from the Save as type box **(Figure 2.12)**, and then change the default .txt extension to .htm or .html **(Figure 2.13)**.

✔ Tips

- When you choose Plain Text (*.txt), Word gives you the option of saving your file with a different encoding. Click Other encoding and then choose the one you want from the list **(Figure 2.14)**. For more details, consult *Saving Your Page with the Proper Encoding* on page 333.

- Other versions of Word may have slightly different wording or dialog boxes.

Figure 2.11 *Don't choose Word's Web Page option next to Save as type! (And don't choose Save as Web Page from the File menu!) It's for converting regular Word documents into Web pages and will mess up hand-coded markup.*

Figure 2.12 *Instead, first choose Plain Text (*.txt) in the Save as type: pop-up menu and then...*

Figure 2.13 *...manually type the .html extension. Then click Save.*

Figure 2.14 *When you save a file in Plain Text (*.txt), Word gives you the option of choosing a different encoding. I recommend UTF-8.*

About Microsoft Word and Web Pages

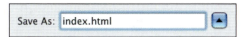

Figure 2.15 *Save the file as either* index.html *or* default.htm *in order to designate the file as the default page that should be opened in that directory.*

Figure 2.16 *When the visitor types the path to the directory, but omits the file name itself, the file with the default name is used.*

Specifying a Default or "Home" Page

Most servers have a system for recognizing a default page in each folder, based on the name of the file. If your visitors type a URL with a directory but don't specify a file name, the default file is used **(Figure 2.16)**.

To specify a default or "home" page:

1. First, ask your ISP how such a default page should be named. On most servers, use *index.html*. (Microsoft servers generally use *default.htm*.)

2. Next, when you save your file *(see page 46)*, use the proper name.

✔ Tips

- You can create a default page for any and every directory on your site.

- The default page that you create at the top level of your Web directory is your site's *home page*, the one that will appear when your visitors type your domain with no additional path information: *http://www.yourdomain.com*

- If you don't have such a default page in each directory, most servers will show a list of the directory's contents (which you may or may not want to reveal to your visitors). To keep those prying eyes out, create a default page for every directory on your site.

Editing Web Pages

Because Web pages are most often viewed with a Web browser, when you double-click them on the Desktop, the default browser cheerily opens up and displays them. If you want to *edit* the Web page, you'll have to manually open it in your word processor.

To edit Web pages:

1. Open your word processor.

2. Choose File > Open.

3. Navigate to the directory that contains the desired file.

4. If you don't see your file listed, choose the All Documents option in the Files of type box **(Figures 2.17** and **2.18)**. The name and location may vary slightly from program to program and platform to platform.

5. Then click Open. Your file is ready to edit.

✔ Tips

■ Usually, once you've made changes to an already saved document, you can simply choose File > Save to save the changes, without having to worry about the format as described on page 46.

■ Right-click the Web page's icon in Windows and then choose Edit to open the Web page in the default HTML editor or Open With and then the program of your choice **(Figure 2.19)**. On a Mac, Control-click the icon in the Finder, select Open With in the pop-up menu, and then choose the desired text editor.

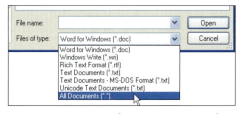

Figure 2.17 *Some word processors in Windows can't automatically see (X)HTML files. Choose All Documents if necessary to view files with any extension.*

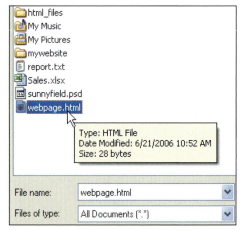

Figure 2.18 *Once files with any extension are displayed, you can choose the desired (X)HTML file and click Open.*

Figure 2.19 *In Windows, you can also right-click the document's icon and then choose Edit or Open With in the pop-up menu that appears. On a Mac, Control-click the icon, select Open With in the pop-up menu, and then choose the desired text editor.*

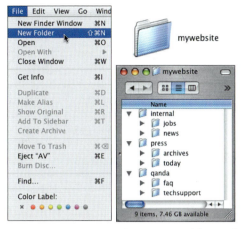

Figure 2.20 *On a Mac, choose New Folder, and then give the folder a name. Then create a separate folder for each section of your site.*

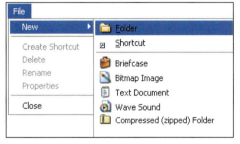

Figure 2.21 *In Windows, from the desktop or the Windows Explorer, choose File > New > Folder.*

Figure 2.22 *You can divide the folder into additional folders if needed.*

Organizing Files

Before you have too many files, it's a good idea to figure out where you're going to put them.

To organize your files:

1. Create a central folder or directory to hold all the material that will be available at your Web site. On the Mac, choose File > New Folder in the Finder **(Figure 2.20)**. In Windows, from the Desktop, choose File > New > Folder **(Figure 2.21)**. Give the folder a name.

2. Divide the folder in a way that reflects the organization of your Web site **(Figures 2.20** and **2.22)**.

3. You may decide to create a separate folder for each section of your site, along with individual subfolders for images and other external files.

4. You can create a top-level *images* folder for images that are common to all areas of your Web site.

✔ Tip

- Use simple, one-word names without symbols or punctuation for your files *and* folders. Use all lowercase letters so that your URLs are easier to type and thus your pages are easier to reach. For more details on how to create good file names, consult *File Names* on page 34.

Organizing Files

Viewing Your Page in a Browser

Once you've created a page, you'll want to see what it looks like in a browser. In fact, since you don't know which browser your visitors will be using, it's a good idea to look at the page in *several* browsers.

To look at your page in a browser:

1. Open a browser.

2. Choose File > Open, Open File, or Open Page (just *not* Open Location), depending on the browser **(Figure 2.23)**.

3. In the dialog box that appears, either type the location of the page on your hard disk, or click Browse to find it **(Figure 2.24)**.

4. If you've clicked Browse in step 3, in the new dialog box that appears, navigate to the folder on your hard disk that contains the desired Web page and click Open **(Figure 2.25)**.

5. Back in the Open dialog box, click OK. The page is displayed in the browser just as it will appear when you actually publish it on the server *(see page 353)*.

✔ Tips

■ You can (usually) also double-click a Web page's icon to view it in a browser.

■ If your Web page does not appear in the Open dialog box, make sure that you have saved it as text-only and given it the .htm or .html extension *(see page 46)*.

■ You don't have to close the document in the text editor before you view it with a browser. You do have to save it.

■ Your visitors won't be able to view your Web site until you publish it *(see page 353)*.

Figure 2.23 *From the desired browser (this is Firefox for Windows), choose File > Open File. In Explorer for Windows, it's called File > Open. In Explorer for Mac, it's File > Open File.*

Figure 2.24 *In Explorer for Windows, you'll get an intermediary box asking if you want to type the path in by hand. If you don't (and why would you?), click the Browse button.*

Figure 2.25 *Choose the file that you want to open and click the Open button (not shown).*

Figure 2.26 *The page appears in the browser. Check it over well to see if it's coming out the way you planned.*

Figure 2.27 *All browsers have a menu command that lets you view a page's (X)HTML code. The name varies from Page Source (in Firefox, shown) to View Source, to just Source.*

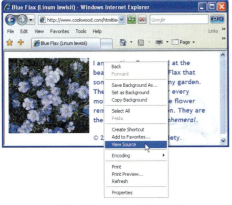

Figure 2.28 *Most browsers will also let you right-click (Control-click on a Mac) and choose the Source command (however it's called) from the pop-up menu that appears. This is Explorer for Windows.*

Figure 2.29 *Some browsers display the code in a specified text editor. Others let you choose between the default window in the browser (as shown) or your preferred text editor.*

The Inspiration of Others

One of the easiest ways to expand your (X)HTML fluency is by looking at how other page designers have created *their* pages. Luckily, (X)HTML code is easy to view and learn from. However, text content, graphics, sounds, video, style sheets, and other external files may be copyrighted. As a general rule, use other designers' pages for inspiration for your (X)HTML, and then create your own content.

To view other designers' (X)HTML code:

1. Open a Web page with any browser.

2. Choose View > Source (in some browsers, it's View > Page Source) **(Figure 2.27)**. The (X)HTML code will be displayed **(Figure 2.29)**.

3. If desired, save the file for further study.

✔ Tips

■ You can also save the source code by selecting File > Save As or File > Save Page As in most browsers.

■ Most browsers also let you right-click (or Control-click on a Mac) and then choose a source command (of varying wording) from the pop-up menu **(Figure 2.28)**.

■ For viewing CSS, see *The Inspiration of Others: CSS* on page 136.

The Inspiration of Others

BASIC (X)HTML STRUCTURE

3

This chapter covers the most basic (X)HTML elements—the ones you need to create the structure of your document. You'll learn how to create new paragraphs, headers, page breaks, comments, and more.

Creating a clear and consistent structure makes it that much easier to apply styles to your document.

Starting Your Web Page

Begin your page by using a DOCTYPE *(see page 40)* to declare what type of HTML or XHTML you're using. The DOCTYPE lets browsers know what to expect and tells validators how to judge your code in order to check its syntax. Then, signal the beginning of the actual code with the opening html tag.

To start a transitional HTML 4 page:

1. Type **<!DOCTYPE HTML PUBLIC "-//W3C //DTD HTML 4.01 Transitional//EN" "http://www.w3.org/TR/html4/ loose.dtd">** to declare that you're using transitional HTML 4.01 in your Web page.

2. Type **<html>** to begin the actual HTML portion of your document.

3. Leave a few spaces for creating the rest of your page (using the rest of this book).

4. Type **</html>**.

To begin a transitional XHTML page:

1. Type **<!DOCTYPE html PUBLIC "-//W3C //DTD XHTML 1.0 Transitional//EN" "http://www.w3.org/TR/xhtml1/DTD/ xhtml1-transitional.dtd">** to declare that you're using transitional XHTML in your Web page.

2. Type **<html xmlns="http://www.w3.org/ 1999/xhtml">** to begin the XHTML portion of your page and declare its namespace.

3. Leave a few spaces for creating the rest of your page (using the rest of this book).

4. Type **</html>**.

✔ Tips

■ Create a template with the appropriate DOCTYPE declaration and html tag as a starting point for all your pages.

```
<!DOCTYPE HTML PUBLIC
"-//W3C//DTD HTML 4.01 Transitional//EN"

"http://www.w3.org/TR/html4/loose.dtd">

<html>




</html>
```

Figure 3.1 *Here's the DOCTYPE for a transitional HTML document as well as the opening and closing* html *tags. It's a gruesome bit of text. I recommend just copying it from one document to the next instead of trying to type all that gobbledy-gook.*

HTML vs. XHTML

For a thorough discussion on whether you should use HTML or XHTML to write your Web pages, see *XHTML vs. HTML: What Should You Use?* on page 21 and *HTML vs. XHTML* on page 38. The short answer is that right now, it doesn't matter much as long as you are consistent and don't mix. If you're writing HTML, write HTML; if you choose XHTML, follow the XHTML rules. In this book, the examples are written in XHTML because XHTML encourages consistency and standards, and consistent, standards-conscious Web pages have a better chance of displaying properly and consistently across Web browsers and platforms. HTML, because it is less picky, sometimes engenders laziness. That laziness can translate to erratic or unexpected Web page display when viewed on a variety of browsers and platforms.

```
<!DOCTYPE html PUBLIC "-//W3C//DTD XHTML
1.0 Transitional//EN"

"http://www.w3.org/TR/xhtml1/DTD/xhtml1-
transitional.dtd">

<html xmlns="http://www.w3.org/1999/xhtml">




</html>
```

Figure 3.2 *Here's the* DOCTYPE *for a transitional XHTML document, the opening* html *tag and required namespace declaration, and the closing* html *tag.*

■ Both the DOCTYPE and the html element are optional in HTML (even strict HTML). XHTML requires both (with the namespace declaration in the opening html tag). Note that there is no xhtml element.

■ I've only shown how to write the DOCTYPE for transitional HTML and XHTML. You can find a list of common DOCTYPE declarations on my Web site *(see page 26)* or at *http://www.w3.org*. For help choosing an appropriate DOCTYPE, see page 40.

■ Declaring a DOCTYPE with a URL at the top of your Web page generally puts current browsers into *standards* mode— letting you use standards-compliant code in order to have more control over the display of your Web page *(see page 41)*.

■ If you use non-standard HTML tags, there's no point in specifying a DOCTYPE. Just enclose your page in opening and closing html tags. Current browsers will use quirks mode when displaying your pages *(see page 41)*.

■ Declaring the appropriate DOCTYPE tells validators which specifications to compare your code against *(see page 345)*.

■ Note that the word DOCTYPE (since it actually originated from *another* language called SGML) is typed in all uppercase letters, both in HTML and in XHTML.

■ XHTML pages, because they are XML, should technically begin with an *XML declaration* like **<?xml version="1.0" encoding="ISO-8859-1"?>**. However, such a declaration throws IE 6 for Windows unaccountably into quirks mode *(see page 41)*. It's a huge bug. Luckily, since most XHTML files are not served or otherwise treated as XML, the declaration can and should be omitted (and the encoding declared as on page 59).

Creating the Foundation

Most Web pages are divided into two sections: the *head* and the *body*. The head section is where you define the title of your page, include information about your page for search engines like Google, set the location of your page, add style sheets, and write scripts. Except for the title *(see page 60)*, the content of the head section is not readily visible to the visitor.

To create the head section:

1. Directly after the opening html tag *(see page 56)*, type **<head>**.

2. Leave a few spaces for the contents of the head section.

3. Type **</head>**.

The *body* of your (X)HTML document encloses the content of your Web page, that is, the part that your visitors will see, including the text and graphics.

To create the body:

1. After the final </head> tag, type **<body>**.

2. Leave a few spaces for the contents of your Web page (which you'll create with the help of the rest of this book).

3. Type **</body>**.

✔ Tips

■ The head and body tags are required in XHTML. They're optional in HTML but even if you don't physically type them, the browser acts as if they are there and even lets you assign styles to them.

■ Another reason to use head and body tags is for controlling when a particular script will run *(see page 312)*.

```
<!DOCTYPE html PUBLIC "-//W3C//DTD XHTML
1.0 Transitional//EN"

"http://www.w3.org/TR/xhtml1/DTD/xhtml1-
transitional.dtd">

<html xmlns="http://www.w3.org/1999/xhtml">

<head>

</head>
<body>


</body>
</html>
```

Figure 3.3 *The* head *and* body *elements help you structure your (X)HTML documents.*

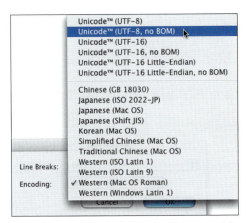

Figure 3.4 *I've saved my files in Unicode, with the UTF-8 encoding. (This is BBEdit. For more details about saving files with encodings other than the default for your system, consult Chapter 21, Symbols and Non-English Characters.)*

```
<!DOCTYPE html PUBLIC "-//W3C//DTD XHTML
1.0 Transitional//EN"

"http://www.w3.org/TR/xhtml1/DTD/xhtml1-
transitional.dtd">

<html xmlns="http://www.w3.org/1999/xhtml">
<head>
<meta http-equiv="content-type"
content="text/html; charset=utf-8" />

</head>
<body>


</body>
</html>
```

Figure 3.5 *When the visitor's browser sees this* meta *tag, it will know that the page was encoded with UTF-8, and will display it properly. The key is that the encoding that you declare in the* meta *tag match the one with which you actually saved the file.*

Declaring the Encoding

All text documents, (X)HTML files included, are saved with a character *encoding*. Since there are many encodings in use in the world, it's a good idea to declare which encoding your page was saved in right in the (X)HTML code. This makes it easier for browsers on systems with different default encodings to view the characters in your pages correctly.

To declare the character encoding:

In the head section of your page, type **<meta http-equiv="content-type" content="text/html; charset=encoding" />**, where *encoding* is the character encoding with which you saved the file.

Your Web page's character encoding depends on the way you saved it. If you saved it in a text-only format—and didn't choose a special encoding—it's a safe bet that your document was saved with the default encoding for your language. For example, the default encoding for English Windows is `windows-1252` and for English Macintosh is `x-mac-roman`.

✔ Tips

- While an encoding is not technically required by the specs, I strongly recommend you declare one.

- If you chose a particular encoding upon saving the file, that's the encoding you should use in the `meta` tag.

- You can find a list of common character set codes at *http://www.w3.org/ International/O-charset-lang.html.*

- XHTML requires that you declare the encoding if it is anything other than the default UTF-8 or UTF-16.

- For more about encodings, see Chapter 21, *Symbols and Non-English Characters.*

Creating a Title

Each (X)HTML page must have a `title` element. A title should be short and descriptive. In most browsers, the title appears in the title bar of the window **(Figure 3.7)**. Perhaps even more importantly, the title is used by search indexes like Yahoo and Google as well as in your visitors' browsers' history lists and bookmarks.

To create a title:

1. Place the cursor between the opening and closing `head` tags *(see page 58)*.

2. Type **<title>**.

3. Enter the title of your Web page.

4. Type **</title>**.

✔ Tips

■ The `title` element is required.

■ A title cannot contain any formatting, images, or links to other pages.

■ A page's title directly affects its ranking in many search engines. The closer a title is to the exact words that a potential visitor types—without any extra words—the higher up it will appear in the listings. It is also used to identify your page in the search results **(Figure 3.8)**.

■ The title is also used in History lists, Favorites lists, and Bookmarks menus to identify your page **(Figure 3.9)**.

■ If your title contains special characters like accents or some symbols, they'll either have to be part of your encoding *(see page 59)* or you'll have to write them with references *(see page 336)*.

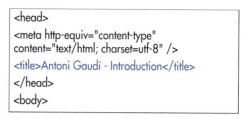

```
<head>
<meta http-equiv="content-type"
content="text/html; charset=utf-8" />
<title>Antoni Gaudí - Introduction</title>
</head>
<body>
```

Figure 3.6 *The* `title` *element should be placed in the head section. It is required.*

Figure 3.7 *The title of a Web page is shown in the title bar of the window.*

Figure 3.8 *Perhaps most importantly, the title is used to describe your page in search results from Google and others. In addition, it's purportedly one of the more important factors for determining a page's relevance and rank in search results.*

Figure 3.9 *The title also appears in your visitor's History pane (shown), Favorites list, and Bookmarks list.*

```
<head>
<meta http-equiv="content-type"
content="text/html; charset=utf-8" />
<title>Antoni Gaudí - Introduction</title>
</head>
<body>


<h1>Antoni Gaudí</h1>


<h2>La Casa Milà</h2>


<h2>La Sagrada Família</h2>



</body>
```

Figure 3.10 *You can use headers to give your document structure, like an outline.*

Figure 3.11 *The most common default display for first level headers is 24 pixels, Times New Roman, in boldface.*

Creating Section Headers

(X)HTML provides for up to six levels of headers in your Web page for separating your page into manageable chunks.

To organize your Web page with headers:

1. In the body section of your (X)HTML document, type **<hn>**, where *n* is a number from 1 to 6, depending on the level of header that you want to create.

2. Type the contents of the header.

3. Type **</hn>** where *n* is the same number used in step 1.

✔ Tips

■ Think of your headers as hierarchical dividers. Use them consistently.

■ The only official rule about headers is that the higher the level (the smaller the number), the more prominently they should be displayed. Nevertheless, the major browsers currently display them all the same: in Times New Roman, bold-face, at 24, 18, 14, 12, 10 and 8 pixels (9 pixels on the Mac), respectively.

■ You can use styles to format headers with a particular font, size, or color (and more). For details, consult Chapter 10, *Formatting with Styles*.

■ Add a named anchor (or `id`) to your headers so that you can create links directly to that header *(see page 106)*.

■ If desired, you can align the text in the header by typing **align="direction"** in the opening tag, where *direction* is `left`, `right`, `center`, or `justify`. But note that the `align` attribute has been deprecated in favor of style sheets *(see page 165)*.

Starting a New Paragraph

(X)HTML does not recognize the returns or other extra white space that you enter in your text editor (*see page 32*). To start a new paragraph in your Web page, you use the p tag.

To begin a new paragraph:

1. Type **<p>**.

2. Type the contents of the new paragraph.

3. Type **</p>** to end the paragraph.

✔ Tips

- The closing </p> tag is required both in XHTML and when applying styles to a paragraph. Therefore, I recommend always ending a paragraph with </p>. In HTML, the closing </p> tag is optional.

- You can use styles to format paragraphs with a particular font, size, or color (and more). For details, consult Chapter 10, *Formatting with Styles*.

- To control the amount of space between lines, consult *Setting the Line Height* on page 158. To control the amount of space after a paragraph, consult *Setting the Margins around an Element* on page 176 or *Adding Padding around an Element* on page 177.

- One quick and dirty (and valid) trick for adding extra space between paragraphs is to type ** ** (a non-breaking space) between each additional p element. Still, it's better to use CSS (*see pages 176–177*).

- You can align the text in the paragraph by typing **align="direction"** in the opening p tag, where *direction* is left, right, center, or justify. But note that the align attribute has been deprecated in favor of style sheets (*see page 165*).

```
</head>
<body>
<h1>Antoni Gaudí</h1>
<p>Many tourists are drawn to Barcelona to see
Antoni Gaudí's incredible architecture. </p>
<p>Barcelona celebrates the 150th anniversary of
Gaudí's birth in 2002.</p>
<h2>La Casa Milà</h2>
<p>Gaudí's work was essentially useful. La Casa
Milà is an apartment building and real people live
there.</p>
<h2>La Sagrada Família</h2>
<p>The complicatedly named and curiously
unfinished Expiatory Temple of the Sacred Family is
the most visited building in Barcelona. </p>
</body>
```

Figure 3.12 *Enclose each paragraph in opening and closing p tags. If you don't close them (which is perfectly legal in HTML but not XHTML), styles won't be applied properly.*

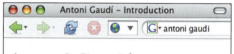

Antoni Gaudí

Many tourists are drawn to Barcelona to see Antoni Gaudí's incredible architecture.

Barcelona celebrates the 150th anniversary of Gaudí's birth in 2002.

La Casa Milà

Gaudí's work was essentially useful. La Casa Milà is an apartment building and real people live there.

La Sagrada Família

The complicatedly named and curiously unfinished Expiatory Temple of the Sacred Family is the most visited building in Barcelona.

Figure 3.13 *The amount of space between each paragraph is proportional to the size of the text.*

```
</head>
<body>
<h1 id="gaudi">Antoni Gaudí</h1>

<p>Many tourists are drawn to Barcelona to see
Antoni Gaudí's incredible architecture. </p>

<p>Barcelona celebrates the 150th anniversary of
Gaudí's birth in 2002.</p>

<h2 class="building">La Casa Milà</h2>

<p>Gaudí's work was essentially useful. La Casa
Milà is an apartment building and real people live
there.</p>

<h2 class="building">La Sagrada Família</h2>

<p>The complicatedly named and curiously
unfinished Expiatory Temple of the Sacred Family is
the most visited building in Barcelona. </p>

</body>
```

Figure 3.14 *Add an* id *attribute to a unique element in order to identify it for later formatting or links. Add a* class *attribute to a group of elements to be able to format them all in one fell swoop.*

Antoni Gaudí

Many tourists are drawn to Barcelona to see Antoni Gaudí's incredible architecture.

Barcelona celebrates the 150th anniversary of Gaudí's birth in 2002.

La Casa Milà

Gaudí's work was essentially useful. La Casa Milà is an apartment building and real people live there.

La Sagrada Família

The complicatedly named and curiously unfinished Expiatory Temple of the Sacred Family is the most visited building in Barcelona.

Figure 3.15 *The* id *and* class *attributes do not by themselves modify an element's appearance. They must be combined with CSS formatting to show their full strength (as described in Chapters 10 and 11).*

Naming Elements

You can give your (X)HTML elements either a unique name or one that identifies them as belonging to a particular class. You can then apply styles to all elements with a given name.

To name unique elements:

Within the opening tag of the element, type **id="name"**, where *name* uniquely identifies the element.

To name groups of elements:

Within the opening tag of the element, type **class="name"**, where *name* is the identifying name of the class.

✔ Tips

- Each id in an (X)HTML document must be unique. In other words, no two elements can be named with the same id.

- More than one element may belong to, and thus be marked with, the same class.

- For information about applying styles to an element with a particular id or class, consult *Selecting Elements by ID or Class* on page 140.

- The class and id attributes may be added to most (X)HTML elements but are particularly useful with the div and span elements *(see pages 64–65).*

- The id attribute automatically turns the element into an anchor, to which you can direct a link. For more details, consult *Creating Anchors* on page 106.

- Finally, the id attribute can also be used to identify elements that will be affected by a scripting language, such as JavaScript.

Naming Elements

Breaking up a Page into Divisions

Breaking up your page into divisions allows you to apply styles to an entire chunk of your page at once. This is particularly useful for designing layouts with CSS *(see page 169).*

To break up a page into divisions:

1. At the beginning of the division, type **<div**.

2. If desired, type **id="name"**, where *name* uniquely identifies the division.

3. If desired, type **class="name"**, where *name* is the identifying name of the class that the division belongs to.

4. Type **>** to complete the opening div tag.

5. Create the contents of the division.

6. At the end of the division, type **</div>**.

✔ Tips

■ A division is a block-level element. That means that its contents automatically start on a new line.

■ In fact, the line breaks are the only formatting inherent to a division. Apply additional formatting by assigning styles to the division's class or id, as described in Chapters 7–14.

■ You're not required to label each division with a class or id, though they're much more powerful if you do.

■ You may apply both a class and id attribute to the same div element, although it's probably more usual to apply one or the other. The principal difference is that class is for a group of elements while id is for identifying individual, unique elements.

```
</head><body>
<div id="gaudi">
<h1>Antoni Gaudí</h1>
<p>Many tourists are drawn to Barcelona to see Antoni Gaudí's incredible architecture. </p>
<p>Barcelona celebrates the 150th anniversary of Gaudí's birth in 2002.</p>

<div class="works">
<h2>La Casa Milà</h2>
<p>Gaudí's work was essentially useful. La Casa Milà is an apartment building and real people live there.</p>
</div>

<div class="works">
<h2>La Sagrada Família</h2>
<p>The complicatedly named and curiously unfinished Expiatory Temple of the Sacred Family is the most visited building in Barcelona. </p>
</div>

</div>
</body></html>
```

Figure 3.16 *There is one large enclosing division (that begins with the level one header and goes to just before the closing body tag) and two inner divisions (that include the level two headers and their paragraphs).*

Figure 3.17 *You generally can't see the effect of divisions until you add styles (see page 127). Then they really shine. You can see this page with styles on my Web site (see page 26).*

```
<body>
<div id="gaudi">
<h1>Antoni Gaudí</h1>
<p>Many tourists are drawn to Barcelona to see
Antoni Gaudí's incredible architecture. </p>
<p>Barcelona celebrates the 150th anniversary of
Gaudí's birth in 2002.</p>

<div class="works">
<h2>La Casa Milà</h2>
<p>Gaudí's work was essentially useful. La Casa
Milà is an apartment building and <span
class="emph">real people</span> live there.</p>
</div>

<div class="works">
<h2>La Sagrada Família</h2>
<p>The complicatedly named and curiously
unfinished Expiatory Temple of the Sacred Family is
the <span class="emph">most visited</span>
building in Barcelona. </p>
</div>

</div>
</body></html>
```

Figure 3.18 *The* span *tag is used to mark a bunch of inline content. You can then format the marked content however you like (which we'll do in Chapters 10 and 11).*

Figure 3.19 *Again, the* span *element gives your document underlying structure. You can't see its effect until you apply styles (see page 127). You can see this page with styles on my Web site (see page 26).*

Creating Inline Spans

While you can organize big chunks of your Web page into head and body sections, into divisions, or even with headers (h1, h2, etc.), you can name smaller chunks or *spans* of text or other inline elements in order to identify them and apply styles to them.

To name inline spans:

1. At the beginning of the inline content, type **<span**.

2. If desired, type **id="name"**, where *name* uniquely identifies the spanned content.

3. If desired, type **class="name"**, where *name* is the identifying name of the class that the spanned content belongs to.

4. Type **>** to complete the opening span tag.

5. Create the inline contents you wish to label.

6. At the end of the span, type **</span>**.

✔ **Tips**

■ For more details on the differences between block-level and inline content, consult *Block vs Inline* on page 30.

■ A span has no inherent formatting. It becomes useful when you apply styles to it, generally through its class or id, as you'll see in Chapters 9–14.

■ You may apply both a class and id attribute to the same span element, although it's probably more usual to apply one or the other. The principal difference is that class is for a group of elements while id is for identifying individual, unique elements.

Creating Inline Spans

Creating a Line Break

Browsers automatically wrap text according to the width of the block or window, creating new lines as necessary. While you can start a new paragraph with the p tag *(see page 62)*, you can also create manual line breaks anywhere you like.

The br tag is perfect for poems or other short lines of text that should appear one after another without a lot of space in between.

To insert a line break:

Type **
** where the line break should occur. There is no separate closing br tag.

✔ Tips

■ The closing slash (/) is only required in XHTML documents to satisfy the rule that all elements be properly closed *(see page 38)*. Make sure there is a space between *br* and the slash. You may omit the slash entirely in HTML documents, though it does no harm to include it.

■ You can use multiple br tags to create extra space between lines or paragraphs.

■ Styles can help you control the space between lines in a paragraph *(see page 158)* and between the paragraphs themselves *(see pages 176–177)*.

■ The br tag used to be used with the deprecated clear attribute to control text that is wrapped around images *(see page 98)*. Its function has been replaced by the CSS clear property *(see page 182)*.

■ The CSS white-space property is great for maintaining original page breaks *(see page 164)*.

```
<body>
<div id="toc">Antoni Gaudí<br />La Casa
Milà<br />La Sagrada Família</div>
<div id="gaudi">
<h1>Antoni Gaudí</h1>
<p>Many tourists are drawn to Barcelona to see
Antoni Gaudí's incredible architecture. </p>
<p>Barcelona celebrates the 150th anniversary of
```

Figure 3.20 *I've created a new division at the top of the page that can serve as a table of contents. There will be three lines (thanks to the* br *tag) with the minimum amount of space between each one.*

```
<body>
<div id="toc">Antoni Gaudí
<br />La Casa Milà
<br />La Sagrada Família</div>
<div id="gaudi">
<h1>Antoni Gaudí</h1>
<p>Many tourists are drawn to Barcelona to see
Antoni Gaudí's incredible architecture. </p>
<p>Barcelona celebrates the 150th anniversary of
```

Figure 3.21 *Remember that the returns in your code are always ignored. This code is equivalent to that shown above in Figure 3.20 though it's easier to read.*

Figure 3.22 *The* br *element starts the subsequent elements on a new line.*

Creating a Line Break

```
<body>
<!--Here is the table of contents, which in a real
document might be a good deal longer.-->
<div id="toc">Antoni Gaudí<br />La Casa
Milà<br />La Sagrada Família</div>
<div id="gaudi">
<h1>Antoni Gaudí</h1>
<p>Many tourists are drawn to Barcelona to see
Antoni Gaudí's incredible architecture. </p>
<p>Barcelona celebrates the 150th anniversary of
Gaudí's birth in 2002.</p>
```

Figure 3.23 *Comments are a great way to add reminders to your text. You can also use them to keep track of revisions.*

Figure 3.24 *Comments are invisible (though they readily appear when the source code is displayed—see page 53).*

Adding Comments

You can add comments to your (X)HTML documents in order to remind yourself (or future editors) what you were trying to achieve with your (X)HTML tags. These comments only appear when the document is opened with a text editor. They are invisible to visitors in the browser.

To add comments to your HTML page:

1. In your (X)HTML document, where you wish to insert comments, type **<!--**.

2. Type the comments.

3. Type **-->** to complete the commented text.

✔ Tips

■ Comments are particularly useful for describing why you used a particular tag and what effect you were hoping to achieve.

■ Another good use for comments is to remind yourself (or future editors) to include, remove, or update certain sections.

■ You should view your commented page with a browser before publishing to avoid sharing your (possibly) private comments with your public.

■ Beware, however, of comments that are *too* private. While invisible in the browser, they cheerfully reappear when the user saves the page as (X)HTML code (source). For more information on viewing a page's code, consult *The Inspiration of Others* on page 53.

■ Comments may not be nested within other comments.

Labeling Elements in a Web Page

You can use the `title` attribute to add a tool tip label to practically every part of your Web site. It's particularly helpful for giving your visitors clues about what's needed in form elements, but you can use it to label just about anything.

To label elements in a Web page:

In the (X)HTML tag for the item you want to label, add **title="label"**, where *label* is the text that should appear in the tool tip when a visitor points at the element.

✔ Tip

■ Explorer for Windows also makes pop-up labels or tool tips out of the `alt` attribute used in image tags (*see page 91*). However, if both the `title` and `alt` attributes are present in an image tag, the tool tip is set to the contents of the `title` tag, not the `alt` tag. So, if you don't want Explorer for Windows to use your `alt` tag as a tool tip, use an empty `title`: **title=""**.

```
<body>
<!--Here is the table of contents, which in a real
document might be a good deal longer.-->
<div id="toc" title="Table of Contents">Antoni
Gaudí<br />La Casa Milà<br />La Sagrada
Família</div>
<div id="gaudi">
<h1>Antoni Gaudí</h1>
<p>Many tourists are drawn to Barcelona to see
Antoni Gaudí's incredible architecture. </p>
<p>Barcelona celebrates the 150th anniversary of
Gaudí's birth in 2002.</p>

<div class="works">
<h2>La Casa Milà</h2>
<p>Gaudí's work was essentially useful. La Casa
Milà is an apartment building and <span
class="emph">real people</span> live there.</p>
</div>
```

Figure 3.25 *You can add a title to any element you wish.*

Figure 3.26 *When your visitors point at the labeled element, the title will appear.*

Basic (X)HTML Formatting

While it's a good idea to try to separate formatting from content and to use style sheets for controlling the appearance of your page, there are a few simple ways to format text in (X)HTML that are handy to know.

When should you use basic (X)HTML formatting instead of CSS? There are two main situations. First, most of the elements discussed in this chapter are *logical* elements, that is, they give structure to your document by describing what they contain. For example, the `code` element is specifically designed for formatting lines of code from a script or program. While it formats such content in a monospace font, it also more importantly *identifies* the text as code.

The second reason to use the basic formatting elements in this chapter is because CSS is sometimes too big a bazooka for the job. If you want to highlight a word or phrase on your page, instead of enclosing it in a `span` element with a particular class and then creating a style sheet for that class, you can just wrap it in a simple formatting element and be done with it.

There are a number of formatting elements—for changing the font, size, and color, for example—that, while still technically legal and widely supported, are being phased out of (X)HTML in favor of style sheets. You can find more information about them in Appendix A, *(X)HTML Reference* as well as on my Web site *(see page 25).*

Making Text Bold or Italic

One way to make text stand out is to format it in boldface or italics.

To make text bold:

1. Type **\<b\>**.

2. Type the text that you want to make bold.

3. Type **\</b\>**.

To make text italic:

1. Type **\<i\>**.

2. Type the text that you want to make italic.

3. Type **\</i\>**.

✔ Tips

- You can also use the less common `em` and `strong` tags to format text **(Figures 4.2)**. These are *logical* formatting tags for "emphasizing" text or marking it as "strong". In most browsers, `em` is displayed in italics and `strong` in bold. On some browsers, though, they're displayed differently. For example, some handhelds can't display italics and use underlining instead.

- You may also use `cite` (for citations), `dfn` (for definitions), and `var` (for variables) to make text italic while giving information about the content.

- The `address` tag—old-fashioned but still valid—is another logical tag for making text italic. It's usually only used to format the Web page designer's email address.

- For more control over bold and italics, try style sheets. For details, consult *Creating Italics* on page 154 and *Applying Bold Formatting* on page 155.

\<h1\>Barcelona Night Life\</h1\>

\<p\>Barcelona is such a great place to live. People there really put a premium on \<b\>socializing\</b\>. Imagine it being more important to go out with your friends than to get that big promotion. Even when you're, gasp, \<i\>pushing 30\</i\>. They say there are more bars in Barcelona than in the rest of the European community \<i\>combined\</i\>.\</p\>

Figure 4.1 *You may use bold or italic formatting anywhere in your (X)HTML document, except in the* `title`.

\<h1\>Barcelona Night Life\</h1\>

\<p\>Barcelona is such a great place to live. People there really put a premium on \<strong\>socializing \</strong\>. Imagine it being more important to go out with your friends than to get that big promotion. Even when you're, gasp, \<em\>pushing 30\</em\>. They say there are more bars in Barcelona than in the rest of the European community \<em\>combined\</em\>.\</p\>

Figure 4.2 *If you prefer, you can use the logical* em *and* `strong` *tags to add both structure and formatting at the same time.*

Figure 4.3 *Bold and italic formatting are the simplest and most effective ways to make your text stand out.*

```
<h1>Barcelona Night Life</h1>

<p>Barcelona is such a great place to live. People
there really put a premium on <strong>socializing
</strong>. Imagine it being more important to go
out with your friends than to get that big promotion.
Even when you're, gasp, <em>pushing 30</em>.
They say there are more bars in Barcelona than in
the rest of the European community
<em>combined</em>.</p>

<p><big>Don't get me wrong,</big> I don't mean
that everyone gets drunk all the time--bars are for
hanging out and talking or for having a cup of
coffee (espresso, of course).</p>

<p><small>The opinions expressed on this page
are mine and mine alone. </small></p>
```

Figure 4.4 *The* big *and* small *tags are a fast and easy way to make text stand out.*

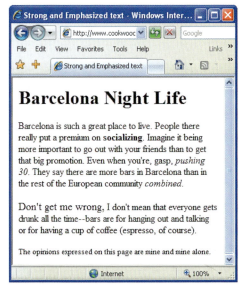

Figure 4.5 *The* big *and* small *elements enjoy wide support. They have identical effects in most browsers. (This is Internet Explorer 7 for Windows.)*

Changing the Size of Text

The big and small tags change the relative size of a given word or phrase with respect to the surrounding text.

To make the text bigger or smaller than the surrounding text:

1. Type **<big>** or **<small>**.

2. Type the text that should be bigger or smaller.

3. Type **</big>** or **</small>** depending on the tag used in step 1.

✔ Tips

- Of course, "big" and "small" are relative, and the specifications do not dictate just how much bigger or smaller browsers are supposed to make the text. In general, they stick to typical font sizes, like 8, 9, 10, 12, 14, 16, 18, 24, 36, and 48, moving one step up or down the ladder depending on the element used. The default size for most browsers is 16px.

- Although the big and small tags have not been deprecated in (X)HTML, you may still want to use style sheets in order to have more control over the size of the text. For more information, consult *Setting the Font Size* on page 156.

- Both the big and small tags have a cumulative effect if used more than once. So **<small><small>teensy text</small></small>** would be *two* sizes smaller than surrounding text.

Changing the Size of Text

Using a Monospaced Font

Every visitor to your page has two fonts specified in their browser's preferences: one regular, proportionally spaced one, and the other monospaced, like a typewriter's text. These are usually Times and Courier, respectively. If you are displaying computer codes, URLs, or other information that you wish to offset from the main text, you might want to format the text with the monospaced font.

Use `code` for formatting computer *code* in languages like C or Perl. The `tt` element (it stands for *typewriter text)* is for general monospaced text. Use `kbd` for formatting *keyboard* instructions. And `samp` is for displaying *sample* text. None of these tags is used very often. The truth is that monospaced text is kind of ugly.

To format text with a monospaced font:

1. Type **<code>**, **<tt>**, **<kbd>**, or **<samp>**.

2. Type the text that you want to display in a monospaced font.

3. Type **</code>**, **</tt>**, **</kbd>**, or **</samp>**. Use the tag that matches the one you chose in step 1.

✔ Tips

- Remember that the monospaced font tags will not have a very dramatic effect in browsers that display all their text in monospaced fonts (like Lynx: *http://www.delorie.com/web/lynxview.html*).

- You can also format several lines of monospaced text with the `pre` tag *(see page 73).*

- You can apply *any* font (that your visitor has installed) to your text with styles *(see page 152).*

```
<h2>Perl Tutorial, Lesson 1</h2>

<p>If you're on a UNIX server, every Perl script
should start with a shebang line that describes the
path to the Perl interpreter on your server. The
shebang line might look like this:</p>

<p><code>#!/usr/local/bin/perl</code></p>
```

Figure 4.6 *The* `code` *element not only formats its contents with a monospaced font but also indicates that the contents are computer code. It's a* logical *tag.*

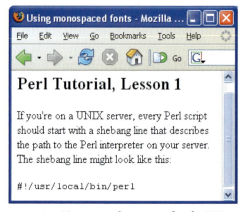

Figure 4.7 *Monospaced text is perfect for URLs and computer code.*

Figure 4.8 *Text tagged with* `code`, `kbd`, `samp`, *or* `tt` *will be displayed in the font that your visitors have chosen for monospaced text in their browser. The Fonts box from IE 7 (shown) comes up when you choose Tools > Internet Options and then click the Fonts button in the General tab.*

```
<body>

<p>Here's the first part of the Cat and Otter Bistro
script (see the WAP/WML chapter), where the
variables are declared, and the $number variable
is screened to make sure it's actually a number:

<pre>my $number = param('number');

my $smoke = param('smoke');

my $dinner_index = param('dinner_index');


$number =~ /([0-9]*)/ ;

$number = $1;

</pre>
```

Figure 4.9 *The* pre *element is ideal for text that contains important spaces and line breaks, like the chunk of Perl CGI code shown above.*

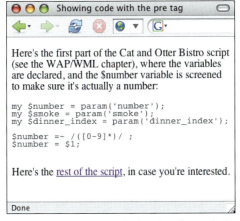

Figure 4.10 *Notice how the line breaks, including the extra return between the third and fourth lines of code, are maintained.*

Using Preformatted Text

Usually, browsers collapse all extra returns and spaces and automatically break lines according to the size of the window. Preformatted text lets you maintain the original line breaks and spacing that you've inserted in the text. It is ideal for computer code examples.

To use preformatted text:

1. Type **<pre>**.

2. Type or copy the text that you wish to display as is, with all the necessary spaces, returns, and line breaks.

3. Type **</pre>**.

✔ Tips

■ Preformatted text is generally displayed with a monospaced font like Courier. You can use styles to change the font, if you like *(see page 152)*.

■ If what you want to display contains (X)HTML elements, you'll have to substitute the appropriate character entities for the greater than and less than signs (namely **>** and **<**, respectively). Otherwise the browser will try to display those elements; the pre tag works no magic on them. For more information, consult *Adding Characters from Outside the Encoding* on page 336.

■ You can also use styles to maintain line breaks and spaces *(see page 164)*.

■ Note that pre is block-level while the tags on page 72 are all inline.

Using Preformatted Text

Quoting Text

There are two special tags for marking quoted text so that you can identify its author, origin, and language. Block-level quotes are generally indented by browsers. Inline quotes are supposed to be automatically enclosed in quotation marks but are not widely supported.

To quote block-level text:

1. Type **<blockquote** to begin a block-level quote.

2. If desired, type **cite="url"**, where *url* is the address of the source of the quote.

3. Type **>** to complete the opening tag.

4. Type the text that you wish to appear set off from the preceding and following text, including any desired (X)HTML tags.

5. Type **</blockquote>** to complete the element.

To quote inline text:

1. Type **<q** to begin.

2. If desired, type **xml:lang="xx" lang="xx"**, where *xx* is the two-letter code for the language the quote will be in. This code is supposed to determine the type of quote marks that will be used ("" for English, « » for many European languages, etc.).

3. Type **>** to complete the opening tag.

4. Type the text that should be quoted.

5. Type **</q>**.

6. If desired, in the html tag, add **xml:lang="xx" lang="xx"**, where *xx* is the two-letter code for the language that most of your Web page is in.

<p>Sometimes I get to the point where I'm not sure anything matters at all. Then I read something like this and I am inspired: </p>

<blockquote cite="http://www.kingsolver.com">

<p>It's not hard to figure out what's good for kids, but amid the noise of an increasingly antichild political climate, it can be hard to remember just to go ahead and do it: for example, to vote to raise your school district's budget, even though you'll pay higher taxes. ... To volunteer time and skills at your neighborhood school and also the school across town. To decide to notice, rather than ignore it, when a neighbor is losing it with her kids, and offer to babysit twice a week. This is not interference. Getting between a ball player and a ball is interference. The ball is inanimate.</p>

</blockquote>

<p>This is from Barbara Kingsolver's brilliant collection of essays, <cite>High Tide in Tucson</cite> (1995, HarperCollins)</p>.

Figure 4.11 *A block quote can be as short or as long as you need. You can even divide it into various paragraphs by adding* p *tags as necessary.*

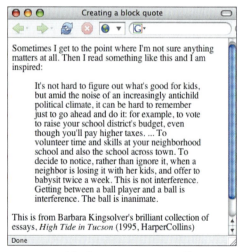

Figure 4.12 *Block quotes are generally indented from both sides. The* cite *attribute is not yet recognized by any browser I've seen.*

```
<html xmlns="http://www.w3.org/1999/xhtml"
xml:lang="en lang="en">

[snip]

<p>And then she said <q>Have you read
Kingsolver's <q>High Tide in Tucson</q>? It's
inspiring.</q></p>

<p>She tried again, this time in French: <q
lang="fr">Avez-vous lu le livre <q lang="fr">High
Tide in Tucson</q> de Kingsolver? C'est
inspirational.</q></p>
```

Figure 4.13 *The* `lang` *attribute in the* `html` *tag is supposed to be a default for the other tags. In my tests, it has no effect on the* `q` *element.*

Figure 4.14 *Firefox adds curly double quotes around* `q` *elements and curly single quotes around nested* `q` *elements.*

✔ Tips

- Text and inline elements should not be placed directly between the opening and closing `blockquote` tags. Instead, enclose the text and inline elements in a block-level tag—like p, for example—*within* the `blockquote` tags.

- You can nest both `blockquote` and `q` elements. Nested `q` elements should automatically have the appropriate quotation marks—in English the outer quotes should be double and the inner ones should be single.

- Proper support for `q` varies widely from one browser to the next. Firefox offers double and single curly quotes on Mac and Windows. Opera 8 uses straight double quotes for everything, including nested `q` elements. Explorer for Windows (up to and including version 7) ignores the `q` element completely.

- No current browsers pay any attention to the `lang` attribute, either in the `q` element or in the `html` element. Internet Explorer 5 for Macintosh was the only browser I've found that ever did.

- The `cite` attribute may also be used with the `q` element, although it makes less sense. I haven't seen a browser that does anything with it in either element.

- For more details on the `xml:lang` and `lang` attributes, consult *Specifying A Page's Language* on page 338.

- You can find a complete list of language codes at *http://www.w3.org/WAI/ER/IG/ert/iso639.htm.*

Quoting Text

Creating Superscripts and Subscripts

Letters or numbers that are raised or lowered slightly relative to the main body text are called *superscripts* and *subscripts*, respectively. (X)HTML includes tags for defining both kinds of offset text.

To create superscripts or subscripts:

1. Type **<sub>** to create a subscript or **<sup>** to create a superscript.

2. Type the characters or symbols that you wish to offset relative to the main text.

3. Type **</sub>** or **</sup>**, depending on what you used in step 1, to complete the offset text.

✔ Tips

■ Most browsers automatically reduce the font size of a sub- or superscripted character by a few points.

■ Superscripts are the ideal way to format certain foreign language abbreviations like Mlle for *Mademoiselle* in French or 3^{a} for *Tercera* in Spanish.

■ Subscripts are perfect for writing out chemical molecules like H_2O.

■ Superscripts are also handy for creating footnotes. You can combine superscripts and links to make active footnotes (the visitor jumps to the footnote when they click the number or asterisk). For more information, see Chapter 6, *Links*.

■ Super- and subscripted characters gently spoil the even spacing between lines **(Figure 4.16)**. You can remedy this by changing the size of the sub or sup text *(see pages 71 and 156)* and adjusting its line height *(see page 158)*.

```
<body>

<h1>Famous Catalans</h1>

<p>When I was in the sixth grade, I played the
cello. There was a teacher at school who always
used to ask me if I knew who "Pablo Casals" was. I
didn't at the time (although I had met Rostropovich
once at a concert). Actually, Pablo Casals' real
name was <i>Pau</i> Casals, Pau being the
Catalan equivalent of Pablo<sup>1</sup>.</p>

<p>In addition to being an amazing cellist, Pau
Casals is remembered in this country for his
empassioned speech against nuclear proliferation
at the United Nations<sup>2</sup> which he
began by saying "I am a Catalan. Catalonia is an
oppressed nation."</p>

<p><sup>1</sup>It means Paul in English.<br />
<sup>2</sup>In 1963, I believe.</p>

</body>
```

Figure 4.15 *The opening* sup *or* sub *tag precedes the text to be affected.*

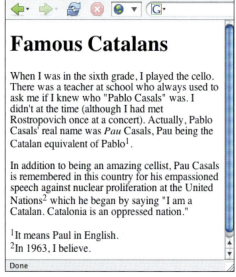

Figure 4.16 *Unfortunately, the* sub *and* sup *elements spoil the line spacing. Notice that there is more space between lines 6 and 7 of the first paragraph and lines 4 and 5 of the second than between the other lines.*

```
<body>

<p><big>I promise to do all of my homework,<ins>
all of my chores,</ins> clean the cat litter, and not
watch more than <del>six</del> a half
hour<del>s</del> of tv.</big></p>


<p>signed</p>
```

Figure 4.17 *You have to be a little bit careful to include the associated punctuation with the* ins *and* del *elements.*

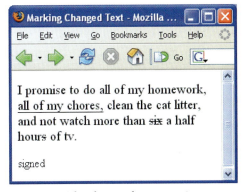

Figure 4.18 *The changes become quite apparent.*

Marking Changed Text

Another set of logical tags that you might find useful are the ones for marking text that has changed from one version to the next. Lawyers and bloggers do this all the time.

To mark newly inserted text:

1. Type **<ins>**.

2. Type the new text.

3. Type **</ins>**.

To mark deleted text:

1. Place the cursor before the text you wish to mark as deleted.

2. Type **<del>**.

3. Place the cursor after the text you wish to mark as deleted.

4. Type **</del>**.

✔ Tips

- Text marked with the ins tag is generally underlined. Since links are often underlined as well (if not in your site, in many others), this may be confusing to visitors. You may want to add an explanation at the beginning of your page and/or use styles to change how inserted passages (or links) are displayed *(see page 151)*.

- Text marked with the del element is generally stricken out. Why not just erase it and be done with it? Striking it out makes it easy for others to see what has changed.

- You can also use styles to underline and strike out text *(see page 168)*. The advantage of the ins and del elements is that they identify the text as being *inserted* or *deleted*, and not just underlined or stricken.

Marking Changed Text

Explaining Abbreviations

Abbreviations and acronyms (an abbreviation that can be pronounced as a word) abound. Unfortunately, people use them so often that they sometimes forget that not everyone knows what they mean. You can use the `abbr` and `acronym` elements to add meaning to the abbreviation or acronym in question without breaking the flow of your Web page or distracting your readers with extra links.

To explain abbreviations:

1. Type **<abbr**.

   Or type **<acronym** if the abbreviation can be pronounced as a word.

2. Next type **title="explanation"**, where *explanation* gives more details about the abbreviation.

3. Type **>**.

4. Then type the abbreviation itself.

5. Finally, finish up with **</abbr>** or **</acronym>** depending on what you used in step 1.

✔ Tips

- Firefox (on both platforms) supports both `abbr` and `acronym`, highlighting both elements with a dotted underline and providing the `title` attribute's contents as a tool tip **(Figure 4.20)**.

- Internet Explorer for Windows (up to version 7) doesn't change the display of `acronym` or `abbr` elements, but does show titles as tool tips. IE 6 and earlier didn't support `abbr`.

```
<p><abbr title="Lyndon Baynes Johnson">LBJ
</abbr> took the <abbr title="Interborough Rapid
Transit">IRT</abbr> down to 4th Street <abbr
title="United States of America">USA</abbr>.

<br />When he got there, what did he see?

<br />The youth of America on <abbr title="d-
Lysergic Acid Diethylamide">LSD</abbr>.</p>

<p>--Hair, the Musical, 1967</p>

<p>Or perhaps you'd rather talk about something
slightly less political, like <acronym title="Light
Amplification By Stimulated Emission of Radiation">
laser</acronym>, or <acronym title="Radio
Detection And Ranging">radar</acronym>, or
<acronym title="Self-Contained Underwater
Breathing Apparatus">scuba</acronym>? </p>
```

Figure 4.19 *It seems an awful lot of code for just a few words. Still, it can be very helpful to get immediate information about an abbreviation, at least the first time it is used.*

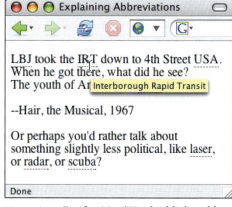

Figure 4.20 *Firefox Mac/Win highlights abbreviations and acronyms with a dotted underline and when your visitors hover, the contents of the element's* `title` *attribute are shown in a tool tip.*

> Or perhaps you'd rather talk about something slightly less political, like laser, or radar, or scuba?
> Light Amplification By Stimulated Emission of Radiation

Figure 4.21 *Explorer displays the title of abbreviations as a tool tip, but doesn't display the abbreviation itself any differently.*

```
<body>

<center>

<h2>The Earth's Core</h2>

<p>At the center of the earth, more than 6000
kilometers from the surface, the temperature is a
toasty 6500 degrees Kelvin.</p>

</center>

<p>Not bad for a little planet.</p>

</body>
```

Figure 4.22 *The* center *element acts like a* div *element with the* align *attribute set to* center.

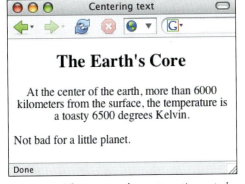

Figure 4.23 *The* center *element continues to be well supported.*

Centering Elements on a Page

The center tag is one of those elements that has been deprecated but not forgotten. When centering with CSS seems like too much of a hassle, many continue to use the center tag. It remains well supported and can be used with virtually any element on your page.

To center elements on a page:

1. Type **<center>**.

2. Create the element that you wish to center.

3. Type **</center>**.

✔ Tips

■ The center element is nothing more than an abbreviation of **<div align= "center"> ... </div>**.

■ For more details on dividing your document into sections that you can then align, consult *Breaking up a Page into Divisions* on page 64.

■ For more on the (deprecated) align attribute, in particular with paragraphs and headers, see the last tips on pages 61–62.

■ If you use the center element, you should make sure to also declare a *transitional* DOCTYPE *(see page 56).*

■ For information on using styles to center text, consult *Aligning Text* on page 165.

■ For information on aligning images with text, consult *Aligning Images* on page 100.

Centering Elements on a Page

5

IMAGES

Creating images for the Web is a bit different from creating images for output on paper. Although the basic characteristics of Web images and printable images are the same, six main factors distinguish them: format, color, size/resolution, speed, transparency, and animation. This chapter will explain the important aspects of each of these six factors and how to use that knowledge to create the most effective images for your Web site.

Once you've created your images, we'll go on to insert them on your Web page.

About Images for the Web

Now let's look at those six factors that you should keep in mind as you create Web images.

Format

People who print images on paper don't have to worry about what their readers will use to look at the images. You do. The Web is accessed every day by millions of Macs, Windows-based PCs, Unix machines, and other kinds of computers. The graphics you use in your Web page should be in a format that each of these operating systems can recognize. Presently, the two most widely used formats on the Web are GIF and JPEG, with PNG gaining in popularity. Current browsers can view all three image formats.

Color

Currently (mid 2006), around 80% of the Web surfing public use 24- or 32-bit monitors, 16% use 16-bit monitors, and fewer than 1% use 8-bit monitors. In 2002, those numbers were quite different: 50% on 24-bit, 40% on 16-bit and 10% on 8-bit. The trend is clearly toward so-called "True Color" monitors in which any of 16 million colors can be displayed.

In the days when 8-bit monitors were the norm, you had to restrict yourself to only the *browser safe colors* in order to ensure that the colors you chose would appear correctly on your Web pages. However, as the numbers show, so few people are using 8-bit monitors, that it is no longer an issue. You may use any colors you like. (If you're interested in the whys and wherefores of browser safe colors, I have maintained some information about them on my Web site.)

Check the inside back cover of this book for a handy table for choosing colors.

Figure 5.1 *Logotypes and other computer-generated images or images with few colors are compressed efficiently with LZW and thus are often saved in GIF format.*

Figure 5.2 *Full-color photographs and other naturally created images, or images with more than 256 colors, should be saved in JPEG format.*

Figure 5.3 *This particular image is 1704 pixels wide and in Photoshop has an output resolution of 284 ppi and only measures 6 x 8 inches. Here in Firefox, its resolution is determined by the visitor's monitor—about 86ppi—which means the picture is 20 inches wide!*

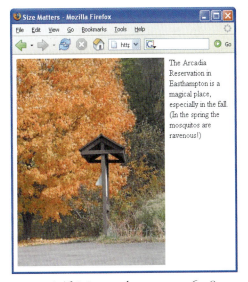

Figure 5.4 *This image also measures 6 x 8 inches in Photoshop, though it has an output resolution of 50ppi. Again, however, these relative measurements are irrelevant. What counts is that it measures 300 pixels wide, which is about half the width of an average browser window.*

Size and Resolution

Digital images are measured in pixels. A 4 megapixel digital camera can take pictures that are 1600 pixels wide by 1200 pixels high. How big is that? It depends. If you print the image to a printer at 200 ppi (pixels per inch), it will measure 8 by 6 inches. But if you're using that page on the Web, the image's size will depend on your visitor's monitor's resolution, which is more likely to be around 86 ppi (and might be as low as 72 or as high as 100 or so), and thus will display as big as 18 x 14 inches (about 46 x 36 cm). Too big.

Perhaps a better way to think of image size is with respect to the average Web page. Since monitors with a resolution of 640 pixels wide by 480 pixels high were the standard for so long, Web page designers got used to keeping their pages around 600 pixels wide, so that viewers could see the entire contents of the page without scrolling horizontally.

While it's true that there are more and more people who have bigger monitors (these days more than half are 1024 x 768), it doesn't necessarily follow that folks will fill up those bigger monitors with a single browser window. Aside from having other programs to consult (or even other browser windows), it's cumbersome to read text in a browser that's too wide. Still, designers have tended to widen their designs as well as use flexible-width designs that expand and contract with a visitor's browser window. Keep this in mind as you plan and create your images.

Note that *resolution* can mean one of two quite distinct concepts: the actual number of pixels on a monitor or in an image, say 640 x 480, *or* the number of pixels in an inch of that monitor or image, say 72 or 86 ppi. Regardless, the higher the resolution, the more pixels. On paper, pixels can add details *or* size. On screen, more pixels *always* translate to a bigger size image.

Speed

The next principal difference between Web images and printed images is that your visitors have to wait for Web images to download. (Imagine waiting for pictures to appear in your morning paper!)

How can you keep download time to a minimum? The easiest way is to use small images. The larger an image's file size, the longer it takes to appear before your visitors' eyes.

The second way to speed up download time is by compressing the image. There are three popular compression methods (that correspond to the three major formats): LZW (for GIF images), JPEG, and PNG. LZW is particularly effective for computer-generated art like logos, rendered text, and other images that have large areas of a single color. In fact, if you can reduce the number of colors in an image, LZW can often (but not always) compress the image even more. JPEG, on the other hand, is better at compressing photographs and other images that have many different colors.

Each method has its drawbacks. Because LZW used to be patented (until 2004), developers had to pay royalties on software that used it. (This is one of the principal reasons that PNG was developed.) And GIF images are limited to 256 colors. JPEG has two main disadvantages. First, its compression information takes up a lot of space and is simply not worth it for very small images. Second, it is *lossy* compression—permanently eliminating details in order to save space. Uncompressing the image will not restore the lost data. If you plan on editing an image in the future you should save a copy in an uncompressed format (e.g., PSD or TIFF) and only save it as a JPEG after you have made your final edits.

PNG compresses better than LZW without losing information like JPEG. However, it does not allow animation, as GIF does. It used to have limited support in browsers, but current browsers, including IE 6 and up, Firefox, and Safari display PNG images just fine. (However, Internet Explorer doesn't display PNG images with Alpha channels properly.)

Transparency

Transparency is important for two reasons. First, you can use it to create complex layouts by making one image move behind another. Second, you can take advantage of transparency to give an image a non-rectangular outline, adding visual interest to your pages. Both GIF and PNG allow transparency; JPEG does not.

Animation

One thing you won't be seeing on paper anytime soon are moving images. On the Web, they're everywhere. Animated images can be saved in GIF format, but not JPEG or PNG. You can also create animation with Flash *(see page 436)*.

About Images for the Web

Getting Images

So how do you get an image that you can use for your Web page? There are several ways. You can buy or download ready-made images, digitize photographs or hand drawn images with a scanner, use a digital camera, or draw images from scratch in an image editing program like Photoshop. Once you've got them in your computer, you can adapt them to the Web, as necessary.

To get images:

- You can use Google to find images on the Web by clicking the Images link above the Search box and entering criteria as usual. See sidebar at right for more information on copyrights for those images.

- Generally, even free images found on the Web are restricted in one form or another (again, see sidebar). Images you buy can usually be used for any purpose (except for reselling the images themselves). Read any disclaimers or licenses carefully.

- Many companies sell stock photography and images on CD. Such disks often have several versions of each image for different purposes. For Web sites, use the Web or Multimedia version.

- Many photo processing outfits will develop a roll of film directly onto a CD.

- Scanners and digital cameras have grown in quality as they've plummeted in price. They are an ideal way to convert print photographs into digital ones, or to create digital ones from scratch.

- If you create your own images, save them as GIF, JPEG, or PNG. Don't save them as BMP—only Explorer for Windows users will be able to see them.

Creative Commons Licenses

Creative Commons *(http://www.creative-commons.org)* is a non-profit organization that has developed a system of copyrights that let artists share their work in specified ways without giving up all their rights over their works. Web site designers, musicians, and photographers are some of the many artists who are using Creative Commons licenses to get their work out in the marketplace without fear that it will be used in a way they don't agree with.

Flickr, the popular photo-sharing Web application *(http://www.flickr.com/)*, asks its users to designate a Creative Commons license for each of the photos that they upload. Flickr then lets visitors search for photos according to the licenses assigned to them. It can be a great place to find photos for your Web site.

You can also use Google to restrict searches based on usage rights. (Click Advanced Search and then choose the desired option next to Usage Rights.)

Choosing an Image Editor

There are many, many different software programs that you can use to create and save images for the Web. Most modern image editors have special tools for creating Web images, which take into account the factors discussed earlier in this chapter.

The industry standard is no doubt Adobe Photoshop ($650) though its less expensive cousin, Photoshop Elements ($90) is a very powerful program in its own right. Both are available for Macintosh and Windows. I have used these two programs to illustrate a few techniques in this chapter.

Let me stress, however, that the basic strategies for optimizing images for the Web are the same regardless of the software you choose. The command names may be slightly different and there may be more or fewer steps, but the ideas remain the same.

There are many alternatives to Photoshop, including Paint Shop Pro for Windows by Corel (formerly by Jasc Software) and GraphicConverter for Macintosh by Lemke Software. Feel free to use whatever program you're most comfortable with.

Choosing an Image Editor

The Save for Web Command

Both Adobe Photoshop and Adobe Photoshop Elements offer the awesome Save for Web command. It lets you visually compare the original image with up to three versions that you can optimize while keeping an eye on any resulting savings in file size and download time.

To use Adobe's Save for Web command:

1. Create your image.

2. Choose File > Save for Web. The Save For Web window appears.

3. In Photoshop, click the 2-up tab to see one optimized version or the 4-up tab to see three. Photoshop Elements always shows a single alternative.

4. Click an optimized version, if necessary.

5. Choose the desired format.

    In general, images that have been created on a computer, including logos, banners, line art, text, and any graphic with large areas of a single color and sharp detail should be saved in GIF or PNG-8 format **(Figure 5.5)**.

    Images with continuous tones, like photographs, should be saved in either JPEG or PNG-24 format **(Figure 5.6)**.

6. Adjust the additional settings that appear until you get the smallest file possible with an acceptable quality.

7. Click OK in Photoshop Elements or Save in Photoshop. Choose a directory and name the new file. It will automatically carry the extension of the selected format (and thus normally will not replace the original image).

Figure 5.5 *Here is part of the Save for Web box that shows the original image (upper left) and three possible compressed versions. This image has a lot of flat color, as well as text, which should be kept sharp. Note how the GIF format (lower left), compresses the image the best, to just over 8K. JPEG at high quality is huge. At medium quality, it's big and ugly.*

Figure 5.6 *The GIF compression leaves banding in the photograph (bottom left). The two JPEG options on the right are smaller and better quality.*

✔ Tips

- Remember that your main objective is to get the smallest file size possible while still maintaining acceptable image quality.

- Images should be created in RGB mode, not CMYK (which is for print).

- If you're not sure which format to choose, compare two optimizations and see which format compresses better while leaving the image at the best quality.

- PNG is a powerful lossless format that can be used for both computer-generated and "natural" color images. It is often better than GIF but not quite as good as JPEG. Unfortunately, Photoshop is probably not the best tool for creating PNG images, as its compression algorithms aren't as tight as they might be. Fireworks (formerly from Macromedia but now also from Adobe) is reportedly much better at saving in PNG format.

- If you have an image with both types of content, you can either slice it into distinct chunks and compress them separately (and then reassemble them with a borderless table—see page 227) or you can just use a single format and let it do its best.

- The Save for Web command creates a new, independent image and leaves the original image intact. The exception, of course, is if you save the new image with the same name and extension as the old.

- Only an image's visible layers are saved in the optimized version.

The Save for Web Command

Inserting Images on a Page

You can place all kinds of images on your Web page, from logos to photographs. Images placed as described here appear automatically when the visitor jumps to your page, as long as the browser is set up to view them.

To insert an image on a page:

1. Place the cursor where you want the image to appear.

2. Type **<img src="image.url"** where *image.url* indicates the location of the image file on the server *(see page 35)*.

3. Type a space and then the final **/>**.

✔ Tips

- Add a p or br tag before an image to start it on its own line.

- Images must be uploaded to the server before visitors will be able to see them *(see page 353)*.

- Don't expect your visitors to wait very long for your page to load and view. Test it (keeping in mind you may have a faster connection than your visitors). If you can't wait, they won't either. One alternative is to create miniatures *(see page 95)* of large images and let visitors *choose* to view the larger images through a link *(see page 115)*.

- There is a deprecated border attribute (border="n", where *n* is the width in pixels) that adds or eliminates a border around images, especially the automatic border that appears around images used in links *(see page 114)*. Better yet, you can use styles to control this and all other aspects of images *(see page 184)*.

```
<h1>Barcelona's Market</h1>

<img src="cornermarket.jpg" />

<p>This first picture shows the entranceway to the Mercat de la Boquería, the central market that is just off the Rambles. It's an incredible place, full of every kind of fruit, meat, fish, or whatever you might happen to need. It took me a long time to get up the nerve to actually take a picture there. You might say I'm kind of a chicken, but since I lived there, it was just sort of strange. Do you take pictures of your supermarket?</p>
```

Figure 5.7 *The URL for this image, since it contains only the file name and no path, indicates that the image is located in the same folder as this Web page.*

Figure 5.8 *Images are aligned to the left side of the page, by default. You can change the alignment or wrap text around an image.*

```
<h1>Barcelona's Market</h1>

<img src="cornermarket.jpg" alt="Fruit Stand in Market" />

<p>This first picture shows the entranceway to the Mercat de la Bouqería, the central market that is just off the Rambles. It's an incredible place, full of every kind of fruit, meat, fish, or whatever you might
```

Figure 5.9 *While the alternate text can theoretically be as long as you like, most browsers don't automatically wrap long lines. Therefore, it's a good idea to keep it under 50 characters or so.*

Figure 5.10 *In Internet Explorer, the alternate text appears next to a small box with a red x. In other browsers, the text appears alone.*

Figure 5.11 *On Explorer for Windows, when the visitor points at an image with alternate text, the alternate text appears in a tool tip. You can create tool tips for all current browsers by using the* title *tag (see page 68).*

Offering Alternate Text

While images are great on a big screen with a fast connection, they can be less useful—and downright problematic—on handhelds, phones, slow connections, or for the blind. You can add descriptive text that will appear if the image, for whatever reason, does not.

To offer alternate text when images don't appear:

1. Within the img tag, after the src attribute and value, type **alt="**.

2. Type the text that should appear if, for some reason, the image itself does not.

3. Type **"**.

✔ Tips

- The alt attribute is required for *all* img tags in both XHTML and HTML.

- On IE Win 5+, the alt tag text is automatically used as a *tool tip* **(Figure 5.11)**, similar to the effect of the title tag in *all* current browsers *(see page 68)*. If you'd like tool tips on images in all browsers, use the title tag in addition to alt (which will still appear when the image does not). If you don't want tool tips at all, set **title=""**.

- If the image is just for formatting, like a horizontal line or a bullet image, the W3C suggests you use **alt=""**.

- Screen readers for the blind, like JAWS, can read the alternate text out loud so that blind visitors can get an idea of what the image is about.

- You can format the alternate text with different fonts and sizes by applying styles to the img tag. For details on styles, see Chapter 10, *Formatting with Styles*.

Specifying Size for Speedier Viewing

When a browser gets to the (X)HTML code for an image, it must load the image to see how big it is and how much space must be reserved for it. If you specify the image's dimensions, the browser can fill in the text around the image as the image loads, so that your visitors have something to read while waiting for the images.

You can either use your browser or your image editing program to get the exact dimensions of your image.

To find the size of your image with your browser:

1. Right-click (in Windows) or Control-click (in Macintosh) the image. A contextual pop-up menu appears (**Figure 5.12**).

2. Choose Properties or Get Image Info (depending on your browser). A box appears that shows the dimensions of your image, in pixels (**Figure 5.13**).

To figure out the size of your image with Photoshop or Photoshop Elements:

1. Open the image in Photoshop or Photoshop Elements.

2. Make the document window wide enough so that the document info ("Doc") bar is visible in the lower-left border of the window.

3. Hold down the Option key (or Alt on Windows) and click in the document info bar. A small box appears with information about the image, including its size (**Figure 5.14**).

Figure 5.12 *Right-click or Control-click the image in the browser to make the contextual pop-up menu appear. Then choose Properties (or Get Image Info).*

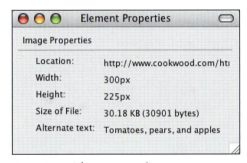

Figure 5.13 *A box appears (its appearance varies depending on the browser you're using) that shows the size of the image in pixels.*

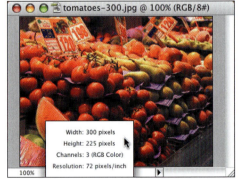

Figure 5.14 *In Photoshop, Alt or Option Click the document info bar at the bottom of a document window to see the image's properties. (If the document info bar doesn't show, make the window a little wider.)*

[snip] just sort of strange. Do you take pictures of your supermarket?</p>

<img src="vegetables.jpg" width="417" height="283" alt="Peppers and Cucumbers" />

<p>I love how they stack up the fruit and vegetables. I'm always tempted to take a pepper out of the bottom row, but of course, you're not supposed to touch them at all. Which I guess makes sense. Sort of. Ok, so you're at the market and there are ten thousand other people milling around.

Figure 5.15 *If you specify the exact height and width in pixels, the browser won't have to spend time doing it and will display the image more quickly.*

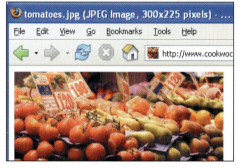

Figure 5.16 *If you open an image directly in a browser (this is Firefox for Windows), its dimensions are displayed in the title bar.*

To specify the size of your image for speedier viewing:

1. Figure out the size of your image using one of the techniques described on page 92.

2. Within the img tag, after the src attribute, type **width="x" height="y"**, using the values you jotted down in step 1 to specify the values for *x* and *y* (the width and height of your image) in pixels.

✔ Tips

■ The width and height attributes don't necessarily have to reflect the actual size of the image. For more details, consult *Scaling an Image* on page 94.

■ If you have several images that are all the same size, you can set their height and width all at the same time with styles *(see page 174)*.

■ You can also find the size of an image in a browser by opening the image in its own window. The size is shown in the title bar **(Figure 5.16)**.

■ In Photoshop or Photoshop Elements, you can also select the entire image and then view the Info palette for the image's dimensions.

Specifying Size for Speedier Viewing

Scaling an Image

You can change the display size of an image just by specifying a new height and width in pixels. This is an easy way to have large images on your page without long loading times. Beware, though, if you enlarge your pictures too much, they'll be grainy and ugly.

To scale an image:

1. Type **<img src="image.url"**, where *image.url* is the location on the server of the image.

2. Type **width="x" height="y"** where *x* and *y* are the desired width and height, respectively, in pixels, of your image.

3. Add any other image attributes as desired and then type the final **/>**.

✔ Tips

■ You can also use a percentage value in step 2, with respect to the browser window (not the original image size).

■ Using the width and height attributes is a quick and dirty way to change how the image is displayed on a Web page, especially if you don't have an image editor (or don't have the time or inclination to use it). However, since the file itself is not changed, the visitor always gets cheated. Reduced images take longer to view than images that are really that size; enlarged images appear grainy. A better solution is to use your image editor to change the size of the image *(see page 95)*.

■ You can set just the width or just the height and have the browser adjust the other value proportionally.

■ You can also use styles to control the width and height of elements. For more information, consult *Setting the Height or Width for an Element* on page 174.

Figure 5.17 *At its original size of 396 by 439 pixels, the image is way too big on the page.*

```
<h1>Fish Ladies</h1>

<img src="fishlady.jpg" width="198"
height="219" alt="One of the fish ladies" />

<p>The fish ladies hold a special place in the
market's heart, where the floors are wet and kind of
slimy, the pervasive smell of fish floats in the air, and
the cold chill from the ice makes you forget the
sunny day you left outside. Unless they're helping
```

Figure 5.18 *Don't specify pixels with the numbers. Just use bare numbers.*

Figure 5.19 *The image appears at half its original size. It's important to note, however, that it takes the same time to load as before. After all, it's the same file.*

Scaling an Image

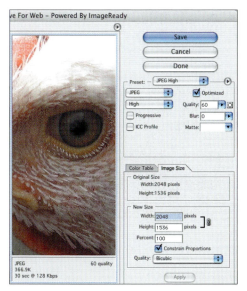

Figure 5.20 *The original image, snapped with my digital camera's default values measured 2048 by 1536 pixels, which besides being big enough for almost four browsers, weighed in at a whopping 366.9K, when compressed as a high quality JPEG.*

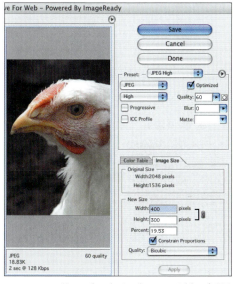

Figure 5.21 *Type the desired new width of 400 pixels in the Width box and click Apply. The reduced-size image will fit properly on my page and will take only 2 seconds to download at 128Kbps (or less with a faster connection).*

Making Images Smaller

Most images are simply too big for a Web page. While an image destined for print might measure 1800 pixels across (in order to print at 300 dpi and be six inches wide), images for Web pages should rarely be wider than 600 pixels, and often more like 200, depending, of course, on what you're doing.

To make images smaller:

1. In the lower right portion of the Save For Web window, click the Image Size tab **(Figure 5.20)**.

2. Enter a new width or height in pixels, or a percentage, and then click Apply **(Figure 5.21)**.

✔ Tips

- You can continue to adjust the size up or down until you're satisfied. The image is not resampled until you press Save.

- Don't use this technique to make an image *bigger* than its original. Adding pixels with Photoshop increases the file size but doesn't add any image data. If you must increase the image's size, use (X)HTML *(see page 94)* or better yet, rescan or redigitize your image.

- You can also use the Image Size command to change the size of an image. Remember that the Resolution box is irrelevant (it refers to the *output resolution*, which is determined on the Web not by you or Photoshop, but rather by the visitor's monitor). Instead, base the size on the number of pixels in the image. You will have to check the Resample Image box to get it to change the image's size (as opposed to its output resolution).

- Another great way to reduce the size of an image is to crop out unwanted areas.

Making Images Smaller

Making Images Float

You can use the `align` attribute (with the *left* and *right* values only) to make images float along one side of your page, with text and other elements wrapping around the other.

To make images float:

1. Type **<img src="image.jpg"** where *image.jpg* indicates the location of the image on the server.

2. *Either* type **align="left"** to float the image on the left of the screen while the text flows to the right, *or* type **align="right"** to float the image on the right edge of the screen while the text flows on the left side of the image.

3. Add other image attributes, as described in other parts of this chapter, if desired.

4. Type the final **/>**.

5. Create the elements that should flow next to the image.

✔ Tips

- Don't get confused about right and left. When you choose **align="right"**, it's the *image* that goes to the right (while the text goes to the left). When you choose **align="left"**, again, the image will be on the left side with the text flowing around the right side.

- The `align` attribute is deprecated. Nevertheless, I think it's a useful trick to have in your bag. If you're doing (X)HTML strict, use the CSS `float` property *(see page 181)* instead.

- Why use the word *align* for floating images? I don't know. Personally, I'd prefer a `float` attribute, but it doesn't exist. For more details about what you can do with `align`, see page 100.

```
<body>

<img src="house.jpg" align="right" alt="house"
width="237" height="225" />

<h2>The Pioneer Valley: Northampton</h2>

<p>This triplex on South Street is a good [snip]
```

Figure 5.22 *When you align an image to the right, you are actually wrapping text to its left.*

Figure 5.23 *The image is aligned to the right and the text wraps around it.*

```
<body>

<img src="house.jpg" align="left" alt="house"
width="237" height="225" />

<h2>The Pioneer Valley: Northampton</h2>

This triplex on South Street is a good [snip]
```

Figure 5.24 *To make the image appear on the left with the text wrapped around the right side, use* `align="left"`.

Figure 5.25 *With the image floated on the left, the text wraps around on the right side (rather closely, but we'll fix that pretty soon).*

```
<body>

<img src="courthouse.jpg" alt="courthouse"
align="right" width="256" height="229" />

<h2>The Pioneer Valley: Northampton</h2>

<p>This building, that some might say looks like a
church, is actually the Hampshire County
Courthouse. If you ever get called to be [snip] </p>

<img src="house.jpg" alt="house" align="left"
width="237" height="225" />

<p>This triplex on South Street is a good example
of multi-family dwellings in the area. Built as a one
family home in the 30s, it has been [snip].</p>

</body>
```

Figure 5.26 *The image always precedes the text that should flow around it.*

Figure 5.27 *The first image is floated to the right and the text flows to its left. The next image appears after the last line of text in the preceding paragraph and pushes the following paragraph to the right.*

To float images on both sides:

1. Type **<img src="right.image" align="right">** where *right.image* indicates the location on the server of the image that should appear on the right side of the screen.

2. Type the text that should flow around the first image.

3. Type **<img src="left.image" align="left">** where *left.image* indicates the location on the server of the image that should appear on the left side of the screen.

4. If desired, type **<p>** to begin a new paragraph, that will be aligned with the image placed in step 3.

5. Type the text that should flow around the second image. Type **</p>** to complete that paragraph, if necessary.

✔ Tips

- The key is to place each image *directly before* the text it should "disrupt."

- Each image will continue to push the text to one side until it either encounters a break *(see page 98)* or until there is no more text.

Stopping Elements from Wrapping

A floated image affects all the elements that follow it, unless you insert a special line break. The `clear` attribute added to the regular `br` tag indicates that the text should not begin until the specified margin is clear (that is, at the end of the image or images).

To stop elements from wrapping:

1. Create your image and the text or other elements (*see pages 96 and 97*).

2. Place the cursor where you want to stop wrapping text and elements to the side of the image.

3. *Either* type **<br clear="left" />** to stop flowing content until there are no more floating objects aligned to the left margin.

   Or type **<br clear="right" />** to stop flowing content until there are no more floating objects aligned to the right margin.

   Or type **<br clear="all" />** to stop flowing content until there are no more floating objects on either margin.

✔ Tips

- The `clear` attribute is deprecated in favor of style sheets. However, I think it's important to know about the `clear` attribute. For information on using styles to control the text flow, consult *Controlling Where Elements Float* on page 182.

- Note that the `clear` attribute affects the elements that follow a floated image, while the CSS `clear` property described on page 182 more directly affects the floated element itself. It's just a slightly different perspective.

```
<img src="house.jpg" align="right" height="200" alt="house" />

<h1>The Pioneer Valley: Northampton</h1>

<img src="flower.gif" align="left" alt="flower" width="43" height="43" />

<br clear="left" />

<p>This triplex on South Street is a good example
```

Figure 5.28 *Notice the order: first the house, then the header, then the flower logo, then more text.*

Figure 5.29 *The* `clear="left"` *attribute makes the text stop flowing until it reaches an empty left margin (that is, below the bottom of the left-aligned flower).*

Figure 5.30 *With* clear="all" *the text won't flow until both the left and right margins are completely clear.*

Figure 5.31 *No space is left, by default, between floating images and the elements they float next to.*

```
<body>

<p><img src="house.jpg" align="left"
height="190" width="200" alt="house"
hspace="10" vspace="10" /></p>

<h2>The Pioneer Valley: Northampton</h2>

<p>This triplex on South Street is a good example
of multi-family dwellings in the area. Built as a one
```

Figure 5.32 *You can add horizontal space or vertical space, or both, to your images.*

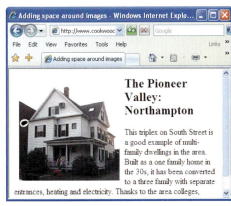

Figure 5.33 *One big limitation of* hspace *and* vspace *is that they add space to* both *sides of an image. Note, for example, that the photo is no longer aligned with the left edge of the text.*

Adding Space around an Image

Look carefully at the image in Figure 5.31. If you don't want your text butting right up to the image, you can use the deprecated vspace and hspace attributes to add a buffer around your image.

To add space around an image:

1. Type **<img src="image.location"** where *image.location* indicates the location on the server of your image.

2. If desired, type **hspace="x"** where *x* is the number of pixels of space to add on *both* the right and left sides of the image.

3. If desired, type **vspace="x"** where *x* is the number of pixels of space to add on *both* the top and bottom of the image.

4. Add other image attributes as desired and type the final **/>**.

✔ Tips

- You don't have to add both hspace and vspace at the same time.

- Both hspace and vspace are deprecated in favor of style sheets which are much more powerful and flexible. For information about using styles to control the space around your images, consult *Setting the Margins around an Element* on page 176 and *Adding Padding around an Element* on page 177.

- The worst part about hspace and vspace is that you can't add space to just one side. This is a perfect example where styles really are worth the extra trouble.

- If you just want to add space to one side of the image, you could use Photoshop to add blank space to that side, and skip hspace and vspace altogether. Then, make the blank space transparent.

Aligning Images

Perhaps the more expected use of the align attribute is for aligning images with text. You can align an image in various ways to a single line in a paragraph. However, be careful with multiple images on the same line—different align options have different effects depending on which image is taller and which appears first.

To align an image with text:

1. Type **<img src="image.location"** where *image.location* indicates the location on the server of the image.

2. Type **align="direction"** where *direction* is top, middle, or bottom **(Figure 5.35)**.

3. Add other attributes as desired and then type the final **/>**.

4. Type the text with which you wish to align the image. (This text may also precede the image.)

✔ Tips

■ The align attribute is deprecated. That means the W3C recommends you start using style sheets to control how elements are aligned on your page *(see page 188)*.

■ Firefox and Internet Explorer don't treat the middle value the same way. Firefox aligns images with the middle of the line of text in which they appear; Explorer aligns images with the middle of the other images on the line.

<h3>Aligned to the top</h3>

<p>If you put an image with a line of text, it might look better if it's aligned with the top of the line <img src="orangecircle.gif" align="top"> and then followed by another couple of lines of interesting text</p>

<h3>Aligned to the middle</h3>

<p>Or it might look better if it's in the middle of the line <img src="orangecircle.gif" align="middle"> depending on what's around it, although it doesn't look much like the middle to me...</p>

<h3>Aligned to the bottom</h3>

<p>Or it might look better at the bottom <img src="orangecircle.gif" align="bottom"> of the line with lots of text in it that is very important and that says something crucial</p>

<p>Then again, maybe it doesn't matter much.

Figure 5.34 *You can align an image with the top, middle, or bottom of the line in which it appears.*

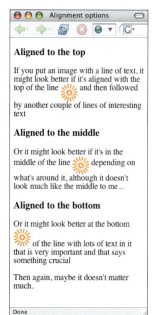

Figure 5.35 *Notice that the height of the image affects the line height of the entire line.*

```
<p>AstroFinder 3
<br />Pleiades Expander
<br />Southern Cross</p>
<hr />
<p>The AstroFinder3 is a revolutionary new
```

Figure 5.36 *The* hr *tag includes an automatic line break both before and after the rule.*

Figure 5.37 *Horizontal rules can be helpful for dividing sections on your page.*

```
<br />Southern Cross</p>
<hr size="10" width="80%" align="center"
noshade="noshade" />
<p>The AstroFinder3 is a revolutionary new
product t
```

Figure 5.38 *The* hr *attributes are deprecated but well supported.*

Figure 5.39 *You can make horizontal rules thicker and narrower.*

Adding Horizontal Rules

One graphic element that is completely supported by the majority of the browsers is the horizontal rule. There are several attributes you can use to jazz up horizontal rules, although they've all been deprecated in favor of styles.

To insert a horizontal rule:

1. Type **<hr** where you want the rule to appear. The text that follows will appear in a new paragraph below the new rule.

2. If desired, type **size="n"**, where *n* is the rule's height in pixels.

3. If desired, type **width="w"**, where *w* is the width of the rule in pixels, or as a percentage of the document's width.

4. If desired, type **align="direction"**, where *direction* refers to the way a rule should be aligned on the page; either left, right, or center. The align attribute is only effective if you have made the rule narrower than the browser window.

5. If desired, type **noshade** to create a solid bar, with no shading. Add **="noshade"** in XHTML.

6. Type the final **/>** to complete the horizontal rule definition.

✔ Tips

■ All of the attributes for hr (but not hr itself) are deprecated. The W3C recommends using styles to format your horizontal rules *(see page 169)*.

■ There is no CSS equivalent to noshade. One solution is to omit rules and just apply borders *(see page 184)*.

Adding Horizontal Rules

Adding an Icon for Your Web Site

Most browsers now support associating a small image with your Web site and displaying it in the Address bar, Favorites menu, or elsewhere. These little images are called *favicons*, which is short for Favorites Icon.

To add an icon for your Web site:

1. Create a 16 pixel by 16 pixel image.

2. In the head section of your (X)HTML document, type **<link rel="icon" href="favicon.ico" type="image/x-icon" />**, where *favicon.ico* is the name and location of your icon on your server.

3. For compatibility with Internet Explorer, add Microsoft's proprietary syntax as well: **<link rel= "shortcut icon" href= "favicon.ico" type="image/x-icon" />**

✔ Tips

- Favicons should generally be saved in .ico format, an icon format developed by Microsoft that contains various sizes and bit depths of a small image. You can find a useful plug-in from Telegraphics for creating .ico format icons in Photoshop (*http://www.telegraphics.com.au/sw/*).

- Some browsers, but not Internet Explorer, also support favicons in GIF (including animated GIFs) and PNG format. Be sure to use the proper MIME type for type.

- Internet Explorer originally required the favicon.ico file to be placed in the root directory of your Web site. This is no longer the case, though browsers may still look there if the link element is not present (or is not understood, say by older browsers).

Figure 5.40 *Favicon icons, in real life, are even smaller than the one shown at left. They measure a measly 16 by 16 pixels.*

Figure 5.41 *Use both link syntaxes to ensure compatibility across browsers.*

Figure 5.42 *The favicon is typically used in the Address bar, Favorites menu, and in Tabs.*

Figure 5.43 *Because Tabs are often gray or colored, you may want to make your icon's background transparent.*

Adding an Icon for Your Web Site

LINKS

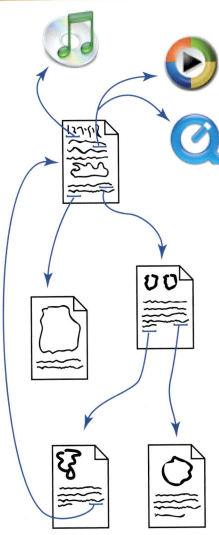

Links are the distinguishing feature of the World Wide Web. They let you skip from one page to another, call up a movie or a recording of The Nields (or *your* favorite band), and download files with FTP.

A link has three parts: a destination, a label, and a target. The first part, the *destination*, is arguably the most important. You use it to specify what will happen when the visitor clicks the link. You can create links that show an image, play a sound or movie, download files, open a newsgroup, send an email message, run a CGI program, and more. The most common links, however, connect to other Web pages, and sometimes to specific locations on other Web pages called *anchors*. All destinations are defined by writing a URL *(see page 35)* and are generally only visible to the visitor in the status area of the browser.

The second part of the link is the *label*, the part the visitor sees and clicks on to reach the destination. It can be text, an image, or both. Label text is often, but not always, shown underlined and in blue. The more appealing, enticing, and attractive the label, the more likely a visitor will click on it. In fact, eliciting Web visitors' clicks is an art.

The last part of the link, the *target*, is often ignored or left up to the browser. The target determines where the destination will be displayed. The target might be a particular named window or frame, or a *new* window or frame.

Figure 6.1 *Some of your pages may have links to many other pages. Other pages may have only one link. Others may link to multimedia files. And still others may have no links at all.*

Creating a Link to Another Web Page

If you have more than one Web page, you will probably want to create links from one page to the next (and back again). You can also create connections to Web pages designed by other people on other servers.

To create a link to another Web page:

1. Type **<a href="page.html">** where *page.html* is the URL of the destination Web page.

2. Type the label text, that is, the text that is highlighted (usually blue and underlined), and that when clicked upon will take the user to the page referenced in step 1.

3. Type **</a>** to complete the definition of the link.

✔ Tips

■ As a general rule, use relative URLs for links to Web pages on your site and absolute URLs for links to Web pages on other sites. For more details, consult *URLs* on page 35.

■ So, a link to a page at another site might look like: **<a href="http://www.site.com/directory/page.html"> Label text</a>** (**Figures 6.5**, **6.6**, and **6.7**).

■ Specify the path but omit the file name to link to the default file for a directory, usually one of *index.html* or *default.htm*: **http://www.site.com/directory/**. Omit the path as well to link to a *site's* default (home) page: **http://www.site.com/**.

■ It's a good idea to use all lowercase letters for your URLs to avoid problems on the many servers that are case sensitive.

■ href stands for *hypertext reference*.

```
<body>

<h1>Cookie and Woody</h1>

<img src="woodygran.jpg" alt="Woody"
width="202" height="131" /> <img src=
"cookiefora.jpg" width="143" height="131" />

<p>Generally considered the sweetest and yet most
independent cats in the <a href="pioneerval.html">
Pioneer Valley,</a> Cookie and Woody are
consistently underestimated by their humble
humans.</p>
```

Figure 6.2 *Since there is only a file name (and no path) referenced in the* href *attribute, the file* pioneerval.html *must be in the same directory as this Web page that contains the link.*

Figure 6.3 *When a visitor points at a link (displayed in blue underlined text, by default), the destination URL is shown in the status area. If they actually click on a link...*

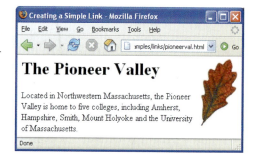

Figure 6.4 *...the page associated with that destination URL is displayed in their browser.*

```
<body>

<h1>Pixel</h1>

<p>If you'd like to meet a JavaCat, check out <a
href="http://www.pixel.mu/">Pixel</a> at Tom
Negrino and Dori Smith's great site about their <a
href="http://www.javascriptworld.com/">
<em>JavaScript for the World Wide Web: Visual
QuickStart Guide</em></a>.</p>

</body>
```

Figure 6.5 *If you're creating links to someone else's Web site, you'll have to use an absolute URL, with the http://, server, full path, and file name.*

Figure 6.6 *When a visitor points at a link (displayed in blue underlined text, by default), the destination URL is shown in the status area. If they click on a link...*

Figure 6.7 *...the page associated with that destination URL is displayed in their browser.*

■ There seems to be some question in the Web community about whether it's OK to link to any page on a site besides the home page. A direct "deep" link, as they're sometimes called, helps your visitor arrive promptly at their destination. However, they may miss important information or advertising that the site's creators left on the home page. One possible compromise is to give the direct connection *as well as* a connection to the site's home page. You may also want to create a link to *your* home page from every other page on your site in case other sites create deep links to your inner pages.

■ Don't make the link's label too long. If the label is part of a sentence, keep only the key words within the link definition, with the rest of the sentence before and after the less than and greater than signs.

■ Try not to use "Click here" for a label. Instead use the key words that already exist in your text to identify the link.

■ You may apply styles *(see page 151)* or (X)HTML basic text formatting *(see page 69)* to the label or even use an image as a label *(see page 114)*.

■ To create a link to a particular place on a page, use an anchor *(see pages 106–107)*.

■ To make the link appear in a given window or frame, use a target *(see page 108)*.

■ You can create keyboard shortcuts for links. For more details, see page 112.

■ You can determine the tab order for visitors who use their keyboards to navigate your page. For more details, consult *Setting the Tab Order for Links* on page 113.

■ An a element may contain any kind of inline tag except another a element. It may not contain block-level elements.

Creating Anchors

Generally, a click on a link brings the user to the *top* of the corresponding Web page. If you want to have the user jump to a specific section of the Web page, you have to create an *anchor* and then reference that anchor in the link.

To create an anchor:

1. Place the cursor in the part of the Web page that you wish the user to jump to.

2. Type **<a name="anchor name">**, where *anchor name* is the text you will use internally to identify that section of the Web page.

3. Add the words or images that you wish to be referenced.

4. Type **</a>** to complete the definition of the anchor.

✔ Tips

■ You can also create an anchor by adding an `id` attribute to the desired element *(see page 63)*.

■ Quotes are *always* required around the anchor name in XHTML. While they're sometimes optional in HTML *(see page 38)*, I highly recommend them.

■ In a long document, create an anchor for each section and link it to the corresponding item in the table of contents.

■ The W3C, Netscape, and others are not at all consistent with the terminology. Some folks call links anchors—a is for anchor, after all—others call targets anchors. In this book, the word *anchor* refers to a specific location in a document that you link to. (A *target* is the window or frame where a link will appear. See page 108.)

```
<body>
<div class="toc">
<h2>Table of Contents</h2>
<a href="#intro">Introduction</a><br />
<a href="#descrip">Description of the Main
Characters</a><br />
<a href="#rising">Rising Action</a><br />
<a href="#climax">Climax</a><br />
<a href="#denoue">Denouement</a>
</div>

<h2><a name="intro">Introduction</a></h2>

<p>This is the intro. If I could think of enough things
to write about, it could span a few pages, giving all
the introductory information that an introduction
should introduce. </p>

<h2><a name="descrip">Description of the Main
Characters</a></h2>

<p>Frankie and Johnny are the main characters.
She's jealous, and seems to have a reason to be.
He's a sleaze, and will pay the price. </p>

<h2><a name="rising">Rising Action</a></h2>

<p>This is where everything starts happening.
Johnny goes out, without Frankie, without even tellin'
her where he's going. She's not crazy about it, but
she lets him go. A while later, she gets thirsty and
decides to go down to the corner bar for some beer.
Chatting with the bartender, she learns that Johnny
has been there with no other than Nellie Bly. Furious,
she catches the cross town bus to find him.</p>

<h2><a name="climax">Climax</a></h2>

<p>When Frankie gets to Nellie's house, she looks
up and sees them kissing on the balcony. With tears
in her eyes, she picks up her shotgun and kills her
Johnny. He falls to the ground.</p>

<h2 id="denoue">Denouement</h2>

<p>Frankie feels bad but it's kind of late now, and
Johnny <em>was</em> a lech. But the police come
and cart her off anyway.</p></body>
```

Figure 6.8 *Notice that most of the anchors are created with the* a *element and* name *attribute, while the last is created by simply adding an* id *attribute to the existing* h2 *element (see first tip). The* id *attribute does double duty as an anchor in all but the oldest browsers.*

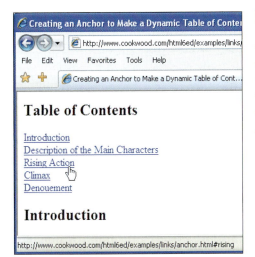

Figure 6.9 *When the visitor points at a link with an anchor, the URL and the anchor name appear in the status bar (in the lower-left corner of the window).*

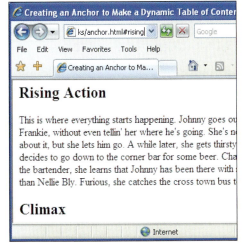

Figure 6.10 *Once the visitor clicks the link, the particular part of the page that the anchor references is displayed at the top of the browser window.*

Linking to a Specific Anchor

Once you have created an anchor, you can define a link so that a user's click brings them directly to the section of the document that contains the anchor, not just the top of that document.

To create a link to an anchor:

1. Type **<a href="#anchor name">**, where *anchor name* is the value of the name attribute in the destination's a tag *(step 2 on page 106)* or the value of the destination's id attribute *(see first tip on page 106).*

2. Type the label text, that is, the text that is highlighted (usually blue and underlined), and that when clicked upon will take the user to the section referenced in step 1.

3. Type **</a>** to complete the definition of the link.

✔ Tips

- If the anchor is in a separate document, use **<a href="page.html#anchorname">** to reference the section. (There should be no space between the URL and the *#*.) If the anchor is on a page on a different server, you'll have to type **<a href= "http://www.site.com/path/page.html #anchorname">** (with no spaces).

- While you obviously can't add anchors to other people's pages, you can take advantage of the ones that they have already created. View the source code of their documents to see which anchor names correspond to which sections. (For help viewing source code, consult *The Inspiration of Others* on page 53.)

- If the anchor is at the bottom of the page, it may not display at the top of the window, but rather towards the middle.

Targeting Links to Specific Windows

Targets let you open a link in a particular window, or even in a new window created especially for that link. This way, the page that contains the link stays open, enabling the user to go back and forth between the page of links and the information from each of those links.

To target links:

Within the link definition, type **target= "window"**, where *window* is the name of the window where the corresponding page should be displayed.

✔ Tips

■ Target names are case sensitive! In addition, you should always enclose them in quotation marks.

■ Open a link in a completely new window by using **target="_blank"**.

■ If you target several links to the same window (e.g., using the same name), the links will all open in that same window.

■ If a named window is not already open, the browser opens a new window and uses it for all future links to that window.

■ Targets are most effective for opening Web pages (or even FTP links) in particular windows. They don't make sense for email or news links which open in different kinds of windows.

■ The W3C has removed the `target` attribute from (X)HTML strict to promote accessibility. Instead, they suggest using JavaScript or the yet-to-be-finalized XLink. I say, use `target`. (It *is* part of both (X)HTML transitional and frameset.)

```
<h1>Nathaniel Hawthorne</h1>

<p>Nathaniel Hawthorne was one of the most
important writers of 19th century America. His most
famous character is <a href="hester.html" target=
"characters">Hester Prynne</a>, a woman living
in Puritan New England. [snip]</p>

<p>Besides <a href="scarlet.html" target=
"books"><em>The Scarlet Letter</em></a>,
Hawthorne wrote <a href="gables.html" target=
"books"><em>The House of Seven Gables</em>
</a>, <a href="blithedale.html" target="books">
<em>The Blithedale Romance</em></a>, <a
href="faun.html" target="books"><em>The Marble
```

Figure 6.11 *In this example, some links will appear in the* characters *window and others will appear in the* books *window.*

Figure 6.12 *When the visitor clicks a link with a target...*

Figure 6.13 *...the corresponding page is shown in the targeted window. In this example, it's the* characters *window.*

```
<!DOCTYPE html PUBLIC "-//W3C//DTD XHTML
1.0 Transitional//EN"

"http://www.w3.org/TR/2000/REC-xhtml1-
20000126/DTD/xhtml1-transitional.dtd">

<html xmlns="http://www.w3.org/1999/xhtml">

<head>

<meta http-equiv="content-type"
content="text/html; charset=iso-8859-1" />

<title>American Writers of the 19th Century</title>

<base target="characters" />

</head>

<body>

<h1>Nathaniel Hawthorne</h1>

<p>Nathaniel Hawthorne was one of the most
important writers of 19th century America. His most
famous character is <a href="hester.html">Hester
Prynne</a>, a woman living in Puritan New
England. Another famous object of Hawthorne's
writing was <a href="http://www.ripon.edu/
dept/pogo/presidency/Pierce/">Franklin Pierce
</a>, the 14th president of the United States.</p>

<p>Besides <a href="scarlet.html" target="books">
<em>The Scarlet Letter</em></a>, Hawthorne
wrote <a href="gables.html" target="books">
<em>The House of Seven Gables</em></a>, <a
```

Figure 6.14 *Use the* base *tag to set the default target (in this case the* characters *window) in order to save typing. Notice that I no longer have to specify the target for the links in the first paragraph. This document is equivalent to the one shown in Figure 6.11.*

Setting the Default Target

A link, by default, opens in the same window or frame that contains the link. You can choose another target for each link individually, as described on page 108, or specify a default target for all the links on a page.

To set a default target for a page:

1. In the head section of your Web page, type **<base**.

2. Type **target="title"**, where *title* is the name of the window or frame in which all the links on the page should open, by default.

3. Type **/>** to complete the base tag.

✔ Tips

■ Target names are case sensitive! In addition, you should always enclose them in quotation marks.

■ You can override the default target specified in the base tag by adding a target attribute to an individual link *(see page 108)*.

■ While the base tag is part of (X)HTML strict, the target attribute is not. I use it anyway (see the last tip on page 108).

■ You can also use the base tag to set the base URL for constructing relative URLs. This can be particularly useful when a Perl CGI script *(see page 253)*, located off in the cgi-bin directory, is generating the (X)HTML page, and you want to reference a bunch of images or links in the main part of your server. Use **<base href="base.url" />** where *base.url* is the URL that all relative links should be constructed from. Put another way, the URL reflects the *virtual* location of the generated (X)HTML page.

Creating Other Kinds of Links

You are not limited to creating links to other Web pages. You can create a link to any URL—FTP sites, files that you want visitors to be able to download, newsgroups, and messages. You can even create a link to an email address.

To create other kinds of links:

1. Type **<a href="**.

2. Type the URL:

   For a link to any file on the Web, including movies, sounds, programs, Excel spreadsheets, or whatever, type **http://www.site.com/path/file.ext**, where *www.site.com* is the name of the server and *path/file.ext* is the path to the desired file, including its extension.

   For a link to an FTP site, type **ftp:// ftp.site.com/path**, where *ftp.site.com* is the server and *path* is the path to the desired directory or file.

3. Type **">**.

4. Type the label for the link, that is, the text that will be underlined or highlighted, and that when clicked upon will take the visitor to the URL referenced in step 2.

5. Type **</a>**.

✔ Tips

- If you create a link to a file that a browser doesn't know how to handle (an Excel file, for example), the browser will either try to open a helper program to view the file or will try to download it to the visitor's hard disk. For more information, consult *Of Plugins and Players* on page 282.

```
<p>There are lots of different kinds of links that you
can create on a Web page. More precisely, there
are a lot of different files you can link to on your
Web page.</p>

<p>You can create links to <a
href="http://static.flickr.com/73/167700314_f7a
773f73d.jpg">photos</a> or even make a link out
of a photo like this: <a
href="http://www.flickr.com/photos/cookwood/1
67700314/" title="Lemurs"><img
src="http://static.flickr.com/73/167700314_f7a
773f73d_m.jpg" width="240" height="180"
alt="Lemurs" /></a></p>

<p>You can link to <p>You can link to <a
href="http://www.sarahsnotecards.com/cataluny
alive/segadors.mov">videos</a> too.</p>

<p>Although you can make links to <a
href="mailto:chokeonthis@stupidspambots.com">e
mail addresses</a> with the mailto: protocol, I
don't recommend it since spambots pick those up
and then bombard them with spam. It's too bad
because they are so convenient. Click it to see how
it opens your Mail program. It's probably better to
offer your email address in the body of your Web
page in a descriptive way, like <i>html at
cookwood.com</i>, although I doubt that's
foolproof either.</p>

<p>You can create links to ftp sites by using the ftp
protocol. There are very few public (anonymous)
FTP sites anymore, since it's just as easy for most
people to download through the Web (that is,
HTTP). But there are a few, like the <a
href="ftp://ftp.gnu.org/gnu">GNU FTP</a> site,
where you can download free software (which is
more complicated than it sounds).</p>

<p>People often offer links to <a
href="http://www.cookwood.com/feed.xml">RSS
feeds</a>, though I don't really get why. They're so
ugly when you click on them. I guess it's just an easy
way to make it available without showing the URL.
Still, I hate a link you're not supposed to click
on.</p>
```

Figure 6.15 *You can create links to all different kinds of URLs.*

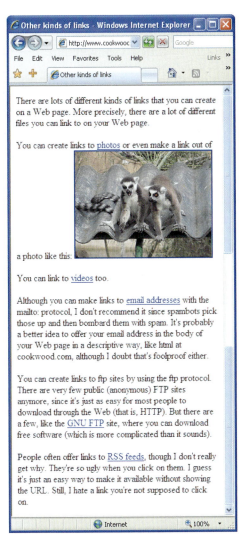

Figure 6.16 *No matter where a link goes, it looks pretty much the same in the browser (unless you wrap it around a photo). Notice that I've tried to create labels that flow with the body of the text, instead of a lot of "click me's". These are all real links. You can see where they lead by opening this page in your own browser:* http://www.cookwood.com/html6ed/examples/links/newotherlinks.html

■ It's a good idea to compress files that you want visitors to download. This makes them faster to download and it also protects them from being corrupted as they go from one system to another. Allume Systems *(www.allume.com)* has some good compression tools for both Macs and Windows machines.

■ Links to Usenet news groups (e.g., news:alt.soc.catalan), Telnet (e.g., telnet://lib.wuacc.edu), or even Gopher and WAIS used to be common. However, their dependence on external applications has meant their demise. Nowadays, most everything is handled directly in a browser with HTTP. For example, you can link to a Yahoo Group with a simple link: **http://groups.yahoo.com/group/ groupname/**, where *groupname* is the official name of the group. Add **message/ number**, where *number* is the message's id number, to link to a specific message. Of course, some Yahoo groups are private and so your visitors may be asked to log in before they reach their destination.

■ You can preface an FTP URL with **name:password@** to access a private FTP site. Beware that browsers keep track of where you've been and the password you used to get there.

■ If you want to create an FTP link to a particular directory on the FTP site (as opposed to an individual file), simply use **ftp://ftp.site.com/directory**.

■ If you want to link to songs at the iTunes Music Store, you can use Apple's Link Maker to generate the URL *(http:// www.apple.com/itunes/ linkmaker/)*. If you are an affiliate *(http://www.apple.com/ itunes/affiliates/)*, Apple pays you a commission on songs people buy through your links.

Creating Keyboard Shortcuts for Links

Keyboard shortcuts let your visitors select and activate links without using a mouse.

To add a keyboard shortcut to a link:

1. Inside the link's tag, type **accesskey="**.

2. Type the keyboard shortcut (any letter or number).

3. Type the final **"**.

4. If desired, add information about the keyboard shortcut to the text so that the visitor knows it exists.

✔ Tips

■ On Firefox (Mac/Win) and Explorer for Mac, typing a keyboard shortcut activates the link, but on Explorer for Windows, it merely gives focus to the link and the visitor must still press Return to actually follow it.

■ On Windows systems, to invoke the keyboard shortcut, visitors use the Alt key plus the letter you've assigned. On a Mac, visitors use the Control key, plus the letter.

■ Keyboard shortcuts don't work at all in Opera and are unreliable with frames, unless the visitor selects the frame—which kind of defeats the purpose.

■ Keyboard shortcuts that you choose can (annoyingly) override the browser's shortcuts. For example, in most Windows programs, Alt-F is for accessing the File menu. If you use Alt-F for a keyboard shortcut, your visitors won't be able to use the keyboard to access their browser's File menu.

```
<h1>Our Cats</h1>

<p>Each of our cats has their own home page.
Click on the corresponding link or use the keyboard
shortcut to see each one.

<br /><a href="gatetseng.html#woody"
accesskey="w">Woody</a> (Alt-W, Ctrl-W)

<br /><a href="gatetseng.html#cookie"
accesskey="c">Cookie</a> (Alt-C, Ctrl-C)

<br /><a href="gatetseng.html#xixona"
accesskey="x">Xixona</a> (Alt-X, Ctrl-X)

<br /><a href="gatetseng.html#llumeta"
accesskey="l">Llumeta</a> (Alt-L, Ctrl-L)</p>

</body>
```

Figure 6.17 *Create a keyboard shortcut for a link by adding the* accesskey *attribute to its tag. The explanatory text (Alt-W, etc.) is optional but helpful.*

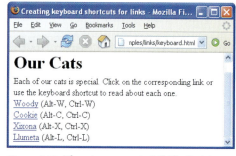

Figure 6.18 *There's no way to tell if a link has a keyboard shortcut unless you've labeled it as such.*

Figure 6.19 *When the keyboard shortcut is used, the link is immediately accessed (and the corresponding page is shown).*

```
<div id="toc"><a href="toc.html" tabindex="2">
Contents</a> <a href="search.html" tabindex
="2">Search</a> <a href="company.html"
tabindex="2">About Us</a></div>

<h1>Our Cats</h1>

<p>Each of our cats is special. Click on the
corresponding link or use the keyboard shortcut to
read about each one.</p>

<p><a href="gatetseng.html#woody"
accesskey="w" tabindex="1">Woody</a> (Alt-
W, Ctrl-W)

<br /><a href="gatetseng.html#cookie"
accesskey="c" tabindex="1">Cookie</a> (Alt-C,
Ctrl-C)

<br /><a href="gatetseng.html#xixona"
accesskey="x" tabindex="1">Xixona</a> (Alt-X,
Ctrl-X)

<br /><a href="gatetseng.html#llumeta"
accesskey="l" tabindex="1">Llumeta</a> (Alt-L,
Ctrl-L)</p>
```

Figure 6.20 *This page begins with a set of links, which, while useful, don't have anything to do with this particular page. So that the first tab selects the first "real" link, I've assigned it the lowest tab index.*

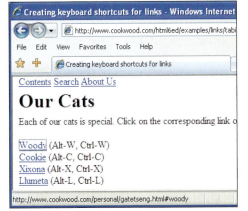

Figure 6.21 *When the visitor hits Tab the first time (OK, the ninth time, see the last tip), the* Woody *link is selected. If they hit Tab again,* Cookie *will be selected, and so on until* Llumeta. *At that point, a tab will bring them up to the* Contents *link.*

Setting the Tab Order for Links

Some browsers let users navigate through the links, image maps, and form elements with the Tab key. You can determine a custom tab order, to emphasize certain elements.

To set the tab order:

In the link's tag, type **tabindex="n"**, where *n* is the number that sets the tab order.

✔ Tips

- To *activate* a link the visitor must tab to it and then press Enter.

- The value for `tabindex` can be any number between 0 and 32767. Use a negative value to take a link out of the tab sequence altogether.

- By default, the tab order depends on the order of the elements in the (X)HTML code. When you change the tab order, the *lower-numbered* elements are activated first, followed by higher-numbered ones.

- Elements with the same tab index value are accessed in the order in which they appear in the (X)HTML document.

- You can also assign tab order to client-side image maps and form elements. For more information, consult *Creating a Client-Side Image Map* on page 117 or *Setting the Tab Order in a Form* on page 277, respectively.

- Currently, browser windows have many elements vying for attention from the Tab key. The first time you hit Tab, you generally get to the Address box. The second Tab often brings you to the Search box. In IE 7, it took me 8 Tabs before I got to the page data, and *then* the link whose `tabindex` was the lowest got the focus.

Setting the Tab Order for Links

Using Images to Label Links

In this age of graphical interfaces, people are used to clicking on images and icons to make things happen. Adding an image to a link creates a navigational button that the visitor can click to access the referenced URL. (For more information about images, see Chapter 5, *Images.*)

To use images to label links:

1. Type **<a href="destination.html">**, where *destination.html* is the URL of the page that the user will jump to when they click the button.

2. Type **<img src="image.jpg"** where *image.jpg* gives the location of the image file on the server.

3. If desired, type **border="n"**, where *n* is the width in pixels of the border. Use a value of 0 to omit the border.

4. Add other image attributes as desired and then type the final **/>**.

5. If desired, type the label text, that is, the text that will be underlined or highlighted in blue, that when clicked upon will take the user to the URL referenced in step 1.

6. Type **</a>** to complete the link.

✔ Tips

■ If you invert steps 5 and 6, only a click on the *image* will produce the desired jump. A click on the text has no effect. (You can also leave the text out altogether.)

■ Most browsers surround clickable images with a border of the same color as the links (generally blue). For no border, use a value of 0 in step 3. Note that the border attribute is deprecated for images. You can use CSS instead *(see page 184).*

```
<body>

<h1>Cookie and Woody</h1>

<p>Generally considered the sweetest and yet most
independent cats in the <a
href="pioneerval.html">Pioneer Valley,</a>
Cookie and Woody are consistently underestimated
by their humble humans.</p>

<p align="right"><a href="firstpage.html"><img
src="rewind.gif" alt="First page" border="0"
/></a>

<a href="prevpage.html"><img src="back.gif"
alt="Previous page" border="0" /></a>

<a href="nextpage.html"><img src="forward.gif"
alt="Next page" border="0" /></a>

<a href="lastpage.html"><img
src="fastforward.gif" alt="Last page" border="0"
/></a></p>
```

Figure 6.22 *I've removed the border from all the image links.*

Figure 6.23 *The images act just like clickable text. The* alt *text can indicate where the link is leading.*

```
<h1>More Market Pictures</h1>

<p><a href="flowers.jpg"><img
src="flowers_little.jpg" alt="Flowers on the
Rambles" width="83" height="125" /></a> <a
href="fruitstand.jpg"><img
src="fruitstand_little.jpg" alt="Fruit stand"
width="103" height="67" /></a> <a
href="ham.jpg"><img src="ham_little.jpg"
alt="Charcuterie" width="123" height="85"
/></a> <a href="cannedgoods.jpg"><img
src="cannedgoods_little.jpg" alt="Canned goods,
hams, wine, oil, olives!" width="84" height="123"
/></a></p>
```

Figure 6.24 *Remember to use the full-size image in the link and the thumbnail in the image definition.*

Figure 6.25 *In this example, the thumbnails are about 4K and take a few seconds to load.*

Figure 6.26 *If the visitor clicks the icon, the full-size image opens in a new window.*

Linking Thumbnails to Images

A very similar technique to using images to label links is to use *thumbnails*, or miniature versions of your images and then link them to larger ones. You can load a lot of small pictures quickly and let your visitor choose which ones they'd like to see full size.

To link a thumbnail to a larger image:

1. Type **<a href="image.jpg">**, where *image.jpg* is the location of the full-sized image on your server *(see page 35)*.

2. Type **<img src="mini.jpg"**, where *mini.jpg* is the location of the thumbnail version of the image on the server.

3. If desired, type **alt="alternate text"**, where *alternate text* is the text that should appear if, for some reason, the thumbnail does not.

4. Type the final **/>** of the thumbnail definition.

5. If desired, type the label text that should accompany the thumbnail. You could include the actual file size of the full-sized image so the visitor knows what they're getting into by clicking it.

6. Type **</a>** to complete the link to the full sized image.

✔ Tips

■ Using miniatures or thumbnails is a good way to get a lot of graphic information onto a page without making your visitors wait too long to see it. Then they can view the images that they are most interested in at their leisure.

■ See *Creating Pop-ups* on page 193 in Chapter 12, *Dynamic Effects with Styles* for a technique that can display the larger images right on the same page.

Dividing an Image into Clickable Regions

A clickable image is like a collection of buttons combined together in one image. A click in one part of the image brings the user to one destination. A click in another area brings the user to a different destination.

There are two important steps to implementing a clickable image: First you must map out the different regions of your image, and second you must define which destinations correspond to which areas of the image.

To divide an image into clickable regions:

1. Create an image, consulting Chapter 5, *Images*, as necessary.

2. Open the image in Photoshop or other image editing program.

3. Choose Window > Info **(Figure 6.27)**.

4. Make sure that the units are pixels (by clicking the tiny arrow next to the cross hairs at the bottom of the Info window).

5. Point the cursor over the upper-left corner of the region you wish to define.

6. Using the Info window, jot down the *x* and *y* coordinates for that corner **(Figure 6.28)**.

7. Repeat steps 5–6 for the rectangle's lower-right corner, for each point of a polygon, or for a circle's center and radius.

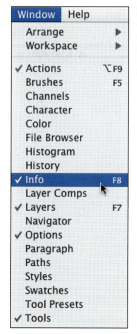

Figure 6.27 *In either Photoshop (shown) or Photoshop Elements, choose Window > Info to show the Info palette.*

Figure 6.28 *Place the cursor in the upper-left corner of the rectangle and jot down the x and y coordinates shown in Photoshop's Info palette. (In this example, x=395 and y=18.) Then do the same with the lower-right corner.*

```
<body><p>

<map name="banner" id="banner">

<area alt="new information" shape="rect"
coords="395, 18, 445, 35" href="newinfo.html" />

<area alt="press releases" shape="rect"
coords="395, 38, 445, 55"
href="pressrelease.html" />

<area alt="events" shape="rect" coords="395, 58,
445, 75" href="events.html" />

</map>

<img src="clickimage.gif" alt="SE banner"
usemap="#banner" width="450" height="100" />

</p>

<div id="content">

<h1>Starsearch Enterprises</h1>

<a href="newinfo.html">New programs</a>
<br />

<a href="pressrelease.html">Press
releases</a><br />

<a href="events.html">Upcoming events</a>
<br />

<a href="infoSE.html">About Starsearch
Enterprises</a><br />

</div>

</body>
```

Figure 6.29 *You can put the* map *anywhere you like in your (X)HTML document. Each clickable area is defined by its own set of coordinates, and has its own corresponding URL. Then, don't forget to add the* usemap *attribute to the image that will serve as the map.*

Creating a Client-Side Image Map

Image maps link the areas of an image with a series of URLs so that a click in a particular area brings the user to the corresponding page. Client-side image maps run quickly because they are interpreted in your visitor's browser and don't have to consult the server for each click. In contrast to server-side image maps, they do not require a CGI script, and thus are simpler to create. Only very old browsers may not understand them.

To create a client-side image map:

1. In the (X)HTML document that contains the image, type **<map**.

2. Type **name="label" id="label">**, where *label* is the name of the map.

3. Type **<area** to define the first clickable area.

4. Type **alt="info"**, where *info* describes what will happen when the visitor clicks.

5. Type **shape="type"**, where *type* represents the area's shape. Use *rect* for a rectangle, *circle* for a circle, and *poly* for an irregular shape.

6. For a rectangle, type **coords="x1, y1, x2, y2"**, where *x1, y1, x2,* and *y2* represent the upper-left and lower-right corners of the rectangle, as obtained on page 116, and shown in Figure 6.28.

   For a circle, type **coords="x, y, r"** where *x* and *y* represent the center of the circle and *r* is the radius.

   For a polygon, type **coords="x1, y1, x2, y2"** (and so on), giving the *x* and *y* coordinates of each point on the polygon.

continued

7. Type **href="url.html"**, where *url.html* is the address of the page that should appear when the user clicks in this area.

Or type **nohref** if a click in this area should have no result. For XHTML add **="nohref"** immediately thereafter.

8. If desired, type **target="name"**, where *name* is the name of the window where the page should appear *(see page 108)*.

9. If desired, add a keyboard shortcut by typing **accesskey="x"** *(see page 112)*.

10. Type **/>** to complete the clickable area.

11. Repeat steps 3–10 for each area.

12. Type **</map>** to complete the map.

13. Type **<img src="image.gif"**, where *image.gif* is the name of the image to be used as an image map.

14. Add image attributes, including `alt`.

15. Type **usemap="#label"**, where *label* is the map name defined in step 2.

16. Type the final **/>** for the image.

✔ Tips

■ Usually, maps are in the same (X)HTML document as the image that uses them. Internet Explorer, however, can use maps that are in an external (X)HTML file. Just add the full URL of that file in front of the label name: **usemap="map.html#label"**.

■ With overlapping areas, most browsers use the URL of the first area defined.

■ The `target` attribute is only allowed in (X)HTML transitional and frameset.

■ The `id` attribute in `map` is required in XHTML strict, but most browsers need the `name` for it to work. So use both.

Figure 6.30 *When your users point at one of the defined areas, the destination URL appears in the status bar at the bottom of the window.*

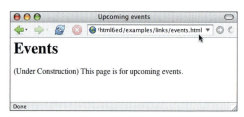

Figure 6.31 *And if a user clicks the link, the browser immediately displays the corresponding page.*

STYLE SHEET BUILDING BLOCKS

7

While (X)HTML gives your Web pages their basic structure, CSS (Cascading Style Sheets) defines their appearance.

A style sheet is simply a text file that contains one or more *rules* that determine—through *properties* and *values*—how certain elements in your Web page should be displayed. There are CSS properties for controlling such basic formatting as font size and color, layout properties such as positioning and float, and print controls for deciding where page breaks should appear. CSS also has a number of dynamic properties, which allow items to appear and disappear and are useful for creating drop-down menus and other interactive components.

While there are various versions of CSS, the version that is best supported, and which we cover in this book, is CSS 2. Most browsers support most of CSS 2. No major current browser supports it all. I'll point out the places to be wary as we go along.

The wonderful thing about CSS is that it can be created outside of a Web page and then applied to all the pages on your site at once. It is flexible, powerful, and efficient and can save you lots of time and bandwidth.

To get the full benefit of CSS, your Web pages must be well structured. CSS appreciates the fastidiousness of XHTML because then it knows just what it has to do.

Constructing a Style Rule

Each style rule in a style sheet has two main parts: the *selector*, which determines which elements are affected and the *declaration*, made up of one or more property/value pairs, which specifies just what should be done (**Figures 7.1** and **7.2**).

To construct a style rule:

1. Type **selector**, where *selector* identifies the elements you wish to format. You'll learn how to create all sorts of selectors in Chapter 9, *Defining Selectors*.

2. Type **{** (an opening curly bracket) to begin the declaration.

3. Type **property: value;**, where *property* is the name of the CSS property that describes the sort of formatting you'd like to apply and *value* is one of a list of allowable options for that property. CSS properties and their values are described in detail in Chapters 10–14.

4. Repeat step 3 as needed.

5. Type **}** to complete the declaration and the style rule.

✔ Tips

■ You may add extra spaces, tabs, or returns between the steps above as desired to keep the style sheet readable (**Figure 7.2**).

■ While each property/value pair should be separated from the next by a semicolon, you may omit the semicolon that follows the *last* pair in the list. Still, it's easier to always use it than to remember when it's possible to omit it.

■ Missing (or duplicate) semicolons can make the browser completely ignore the style rule.

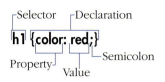

Figure 7.1 *A style rule is made up of a selector (which indicates which elements will be formatted), and a declaration (which describes the formatting that should be executed).*

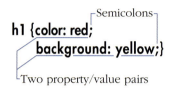

Figure 7.2 *Multiple property/value pairs in the declaration must be separated by a semicolon. Some folks simply end every property/value pair with a semicolon—including the last pair in a list—so that they never forget to add it. That's fine, as shown here, but not required. Note the extra spacing and indenting to keep everything readable.*

```
/* Images will have a solid red 4 pixel border */
img {border: 4px solid red}
```

Figure 7.3 *Comments can be used to describe style rules so that they are easier to edit and update later on. (OK, this one isn't very complicated, but yours might be.)*

```
img {border: 4px solid red} /* Images will have a
solid red 4 pixel border */
```

Figure 7.4 *If you prefer, you can insert comments after a style rule.*

Adding Comments to Style Rules

It's a good idea to add comments to your style sheets so that you can remember what particularly complicated style rules are supposed to do. When you come back later, you'll be happy you left yourself these reminders.

To add comments to style rules:

1. In your style sheet, type **/*** to begin your comments.

2. Type the comments.

3. Type ***/** to signal the end of the comments.

✔ Tips

■ Comments may include returns, and thus span several lines.

■ You can put comments around style rules effectively hiding them from the browser. This is a good way to test style sheets without permanently removing problematic portions.

■ You may not put comments inside other comments. In other words, comments may not include */.

■ You may start comments on their own line **(Figure 7.3)**, or at the end of a style rule **(Figure 7.4)**.

Adding Comments to Style Rules

The Cascade: When Rules Collide

There are many places to apply styles. As we saw back in Chapter 1, every browser has its own default styles *(see page 42)*. Next, you can write style rules and apply them to a specific (X)HTML element right in the code, insert them at the top of an (X)HTML document, and import one or more from an external file *(see page 127)*. And some browsers let your visitors create and apply their own style sheets to any pages they visit—including yours. Finally, some styles are inherited from parent element to child.

What happens, you might ask, when there is more than one style rule that applies to a given element? CSS uses the principle of the *cascade*, from which it gets its initial *C*, to take into account such important characteristics as *inheritance*, *specificity*, and *location* in order to determine which of a group of conflicting rules should win out.

Let's start with inheritance. Many CSS properties affect not only the elements defined by the selector but are also *inherited* by the descendants of those elements. For example, suppose you make all your h1 elements blue with a red border. It so happens that the `color` property is inherited, but the border property is not. Thus, any elements contained within the h1 elements will also be blue, but will *not* have their own red border. You'll learn which properties are inherited in the individual section describing each property (and in Appendix B, *CSS Properties and Values*). You can also use a value of `inherit` with most properties to force inheritance *(see page 124)*.

While inheritance determines what happens if no style rule is applied to an element, *specificity* is the key when more than one rule is applied. The law of specificity states that the more specific the selector, the stronger the

```
body {background:url(bg_flax.jpg) bottom right
no-repeat}

p {font-family: "Trebuchet MS", "Helvetica", sans-
serif; font-weight: bold; color:#3366cc; }

img {float:left;margin-right:10px}
```

Figure 7.5 *Here is the style sheet for this document. Don't worry too much about the details right now, but do notice that there is a rule for* p *elements, but not for* em *elements.*

```
<p>I am continually amazed at the beautiful,
delicate Blue Flax that somehow took hold in my
garden.

They are awash in color every morning, yet not a
single flower remains by the afternoon.

They are the very definition of <em>ephemeral
</em>.</p>

<p>&copy; 2002 by Blue Flax Society.</p>
```

Figure 7.6 *The* em *element is contained within the* p *element, and thus is a* child *of* p.

Figure 7.7 *In the absence of a rule specified explicitly for the* em *element in Figure 7.5, it inherits the font, weight, and color from its parent, the* p *element.*

```
p {color:red}

p.group {color:blue}

p#one {color:green}

p#one {color:magenta}
```

Figure 7.8 *Here are four rules of varying specificity. The first affects any old* p *element, the second affects only those* p *elements with a class equal to* group, *and the third and fourth affect only the single* p *element with an* id *equal to* one.

```
<p>Here's a generic p element. It will be red.</p>

<p class="group">Here's a group-class p element. There are two rules that apply, but since the p.group rule is more specific, this paragraph will be blue.</p>

<p class="group" id="one">Here's a p element with an id of one. There are four rules that could apply to this paragraph. The first two are overruled by the more specific last two. The position breaks the tie between the last two: the one that appears later wins, and thus this paragraph will be magenta.

</p>
```

Figure 7.9 *Here are three paragraphs, one generic one, one with just a class, and one with a class and an id.*

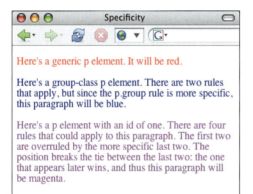

Figure 7.10 *Since the third and fourth rules have the same specificity, their position becomes a factor—and thus the fourth rule wins out since it appears last.*

rule. So if one rule states that all h1 elements should be blue but a second rule states that all h1 elements with a class of *Spanish* be red, the second rule will override the first for all those h1 elements whose class is *Spanish*.

Note that id attributes are considered the most specific (since they must be unique in a document), while the presence of a class attribute makes a selector more specific than a simple selector that has none. Indeed, a selector with more than one class is more specific than a selector with only one. Selectors with just element names come next on the specificity scale; inherited rules are considered to be the most general of all, and are overruled by *any* other rule.

For the exact rules of calculating specificity, see Section 6.4.3 of the CSS specifications (*http://www.w3.org/TR/CSS21/cascade.html #specificity*).

Sometimes, specificity is not enough to determine a winner among competing rules. In that case, the *location* of the rule breaks the tie: Rules that appear later have more weight. For example, rules that are applied locally right in the (X)HTML element *(see page 134)* are considered to appear after (and thus have more weight than) equally specific rules applied internally at the top of the (X)HTML document *(see page 131)*. For details, consult *The Importance of Location* on page 135.

If that isn't enough, you can override the whole system by declaring that a particular rule should be more *important* than the others by adding !important at the end of the rule.

In summary, in the absence of a rule, many styles are inherited from parent element to child. With two competing rules, the more specific the rule, the more weight or importance it has—regardless of its location. With two rules of equal specificity, the one that appears later wins.

A Property's Value

Each CSS property has different rules about what values it can accept. Some properties only accept one of a list of predefined values. Others accept numbers, integers, relative values, percentages, URLs, or colors. Some can accept more than one type of value. While the acceptable values for each property are listed in the section describing that property (mostly in Chapters 10 and 11), I'll discuss the basic systems here.

Inherit

You can use the `inherit` value for any property when you want to explicitly specify that the value for that property be the same as that of the element's parent.

Predefined Values

Most CSS properties have a few predefined values that can be used. For example, the `display` property can be set to **block**, **inline**, **list-item**, or **none**. In contrast with (X)HTML, you don't need to and indeed *must not* enclose predefined values in quotation marks **(Figure 7.11)**.

Lengths and Percentages

Many CSS properties take a *length* for their value. All length values must contain a quantity and a unit, with no spaces between them, for example, **3em** or **10px (Figure 7.12)**. The only exception is **0**, which may be used with or without units.

There are length types that are *relative* to other values. An *em* is usually equal to the element's font-size, so **2em** would mean "twice the font-size". (When the em is used to set the element's `font-size` property itself, its value is derived from the font size of the element's *parent*.) The *ex* should be equal to the font's x-height, that is, the height of a letter *x* in the font, but it's not well supported.

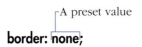

Figure 7.11 *Many CSS properties will only accept values from a predefined list. Type them exactly and do not enclose them in quotation marks.*

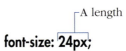

Figure 7.12 *Lengths must always explicitly state the unit. There should be no space between the unit and the measurement.*

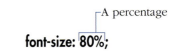

Figure 7.13 *Percentages are generally relative to the parent element. So, in this example, the font would be set to 80% of the parent's font-size.*

Figure 7.14 *Don't confuse numbers and integers with length. A number or integer has no unit (like px). In this case, the value shown here is a factor that will be multiplied by the font-size to get the line-height.*

Figure 7.15 *URLs in CSS properties do not need to be enclosed in quotation marks.*

Pixels (px) are relative to the resolution of the monitor—though not to other style rules. Most monitors these days display about 80 pixels to the inch (though they range from 72 to 96 pixels to the inch), so 16 pixels is about 1/5 of an inch high (or 0.5cm).

There are also the largely self-explanatory *absolute* units—inches (in), centimeters (cm), millimeters (mm), points (pt), and picas (pc). In general, you should only use absolute lengths when the size of the output is known (as with the printed page—see Chapter 14).

Percentage values, **65%**, for example—work much like ems, in that they are relative to some other value **(Figure 7.13)**.

Bare Numbers

A very few CSS properties accept a value in the form of a number, without a unit, like **3**. The most common are `line-height` **(Figure 7.14)** and `z-index`. (The others are mostly for print and aural style sheets and are not yet well supported.)

URLs

Some CSS properties allow you to specify the URL of another file. In that case, use **url(file.ext)**, where *file.ext* is the path and file name of the desired document **(Figure 7.15)**. Note that the specifications state that relative URLs should be relative to the style sheet and not the (X)HTML document.

While you may use quotations around the file name, they're not required. On the other hand, there should be no space between the word **url** and the opening parentheses. White space between the parentheses and the address is allowed but not required.

For more information on writing the URLs themselves, consult *URLs* on page 35.

A Property's Value

CSS Colors

There are several ways to specify colors for CSS properties. First, and easiest, the value can be one of 16 predefined color names **(Figure 7.16)**. Of course, 16 colors get pretty boring pretty quickly.

Instead of limiting yourself to those colors, you can construct your own by specifying the amount of red, green, and blue in the desired color. You can give the values of each of these contributing colors as a percentage, a number from 0–255, or a hexadecimal representation of the number. For example, if you wanted to create a dark purple, you might use 35% red with 50% blue. That color could be written **rgb(%35, 0%, 50%)** as shown in Figure 7.17. If you use numerical values, you could write the same color as **rgb(89, 0, 127)**, since 89 is 35% of 255 and 127 is 50% of 255.

I've saved the most common though most convoluted method for last **(Figure 7.18)**: convert those numerical values to hexadecimals, join them together, and add an initial #: **#59007F**. (59 is the hexadecimal equivalent of 89, 00 is the hexadecimal equivalent of 0, and 7F is the hex equivalent of 127.)

And if that weren't enough, when a hexadecimal color is comprised of three pairs of repeating digits, as in **#ff3344**, you may abbreviate the color to **#f34**.

While most current image editors, including Photoshop and Photoshop Elements, include tools for choosing colors and displaying their hex values, I've also included a do-it-yourself table in Appendix E, along with some esoteric details about hexadecimal conversions.

Perhaps more useful is the inside back cover of this book where you'll find a selection of colors–together with their hex values—that you can use on your Web pages. I'd also recommending taking a look at *Color* on page 82.

I'd also recommending taking a look at *Color* on page 82.

Figure 7.16 *Here are the 16 predefined color names together and their hexadecimal codes.*

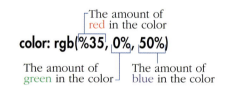

Figure 7.17 *Another way to express the amount of each of the three contributing colors is with a percentage. Define the red first, followed by green, and then blue.*

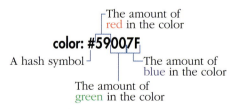

Figure 7.18 *The most common way in both (X)HTML and CSS to define a color is by specifying, with hexadecimal numbers, the amounts of red, green, and blue that it contains.*

A Property's Value

WORKING WITH STYLE SHEET FILES

8

Before you start defining your style sheets, it's important to know how to create and use the files that will contain them. In this chapter, you'll learn how to create a style sheet file, and then apply that style sheet to an individual element, a whole Web page, or an entire Web site.

You'll learn how to create the content of your CSS style sheets in the chapters that follow.

Creating an External Style Sheet

External style sheets are ideal for giving all the pages on your Web site a common look. You can define all your styles in an external style sheet and then tell each page on your site to consult the external sheet, thus ensuring that each will have the same settings.

To create an external style sheet:

1. Create a new text document in your text editor of choice.

2. Define the style rules for your Web pages as described in Chapters 9–14 **(Figure 8.1)**.

3. Save the document in a text-only format in the desired directory **(Figure 8.2)**. Give the document the extension .css to designate the document as a Cascading Style Sheet.

✔ Tips

■ Make sure you save the style sheet in a text-only format (sometimes called Text Document or Plain Text) and give it the .css extension. When you upload it to the server (which we'll get to in Chapter 23), be sure to choose ASCII mode—not Binary—just as you do for (X)HTML files. This goes for Mac folks, too!

■ External style sheets must be either linked to *(see page 129)* or imported *(see page 132)*.

■ If your style sheet will contain non-ASCII characters, you should declare its character encoding on the first line with **@charset "encoding";** *(see page 332)*.

■ XSL (Extensible Stylesheet Language) is another style sheet language for XHTML pages. You can find more information about it at the W3C's XSL site, *http://www.w3.org/Style/XSL/*

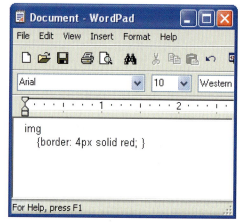

Figure 8.1 *Use any text editor you like to write CSS documents. This is WordPad.*

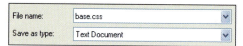

Figure 8.2 *Be sure to save the CSS file with the .css extension and in text-only format (as a Text Document, or Plain Text, or ASCII, or however your text editor calls it).*

```
img {border: 4px solid red;}
```

Figure 8.3 *Here's the external style sheet that we created on page 128 (called* base.css*). Don't worry about the properties and values just yet. (It just means create a solid red border around all the* img *elements.)*

```
<head><meta http-equiv="content-type"
content="text/html; charset=utf-8" />
<title>Palau de la Música</title>
<link rel="stylesheet" type="text/css"
href="base.css" />
</head>
<body>
<img src="palau250.jpg" alt="El Palau de la
Música" width="250" height="163" align="left" />
```

Figure 8.4 *The* link *tag goes inside the* head *section of your (X)HTML document.*

Figure 8.5 *The style rule (a red, solid border) is applied to each* img *element.*

Figure 8.6 *Other documents can link to the very same external style sheet.*

Linking External Style Sheets

The easiest, best supported, and most common way to apply the rules in a style sheet to a Web page is to *link* to the style sheet.

To link an external style sheet:

1. In the head section of each (X)HTML page in which you wish to use the style sheet, type **<link rel="stylesheet" type="text/css"**, where *text/css* indicates that the style sheet is written in CSS.

2. Type **href="url.css"**, where *url.css* is the name of your CSS style sheet *(see step 3 on page 128).*

3. Type the final **/>**.

✔ Tips

- When you make a change to an external style sheet, all the pages that reference it are automatically updated as well.

- URLs in an external style sheet are relative to the location of the style sheet file on the server, not to the (X)HTML page's location.

- Styles that are imported are overridden by styles within an (X)HTML document. The relative influence of styles applied in different ways is summarized on page 135.

- You can link to several style sheets at a time. The later ones take precedence over the earlier ones.

- You can offer alternate versions of linked style sheets and let your visitors choose among them *(see page 130).*

- You can limit style sheets to a particular kind of output by setting the media attribute. For more details, see *Using Media-Specific Style Sheets* on page 133.

Linking External Style Sheets

Offering Alternate Style Sheets

You can link to more than one style sheet and let visitors choose the styles they like best. The specifications allow for a base set of *persistent* styles that are applied regardless of the visitor's preference, a default or *preferred* set of styles that are applied if the visitor makes no choice, and one or more *alternate* style sheets that the visitor can choose, at which point the preferred set (though not the persistent one) is deactivated and ignored.

To offer alternate style sheets:

1. To designate the style sheet that should be used as a base, regardless of the visitor's preferences, use the simple syntax described on page 129, with no `title`.

2. To designate the style sheet that should be offered as a first choice, but that can be deactivated by another choice, add **title="label"** to the `link` element, where *label* identifies the preferred style sheet.

3. To designate a style sheet that should be offered as an alternate choice, use **rel="alternate stylesheet" title="label"** in the `link` element, where *label* identifies the alternate style sheet.

✔ Tips

- Currently, only Firefox **(Figure 8.11)** and Opera offer an easy way to switch from one style sheet to another. However, there are JavaScript solutions for other browsers. For one such solution, check out *http://www.alistapart.com/stories/alternate/*.

- You can also create style sheets just for printing your Web page *(see page 209)* or just for viewing it on handhelds *(see page 199)*. For details, see *Using Media-Specific Style Sheets* on page 133.

```
img {border: 4px solid red;}
```

Figure 8.7 *This CSS file* (base.css) *will be our persistent style sheet, and will be applied no matter what the visitor does.*

```
img {border-style: dashed;}
```

Figure 8.8 *This style sheet* (preferred.css) *is the one that I want loaded by default, when the visitor jumps to my page.*

```
img {border-style: dotted;}
```

Figure 8.9 *The visitor will be able to load this alternate style sheet if they want. Its file name is* alternate.css.

```
<head><meta http-equiv="content-type"
content="text/html; charset=utf-8" />
<title>Palau de la Música</title>
    <link rel="stylesheet" type="text/css"
href="base.css" />
    <link rel="stylesheet" type="text/css"
href="preferred.css" title="Dashed" />
    <link rel="alternate stylesheet" type="text/css"
href="alternate.css" title="Dotted" />
```

Figure 8.10 *In order, I've defined the base or persistent style sheet, the preferred or automatic style sheet, and an alternate style sheet. Each style sheet needs its own* link *element.*

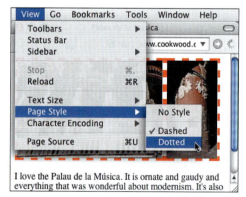

Figure 8.11 *When the page is loaded, it has a dashed border (the preferred value overrides the base value of solid, but the base color is maintained). If the visitor chooses Dotted, the alternate style sheet will be used instead.*

```
<head>
<meta http-equiv="content-type"
content="text/html; charset=utf-8" />
<title>El Palau de la Música</title>
    <style type="text/css">
    img {border: 4px solid red; }
    </style>
    </head>
<body>
<img src="palau250.jpg" alt="El Palau de la
Música" width="250" height="163" align="left"
/>
<img src="tickets.jpg" alt="The Ticket Window"
width="87" height="163" />
```

Figure 8.12 *The* style *element and its enclosed style rules go in the* head *section of your document. Don't forget the closing* </style> *tag, as for some reason I am wont to do.*

Figure 8.13 *The result is exactly the same as if you linked to the styles in an external style sheet. The difference is that no other Web page can take advantage of the styles used on this page.*

Creating an Internal Style Sheet

Internal style sheets let you set the styles at the top of the (X)HTML document to which they should be applied. If you plan to apply the style sheet to more than one page, you're better off using external style sheets *(see page 128)*.

To create an internal style sheet:

1. In the head section of your (X)HTML document, type **<style type="text/css">**.

2. Define as many style rules as desired *(see page 120)*.

3. Type **</style>** to complete the internal style sheet **(Figure 8.12)**.

✔ Tips

■ Styles applied in an internal style sheet override external style sheets if and only if the style tag comes after the link tag. For more details, see *The Importance of Location* on page 135.

■ Add (X)HTML comment tags (**<!--**) after the initial <style> tag and before (**-->**) the final </style> tag to hide styles from very old browsers *(see page 67)*. In XHTML, you can enclose an internal style sheet in **<![CDATA[...]]>** to hide it from XML parsers *(see page 319)*.

■ You can also apply styles to individual (X)HTML tags. For more details, consult *Applying Styles Locally* on page 134.

■ If you want to apply your styles to more than one Web page, you should use an external style sheet. For more information, consult *Creating an External Style Sheet* on page 128.

■ If you use a different style sheet language (like XSL), you'll have to adjust the type attribute accordingly, e.g., *text/xsl*.

Creating an Internal Style Sheet

Importing External Style Sheets

You can also call on an external style sheet by *importing* it.

To import an external style sheet:

Within the `style` element *(see page 131)*, but before any individual style rules, type **@import "external.css";**, where *external.css* is the name of your CSS style sheet *(see step 3 on page 128)* **(Figure 8.15)**.

✔ Tips

■ The `@import` rule can also be written as **@import url(external.css);** or **@import url("external.css");**. Regardless, always put it before any other style rules in the `style` element and don't forget the semicolon.

■ Style rules in an imported style sheet take precedence over any rules that come before the `@import` rule (for example, rules in earlier `@import` rules or in external sheets placed before the `style` element).

■ You may use the `@import` rule in an external style sheet (as always, before any other style rules).

■ The `@import` rule has been used as a way to hide CSS rules from buggy browsers, in particular Netscape 4 **(Figure 8.14)**. For example, you could *link* to style sheets with rules that Netscape 4 understood and then *import* style sheets with advanced techniques it couldn't handle.

■ Since linking style sheets *(see pages 129–130)* gives you the ability to indicate preferred and alternative style sheets (and Netscape 4 is no longer an issue), that's the method I prefer.

■ You can limit imported style sheets to particular outputs, as described on the following page.

Figure 8.14 *Some very old browsers not only didn't support particular CSS features but would create something hideous instead. Such was the case of Netscape 4.x and borders. Look how it created those charming little boxes instead of the borders we asked for. Yuck!*

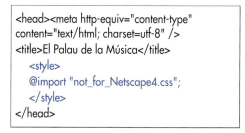

```
<head><meta http-equiv="content-type"
content="text/html; charset=utf-8" />
<title>El Palau de la Música</title>
    <style>
    @import "not_for_Netscape4.css";
    </style>
</head>
```

Figure 8.15 *The* `@import` *rule must be placed before any individual style rules in the* `style` *element. It may come after other* `@import` *rules.*

Figure 8.16 *All major modern browsers support importing styles.*

```
<head>
    <meta http-equiv="content-type"
content="text/html; charset=utf-8" />
    <title>El Palau de la Música</title>
    <link rel="stylesheet" type="text/css"
href="base.css" media="screen" />
<link rel="stylesheet" type="text/css"
href="printstyles.css" media="print" />
</head>
<body>
<img src="palau250.jpg" alt="El Palau de la
Música" width="250" height="163" align="left"
/>
```

Figure 8.17 *Limit the style sheet to a particular output by adding the* media *attribute to the* link *element.*

```
<head>
    <meta http-equiv="content-type"
content="text/html; charset=utf-8" />
    <title>El Palau de la Música</title>
    <style>
    @import "screenstyles.css" screen;
    @import "printstyles.css" print;
    </style>
</head>
```

Figure 8.18 *If you're importing style sheets rather than linking them, you add the* media *attribute's value to the end of the* @import *rule.*

Using Media-Specific Style Sheets

You can designate a style sheet to be used only for a particular output, perhaps only for printing, or only for handhelds. For example, you might create one general style sheet with features common to both the print and screen versions, and then individual print and screen style sheets with properties to be used only for print and screen, respectively.

To designate media-specific style sheets:

Add **media="output"** to the opening `link` or `style` tags, where *output* is one or more of the following: `print`, `screen`, `handheld`, or `all` **(Figure 8.17)**. Separate multiple values with commas.

Or, in an `@import` rule, as described on the previous page, after the URL, add **output**, where *output* has the same values as above, after the URL but before the semicolon **(Figure 8.18)**. Again, separate multiple values with commas.

✔ Tips

- The default value for the `media` attribute is `all`.

- There are ten possible output types: `all`, `aural`, `braille`, embossed, `handheld`, `print`, `projection`, `screen`, `tty`, and `tv`, with varying degrees of support.

- There is also an `@media` rule, though it is less well supported than the options described above.

- For more on style sheets for handhelds, consult Chapter 13, *Style Sheets for Handhelds*. For more information about creating style sheets for print, see Chapter 14, *Style Sheets for Printing*.

Applying Styles Locally

If you are new to style sheets and would like to experiment a bit before taking the plunge, applying styles locally is an easy, small-scale, and rather safe way to begin. Although it doesn't centralize all your formatting information for easy editing and global updating, it does open the door to the additional formatting that is impossible to create with conventional (X)HTML tags.

To apply styles locally:

1. Within the (X)HTML tag that you want to format, type **style="**.

2. Create a style rule without curly brackets or a selector. The selector isn't necessary since you're placing it directly inside the desired element.

3. To create additional style definitions, type a semicolon **;** and repeat step 2.

4. Type the final quote mark **"**.

✔ Tips

- Be careful not to confuse the equals signs with the colon. Since they both assign values it's easy to interchange them without thinking.

- Don't forget to separate multiple property definitions with a semicolon.

- Don't forget to enclose your style definitions in straight quote marks.

- Styles applied locally take precedence over all other styles *(see page 135)*.

- If you specify the font family in a local style declaration, you'll have to enclose multi-word font names with *single* quotes in order to avoid conflict with the style element's double quotes. Actually, the reverse is also fine. You just can't use the same type of quotes in both places.

```
<head>
    <meta http-equiv="content-type"
content="text/html; charset=utf-8" />
    <title>El Palau de la Música</title>
    </head>
<body>
<img src="palau250.jpg" alt="El Palau de la
Música" width="250" height="163"
style="border:4px solid red" align="left" />
<img src="tickets.jpg" alt="The Ticket Window"
width="87" height="163"/>
<br clear="all" />
<p>I love the Palau de la Música. It is ornate and
```

Figure 8.19 *Rules applied locally affect only a single element, in this case, the left* img *tag.*

Figure 8.20 *Only the left image has a border. To repeat the effect shown in the rest of this chapter, you'd have to add* `style="border: 4px solid red"` *to every single* img *tag individually.*

```
<head>
    <title>El Palau de la Música</title>
    <link rel="stylesheet" type="text/css"
href="base.css" />
    <style> img {border-style: dashed} </style>
</head>
```

Figure 8.21 *In this example, the* style *element comes last. Therefore, its rules will have precedence over the rules in the* base.css *style sheet (as long as the conflicting rules have the same inheritance and specificity factors).*

Figure 8.22 *The* style *element's dashed border wins out over the linked solid border.*

```
<head>
    <title>El Palau de la Música</title>
    <style> img {border: dashed} </style>
    <link rel="stylesheet" type="text/css"
href="base.css" />
</head>
```

Figure 8.23 *Here, the linked style sheet comes last and has precedence over rules in the* style *element (all else being equal).*

Figure 8.24 *The solid border from the* base.css *style sheet wins out over the internal* style *element's dashed border.*

The Importance of Location

With so many ways to apply styles, it's not unusual for more than one style rule to apply to the same element. As we discussed in Chapter 7, *Style Sheet Building Blocks*, and specifically on pages 122–123, a style's *location* can break a tie in the contest between inheritance and specificity. The basic rule is, with all else equal, the later the style appears, the more precedence or importance it has.

So, locally applied styles *(see page 134)* have the most precedence and will override any conflicting styles applied earlier.

In a style element, any @import rules present will lose out to any individual style rules that also appear in the style element (since these must follow the @import rules, by definition).

The relationship between the style element and any linked external style sheets depends on their relative positions. If the link element comes later in the (X)HTML code, it overrides the style element. If it comes earlier, the style element (and any imported style sheets it contains) overrides the rules in the linked style sheet.

External style sheets can also contain @import rules. In that case, the imported rules are overridden by the other rules contained in the external style sheet (since, by definition, they must follow the @import rule). Their relationship with the document's other style sheets is determined by the position of the link to the external style sheet, as usual.

The Inspiration of Others: CSS

In Chapter 2, *Working with Web Page Files*, I showed you how to see the source code for a Web page. Viewing someone's CSS is not much more difficult.

To view other designers' CSS code:

1. First view the page's (X)HTML code **(Figure 8.25)**. For more details on viewing (X)HTML source code, see *The Inspiration of Others* on page 53.

   If the CSS code is in an internal style sheet, you'll be able to see it already.

2. If the CSS is in an external style sheet, copy the URL shown in the link element or imported with an `@import` rule.

3. Paste the style sheet's URL in the Address box of your browser and hit Enter. If the style sheet's URL is a relative address *(see page 35)*, you may have to reconstruct the style sheet's URL by combining the Web page's URL with the style sheet's relative URL **(Figures 8.26** and **8.27)**.

✔ Tip

■ As with (X)HTML, use other designers' code for inspiration, then write your own style sheets.

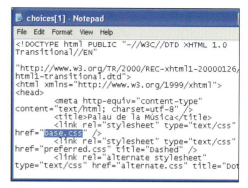

Figure 8.25 *View the source code for the (X)HTML page you're interested in and then copy the URL from the* href *attribute of the* link *element or the* @import *rule.*

Figure 8.26 *This is the URL for the page whose CSS we're interested in.*

Figure 8.27 *Paste the relative URL that you copied in Figure 8.25 in place of the Web page's file name in the full URL. Depending on the relative URL, you may need to remove the Web page's original directory as well. Press Enter.*

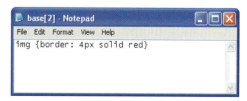

Figure 8.28 *The CSS code is shown either right in the browser source window or in an external text editor (as shown here), depending on your browser and its preferences.*

DEFINING SELECTORS

As you saw in *Constructing a Style Rule* on page 120, there are two principal parts of a CSS style rule. The *selector* determines which elements the formatting will be applied to and the *declarations* define just what formatting will be applied. In this chapter, you'll learn how to define CSS selectors.

While the simplest selectors let you format all the elements of a given type—say, all the h1 headers—more complex selectors let you apply formatting rules to elements based on their class or id, context, state and more.

Once you've defined the selectors, you can go on to create the declarations (with actual properties and values) in Chapters 10–14. Some more specialized style properties are discussed throughout the rest of this book. Until then, we'll use the very simple and relatively obvious {color:red;} in our examples.

Constructing Selectors

The *selector* determines which elements a style rule is applied to. For example, if you want to format all p elements with the Times font, 12 pixels high, you'd need to create a selector that identifies just the p elements while leaving the other elements in your code alone. If you want to format the first p in each division with a special indent, you'll need to create a slightly more complicated selector that identifies only those p elements that are the first element in their division.

A selector can define up to five different criteria for choosing the elements that should be formatted:

- the type or name of the element **(Figure 9.1)**,

- the context in which the element is found **(Figure 9.2)**,

- the class or id of an element **(Figure 9.3)**,

- the pseudo-class of an element or a pseudo-element itself **(Figure 9.4)**. (I'll explain that awful sounding *pseudo-class*, I promise.)

- and whether or not an element has certain attributes and values **(Figure 9.5)**.

Selectors can include any combination of these five criteria in order to pinpoint the desired elements. Mostly, you use one or two. In addition, you can apply the same declarations to several selectors at once if you need to apply the same style rules to different groups of elements *(see page 148)*.

The rest of this chapter explains exactly how to define selectors and gives information about which selectors are best supported by current browsers.

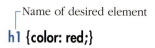

Figure 9.1 *The simplest kind of selector is simply the name of the type of element that should be formatted, in this case,* h1 *elements.*

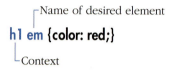

Figure 9.2 *This selector uses context. The style will only be applied to the* em *elements within* h1 *elements. The* em *elements found elsewhere are not affected.*

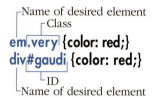

Figure 9.3 *The first selector chooses all the* em *elements that belong to the* very *class. The second selector chooses the one* div *element with an* id *of gaudi.*

Figure 9.4 *In this example, the selector chooses* a *elements that belong to the* link *pseudo-class (in English this means the* a *elements that haven't yet been visited).*

Figure 9.5 *You can use the square brackets to add information to a selector about the desired element's attributes and/or values.*

```
<p>Barcelona <a href="http://www.gaudi2002.
bcn.es/english/">celebrates</a> the 150th
anniversary of Gaudí's birth in 2002.</p>

<div class="works"><h2>La Casa Milà</h2>

<p>Gaudí's work was essentially useful. La Casa
Milà is an apartment building and <em>real
people</em> live there.</p>

</div>

<div class="works"><h2>La Sagrada
Família</h2>

<p>The complicatedly named and curiously
```

Figure 9.6 *Our (X)HTML code has two* h2 *elements.*

```
h2 {color:red;}
```

Figure 9.7 *This selector will choose all of the* h2 *elements in the document.*

Figure 9.8 *All the* h2 *elements are colored red.*

Selecting Elements by Name

Perhaps the most common criteria for choosing which elements to format is the element's name or *type*. For example, you might want to make all of the h1 elements big and bold and format all of the p elements with a sans-serif font.

To select elements to format based on their type:

Type **selector**, where *selector* is the name of the desired type of element, without any attributes **(Figure 9.7)**.

✔ Tips

- Unless you specify otherwise (using the techniques in the rest of this chapter) all the elements of the specified type will be formatted, no matter where they appear in your document.

- Not all selectors need to specify an element's name. If you want to apply formatting to an entire class of elements, regardless of which type of elements have been identified with that class, you'd want to leave the name out of the selector.

- The wild card, ***** (asterisk), matches any element name in your code.

- You can choose a group of element names for a selector by using the comma to separate them. For more details, consult *Specifying Groups of Elements* on page 148.

- Name or type selectors are well supported by current browsers.

Selecting Elements by Name

Selecting Elements by ID or Class

If you've labeled elements with an id or class *(see page 63)*, you can use that criteria in a selector to apply formatting to only those elements that are so labeled.

To select elements to format based on their id:

1. Type **#** (a hash or pound sign).

2. With no intervening space, immediately type **id**, where *id* uniquely identifies the element to which you'd like to apply the styles.

To select elements to format based on their class:

1. Type **.** (a period).

2. With no intervening space, immediately type **label**, where *label* identifies the class to which you'd like to apply the styles.

✔ Tips

- You can use class and id selectors alone or together with other selector criteria. For example, **.news {color: red;}** would affect all elements with the news class, while **h1.news {color: red;}** would affect only the h1 elements with the news class.

- For more information on assigning classes to elements in the (X)HTML code, consult *Naming Elements* on page 63.

- Class and id selectors are well supported by current browsers.

```
<h1>Antoni Gaudí</h1>

<div id="gaudi">

<p>Many tourists are drawn to Barcelona to see Antoni Gaudí's incredible architecture. </p>

<p>Barcelona <a href="http://www.gaudi2002.bcn.es/english/">celebrates </a> the 150th anniversary of Gaudí's birth in 2002.</p>

<div class="works"><h2>La Casa Milà</h2>

<p>Gaudí's work was essentially useful. La Casa Milà is an apartment building and <em>real people</em> live there.</p>

</div>

<div class="works"><h2>La Sagrada Família</h2>
```

Figure 9.9 *The division with an* id *of* gaudi *encloses almost the entire page (everything but the initial* h1*).*

```
div#gaudi {color:red;}
```

Figure 9.10 *This selector will choose the* div *element with an* id *equal to "gaudi".*

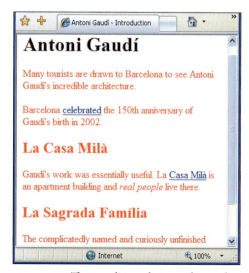

Figure 9.11 *The gaudi* div*, but not the* h1 *element, is displayed in red.*

```
<h1>Antoni Gaudí</h1>

<div id="gaudi">

    <p>Many tourists ... </p>

    <p>Barcelona ...</p>

    <div class="works">

        <h2>La Casa Milà</h2>

        <p>Gaudí's work ...</p>

    </div>

    <div class="works">

        <h2>La Sagrada Família</h2>
```

Figure 9.12 *I've snipped the text to make the relationships between elements easier to see. Each indentation represents a generation. Note that there are two second generation* p *elements, directly within the* gaudi *div, and one third generation* p *element, within the* works *divs (within the* gaudi *div).*

```
div#gaudi p {color:red;}
```

Figure 9.13 *The space between* div#gaudi *and* p *means that this selector will find any* p *element that is a descendant of the* gaudi *div, regardless of its generation.*

Figure 9.14 *All of the* p *elements that are contained within the* gaudi *div are red, even if they're also within other elements within that* gaudi *div.*

Selecting Elements by Context

In CSS you can pinpoint elements depending on their ancestors, their parent, or their siblings *(see page 31).*

An *ancestor* is any element that contains the desired element (the *descendant*), regardless of the number of generations that separate them.

To select elements to format based on their ancestor:

1. Type **ancestor**, where *ancestor* is the name of the element that contains the element you wish to format.

2. Type a space **(Figure 9.13)**.

3. If necessary, repeat steps 1–2 for each successive generation of ancestors.

4. Type **descendant**, where *descendant* is the name of the element you wish to format.

✔ Tips

■ A selector based on an element's ancestor is called a *descendant selector.*

■ Descendant selectors are well supported by current browsers.

■ Don't be thrown off by the **div#gaudi** portion of the example (even though it's ugly). Remember that it simply means "the div whose id is equal to *gaudi*" *(see page 140).* So **div#gaudi p** means "any p element that is contained in the div whose id is equal to *gaudi*".

continued

Selecting Elements by Context

A *parent* is the element that directly contains the desired element (the *child*) with no intermediate containing elements.

To select elements to format based on their parent:

1. Type **parent**, where *parent* is the name of the element that directly contains the element you wish to format.

2. Type **>** (the greater than sign) **(Figure 9.15)**.

3. If necessary, repeat steps 1–2 for each successive generation of parents.

4. Type **child**, where *child* is the name of the element you wish to format.

✔ Tips

■ A selector based on an element's parent is called a *child selector.*

■ Internet Explorer 5.5 and 6 for Windows did not support the child selector. Internet Explorer 7 does **(Figure 9.17)**.

```
div#gaudi > p {color:red;}
```

Figure 9.15 *This selector will only choose those* p *elements that are children of the* gaudi *div. They may not be contained within any other element in order to qualify.*

Figure 9.16 *Only the first two* p *elements are children of the* gaudi *div. The two other* p *elements are children of the* works *div. For the (X)HTML code used in this example, see Figure 9.12 on page 141.*

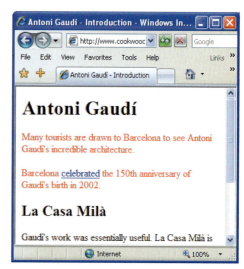

Figure 9.17 *Although Internet Explorer 5.5 and 6 did not recognize the child selector, Internet Explorer 7 does.*

```
div#gaudi p:first-child {color:red}
```

Figure 9.18 *This selector chooses only the p element that is the first child of the gaudi div.*

Figure 9.19 *The first p element contained in the gaudi div is red. The second one isn't.*

```
div#gaudi p+p {color:red}
```

Figure 9.20 *This selector chooses only those p elements which directly follow a sibling p element.*

Figure 9.21 *Only the p elements that directly follow a sibling p element are red. This selector would be useful for indenting all paragraphs except the first.*

It's sometimes useful to be able to select only the *first* child of an element, as opposed to all of the children of an element.

To select elements to format that are the *first* child of their parent:

1. Type **parent**, where *parent* is the selector for the desired element's parent.

2. Type **:first-child** (just like that) **(Figure 9.18)**.

An adjacent sibling is the element that directly precedes the desired element within the same parent element.

To select elements to format based on an adjacent sibling:

1. Type **sibling**, where *sibling* is the selector for the element that directly precedes the desired element within the same parent element.

2. Type **+** (a plus sign).

3. If necessary, repeat steps 1–2 for each successive sibling.

4. Type **tag**, where *tag* is the name of the element you wish to format.

✔ Tips

■ Also see *Parents and Children* on page 31.

■ The :first-child part of the selector is called a *pseudo-class*, because it identifies a group of elements without you, the designer, having to mark them in the (X)HTML code. It is supported by all major current browsers (including IE starting with version 7).

■ Adjacent sibling selectors are currently supported by Firefox, Opera, and IE 7.

Selecting Elements by Context

Selecting Part of an Element

You can also select just the first letter or first line of an element and then apply formatting to that.

To select the first line of an element:

1. Type **tag**, where `tag` is the selector for the element whose first line you'd like to format.

2. Type **:** (the colon).

3. Type **first-line** to select the entire first line of the element referenced in step 1.

To select the first letter of an element:

1. Type **tag**, where `tag` is the selector for the element whose first line you'd like to format.

2. Type **:** (the colon).

3. Type **first-letter** to select the first letter of the element referenced in step 1.

```
<h1>Antoni Gaudí</h1>

<div id="gaudi">

<p>Many tourists are drawn to Barcelona to see
Antoni Gaudí's incredible architecture. </p>

<p>Barcelona <a href="http://
www.gaudi2002.bcn.es/english/">celebrates
</a> the 150th anniversary of Gaudí's birth in
2002.</p>

<div class="works"><h2>La Casa Milà</h2>

<p>Gaudí's work was essentially useful. La Casa
Milà is an apartment building and <em>real
people</em> live there.</p>
```

Figure 9.22 *There is nothing highlighted here because you can't identify the first line until the page is displayed in the browser.*

```
p:first-line {color:red;}
```

Figure 9.23 *Here the selector will choose the first line of each p element.*

Figure 9.24 *Adjusting the width of the window changes the content of the first lines (and thus, what is formatted).*

```
p:first-letter {color:red;}
```

Figure 9.25 *Here the selector will choose just the first letter of each* p *element. For the corresponding (X)HTML code, see Figure 9.22 on page 144.*

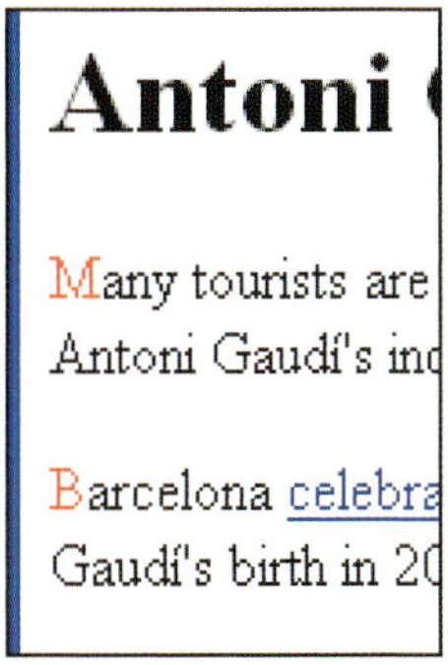

Figure 9.26 *The* first-letter *selector could conceivably be used to create drop caps (once we've learned more properties besides* color*).*

Figure 9.27 *The specifications say the* first-letter *pseudo-element should include any punctuation that precedes the first letter. Firefox and Opera (left) do that, IE (up to and including version 7, shown on the right) does*

✔ **Tips**

■ The first-letter and first-line selectors are called *pseudo-elements*, since they refer to actual content that can't be manually marked as an independent element. OK, you could conceivably mark each first letter of the paragraph with a special span tag (though it would be cumbersome), but the content of the first line depends on a myriad of factors, including such uncontrollable issues as the size of the visitor's window and the visitor's monitor resolution.

■ All current major browsers (including Internet Explorer from version 6 on) support both the first-line and first-letter pseudo-elements.

■ According the CSS specifications, punctuation that precedes the first letter should be included in the selector. Firefox and Opera do this right. IE (as of version 7) doesn't, and instead considers the punctuation itself as the first letter.

■ Only certain CSS properties can be applied to first-letter pseudo-elements: font, color, background, text-decoration, vertical-align (as long as the first-letter is not floated), text-transform, line-height, margin, padding, border, float, and clear. We'll discuss all of these in Chapters 10 and 11.

■ You may combine the first-letter or first-line pseudo-elements with more complicated selectors than that which I've used in this example. For example, if you wanted just the first-letter of the p elements in the *works* divs, your selector would be **div.works p:first-letter**.

Selecting Part of an Element

Selecting Link Elements Based on Their State

CSS lets you apply formatting to links based on their current *state*, that is whether they've been visited, whether the visitor is hovering their cursor on top of them, or whatever.

To select link elements to format based on their state:

1. Type **a** (since *a* is the name of the link tag).

2. Type **:** (the colon).

3. Type **link** to change the appearance of links that haven't yet been or currently aren't being clicked or pointed at.

   Or type **visited** to change links that the visitor has already clicked.

   Or type **focus** if the link is selected via the keyboard and is ready to be activated.

   Or type **hover** to change the appearance of links when pointed to.

   Or type **active** to change the appearance of links when clicked.

✔ Tips

- In most browsers, these *pseudo-classes* (classes for intangible characteristics you can't mark manually) can work with all kinds of elements. IE, up to and including 7, only supports them for the a tag.

- Since a link can be in more than one state at a time (say, simultaneously active *and* hovered above) and later rules override earlier ones, it's important to define the rules in the following order: link, visited, focus, hover, active (LVFHA).

```
<p>Many tourists are drawn to Barcelona to see
Antoni Gaudí's incredible architecture. </p>

<p>Barcelona <http://www.gaudi2002.bcn.es/
english/">celebrated</a> the 150th anniversary
of Gaudí's birth in 2002.</p>

<div class="works"><h2>La Casa Milà</h2>
```

Figure 9.28 *You can't specify in the code what state a link will have. It's controlled by your visitors.*

```
a:link {color:red;}

a:visited {color:orange;}

a:focus {color: purple;}

a:hover {color:green;}

a:active {color:blue;}
```

Figure 9.29 *Styles for links should always be defined in this order, to avoid overriding properties when a link is in more than one state (say, visited and hovered).*

Figure 9.30 *Links will be red when new and not visited.*

Figure 9.31 *Once the link has been visited, it turns orange.*

Figure 9.32 *If the link gets the focus (generally with the Tab key), it is purple.*

Figure 9.33 *When the visitor hovers over the link with the pointer, it is green.*

Figure 9.34 *As the visitor clicks the link, it turns blue.*

```
<h1>Antoni Gaudí</h1>

<div id="gaudi">

<p>Many tourists are drawn to Barcelona... </p>

<p>Barcelona <a href="http://www.gaudi...</p>

<div class="works"><h2>La Casa Milà</h2>

<p>Gaudí's work was essentially useful....</p>

</div>

<div class="works"><h2>La Sagrada
Família</h2>

<p>The complicatedly named and curiously...</p>

</div>

</div>
```

Figure 9.35 *In this code, only the two inner* div *elements have* class *attributes.*

```
div[class] {color:red;}
```

Figure 9.36 *The square brackets enclose the desired attribute and any desired value.*

Figure 9.37 *Every* div *element that contains a* class *attribute, regardless of the class's value, is red.*

Selecting Elements Based on Attributes

You can also apply formatting to those elements that have a given attribute or attribute value.

To select elements to format based on their attributes:

1. If desired, type **element**, where *element* is the selector for the element whose attributes are in question.

2. Type **[attribute**, where *attribute* is the name of the attribute that an element must have to be selected.

3. If desired, type **="value"** if you want to specify the *value* that the attribute must have for its element to be selected.

    Or, if desired, type **~="value"**, to specify a *value* that the attribute can contain (along with other content) for its element to be selected.

    Or, if desired, type **|** (the pipe symbol) **="value"** to specify that the attribute's value begin with *value-*(that is, what you typed followed by a hyphen) in order for its element to be selected. (This is most common when searching for elements in a particular language.)

4. Type **]** **(Figure 9.36)**.

✔ Tip

■ Selecting elements based on the attributes (and values) they contain is supported by all current major browsers (including IE as of version 7).

Selecting Elements Based on Attributes

Specifying Groups of Elements

It's often necessary to apply the same style rules to more than one element. You can either reiterate the rules for each element, or you can combine selectors and apply the rules in one fell swoop.

To apply styles to groups of elements:

1. Type **selector1**, where *selector1* is the name of the first element that should be affected by the style rule.

2. Type **,** (a comma).

3. Type **selector2**, where *selector2* is the next tag that should be affected by the style rule.

4. Repeat steps 2–3 for each additional element.

✔ Tips

■ This is nothing more than a handy shortcut. The rule **h1, h2 {color: red}** is precisely the same as the two rules **h1 {color: red}** and **h2 {color: red}**.

■ You can group any kind of selector, from the simplest (as shown in the example) to the most complex. For example, you could use **h1, div.works p:first-letter** to choose the level one headers *and* the first letter of the p elements in divs whose class is equal to *works* (!).

■ It is sometimes useful to create a single style rule with the common styles that apply to several selectors and then create individual style rules with the styles they do not share. Remember that rules specified later override rules specified earlier in the style sheet (*see page 122*).

```
<h1>Antoni Gaudí</h1>
<div id="gaudi">
<p>Many tourists are drawn to Barcelona .... </p>
<p>Barcelona <a href="http://www.gaudi...</p>
<div class="works"><h2>La Casa Milà</h2>
<p>Gaudí's work was essentially useful...</p>
</div>
<div class="works"><h2>La Sagrada Família</h2>
<p>The complicatedly named and curiously... </p>
</div>
</div>
```

Figure 9.38 *There is one* h1 *and two* h2 *elements.*

```
h1, h2 {color:red;}
```

Figure 9.39 *You can list any number of individual selectors, as long as you separate each with a comma.*

Figure 9.40 *Now both the* h1 *and the* h2 *elements will be colored red with a single rule.*

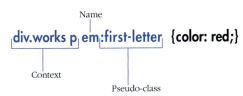

Figure 9.41 *Here's a doozy for you. It says "choose only the first letter of the* em *elements that are found within* p *elements that are in the* div *elements whose class is equal to* works.

Combining Selectors

You can combine any of the techniques that I've explained in the last few pages in order to pinpoint the elements that you're interested in formatting.

To combine selectors:

1. Define the context of the desired element. For more details, consult *Selecting Elements by Context* on page 141.

2. Next, either spell out the element's name *(see page 139)* or use the wild card character *(see page 139).*

3. Then, specify the class or id of the desired element(s). For more details, consult *Selecting Elements by ID or Class* on page 140.

4. Next, specify the pseudo-class or pseudo-element. For more details, consult *Selecting Part of an Element* on page 144 and *Selecting Link Elements Based on Their State* on page 146.

5. Finally, specify which attributes and values must be present for the element to be selected. For more details, consult *Selecting Elements Based on Attributes* on page 147.

✔ Tip

■ You may leave out any of the steps that you don't need. This page is designed to show you the *order* in which the different criteria should be listed.

FORMATTING WITH STYLES

Figure 10.1 *Here is what the page looks like with no style sheet applied. You can find the source XHTML code in the Examples section of my site:* http://www.cookwood.com/html6ed/examples/

As we saw in Chapter 4, *Basic (X)HTML Formatting*, (X)HTML has a rather limited repertoire of text formatting options. Thankfully, CSS offers many more possibilities.

With CSS, you can change the font face, size, weight, slant, line height, foreground and background color, spacing and alignment of text, decide whether it should be underlined, overlined, struck through, or blinking, and convert it to all uppercase, all lowercase, or small-caps. And you can apply those changes to an entire document or an entire site. In this chapter, you'll learn how.

I should probably also note that while many of the properties discussed in this chapter apply mostly to text, that doesn't mean they only work with text. Many of them work just fine on other kinds of content as well.

We'll continue on with CSS layout in Chapter 11, *Layout with Styles.*

Choosing a Font Family

One of the most important choices you'll make for your Web site is the font that you'll use for the body and for headlines.

To set the font family:

After the desired selector in your style sheet, type **font-family: name**, where *name* is your first choice of font.

✔ Tips

- Surround multi-word font names with quotes (single or double).

- If your font names contain non-ASCII characters, you'll have to declare the encoding for your style sheet as described on page 332.

- While you can specify any font you want, your visitor will only see the fonts that they already have installed on their system. See the next page for more details.

- You can set the font family, font size, and line height all at once, using the general font property *(see page 159).*

- The font-family property is inherited.

```
h1, h2 {font-family: "Arial Black"}
p {font-family: "Palatino Linotype"}
```

Figure 10.2 *I've specified the very common Arial Black for the headlines. For paragraphs, I've chosen Palatino Linotype, a font common on Windows systems.*

Figure 10.3 *On this Windows XP system, Palatino Linotype was installed by default and thus displays properly here.*

Figure 10.4 *Palatino Linotype is not installed on most Macintosh systems by default. If you choose a font that is not installed on your visitor's system, their browser, as shown here, will use the default font instead (in this case, that is Times).*

```
h1, h2 {font-family: "Arial Black", sans-serif}

p {font-family: "Palatino Linotype", Palatino, serif}
```

Figure 10.5 *The* `font-family` *property lets you include alternate fonts that the browser should use if the system does not have the first one installed. In this case, we can tell the browser to look for* Palatino *on systems that don't have* Palatino Linotype *installed.*

Figure 10.6 *Systems that have Palatino Lino-type installed will continue to use that font.*

Figure 10.7 *Systems that don't have Palatino Linotype will use Palatino, as long as they have it (as most Mac systems do). If they don't have Palatino either, the browser will try the third choice. Note that the default line height is still different. We'll adjust this a bit later.*

Specifying Alternate Fonts

While you can specify whichever font you want, your visitors will only see that font if they, too, have it installed on their computer. So, it's a good idea to use fonts that you can reasonably expect them to have.

If the font you want comes on both Mac and Windows, you can feel pretty safe simply specifying that font. If the font has different names on each system, you can specify *both* names and each OS will use the one it has installed. If the font you want only comes with one operating system, you can choose an alternate font for the other system, that may or may not match exactly. Finally, if the font you want doesn't come preinstalled on either computer system, you may want to specify alternate standard fonts for both operating systems.

To specify alternate fonts:

1. After typing `font-family:name` as on page 152, type **, name2**, where *name2* is your second font choice. Separate each choice with a comma and a space.

2. Repeat step 1 as desired.

✔ Tips

- You can specify fonts for different alphabets in the same `font-family` rule (say, Japanese and English) to format a chunk of text that contains different languages *and* writing systems.

- You can use the following generic font names—**serif**, **sans-serif**, **cursive**, **fantasy**, and **monospace**—as a last ditch attempt to influence which font is used for display.

Creating Italics

Italics are often used to set off quotations, emphasized text, foreign words, magazine names and much more.

To create italics:

1. Type **font-style:**.

2. Type **italic** for italic text, or **oblique** for oblique text.

To remove italics:

Type **font-style: normal**.

✔ Tips

- It used to be that the italic version of a font was created by a font designer from scratch, while the oblique version was created by the computer, by simply slanting the letters, especially of sans-serif fonts, on the fly. This distinction has blurred somewhat, but generally holds.

- If you set the font style as italic and there is no italic style available, the browser should try to display the text as oblique.

- One reason you might want to remove italics is to emphasize some text in a paragraph that has inherited italic formatting from a parent tag. For more details about inheritance, consult *The Cascade: When Rules Collide* on page 122.

- You can also use the i or em tags in the (X)HTML code to create italics. For details, see page 70.

- The font-style property is inherited.

```
h1, h2 {font-family: "Arial Black", sans-serif}
p {font-family: "Palatino Linotype", Palatino, serif}
.emph {font-style: italic}
```

Figure 10.8 *In this example, I've made the* .emph *class display in italics.*

```
<p>The complicatedly named and curiously
unfinished masterpiece that is the Expiatory Temple
of the Sacred Family is the most visited building in
Barcelona. In it, Gaudí combines his vision of
nature and architecture with his devotion to his
<span class="emph">faith</span>. His focus on
this project was so intense that he shunned all other
projects, slept in an apartment at the work site
```

Figure 10.9 *Remember that in the (X)HTML code, the word* faith *is marked with the* emph *class.*

d masterpiece that is the Expiatory Temple
Barcelona. In it, Gaudí combines his
to his *faith*. His focus on this project was so
an apartment at the work site surrounded
his dissheveled appearance that when, in
urch, he was mistaken for an indigent and
on thereafter.

Figure 10.10 *Palatino Linotype has a true italic font as you can see here in the third line. The letter* a *in particular is clearly not just slanted.*

h1, h2 {font-family: "Arial Black", sans-serif; font-weight:normal}

p {font-family: "Palatino Linotype", Palatino, serif}

.emph {font-style: italic;font-weight:bold}

a:link, a:hover {font-weight:bold}

Figure 10.11 *Browsers add bold formatting to headers (like* h1 *and* h2*) automatically. I can apply a normal font weight to remove it (since it's a bit much on this page). I've also added bold formatting to the* emph *class and to new and hovered links.*

Figure 10.12 *The headers are not so overbearing with the extra bold formatting removed. New links stand out (while visited ones are less obtrusive).*

Figure 10.13 *The emphasized text (the word* faith *in the second to last line shown) is not only italic (from the preceding page) but also bold.*

Applying Bold Formatting

Bold formatting is probably the most common and effective way to make text stand out. Using style sheets gives you much more flexibility with bold text, providing relative values or allowing you to get rid of it altogether.

To apply bold formatting:

1. Type **font-weight:**.

2. Type **bold** to give an average bold weight to the text.

   Or type **bolder** or **lighter** to use a value relative to the current weight.

   Or type a multiple of **100** between 100 and 900, where 400 represents normal or book weight and 700 represents bold.

To remove bold formatting:

Type **font-weight: normal**.

✔ Tips

■ Since the way weights are defined varies from font to font, the predefined values may not be relative from font to font. They are designed to be relative *within* a given font family.

■ If the font family has fewer than nine weights, or if they are concentrated on one end of the scale, it is possible that some numeric values will correspond to the same font weight.

■ What can you remove bold formatting from? Any tag where it's been applied automatically (strong and h1 come to mind) and where it's been inherited from a parent tag *(see page 122)*.

■ The font-weight property is inherited.

Setting the Font Size

There are two basic ways to set the font size for the text in your Web page. You can mandate that a specific size be used or you can have the size depend on the element's parent.

To mandate a specific font size:

1. Type **font-size:**.

2. Type an exact size: say, **16px** or **1em**.

   Or use a keyword to specify the size: **xx-small**, **x-small**, **small**, **medium**, **large**, **x-large**, or **xx-large**.

✔ Tips

- See page 124 for details about units.

- There shouldn't be any spaces between the number and the unit.

- The average pixel is about 1/80th of an inch high (1/32 cm), though it depends on the screen resolution. Imagine a 17" monitor, whose screen is roughly 12.5" wide, with a resolution of 1024 x 768. At that resolution, text at 16 pixels would be about 1/5 of an inch high (about 1/2 cm).

- If you set the font size with pixels, visitors using Internet Explorer (up to and including version 7) will not be able to make the text bigger or smaller with the Text Size option. (Zoom still works.)

- Only use points, cm, mm, or picas in style sheets that format printed output (*see page 209*).

- Different browsers interpret the keywords in different ways. Explorer 5.x uses `small` as its base size while IE 6, Opera, and Netscape use `medium`.

- The `font-size` property is inherited.

```
h1, h2 {font-family: "Arial Black", sans-serif;
font-weight: normal}

h1 {font-size: 22px}

h2 {font-size: 16px}

p {font-family: "Palatino Linotype", Palatino, serif;
font-size: 14px}

.emph {font-style: italic; font-weight:bold}

a:link, a:hover {font-weight:bold}

#toc {font-size:12px}
```

Figure 10.14 *Here I use pixel values to have control over the initial size of the text (which I've decreased in size throughout, compared with most browsers' defaults).*

Figure 10.15 *The sizes I've specified are displayed in the browser. Internet Explorer will use these sizes even if the visitor chooses a different size with the Text Size command.*

Setting the Font Size

```
h1 {font-size: 1.37em}

h2 {font-size: 1em}

p {font-family: "Palatino Linotype", Palatino, serif;
font-size:87%}

.emph {font-style: italic; font-weight:bold}

a:link, a:hover {font-weight:bold}

#toc {font-size:75%}
```

Figure 10.16 *Assuming a default text size of 16 pixels, this style sheet will be equivalent to the one shown in Figure 10.14 on page 156.*

Figure 10.17 *The difference comes if your visitor tries to resize the text in their browser.*

Figure 10.18 *As long as you have used relative sizing, the Text Size command will change the size of all the text (but not the graphics) on your page, in proportion to its original sizes.*

To set a size that depends on the parent element's size:

1. Type **font-size:**.

2. Type the relative value, say **1.5em** or **150%**.

    Or use a relative keyword: **larger** or **smaller**.

✔ Tips

■ The new size is determined by multiplying the percentage or em factor by the parent element's size. For example, if the body is set to 16 pixels, a p element contained in it with a relative value of 75% will be displayed at 12 pixels.

■ The parent element's size may be set by you (the designer), may be inherited, or may come from the browser's defaults. On most current browsers, the default size for the body element is 16 pixels.

■ The child of an element with a relative size inherits the size, not the factor. So, an em element in the p in the first tip would inherit a size of 12 pixels, not a relative value of 75% (which would be strange).

■ An em is equal to the size of the font. So 1 em equals 100%.

■ Ems and percentages are well supported in current browsers.

■ You can set font size together with other font values *(see page 159)*.

■ Sizes specified with ems and percentages are more elastic. You can change the design by changing just the base size. And visitors can change the base size with their browser's Text Size command.

■ There's also an ex unit, which refers to the x-height of the parent element, but it is not widely supported.

Setting the Line Height

Line height refers to a paragraph's leading, that is, the amount of space between each line in a paragraph. Using a large line height can sometimes make your body text easier to read. A small line height for headers (with more than one line) often makes them look classier.

To set the line height:

1. Type **line-height:**.

2. Type **n**, where *n* is a number that will be multiplied by the element's font size *(see page 156)* to obtain the desired line height.

    Or type **p%**, where *p%* is a percentage of the font size.

    Or type **a**, where *a* is an absolute value in pixels, points, or whatever.

✔ Tips

- You can specify the line height together with the font family, size, weight, style, and variant, as described on page 159.

- If you use a number to determine the line height, this factor is inherited by all child items. So if a parent's font size is 16 pixels and the line height is 1.5, the parent's line height will be 24 (16 x 1.5). If the child's font size is 10, its line height will be 15 (10 x 1.5).

- If you use a percentage or em value, only the resulting size (or "computed value") is inherited. So, given a parent at 16 pixels with a line height of 150%, the parent's line height will still be 24 pixels. However, all child elements will also inherit a line height of 24 pixels, regardless of their font size.

h1, h2 {font-family: "Arial Black", sans-serif; font-weight: normal}

h1 {font-size: 1.37em}

h2 {font-size: 1em}

p {font-family: "Palatino Linotype", Palatino, serif; font-size: 87%; line-height: 170%}

.emph {font-style: italic; font-weight:bold}

a:link, a:hover {font-weight:bold}

#toc {font-size: 75%}

Figure 10.19 *Assuming a default body element of 16 pixels, the font size of the* p *element will be 87% or about 14 pixels. The line height will be 170% of those 14 pixels, or about 24 pixels.*

Barcelona's Architect - **La Sagrada Família** - **Park Guell**

Barcelona's Architect

Antoni Gaudí's incredible buildings bring millions of tourists to

Gaudí's non-conformity, already visible in his teenage years, cou church, made a unique foundation for his thoughts and ideas. H observations of nature are quite apparent in his work, from the P mosaics, to the Church of the **Sacred Family** and its organic, bul

La Sagrada Família

The complicatedly named and curiously unfinished masterpiece Family is the most visited building in Barcelona. In it, Gaudí con with his devotion to his *faith*. His focus on this project was so in

Figure 10.20 *Spacing out the lines makes them more attractive and easier to read.*

```
h1, h2 {font: 1.37em "Arial Black", sans-serif}

h2 {font-size: 1em}

p {font: 87%/170% "Palatino Linotype", Palatino,
serif}

.emph {font-style: italic; font-weight:bold}

a:link, a:hover {font-weight:bold}

#toc {font-size: 75%}
```

Figure 10.21 *This style sheet is equivalent to the one shown in Figure 10.19 on page 158. I've simply consolidated the* font *properties for the* h1, h2 *and* p *rules. Note that I don't have to specify that the* font-weight *be* normal *for* h1, h2, *since* normal *is the default for the* font *property.*

Figure 10.22 *This page is identical to the one shown in Figure 10.20 on page 158.*

Setting All Font Values at Once

You can set the font style, weight, variant, size, line height, and family all at once.

To set all font values at once:

1. Type **font:**.

2. If desired, type **normal**, **oblique**, or **italic** to set the font style *(see page 154)*.

3. If desired, type **normal**, **bold**, **bolder**, **lighter**, or a multiple of **100** (up to 900) to set the font weight *(see page 154)*.

4. If desired, type **normal** or **small-caps** to remove or set small caps *(see page 167)*.

5. Type the desired font size *(see pages 156–157)*.

6. If desired, type **/line-height**, where *line-height* is the amount of space there should be between lines *(see page 156)*.

7. Type a space followed by the desired font family or families, in order of preference, separated by commas, as described on page 152.

✔ Tips

■ You can also set each property separately. See the page referenced with the desired step.

■ The first three properties may be specified in any order or omitted. If you omit them, they are set to normal—which may not be what you expected.

■ The size and family properties must always be explicitly specified: first the size, then the family.

■ The line height, which is optional, must come directly after the size and the slash.

■ The font property is inherited.

Setting All Font Values at Once

Setting the Color

You can change the color of the elements on your Web page.

To set the color:

1. Type **color:**.

2. Type **colorname**, where *colorname* is one of the 16 predefined colors *(see page 126 and the inside back cover)*.

   Or type **#rrggbb**, where *rrggbb* is the color's hexadecimal representation.

   Or type **rgb(r, g, b)** where *r*, *g*, and *b* are integers from 0–255 that specify the amount of red, green, or blue, respectively, in the desired color.

   Or type **rgb(r%, g%, b%)** where *r*, *g*, and *b* give the percentage of red, green, and blue, respectively, in the desired color.

✔ Tips

- You can use the `color` property to change the color of *any* (X)HTML element, not just text.

- If you type a value for r, g, or b higher than 255, 255 will be used. Similarly a percentage higher than 100% will be substituted with 100%.

- You can also use **#rgb** to set the color where the hex values are repeated digits. So you could write **#FF0099** as **#F09**. (Don't do this in (X)HTML.)

- The hex number should *not* be enclosed in double quotes (as it used to be when used in an (X)HTML tag.)

- The `color` property is inherited.

- The inside back cover of this book offers sample colors and their hex values.

h1, h2 {font: 1.37em "Arial Black", sans-serif; color: navy}

h2 {font-size: 1em}

p {font: 87%/170% "Palatino Linotype", Palatino, serif; color:#909}

.emph {font-style: italic;font-weight:bold}

a:link {font-weight:bold; color:#74269D}

a:visited {font-weight:normal; color:#909}

a:hover {font-weight: bold; color: #74269D}

#toc {font-size: 75%}

Figure 10.23 *You can use color names, hexadecimals, or even RGB values to define your colors. Note that the second color (#909) uses the abbreviation discussed in the third tip.*

Figure 10.24 *The headers are navy blue, the text is light purple, and the links are dark purple, but turn lighter after being visited, and dark purple again when hovered over.*

body {background:#eef}

h1, h2 {font: 1.37em "Arial Black", sans-serif; color: navy}

h2 {font-size: 1em}

p {font: 87%/170% "Palatino Linotype", Palatino, serif; color:#909}

.emph {font-style: italic;font-weight:bold}

a:link {font-weight:bold; color:#74269D}

a:visited {font-weight:normal; color:#909}

a:hover {font-weight: bold; color: #74269D}

#toc {font-size: 75%; background:#EBC6F9}

Figure 10.25 *It's a good idea to set the background color for every element that you've set a foreground color for. Setting the background color of the* body *element, covers the background of all of its child elements.*

Figure 10.26 *The background of the* body *element is light blue. The background of the table of contents is light purple.*

Changing the Text's Background

The background refers not to the background of the entire page, but to the background of the specified element. In other words, you can change the background of just a few paragraphs or words, by setting the background of those words to a different color.

To change the text's background:

1. Type **background:**.

2. Type **transparent** or **color**, where *color* is a color name or hex color *(see page 160)*.

3. If desired, type **url(image.gif)**, to use an image for the background.

   If desired, type **repeat** to tile the image both horizontally and vertically, **repeat-x** to tile the image only horizontally, **repeat-y** to tile the image only vertically, and **no-repeat** to not tile the image.

   If desired, type **fixed** or **scroll** to determine whether the background should scroll along with the canvas.

   If desired, type **x y** to set the position of the background image, where *x* and *y* can be expressed as a percentage or an absolute distance from the top-left corner. Or use values of `left`, `center`, and `right` for *x* and `top`, `center`, or `bottom` for *y*.

✔ Tips

■ You can specify both a color and an image's URL for the background. The color will be used until the image is loaded—or if it can't be loaded for any reason—and will be seen through any transparent portions of the image.

■ Create enough contrast between the background and the foreground so that your visitors can actually read the text.

■ The `background` property is not inherited.

Controlling Spacing

You can add or reduce space between words (tracking) or between letters (kerning).

To specify tracking:

Type **word-spacing: length**, where *length* is a number with units, as in **0.4em** or **5px**.

To specify kerning:

Type **letter-spacing: length**, where *length* is a number with units, as in **0.4em** or **5px**.

✔ Tips

- You may use negative values for word and letter spacing, although the actual display always depends on the browser's capabilities.

- Word and letter spacing values may also be affected by your choice of alignment.

- Use a value of **normal** or **0** to set the letter and word spacing to their defaults (that is, to add no extra space).

- If you use an em value, only the resulting size (or "computed value") is inherited. So, a parent at 16 pixels with .1em of extra word-spacing, will have 1.6 pixels of extra space between each word. And all child elements will also have 1.6 pixels of extra space between words, regardless of their font size. Set the extra spacing explicitly for the child elements if you need to override such a value.

- Both the `word-spacing` and `letter-spacing` properties are inherited.

```
body {background:#eef}

h1, h2 {font: 1.37em "Arial Black", sans-serif;color:
navy; letter-spacing:0.4em}

h2 {font-size: 1em}

p {font: 87%/170% "Palatino Linotype", Palatino,
serif; color:#909}

.emph {font-style: italic;font-weight:bold}

a:link {font-weight:bold; color:#74269D}

a:visited {font-weight:normal; color:#909}

a:hover {font-weight: bold; color: #74269D}

#toc {font-size: 75%; background:#EBC6F9}
```

Figure 10.27 *Here I've added .4em of extra space between letters (which at a font size of 22px will mean almost 9 pixels between each letter).*

Figure 10.28 *I rather like the effect of spaced out headers.*

```
body {background:#eef}

h1, h2 {font: 1.37em "Arial Black", sans-serif;color:
navy; letter-spacing:0.4em}

h2 {font-size: 1em}

p {font: 87%/170% "Palatino Linotype", Palatino,
serif; color:#909; text-indent:1.5em}

.emph {font-style: italic;font-weight:bold}

a:link {font-weight:bold; color:#74269D}

a:visited {font-weight:normal; color:#909}

a:hover {font-weight: bold; color: #74269D}

#toc {font-size: 75%; background:#EBC6F9}
```

Figure 10.29 *I added a 1.5 em indent to the* p *elements (which, since their font size is about 14 pixels, will be an indent of about 21 pixels).*

Figure 10.30 *Each paragraph is indented 21 pixels.*

Adding Indents

You can determine how much space should precede the first line of a paragraph.

To add indents:

Type **text-indent: length**, where *length* is a number with units, as in **1.5em** or **18px**.

✔ Tips

■ A positive value creates a typical paragraph indent and serves as a visual clue as to where new paragraphs begin.

■ A negative value creates a hanging indent. You may need to increase the padding *(see page 177)* or margins *(see page 176)* around a text box with a hanging indent in order to accommodate the overhanging text.

■ Em values, as usual, are calculated with respect to the element's font size. Percentages are calculated with respect to the width of the *parent* element.

■ The `text-indent` property is inherited.

■ If you use a percentage or an em value, only the resulting size (or "computed value") is inherited. So, if the parent is 300 pixels wide, a text-indent of 10% will be 30 pixels. And all child elements will also have their first lines indented 30 pixels, regardless of the width of their respective parents.

■ Use a value of 0 to remove an inherited indent. For example, you might want to create a special class for the first paragraph in each section and set its text indent to 0.

Adding Indents

Setting White Space Properties

By default, multiple spaces and returns in an (X)HTML document are either displayed as a single space or ignored outright. If you want the browser to display those extra spaces, use the `white-space` property.

To set white space properties:

1. Type **white-space:**.

2. Type **pre** to have browsers display all the spaces and returns in the original text.

   Or type **nowrap** to treat all spaces as non-breaking.

   Or type **normal** to treat white space as usual *(see page 32)*.

✔ Tips

- The value of `pre` for the `white-space` property gets its name from the `pre` tag, which is an old-fashioned HTML tag that displays text in a monospace font while maintaining all of its spaces and returns. The `pre` tag, in turn, got its name from the word "pre-formatted". You can find more information about the `pre` tag on page 73.

- Note that the `pre` value for the `white-space` property has no effect on an element's font (in contrast with the `pre` tag, which changes the display to a monospace font).

- You may use the `br` tag to manually create line breaks in an element styled with `white-space:nowrap`. For details about the `br` tag, consult *Creating a Line Break* on page 66.

- IE versions earlier than 6 don't support the `pre` value for `white-space`.

```
body {background:#eef}

h1, h2 {font: 1.37em "Arial Black", sans-serif;color:
navy; letter-spacing:0.4em}

h2 {font-size: 1em}

p {font: 87%/170% "Palatino Linotype", Palatino,
serif; color:#909; text-indent:1.5em}

.emph {font-style: italic;font-weight:bold}

a:link {font-weight:bold; color:#74269D}

a:visited {font-weight:normal; color:#909}

a:hover {font-weight: bold; color: #74269D}

#toc {font-size: 75%; background:#EBC6F9;
white-space: nowrap}
```

Figure 10.31 *The* nowrap *value for* white-space *treats spaces as non-breaking.*

Figure 10.32 *The table of contents line won't wrap, even when the browser window is too narrow to display the entire line.*

```
body {background:#eef}

h1, h2 {font: 1.37em "Arial Black", sans-serif;color:
navy; letter-spacing:0.4em; text-align:center}

h2 {font-size: 1em}

p {font: 87%/170% "Palatino Linotype", Palatino,
serif; color:#909; text-indent:1.5em;
text-align:justify}

.emph {font-style: italic;font-weight:bold}

a:link {font-weight:bold; color:#74269D}

a:visited {font-weight:normal; color:#909}

a:hover {font-weight: bold; color: #74269D}

#toc {font-size: 75%; background:#EBC6F9;
white-space: nowrap; text-align:center}
```

Figure 10.33 *Don't forget the hyphen in* text-
align.

Figure 10.34 *The table of contents and headers
are centered while the paragraph text is
justified.*

Aligning Text

You can set up certain (X)HTML elements to
always be aligned to the right, left, center, or
justified, as desired.

To align text:

1. Type **text-align:**.

2. Type **left** to align the text to the left.

    Or type **right** to align the text to the right.

    Or type **center** to center the text in the
    middle of the screen.

    Or type **justify** to align the text on both
    the right and left.

✔ Tips

■   If you choose to justify the text, be aware
    that the word spacing and letter spacing
    may be adversely affected. For more
    information, consult *Controlling
    Spacing* on page 162.

■   Note that the text-align property can
    only be applied to block-level elements.
    If you want to align inline content, you
    must place that inline content within a
    block-level element like p or div to
    which you've applied the text-align
    property. Also see pages 174–175.

■   The text-align property is inherited.
    Its default value is supposed to depend
    on the document's language and writing
    system, but in most cases it's indiscrimi-
    nately set to left.

Aligning Text

Changing the Text Case

You can define the text case for your style by using the `text-transform` property. In this way, you can display the text either with initial capital letters, in all capital letters, in all small letters, or as it was typed.

To change the text case:

1. Type **text-transform:**.

2. Type **capitalize** to put the first character of each word in uppercase.

   Or type **uppercase** to change all the letters to uppercase.

   Or type **lowercase** to change all the letters to lowercase.

   Or type **none** to leave the text as is (possibly canceling out an inherited value).

✔ Tips

■ I'm unimpressed with the `capitalize` value. While I sometimes need to capitalize all the important words in a sentence, or even just the first word in a sentence, I am hard pressed to think of an example where I'd need to capitalize everything. Now, a true headline-style capitalization property would be welcome. Of course it would have to be language dependent.

■ The `lowercase` value can be useful for creating stylish headers (or if you're e.e. cummings).

■ The `text-transform` property is inherited.

```
body {background:#eef}

h1, h2 {font: 1.37em "Arial Black", sans-serif;color:
navy; letter-spacing:0.4em; text-align:center}

h1 {text-transform: uppercase}

h2 {font-size: 1em}

p {font: 87%/170% "Palatino Linotype", Palatino,
serif; color:#909; text-indent:1.5em;
text-align:justify}

.emph {font-style: italic;font-weight:bold}

a:link {font-weight:bold; color:#74269D}

a:visited {font-weight:normal; color:#909}

a:hover {font-weight: bold; color: #74269D}

#toc {font-size: 75%; background:#EBC6F9;
white-space: nowrap; text-align:center}
```

Figure 10.35 *I've decided to display the level 1 header in all uppercase letters for emphasis.*

Figure 10.36 *Now the header really stands out.*

```
body {background:#eef}

h1, h2 {font: 1.37em "Arial Black", sans-serif;color:
navy; letter-spacing:0.4em; text-align:center}

h1 {text-transform: uppercase}

h2 {font-size: 1em; font-variant: small-caps}

p {font: 87%/170% "Palatino Linotype", Palatino,
serif; color:#909; text-indent:1.5em;
text-align:justify}

.emph {font-style: italic;font-weight:bold}

a:link {font-weight:bold; color:#74269D}

<snip>
```

Figure 10.37 *Don't forget the hyphen in both* font-variant *and* small-caps*!*

Figure 10.38 *Small caps vary a tiny bit from browser to browser. From top to bottom, there is Firefox for Windows (which is identical to Internet Explorer 7), Internet Explorer 6, and Opera 8.5 for Windows.*

Using Small Caps

Many fonts have a corresponding small caps variant that includes uppercase versions of the letters proportionately reduced to small caps size. You can call up the small caps variant with the font-variant property.

To use a small caps font:

Type **font-variant: small-caps**.

To remove small caps:

Type **font-variant: none**.

✔ Tips

■ Small caps are not quite as heavy as uppercase letters that have been simply reduced in size.

■ Not all fonts have a corresponding small caps design. If the browser can't find such a design, it has a few choices. It can fake small caps by simply reducing the size of uppercase letters (which tends to make them look a bit squat), it can forget about small caps altogether and display the text in all uppercase (similar to text-transform: uppercase as described on page 166), or, theoretically, it can choose the next font in the list to see if it has a small caps design (though I've never seen this happen).

■ The font-variant property is inherited.

Using Small Caps

Decorating Text

Style sheets let you adorn your text with underlines, overlining, lines through the text (perhaps to indicate changes), and even blinking text.

To decorate text:

1. Type **text-decoration:**.

2. To underline text, type **underline**.

   Or, for a line above the text, type **overline**.

   Or, to strike out the text, type **line-through**.

   Or to make the text appear and disappear intermittently, type **blink**.

To get rid of decorations:

1. Type **text-decoration:**.

2. Type **none**.

✔ Tips

- You can eliminate decorations from elements that normally have them (like a, strike, or ins) or from elements that inherit decorations from their parents.

- Many graphic designers hate underlining and consider it a relic from the typewriter age. While it's perfectly fine to remove underlining from link elements, you'll have to identify the links some other way or nobody will know to click on them.

- The blink value has a troubled past. Originally designed by Netscape to add pizzazz to Web pages and get an edge over its competition, it was soon scorned by both graphic designers and Internet Explorer, which never deigned to support it. (Firefox and Opera do.)

```
[snip]

a:link {font-weight:bold; color:#74269D;
text-decoration:none;}

a:visited {font-weight:bold; color:#909;
text-decoration:none;}

a:hover {font-weight:bold; color:#74269D;
text-decoration: underline;}

#toc {font-size: 75%; background:#EBC6F9;
white-space:nowrap; text-align:center;}
```

Figure 10.39 *You don't have to restrict underlining, or other text decorations to link elements, as I have done here. They can be applied to any element.*

Figure 10.40 *I've removed the underlining from both new and visited links. Then, I added underlining to links that are being hovered over to help visitors know that they are links. It's in italics because it's the title of a book.*

LAYOUT WITH STYLES

Figure 11.1 *This page, with two fluid columns, a header and footer, was laid out with CSS. It is explained step-by-step throughout this chapter.*

There are two principal methods for laying out Web pages: CSS and tables (which we'll discuss in Chapter 16). Using CSS has several advantages. First, CSS is good for creating *liquid layouts* that expand or contract depending on the size of your visitor's monitor. In addition, keeping content separate from layout instructions means you can easily apply the same layout to an entire Web site all at once. You can then change the layout of the whole site simply by modifying the CSS file. The CSS + (X)HTML combination also tends to produce smaller file sizes, which means your visitors don't have to wait as long to see your site. Finally, since CSS and XHTML are the current standards, pages that adhere to their rules are guaranteed to be supported in future browsers (and required of professional Web designers).

The principal disadvantage of CSS, especially for layout, is that not all browsers support it exactly the same way. Internet Explorer in particular, has been slow to fully support CSS, although IE 6 was much better than earlier versions and IE 7 continues that trend. There are strategies you can use to provide styled content to users of older browsers and to accommodate buggy current browsers.

Structuring Your Pages

The whole point of using CSS is to separate the formatting and styling rules from the content of your page. This frees your page from rigid appearance directives and gives it the flexibility to work well in different browsers, platforms, media, and even print. Perhaps the most important aspect of a page to be styled with CSS is its structure. A reasonable, logical structure can be easily adapted for more than one kind of output device.

To structure your page:

1. Divide logical sections of your document into `div` elements. In our example, we have *wrap* and *screen* divisions that are used to make the design liquid, a *header* division for the title and description of the site, a *main* division divided into multiple *entry* divisions to contain the main content, a *sidebar* division to house a monthly opinion in the right column and a *footer* division for an "about" blurb **(Figure 11.2)**.

2. Put your `div` elements in an order that would be the most useful if the CSS were not used, for example, a title at the top, followed by the main content, followed by a sidebar. The people most likely to view your site without CSS are those using handhelds. You want to get the main content to them without making them scroll too far—or load too many bytes. In addition, if search engines see your main content first, they'll be better able to properly catalog your site.

3. Use header elements (`h1`, `h2`, etc.) consistently to identify and prioritize information on your page.

4. Use comments to identify different areas of your page and their contents. I also use comments to identify closing `</div>` tags so I can keep them straight.

```
<body>
<div id="wrap"><div id="screen">
<div id="header">
    <h1>photobarcelona . . . </h1> ...snip...
    </div> <!-- end #header -->

<div id="main">
<div class="entry">
    <h2>Hospital Sant Pau</h2> ...snip...
    <p>The Saint Paul Hospital at the top of...</p>
</div> <!--end entry div -->
<div class="entry">
    <h2>Cathedral Cloister</h2>...snip...
    <p>Outside it feels like a battle is raging... </p>
</div> <!--end entry div -->...snip...
</div> <!-- end main div -->

<div id="sidebar">
    <h3>from my window</h3>...snip...
</div> <!-- end sidebar div -->

<div id="footer">
    <h2>about this photoblog</h2>...snip...
</div> <!-- end footer div -->

</div></div> <!-- end screen and wrap divs -->
</body>
```

Figure 11.2 *This is the document I use throughout this chapter. There are four divisions:* header, main, sidebar, *and* footer, *enclosed in two outer wrapper divisions (*wrap *and* screen*). You can find the complete file on my Web site (see page 26).*

photobarcelona . . .

home• faq• resources• previous• archives

capturing barcelona's cultural treasures on film

Hospital Sant Pau

June 23, 2006

The Saint Paul Hospital at the top of Gaudi Avenue in the Sagrada Familia neighb oft-overlooked gem of modernist architecture. Although the building was begun in direction of the architect Lluis Domènec i Montaner, the hospital itself dates from

Figure 11.3 *Here's what our example looks like with no styles at all. Thanks to its decent structure, it is perfectly intelligible, if a bit spartan.*

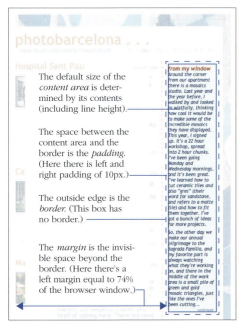

Figure 11.4 *Each element's box has four important properties that determine its size: in order from the center to the outside they are the* content area, *the* padding, *the* border, *and the* margin. *You can control each property (and even* parts *of each of these properties) individually.*

The Box Model

CSS treats your Web page as if every element it contains is enclosed in an invisible box. The box is comprised of a content area, the space surrounding that area (padding), the outside edge of the padding (border), and the invisible space around the border (margin).

You can use CSS to determine both the appearance and the position of each element's box, and in so doing, have considerable control over the layout of your Web page.

As we discussed earlier *(see page 30)*, an element's box may be *block-level* (thereby generating a new paragraph) or *inline* (not generating a new paragraph). This trait governs the initial layout of the Web page: by default, elements are displayed in the order that the (X)HTML *flows* from top to bottom, with line breaks at the beginning and end of each block-level element's box.

There are four principal ways to position an element box: you can leave the box in the flow (the default, also called *static*), you can remove the box from the flow and specify its exact coordinates with respect to either its parent element (*absolute*) or the browser window (*fixed*), or you can move the box with respect to its default position in the flow (*relative*). In addition, if boxes overlap one another, you can specify the order in which they should do so (*z-index*).

Once you've determined where the box should go, you can control its appearance, including its padding, border, margins, size, alignment, color, and more. We'll discuss all of these properties in this chapter.

Note that some layout properties, particularly em and percentage values, depend on an element's parent. Remember that a *parent* is the element that contains the current element *(see page 30)*.

The Box Model

Changing the Background

The background refers not to the background of the entire page, but to the background of a particular element. In other words, you can change the background of any element—including images, form elements, and tables.

To use a background image:

1. Type **background-image:**

2. Then type **url(image.gif)**, where *image.gif* is the name of the image that should be used for the background, or **none** to use no image at all **(Figure 11.5)**.

To repeat a background image:

Type **background-repeat: direction**, where *direction* is either `repeat` (to tile the image both horizontally and vertically), `repeat-x` (to tile the image horizontally), `repeat-y` (to tile the image vertically), or `no-repeat` (to not tile the image at all) **(Figure 11.5)**.

To control whether the background image is attached or not:

1. Type **background-attachment:**.

2. Then type **fixed** to stick the background image to the browser window or **scroll** to let it move when the visitor scrolls.

To specify the position of an element's background image:

Type **background-position: x y**, where *x* and *y* can be expressed as a percentage or as an absolute distance. Or use values of `left`, `center`, or `right` for *x* and `top`, `center`, or `bottom` for *y* **(Figure 11.5)**.

To change the background color:

1. Type **background-color:**

2. Type **transparent** (to let the parent element's background show through) or **color**, where *color* is a color name or rgb color *(see page 126 and the inside back cover)* **(Figures 11.8, 11.9, and 11.10)**.

```
#wrap {background-image: url(bluebench.jpg);
       background-position: left top;
       background-repeat: repeat;}
```

Figure 11.5 *First, we apply a background image to the outermost division, the* wrap *div. Then we position the image in the left, top corner of the* wrap *div and repeat it in both directions.*

```
#wrap {background: url(bluebench.jpg) left top
       repeat;}
```

Figure 11.6 *You can use the shortcut* background *property described on the next page to apply more than one background related property at once.*

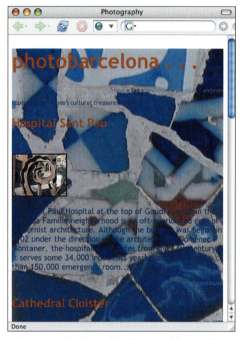

Figure 11.7 *Setting a background image for your page is always a dangerous mission. On the next page, we'll cover up the background so that the text is once again legible. Later on, we'll peel back the cover to let some of the background peek through.*

```
#wrap {background: url(bluebench.jpg) left top
repeat;}
#screen {background: #FEF6F8;}
a:focus, a:hover, a:active {background: #F3CFB6;}
#sidebar {background: #F5F8FA;}
```

Figure 11.8 *The background for the* screen *div will make the text legible. Its color is temporary. Next, we add a background to links when they're hovered over, in order to make it clear that they really are links. Finally, we'll add a background color to the monthly opinion column in the* sidebar *div.*

Figure 11.9 *The screen div's background completely covers our new background image from the preceding page. We'll remedy that shortly (with* padding, *on page 177). Notice how the links that are not being hovered over share the same background as the screen, while the hovered* resources *link has a higher contrast background to show it off.*

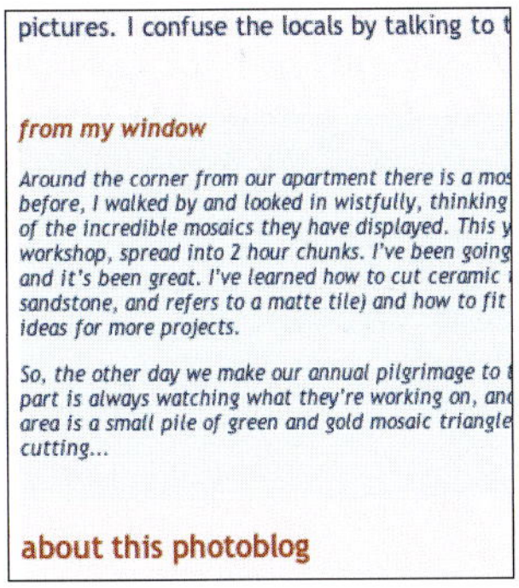

Figure 11.10 *The background color for the sidebar is the lightest shade of blue I could manage. Just enough to set it off.*

To change all the background properties at once:

1. Type **background:**

2. Specify any of the accepted background property values (as described on the preceding page), in any order **(Figures 11.6 and 11.7)**.

✔ Tips

■ The default for `background-color` is `transparent`. The default for `back-ground-image` is `none`. The default for `background-repeat` is `repeat`. The default for `background-attachment` is `scroll`. The default for `background-position` is `top left`.

■ When using the `background` shortcut property (above), you needn't specify all of the properties. But beware that any non-specified properties are set to their defaults (and thus may override earlier style rules).

■ The `background` properties are not inherited. You only need to explicitly set default values like `transparent` or `scroll` when you want to override another style rule.

■ If you use the `background-position` property with a repeat, the position specifies where the first image in the repeat starts, e.g., from the `top right`.

■ To create a background for the entire page, set the `background` property for the `body` element.

■ If you specify both a color and a URL for the background, the color will be used until the URL is loaded, and will be seen through any transparent portions of the background image.

Changing the Background

Setting the Height or Width for an Element

You can set the height and width for most elements, including images, form elements, and even blocks of text.

To set the height or width for an element:

- Type **width: w**, where *w* is the width of the element's content area, and can be expressed either as a length (with units) or as a percentage of the parent element. Or use `auto` to let the browser calculate the width.

- Type **height: h**, where *h* is the height of the element, and can be expressed only as a length (with units). Or use `auto` to let the browser calculate the height.

✔ Tips

- If you don't explicitly set the `width` or `height`, `auto` is used *(see page 175)*.

- Remember that a percentage value is relative to the width *of the parent element*—not the original width of the element itself.

- The padding, borders, and margin are not included in the value of `width` (except in IE 5.x for Windows, which quite erroneously considers the `width` to be the sum of the content area, borders, and padding—see next page).

- Widths and heights are not inherited.

- There are also `min-width`, `min-height`, `max-width` and `max-height` properties **(Figure 11.13)** but they are not supported by Internet Explorer, up to and including version 7.

```
#wrap {width: 90%;}

#main {width: 75%;}

.photo {width:100px;height: 75px;}
```

Figure 11.11 *Limiting the* wrap *div to 90% of the browser window gives it some air and helps it not look so cramped. By reducing the* main *div to 75% of the screen div (which is the same size as the* wrap *div), we leave room for the* sidebar.

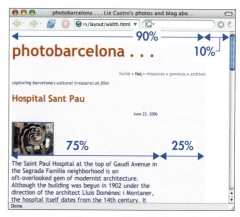

Figure 11.12 *The* wrap *div, which encloses the shaded screen div completely, now occupies only 90% of the browser window.*

```
#wrap {max-width: 900px; min-width: 480px;}
```

Figure 11.13 *The* max-width *and* min-width *properties are ideal for setting the outside limits of our liquid layout. We don't want it to get too wide, even if visitors have huge monitors, nor too narrow, even if visitors squeeze it beyond recognition. While Firefox and Opera support these properties, unfortunately, Internet Explorer (up to and including version 7) does not.*

```
div {width:300px; height: 500px;
   background: yellow;}


p.auto {width:auto; margin: 10px; padding: 5px;
border: 5px solid blue; background: white;}


p {width: 200px; margin: 10px; padding: 5px;
border: 5px solid purple; background: white;}
```

Figure 11.14 *In this mini-example, I've set the* width *of the* parent *div to 300 pixels. This will be our containing block. Then, both paragraphs have 10 pixel margins, 5 pixel padding and 5 pixel borders on all sides. The first paragraph has the width set automatically, the second is set at 200 px.*

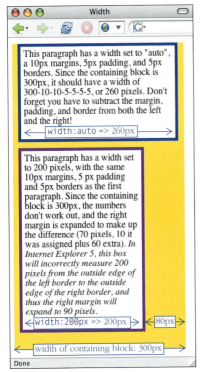

Figure 11.15 *If the* width *is auto, as in the top paragraph, its value is derived from the width of the containing block (yellow) minus the margins, padding, and border. If the* width *is set manually (as in the bottom paragraph), the right margin is usually adjusted to pick up the slack.*

Width, margins, and auto

For most block-level elements, the `auto` value for `width` is calculated from the width of the containing block minus the padding, borders, and margins. The *containing block* is the width that the element gets from its parent and is sometimes confusingly called the *inherited width*, even though it has nothing to do with normal CSS inheritance.

Elements with images and objects *(replaced elements)* have an `auto` width equal to their intrinsic value, that is, the actual dimensions of the external file. Floated elements have an `auto` width of 0. Non-floated inline elements ignore the `width` property altogether.

If you manually set the `width`, `margin-left`, and `margin-right` values, but together with the border and padding they don't equal the size of the containing block, something's got to give. And indeed, the browser will override you and set `margin-right` to `auto` **(Figures 11.14 and 11.15)**. If you manually set the `width` but set one of the margins to `auto`, then that margin will stretch or shrink to make up the difference. If you manually set the `width` but leave both margins set to `auto`, *both* margins will be set to the *same* maximum value (resulting in your element being centered).

Note that browsers never adjust the width of the borders or the padding.

Now those are the rules, for what they're worth. Unfortunately, IE 5 (and IE 6 in quirks mode) thought that when you set the width, you were setting the sum of the content area, the borders, and the padding, instead of just the content area as it should be. And IE 6 lets the margins and replaced elements of a child element affect the width of the containing block while asserting in their documentation that this should not be allowed. As if this weren't all complex enough!

Setting the Margins around an Element

The margin is the amount of transparent space between one element and the next, in addition to and outside of any padding *(see page 177)* or border *(see page 184)* around the element.

To set an element's margins:

Type **margin: x**, where *x* is the amount of desired space to be added, expressed as a length, a percentage of the width of the parent element, or `auto`.

✔ Tips

■ If you use one value for `margin`, that value is applied to all four sides equally. If you use two values, the first value applies to the top and bottom and the second value applies to the right and left. If you use three values, the first applies to the top, the second to the right and left, and the third to the bottom. If you use four values, they are applied to the top, right, bottom, and left, in clockwise order.

■ You can also add one of the following suffixes to the `margin` property to apply a margin to a single side: `-top`, `-bottom`, `-left`, or `-right`. There shouldn't be any space after margin (e.g., `margin-top: 10px`).

■ The `margin` property's `auto` value depends on the value of the `width` property *(see page 174)*.

■ If one element is placed above another, only the greater of the two touching margins is used. The other one is said to *collapse*. Left and right margins don't collapse.

■ Margins are not inherited.

```
#wrap {margin: 20px auto;}
```

Figure 11.16 *One of the principal margin adjustments is to the* wrap *div. When you set two values, the first is applied to the top and bottom margins, the second is applied to the left and right margins. We'll set the top and bottom margins to 20px to give our design a little space.*

Figure 11.17 *The* auto *margin setting centers the layout in the window by dividing up the leftover 10% of the browser window width that is not used by the* wrap *div between the right and left margins.*

```
#sidebar {margin-left: 74%;}
.photo_text {margin-left: 110px;}
```

Figure 11.18 *The* sidebar *div will have a left margin of 74%, which will overlap the space for the main content just enough to allow for some padding around the sidebar text.*

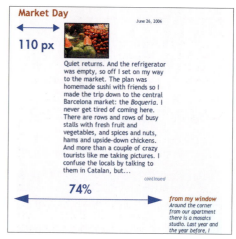

Figure 11.19 *The 110 px margin to the left of the main content will give us room for the photo later.*

```
#wrap {padding: 30px 20px 0 0;}
```

Figure 11.20 *When you set four values for* pad-ding, *they are assigned to the top, right, bottom, and left, in that order. So, here, there will only be padding on the top and right.*

Figure 11.21 *When we add padding to the* wrap *div, we are actually adding padding between its contents (in this case, the* screen *div) and its margin (that we set on the previous page). Padding added to the* wrap *div uses the background image from the* wrap *div.*

```
#screen {padding: 10px 10px 10px 0;}
```

Figure 11.22 *Now we'll add padding to the contents of the* screen *div—to the top, right, and bottom, but not the left.*

Figure 11.23 *Padding added to the* screen *div goes between its contents and its margin. Notice the extra 10 pixels between* photobarcelona *and the top edge and between the word* archives *in the menu and the right edge.*

Figure 11.24 *When the screen background is set to white, it's clear why we didn't need padding to the left as well. I have made a number of other padding adjustments that you can study in the code files on my Web site.*

Adding Padding around an Element

Padding is just what it sounds like: extra space around the contents of an element but inside the border. Think of Santa Claus' belly—nicely padded, while being held in by his belt (the border). You can change the padding's thickness, but not its color or texture. (Margins are Santa's personal space.)

To add padding around an element:

Type **padding: x**, where *x* is the amount of desired space to be added, expressed in units *(10px)* or as a percentage of the width of the parent element *(20%)*.

✔ Tips

- As with the `margin` property, if you use one value, the specified padding is applied to all four sides equally. If you use two values, the first value applies to the top and bottom and the second value applies to the right and left. If you use three values, the first applies to the top, the second to the right and left, and the third to the bottom. If you use four values, they are applied to the top, right, bottom, and left, in clockwise order.

- You can also add one of the following suffixes to the `padding` property to apply padding to a single side: `-top`, `-bottom`, `-left`, or `-right`. There should be no space between the word `padding` and the suffix (e.g., `padding-right: 1em`).

- Padding is not inherited.

- Use percentages or ems to create liquid layouts that expand or contract depending on the visitor's monitor.

- The space after the colon is optional. There is never a space between the number and the unit.

Offsetting Elements In the Natural Flow

Each element has a natural location in a page's flow. Moving the element with respect to this original location is called *relative positioning*. The surrounding elements are not affected—at all.

To offset elements within the natural flow:

1. Type **position: relative;** (don't forget the semicolon; the space is optional).

2. If desired, type **top**, **right**, **bottom**, or **left**.

   Then, type **:v**, where *v* is the desired distance that you want to offset the element from its natural location, either as an absolute or relative value (10ps, or 2em, for example) or as a percentage.

3. If desired, repeat step 2 for additional directions, separating each property/value pair with a semicolon as usual.

✔ Tips

■ The "relative" in *relative positioning* refers to the element's original position, not the surrounding elements. You can't move an element with respect to other elements. Instead, you move it with respect to where it used to be. Yes, this is important!

■ The other elements are not affected by the offsets—they flow with respect to the *original* containing box of the element, and may even be overlapped.

■ Offsets don't work unless you're also using the `position` property.

■ Positioning is not inherited.

Figure 11.25 *Although the date is aligned to the right, it is on a separate line than the header element and thus appears below it.*

```
.date {position: relative; top: -1.1em;}
```

Figure 11.26 *Remember to both specify the relative positioning and also give the offset. Using ems will keep the offset in proportion with the size of the text.*

Figure 11.27 *By applying a negative offset to the date, we push it up into the preceding block's space. In this case, that results in the date being aligned with the section title. The succeeding elements are not affected at all.*

```
.description {position: relative; left: 1em;
             margin-bottom: 0.2em}
```

Figure 11.28 *Here we'll indent the description from the left edge slightly and pull it up slightly with a negative margin.*

Figure 11.29 *Notice how the description (that begins with* capturing*) is now offset to the right under* photobarcelona*.*

Hospital Sant Pau

June 23, 2006

The Saint Paul Hospital at the top of Gaudí Avenue in the Sagrada Família neighborhood is an oft-overlooked gem of modernist architecture. Although the building was begun in 1902 under the direction of the architect Lluís Domènec i

Figure 11.30 *Our photo is still sitting above the text in the* photo_text *div. We want to shift it down into the space that we've set aside in the left margin.*

```
.photo_text {position: relative;}

.photo {position: absolute; left: -112px; top: 3px;}
```

Figure 11.31 *First we set the position for the* photo_text *class so that the photos will be positioned with respect to it (and not to the* body *). The negative left offset will pull the photo left and out of the* photo_text *box.*

Hospital Sant Pau

June 23, 2006

The Saint Paul Hospital at the top of Gaudí Avenue in the Sagrada Família neighborhood is an oft-overlooked gem of modernist architecture. Although the building was begun in 1902 under the direction of the architect Lluís Domènec i

Figure 11.32 *Wherever the* photo_text *class goes, the photo will be stuck to its left side. Remember that the text in* photo_text *does not move out of the way for the photo. We pushed it away by giving it a left margin of 110px on page 176.*

Positioning Elements Absolutely

The elements in your Web page generally flow in the order in which they appear. That is, if the `img` tag comes before the `p`, the image appears before the paragraph. You can take elements out of the normal flow—and position them *absolutely*—by specifying their precise position with respect to the nearest positioned ancestor or to the body.

To position elements absolutely:

1. Type **position: absolute;** (don't forget the semicolon; the space is optional).

2. If desired, type **top**, **right**, **bottom**, or **left**.

   Then, type **:v**, where *v* is the desired distance that you want to offset the element from its ancestor (10px, or 2em, for example), or as a percentage of the ancestor.

3. If desired, repeat step 2 for additional directions separating each property/ value pair with a semicolon as usual.

4. If desired, add **position: relative** to the ancestor element to which you want your absolutely positioned element to be offset. If you skip this step, the element will be offset with respect to the `body`.

✔ Tips

- Use percentages or ems for liquid designs that adapt to your visitors' preferences.

- Because absolutely positioned elements are taken out of the flow of the document, they can overlap each other and other elements. (This is not always bad.)

- If you don't specify an offset for an absolutely positioned item, the item appears in its natural position, but does not affect the flow of subsequent items.

- Positioning is not inherited.

Affixing an Element to the Browser Window

When a visitor scrolls in the browser window, the contents of the window usually move up or down while the Back and Forward buttons, for example, stay stationary or *fixed*. CSS allows you to affix elements to the browser window so that they don't move when the visitor scrolls up or down.

To affix an element to the browser window:

1. Type **position: fixed;** (don't forget the semicolon; the space is optional).

2. If desired, type **top**, **right**, **bottom**, or **left**.

   Then, type **:v**, where *v* is the desired distance that you want to offset the element from the edges of the browser window, either expressed as an absolute or relative value (10px, or 2em, for example), or as a percentage of the browser window.

3. If desired, repeat step 2 for additional directions, separating each property/value pair with a semicolon as usual.

4. Use the `width` property *(see page 174)* to explicitly set the width of the element.

✔ Tips

- Remember that the offsets of a fixed element are relative to the browser window, while the offsets of an element positioned absolutely are relative to that element's positioned ancestor.

- Unfortunately, Explorer for Windows (up to and including version 6) did not support fixed positioning. IE 7 does. Firefox and Opera have for some time.

- Positioning is not inherited.

```
#sidebar {position: fixed; width: 26%;}

#main {padding:4px;}
```

Figure 11.33 *We'll make a momentary digression to show a fixed element, in this case the sidebar. IE needs its width expressed explicitly. In the (X)HTML, I removed the main, wrap, and header divs, since they don't make sense with a fixed element. I also moved the sidebar in front of the main div. We won't use this CSS with the rest of the example in this chapter.*

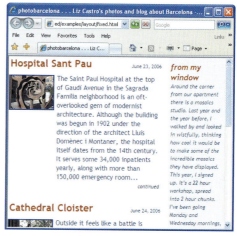

Figure 11.34 *A fixed element lets other elements flow right over it. In addition, it doesn't move when the visitor scrolls through the page.*

Figure 11.35 *Notice how the sidebar remains immobile as the visitor scrolls through the left content.*

```
#main {width: 75%; float: left;}

#navbuttons {width: 22em; float: right;}
```

Figure 11.36 *We already pushed the* sidebar *off to the right, now we'll float the main content in on its left. The* navbuttons *div will float next to the description instead of just under it.*

Figure 11.37 *Note that it's the* main *div that's floating, not the sidebar. The sidebar simply flows along the right side of the iceberg that is the* main *div. Note that it wasn't strictly necessary to give the sidebar a big left margin to get the float effect, but unless the* main *div is exactly the same length as the sidebar, the margin helps maintain that float effect long after the* main *div is done.*

Making Elements Float

You can make elements float in a sea of text (or other elements). You can use this technique to create multi-column layouts, to create callout quotes, and more.

To wrap text around elements:

1. Type **float:**.

2. Type **left** if you want the element on the left and the rest of the content to flow to its right.

   Or type **right** if you want the element on the right and the rest of the content to flow to its left.

3. Use the `width` property *(see page 174)* to explicitly set the width of the element.

✔ Tips

■ Remember, the direction you choose applies to the element you're floating, not to the elements that flow around it. When you **float: left**, the rest of the page flows to the right, and vice-versa.

■ Non-replaced elements (e.g., text) without an explicit width may not float properly.

■ The `float` property is not inherited.

■ For an old-fashioned, deprecated, but well-supported way of flowing text between images, consult *Making Images Float* on page 96.

Making Elements Float

Controlling Where Elements Float

You can control which elements an element can float next to and which it cannot. To keep an element from floating next to something it shouldn't, use the `clear` property.

To control where elements float:

1. Type **clear:**.

2. Type **left** to keep elements from floating to the left of the element you're styling.

   Or type **right** to keep elements from floating to the right of the element you're styling.

   Or type **both** to keep elements from floating to either side of the element you're styling.

   Or type **none** to let elements flow to either side of the element you're styling.

✔ Tips

■ The `clear` property stops the affected element (the one to which the `clear` property is applied) from displaying until the designated side is free of floating elements.

■ You add the `clear` property to the element whose sides you want to be clear of floating objects. So, if you want an element not to be displayed until the right side is clear of floating elements, add `clear:right` to *it* (and *not* to the floating elements).

■ The use of the `clear` property is similar to the `br` tag with the (alas, deprecated) `clear` attribute *(see page 98)*.

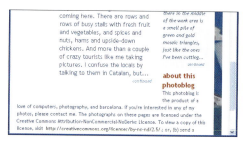

Figure 11.38 *Since it is the* main *div that is floating, all of the other elements, including the footer, flow around it unless we say otherwise.*

```
#footer {clear:both;}
```

Figure 11.39 *We could conceivably use* `clear:left` *here since the only floated element we have to worry about is floating on the left. But it doesn't hurt to clear both sides and it may come in handy if our design becomes more complicated.*

Figure 11.40 *The* `clear` *property indicates that the element in question (the* footer *in this case) must not flow around the floated element but instead be displayed after the floated element.*

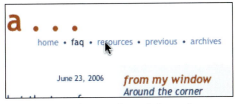

Figure 11.41 *When we floated the* navbuttons *they slid under the description. It's not noticeable at first because the description has a transparent background but when you try to click the links, they balk.*

#navbuttons {position:relative; z-index:1;}

Figure 11.42 *We set the* z-index *level to 1 which pulls the* navbuttons *div above the description. Notice that we must position the* navbuttons *div relatively so that the* z-index *property can work. As long as we don't set the offsets, the* navbuttons *won't go anywhere.*

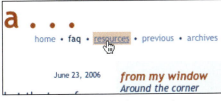

Figure 11.43 *Once the* navbuttons *div is on top, the links work as expected.*

Positioning Elements in 3D

Once you start using relative and absolute positioning, it's quite possible to find that your elements have overlapped. You can choose which element should be on top.

To position elements in 3D:

Type **z-index: n**, where *n* is a number that indicates the element's level in the stack of objects.

✔ Tips

- The z-index property only works on positioned elements.

- The higher the value of the z-index property, the higher up the element will be in the stack. You can think of the z-index property as a measure of elevation, with the visitors in an airplane looking down, seeing the elements on the tops of mountains first.

- You can use both positive and negative values for z-index.

- If you have nested items within an element that has a certain z-index, all those nested items are first ordered according to their own individual z-indexes, and then, as a group, ordered in the larger context.

- The z-index property is not inherited.

Positioning Elements in 3D

Setting the Border

You can create a border around an element and then set its thickness, style, and color. If you've specified any padding *(see page 176)* the border encloses both the padding and the contents of the element.

To define the border-style:

Type **border-style: type**, where *type* is `none`, `dotted`, `dashed`, `solid`, `double`, `groove`, `ridge`, `inset`, or `outset`.

To set the width of the border:

Type **border-width: n**, where *n* is the desired width, including abbreviated units (for example, *4px*).

To set the color of the border:

Type **border-color: color**, where *color* is a color name or rgb color *(see page 126 and the inside back cover)*.

To set one or more border properties at once with a shortcut:

1. Type **border**.

2. If desired, type **-top**, **-right**, **-bottom**, or **-left** to limit the effect to a single side.

3. If desired, type **-property**, where *property* is one of `style`, `width`, or `color`, to limit the effect to a single property.

4. Type **:**.

5. Type the appropriate values (as described in the first three techniques above). If you've skipped step 3, you can specify any or all of the three types of border properties (e.g., `border:1px solid` or `border-right:2px dashed green`). If you have specified a property type in step 3, use an accepted value for just that property (e.g., `border-right-style:dotted`).

```
.entry {border-right: 2px dashed #B74E07;}

.photo img {border: none;}

#footer {border-top: 2px dotted #B74E07;}
```

Figure 11.44 *When you make a link out of an* img *element, the image is displayed with a blue border by default in most browsers. In this example, it's easier to remove the border from the* img *element than from a* elements, *though we could do that, too.*

Figure 11.45 *Notice that since a right border is applied to the* entry *div and not the main* div, *it stops and starts for each entry. Also, now that the photos don't have that annoying default border, there is enough space between them and the text.*

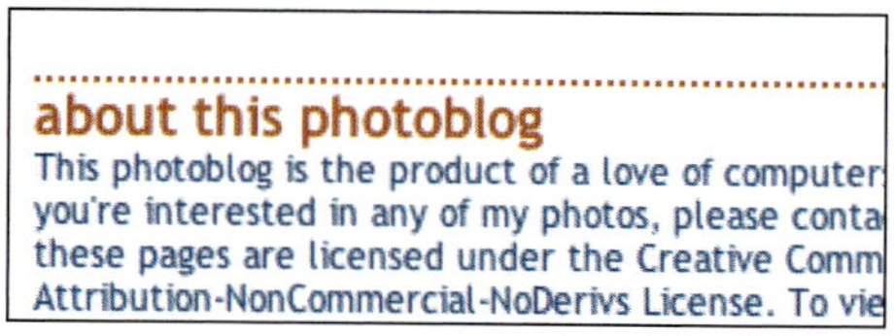

about this photoblog
This photoblog is the product of a love of computer you're interested in any of my photos, please conta these pages are licensed under the Creative Comm Attribution-NonCommercial-NoDerivs License. To vie

Figure 11.46 *The* footer *has a top border that is the same color but that is dotted instead of dashed.*

```
p {padding:15px; border: 10px solid red;}

p.ddd {border-width: 4px; border-style: dotted
dashed double solid;}


p.inset {border: 10px inset blue;}
p.outset {border: 10px outset green;}
p.groove {border: 10px groove purple;}
p.ridge {border: 10px ridge orange;}
```

Figure 11.47 *In this mini-example, I set the padding and default border for each paragraph. Then for the first paragraph, I set the border width for all four sides, and then the style for each side. For the four remaining paragraphs, it was easier to repeat the 10px then to separate the style and color into two separate properties.*

Figure 11.48 *Firefox for Macintosh is shown on the left, IE 7 for Windows is on the right. The styles are very similarly displayed, but not exactly the same. Note, for example, how IE's dots are actually round and how Firefox's shading is lighter and more pronounced.*

✔ Tips

- Borders are not inherited.

- The individual border properties (`border-width`, `border-style`, and `border-color`) can have from one to four values. If you use one value, it is applied to all four sides. If you use two, the first is used for the top and bottom, and the second for the right and left. If you use three, the first is used for the top, the second for the right and left, and the third is used for the bottom. And if you use four, they are applied to the top, right, bottom, and left, in clockwise order.

- You must define at least the style for a border to display. If there's no style, there will be no border. The default is `none`.

- If you use a shortcut, like `border` or `border-left` (etc.), the properties you don't give values for are set to their defaults. So `border: 1px black` means `border: 1 px black none`, which means you won't get a border (even if you specified a style earlier with `border-style`).

- The default color is the value of the element's `color` property *(see page 160)*.

- The width can also be expressed in generic terms: `thin`, `medium`, and `thick`. The default is `medium`.

- IE (up to and including version 7) cannot display very dark two-tone border styles like `groove`, `ridge`, `outset`, and `inset`. They come out solid.18

- The `border` property can be used for tables and their cells. For more details, consult *Adding a Border* on page 230.

- Frankly, I think someone went a bit over the top in thinking up different ways to set the `border` properties.

Setting the Border

Changing the Cursor

Normally, the browser takes care of the cursor shape for you, using an arrow most of the time, and a pointing finger to highlight links. CSS lets you take the reigns.

To change the cursor:

1. Type **cursor:**.

2. Type **pointer** for the cursor that usually appears over links (🖑), **default** for an arrow (🖈), **crosshair** (+), **move** (✛), **wait** (⧗), **help** (🖈?), **text** (I), **progress** (🖈⧗).

    Or type **auto** to get whatever cursor usually appears in that situation.

    Or type **x-resize** to get a double-sided arrow, where *x* is the cardinal direction one of the arrows should point—that is, n (north), nw (northwest), e (east), etc. For example, the e-resize cursor might look like this: ↔.

✔ Tips

■ The illustrations shown above are from IE 6. The cursors vary slightly from browser to browser and system to system. For example, the wait cursor on a Mac is the familiar watch: ⌚.

■ I find the names confusing. The default isn't the default, but instead is an arrow, which I would call a pointer, but pointer means a hand, while hand is a non-standard value created by Microsoft. Ugh.

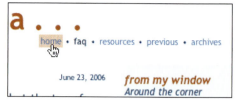

Figure 11.49 *When you point to the home link, the cursor changes to a pointing hand and the link is highlighted, just as for any other link.*

```
a:hover.current {cursor: default;
background: white;}
```

Figure 11.50 *Because we're on the home page, the home link will be part of the* current *class. We can then change the cursor and background of the home link so that it doesn't act like a link.*

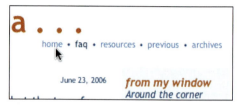

Figure 11.51 *Although this continues to be a real, live link, it no longer looks like one. Since we are already on the page to which this link goes, that makes sense.*

about this photoblog

This photoblog is the product of a love of computers, photography, and barcelona. if you're interested in any of my photos, please contact me. The photographs on these pages are licensed under the Creative Commons Attribution-NonCommercial-NoDerivs License. To view a copy of this license, visit http://creativecommons.org/licenses/by-nc-nd/2.5/; or, (b) send a letter to Creative Commons, 543 Howard Street, 5th Floor, San Francisco, California, 94105, USA.

Figure 11.52 *The images at the bottom of the footer are displayed on multiple lines.*

```
p.miniphotos {height: 33px; overflow: hidden;}
```

Figure 11.53 *In order to display a single line of images, we set the height of the paragraph to the height of the largest images and then set* overflow *to* hidden.

http://creativecommons.org/licenses/by-nc-nd/2.5/; or, (b) send a letter to Creative Commons, 543 Howard Street, 5th Floor, San Francisco, California, 94105, USA.

Figure 11.54 *Now the extra images are hidden.*

http://creativecommons.org/licenses/by-nc-nd/2.5/; or, (b) send a letter to Creative Commons, 543 Howard Street, 5th Floor, San Francisco, California, 94105, USA.

Figure 11.55 *Now the line of images expands and contracts as the browser window expands and contracts, never spilling over into additional lines.*

Determining Where Overflow Should Go

Elements are not always contained in their boxes. Sometimes the box is simply not big enough. Or perhaps you've positioned the content outside of the box, either with negative margins or absolute positioning. Regardless of the cause, you can control the area outside of the element's box with the overflow property.

To determine where overflow should go:

1. Type **overflow:**.

2. Type **visible** to expand the element box so that its contents fit. This is the default option.

   Or type **hidden** to hide any contents that don't fit in the element box.

   Or type **scroll** to always add scroll bars to the element so that the visitor can access the overflow if they so desire.

   Or type **auto**, to have scroll bars appear only when necessary.

✔ Tips

■ Note that IE 6 doesn't think you know what you're doing when you make a child bigger than its parent and will incorrectly extend the parent to be as big as the child. The only exception is if you set the overflow property to any value except visible (the default), in which case the parent will shrink down to its normal size and let the overflow property do its job.

■ The default value for overflow is visible. The overflow property is not inherited.

Aligning Elements Vertically

You can align elements in many different ways to make them look neater on the page.

To position elements vertically:

1. Type **vertical-align:**

2. Type **baseline** to align the element's baseline with the parent's baseline.

   Or type **middle** to align the middle of the element with the middle of the parent.

   Or type **sub** to position the element as a subscript of the parent.

   Or type **super** to position the element as a superscript of the parent.

   Or type **text-top** to align the top of the element with the top of the parent.

   Or type **text-bottom** to align the bottom of the element with the bottom of the parent.

   Or type **top** to align the top of the element with the top of the tallest element on the line.

   Or type **bottom** to align the bottom of the element to the bottom of the lowest element on the line.

   Or type a percentage of the line height of the element, which may be positive or negative.

Figure 11.56 *Images are aligned by default to the bottom of the line.*

```
.miniphotos img {vertical-align:middle;}
```

Figure 11.57 *Notice that the alignment is set on the images themselves, not on the paragraph.*

Figure 11.58 *Now the images are aligned to the middle of the line.*

Dynamic Effects with Styles

There are a few CSS features that lend themselves to creating dynamic effects. These are the `display` and `visibility` properties, and the `:hover` pseudo-class. While the `display` and `visibility` properties control when an element is visible, the `:hover` pseudo-class gives you the power to administer that control.

In this chapter, I'll go over `display` and `visibility` and then show you a few ways that CSS designers are implementing these dynamic effects on their Web sites to make rollover buttons, pop-ups, dynamic menus, and more—all *without* the use of JavaScript.

Displaying and Hiding Elements

The `display` property is useful for hiding or revealing particular elements. You can also override an element's natural display type (from block-level to inline, or vice-versa). Or you can display an element as a list item—even without the `li` tag.

To specify how elements should be displayed:

1. In your style sheet rule, type **display:**.

2. Type **none** to hide the given element and completely remove it from the document flow **(Figures 12.3 and 12.4)**.

    Or type **block** to display the element as block-level (thus starting a new paragraph).

    Or type **inline** to display the element as inline (not starting a new paragraph).

    Or type **list-item** to display the element as if you had used the `li` tag *(see page 216)*.

To control an element's visibility:

1. In your style sheet rule, type **visibility:**.

2. Type **hidden** to make the element invisible without removing it from the document flow **(Figures 12.5 and 12.6)**.

    Or, type **visible** to reveal the element.

✔ Tips

■ If you use `display: none`, no trace remains of the hidden element in the browser window. There is no empty space. When you use `visibility: hidden`, the space that the hidden element would have taken up still takes up room in the document flow.

```
<head>
    <title>Showing the whole tower</title>
    <style type="text/css">
    p {margin:0 0 2px 0;padding:0}
    </style>

</head><body>
<p><img src="towertop.jpg" width="100"
height="134" alt="At the top" /></p>
<p class="hide"><img src="towermiddle.jpg"
width="100" height="134" alt="In the middle"
/></p>
<p><img src="towerbottom.jpg" width="100"
height="134" alt="At the bottom" /></p>
</body>
```

Figure 12.1 *Here's the (X)HTML: three simple paragraphs with an image in each one. The middle paragraph has a* `class` *of* hide.

Figure 12.2 *The only CSS applied here is a 2 pixel bottom margin to the* p *elements. All three paragraphs and their images are visible.*

```
.hide {display: none;}
```

Figure 12.3 *When we hide the display...*

Figure 12.4 *... no trace of the hidden paragraph (or the image within it) remains.*

```
.hide {visibility: hidden;}
```

Figure 12.5 *When we change the visibility to hidden...*

Figure 12.6 *...an empty space remains where the hidden paragraph used to be.*

- If an element is absolutely positioned and thus already taken out of the document flow, `display:none` and `visibility: hidden` are identical in terms of layout. However, some browsers don't load elements whose `display` is set to `none`, saving download time.

- While it's true that the `display` property is not inherited, this may be irrelevant since when an element is hidden, its entire contents (including any descendants) are also hidden.

- The `display` property has a number of other properties for use in tables but they are poorly supported.

- I have some more complex examples of `display` on the following pages.

- The `visibility` property is not inherited.

- The `visibility` property has a third value (apart from `inherit`): `collapse`. When used with table cells, it hides the offending row, removes it from the table, but still uses the content to calculate the height and width of adjacent columns and rows.

- CSS also has a `clip` property which allows you to determine which portion of an element will show through. Its syntax is `clip: rect(top right bottom left)`, where each value is the desired distance in that direction starting from the top or left. Although it is supported relatively widely, I haven't seen it implemented in a useful way that couldn't be more easily handled with `margin` and `padding`.

Displaying and Hiding Elements

Creating Rollover Buttons

Rollover buttons change their appearance when your visitor points at or hovers over them.

To change links on rollover:

1. Create a set of links in the usual way in the (X)HTML document *(see page 103)*.

2. In the CSS, style the `a:link` and `a:visited` selectors with the "initial state" of the links by adding background color or image properties.

3. Modify the colors or backgrounds slightly for the `a:focus` and `a:hover` selectors so that the buttons change appearance when they get the focus or are pointed at.

4. If desired, select a third style for buttons when they're activated by setting the CSS for the `a:active` selector.

✔ Tips

- This is a very simple example. You can do wonders by designing and choosing special images. For more ideas, see the article by Douglas Bowman on Sliding Doors of CSS at *A List Apart*: *http://www.alistapart.com/slidingdoors*

- I used the `display:block` to format the usually inline a elements as block-level elements, each beginning its own line. This is not necessary for rollover buttons; you could just as easily have them in a horizontal row.

```
<title>Rollover Buttons</title>
    <style type="text/css">
    a {display: block; padding: 2px;
text-decoration: none; width: 5em; margin: 2px;
color: #8D4F10; font-family: "Trebuchet MS",
Verdana, sans-serif;}
    a:link, a:visited {background: #efb57c;
border: 2px outset #efb57c;}
    a:focus, a:hover {background: #DAA670;
border: 2px outset #DAA670; color: black;}
    a:active {background: #BB8E60;
border: 2px outset #BB8E60;}
    </style>
</head>
<body>

<a href="home.html">home</a>
<a href="about.html">about</a>
<a href="examples.html">examples</a>
<a href="extras.html">extras</a>
```

Figure 12.7 *In this simple example, the unvisited and visited links have one color for background and border, the focus and hover links have a slightly darker background and border, and black text, and the active links have an even darker background and border.*

Figure 12.8 *The unvisited and visited states are shown at left. When the visitor points (hovers) or gives the focus to the link, it appears darker with black text (as shown on the right).*

```
<style type="text/css">
    img.mini {border: none;}
    div#minis a:hover {background: white;}
    div#minis a img.big {height: 0; width: 0;
border-width: 0;}
    div#minis a:hover img.big {position: absolute;
top: 18px; left: 120px; height: 375px;
width: 500px; border: none;}

    #frame {position: absolute; top: 16px;
left: 118px; height: 355px; width: 480px;
border: 2px solid red; font: 1em "Trebuchet MS",
Verdana, sans-serif; color: red; padding: 10px;}
    p {margin-bottom: 26px;}
    </style>
</head>
<body>
<div id="frame">
<p>Click over the photos to enlarge them into this
box.</p>
</div>
<div id="minis">
<p><a class="photo"
href="http://www.flickr.com/photos/cookwood/1
87664726/"><img class="mini"
src="http://static.flickr.com/68/187664726_5b9
```

Figure 12.9 *You can see a fully commented version of this code on my Web site.*

Figure 12.10 *When the visitor hovers over a photo in the left column, a larger version appears in the right frame.*

Creating Pop-ups

There's nothing that says the second image in a rollover has to appear directly on top of the previous one. If you position the second image some distance away, you can give additional details about the hovered item.

To create pop-ups:

1. Create a set of links in the usual way in the (X)HTML document.

2. In the CSS, style the `a:link` and `a:visited` selectors at the "home" location.

3. Then style the `a:focus` and `a:hover` selectors with absolute positioning so that the additional information—in this case, a larger image—is displayed in a different location.

✔ Tips

- This technique builds on Eric Meyer's work on pure CSS pop-ups: *http://meyerweb.com/eric/css/edge/popups/demo2.html*

- Set the `height` and `width` to 0 instead of `display:none` to make this work on Netscape 6 and IE 6. I also noticed that it was necessary to apply a background color to the `a:hover` (not to the `img`) for it to work properly in IE 6.

- There's no reason you couldn't have the pop-up include text instead of images. Or text *and* images.

- Notice that in the example shown here, the page does not load faster just because the initial images are small. The images are all the same, original size.

Creating Drop-Down Menus with Lists

Although we don't talk about lists until Chapter 15, I'll advance you a technique for using them to format navigation links into drop-down (or pop-out) menus with CSS. You may want to come back to this section after having gone through that chapter.

To create drop-down menus with lists:

1. In the (X)HTML file **(Figure 12.11)**, create navigation links in the form of a nested list like the one on page 224. The first level items will always be visible, the second (and subsequent) level items will only be visible when hovered over.

2. Enclose the entire list in a `div` with a name like `navbar`.

3. Enclose the rest of your page in its own `div` with a name like `content`.

4. In the CSS **(Figure 12.12)**, remove the default list formatting by using **#navbar ul {margin: 0; padding: 0; list-style: none;}**.

5. Next, make the whole link clickable (not just the text) and control its width by typing **#navbar a {display: block; width:10em;}**.

6. To make the first level navbar items appear horizontally, type **#navbar li {float: left; width:10em;}**.

7. To hide the second level list except when hovered over, type **#navbar li ul {display: none}**.

8. To make the second level list appear when hovered over, type **#navbar li: hover ul {display: block;width:10em;**.

```
<div id="navbar">
<ul>
<li><a href="">Products</a>
   <ul>
   <li><a href="">PageWhacker 13.1</a></li>
   <li><a href="">InstaWeb 4.0</a></li>
   <li><a href="">BookWriter 1.0
(beta)</a></li>
   </ul>
</li>
<li><a href="">Support</a>
   <ul>
   <li><a href="">Online Forum</a></li>
   <li><a href="">Contact Us</a></li>
   </ul>
</li>
...snip last top level li ...</ul></div>

<div class="content">
<h1>PageWhacker Incorporated</h1>
<p>PageWhacker Incorporated, founded in 1995,
```

Figure 12.11 *Note that each of the submenus is a* ul *with its* li *elements within opening and closing tags of the top level* li *item. The links are empty to save space in this illustration, but clearly they'd have to have something there in the real world.*

```
#navbar ul {margin: 0; padding: 0; list-style: none;}

#navbar a {display: block; width: 10em;}

#navbar li {float: left; width: 10em;}

#navbar li ul {display: none;}

#navbar li:hover ul {display: block; width: 10em;
position: absolute;}

div.content {clear: left;}
```

Figure 12.12 *The basic code behind CSS drop-down menus is not complicated: remove the default formatting from the* ul, *float the list items horizontally, hide the second tier* ul *and make it appear only when hovered on. Clear floats for any content that follows.*

Figure 12.13 *When no hovering is happening, the top level* li *items are visible but their* ul *babies (with the second level* li *items) are hidden.*

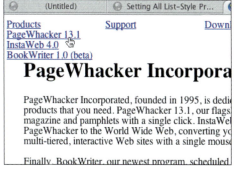

Figure 12.14 *When your visitor hovers over the list, the second level* ul *and its list items become visible.*

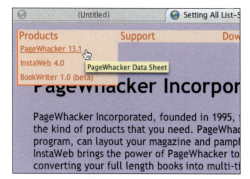

Figure 12.15 *This is the same code with some extra formatting. You can see both CSS files in full on my Web site (see page 26).*

9. To keep the rest of your page from bouncing around when the second level lists appear, add **position: absolute;}** to the previous line.

10. To keep the rest of your page from floating next to the navbar, clear the float from the `content div` by typing **div.content {clear:left}**.

11. Add extra formatting to make the menus pretty **(Figure 12.15)**. You can find the CSS file used for formatting on the Web site *(see page 26)*.

✔ Tips

■ This technique only works on browsers like Firefox and Opera that fully support CSS' `:hover` pseudo-class *(see page 146)*. Unfortunately, Internet Explorer (up to and including version 7), only supports `:hover` with a elements. What a waste! One way to make CSS menus work in IE is to add a bit of JavaScript. See Patrick Griffiths' *Son of Suckerfish Dropdowns* for one such technique *(www.htmldog.com/articles/suckerfish/dropdowns/)*.

■ You might want to set a width *(see page 174)* or minimum width *(also on page 174)* for your page so that your navigation bars don't collapse when the page is too narrow. Unfortunately, as of version 7, IE doesn't support minimum width yet either.

■ You can accommodate browsers like IE that don't fully support `:hover` by making the top level items actual links to pages that contain the second level links. While IE users won't see your drop-down menus, they'll still be able to get to the pages where they lead.

■ You can use this technique to create vertical pull-out menus as well.

Creating Drop-Down Menus with Lists

Replacing Headers with Images

Fahrner's Image Replacement (or FIR) is an extremely popular and equally controversial technique for replacing text with a graphic image of that text. It is one of the principal techniques used at the CSS Zen Garden, that hotbed of avant-garde CSS, but is criticized on accessibility grounds.

To replace a header with images:

1. In the CSS document, set the `background` property of the header (`h1` in the example) to the desired image.

2. Set the height of the header to the height of the image.

3. Hide the text in the `span` element by using **h1 span {display:none}**.

4. Save the CSS document with the .css extension.

5. In the head section of your (X)HTML document type **<style type="text/css">** to begin the internal style sheet.

6. Type **@import "sheet.css" screen;**, where *sheet.css* is the CSS file that you created in steps 1–4 and that will be used only for formatting your page in computer browsers, not in print or in handheld browsers.

7. Import or create any other formatting that should be applied to the screen, print, or handheld versions of your page.

8. Create your header in the desired location in the (X)HTML by typing **<h1>**.

9. Enclose the header text with a `span` element by typing **header**.

10. Complete the header with **</h1>**.

```
h1 {background: url(ftplogo.gif) no-repeat;
    height: 111px;}
h1 span {display: none;}
```

Figure 12.16 *The CSS code for image replacement should go in an external style sheet.*

```
<!DOCTYPE html PUBLIC "-//W3C//DTD XHTML
1.0 Transitional//EN"

"http://www.w3.org/TR/xhtml1/DTD/xhtml1-
transitional.dtd">
<html xmlns="http://www.w3.org/1999/xhtml">
<head>
    <title>Image Replacement</title>
    <style type="text/css">
    @import "imagereplacement.css" screen;
    p {font:italic 1.4em "Trebuchet MS", Verdana,
sans-serif;margin-left:4em; color:#EB7B31}

    </style>
</head>
<body>
<h1><span>Farm Training
Podcasts</span></h1>
<p>This week we go to Blackberry Farm in South
Hills to meet with Farmer Alice who will show us the
proper way to prune those prickly delights.</p>

</body>
</html>
```

Figure 12.17 *It's a good idea to import, rather than link CSS files that use the FIR technique to help keep screen readers and mobile browsers from using those styles.*

Figure 12.18 *The* h1 *element is replaced by the Farm Training Podcasts logo.*

✔ Tips

■ I describe image replacement here because I think it's important to understand the basic concept. Perhaps it will evolve to overcome the obstacles that keep it from complete acceptance.

■ One of the advantages of FIR is that because the header text does exist, search engines will see it in the source code, even though your visitors will not.

■ One problem with image replacement is that screen readers like JAWS sometimes can't read the spanned text. Importing the CSS for screen only (which translates to computer browsers, not screen readers) helps solve that problem.

■ A second problem arises if a visitor uses a browser that does not support CSS (perhaps a mobile browser) and has images turned off. In that case, they will see neither the image nor the text it was meant to replace.

■ There are a number of additional image replacement techniques that have attempted to solve the accessibility issues. Some are discussed by Dave Shea in his article defending FIR, *http://www.digital-web.com/articles/in_defense_of_fahrner_image_replacement/* and in his and Molly Holzschlag's book, *The Zen of CSS Design*, whose signature Web site relies heavily on image replacement. Another source of alternative techniques is the original article by Douglas Bowman popularizing FIR: *http://www.stopdesign.com/articles/replace_text/*, in particular the notes at the end. Finally, you may also want to read Joe Clark's criticisms of FIR at A List Apart, *http://www.alistapart.com/articles/fir* for the other side of the argument.

STYLE SHEETS FOR HANDHELDS

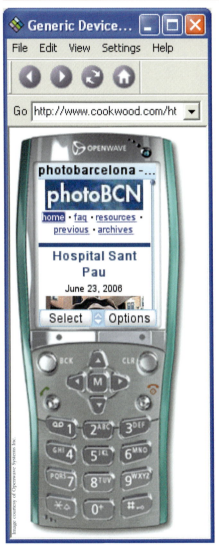

Figure 13.1 *While it's hard to match the layout of a big screen browser, there are a number of techniques that will make your page more accessible and attractive to mobile visitors.*

A last minute decision to go to the movies, a need to settle a bet about the official language of Andorra, the phone number of the company to which you'll arrive fifteen minutes late for your meeting, a map to the company because the reason you're late is you can't find the place. The Mobile Web is upon us. We want information when we need it, not when we get home to our computers.

The Mobile Web's beginnings were marked by its limitations: a tiny screen, little memory, and slow transfer rates. WAP, the *Wireless Application Protocol* was developed to squeak out as much speed as possible. WML, or *Wireless Markup Language*, was designed to streamline sites so that they wouldn't tax those little browsers.

The Mobile Web's adolescence, where we are now, has seen telephones grow more powerful—often with more memory than early desktop computers—and users grow more demanding: access to a tiny fraction of the Web is no longer enough. In response, WAP has expanded to be able to handle a good deal of XHTML and CSS and thus regular Web pages. WML, meanwhile, is headed towards obsolescence *(see page 25)*.

But like any good adolescent, the Mobile Web is unpredictable and frustratingly inconsistent. There are hundreds of handheld devices, sharing perhaps forty different browsers, which (surprise!) don't all support XHTML and CSS the same way. At this time, I recommend simplicity and patience as we wait for the Mobile Web to mature (and for the *mini-browser wars* to settle).

199

Mobilize vs. Miniaturize

There are two schools of thought with respect to creating Web pages for handhelds. The first says the whole reason we have separated content from design in the first place is so we can leverage that content with a CSS style sheet specially designed for the small screen. This system is efficient and agile, and facilitates both the creation and updating of such pages.

The second school says the difference between Web pages for computers and Web pages for handhelds does not end with their display size. What a visitor might need when they're on the road with their phone will be quite different from what they're looking for from home or the office, and simply *miniaturizing* that information is not going to be sufficient. These folks believe that pages should be rewritten with *mobilization* in mind: deciding what information is particularly useful for the mobile visitor and providing it to them with the least amount of scrolling, clicking, waiting, and downloading.

In the short term, I think it makes perfect sense to take advantage of what you already have working and make it as useful and accessible to visitors who come to your site through a handheld screen. In this chapter, I'll discuss what XHTML and CSS features are most appropriate for handheld browsers and how to get a CSS style sheet for handheld browsers up and working.

In the long term, you should probably think about whether you need to create a separate site that caters to the mobile visitor by offering features that are particularly useful to them.

Figure 13.2 *Here is Google's familiar interface for desktop screens. It is clean and clear and could easily be adapted for the small screen.*

Figure 13.3 *Google does not just miniaturize its regular page, however. Besides reducing the size of the graphics and layout, Google offers mobile visitors who visit www.google.com the opportunity to search the Mobile Web, read current news, and check Gmail accounts.*

Looking at Your Site

The first thing you should do in order to adapt your site for handheld screens is look at it with your own telephone (and anyone else's you can lay your hands on).

To look at your site

1. Open your own telephone and view your site. Use any other handhelds you have (including PDAs and smart phones) to view your site.

2. Download the latest version of Opera *(http://www.opera.com)*. Open your site and then choose View > Small Screen. Opera will show you what users of its Opera for Mobile browsers (installed on millions of handheld devices) are seeing.

3. Download Openwave's Phone Simulator *(http://developer.openwave.com)*. Openwave's browsers are on about 50% of the world's handheld devices.

4. Download the Nokia simulators *(http://www.forum.nokia.com)*. Nokia browsers are also very popular.

5. Download simulators from Palm, Blackberry, and other manufacturers of handheld devices.

✔ Tips

■ Unfortunately, most simulators—with Opera being the notable exception—run only on Windows system software.

■ Opera's desktop browsers emulate Opera's Mobile browser when you choose View > Small Screen. If your page has a handheld style sheet, Opera will use that. If your page does not have an associated handheld style sheet, Opera will use its proprietary Small Screen Rendering (SSR) technology to adapt your pages to the small screen on the fly.

Figure 13.4 *The style sheet for big screens looks pretty bad on this Openwave handheld browser.*

Figure 13.5 *Opera's desktop browsers can show you what your page will look like in its Opera Mobile software. If no handheld style sheet is available (as above) Opera adapts it automatically—and not too badly in this case.*

XHTML and CSS for Handhelds

Probably not too far in the future, you'll be able to use whatever (X)HTML and CSS you'd like for handhelds. Right now, however, support is good for some elements and dismal for others. Here's a rundown on what's safe and what's not.

What handhelds can and can't do	What you should do about it
Web access is expensive, mobile visitors often pay for every kilobyte (sometimes up to a penny per K).	Make every K worth it. Hide the extra parts *(see page 205)*, use fewer and smaller images, etc. Note that some handheld browsers will download even those images (and other elements) that are not to be displayed. For them, you'll have to create a super-lean mobile-specific site.
Visitors may choose to show pages without images to speed access (and save connection costs).	Make sure that every meaningful image on your site has alternate text *(see page 91)* so that visitors who view your page without images don't lose any info. Decorative images can use `alt=""`.
Handhelds sometimes filter Web sites through proxy servers, which strip out or shrink whatever the handheld browser can't deal with, like large images and problematic XHTML and/or CSS.	Keep your images really small. Test your site thoroughly.
Handhelds have narrow screens, but vary a fair bit between the smallest and the largest (while most phones average 100 – 150 pixels in width, PDA are in the 200 – 300 range and some Pocket PC type handhelds can be as wide as 600 pixels).	Use one column with narrow margins or preferably, none at all. Don't use floats, absolute positioning, tables (whose contents may be displayed in an order you haven't envisioned), or pop-up windows. Don't make headers so big that they don't fit across the screen. Support for CSS properties `margin` and `padding` is good. It's a good idea to minimize the space between paragraphs, just go easy on the horizontal margins. Avoid fixed width designs. Use ems and percentages instead.

What handhelds can and can't do	What you should do about it
Handheld browsers typically have no mouse or other pointing device and limited text-entry capabilities.	Add navigation systems that make it easier for visitors to get around text-heavy pages *(see page 207)*.
Most handheld browsers support a single font face, two or three font sizes at most, and can do boldface but not italics (at least not well).	With that in mind, forget about the CSS font property and focus on using header tags (h1, h2, etc.) to distinguish titles and section heads. Use paragraphs (p) for regular text. Use bold text for emphasis (b or strong) and use italics sparingly. Use percentages or ems to resize body text, not pixels.
Handhelds are good at lists, and may assign access keys (keyboard shortcuts) to numbered list items.	You can use numbered lists (ol) for navigation bars.
The CSS background-image property is not well supported.	Avoid background images. (And see next tip on background-color.)
More and more handhelds have color screens.	The CSS properties color and background-color are generally supported. Make sure you keep the contrast high between the text color and the background color so that folks looking at your page out on a sunny day can still see what's what.
Borders are supported...	... as long as you like them solid.
CSS properties like max-width, max-height, and overflow would be useful for dealing with varying small screen widths but are not well supported yet.	Keep them in mind and watch for upcoming handheld browser support.
Some handheld browsers will ignore the CSS file altogether.	Make sure your site displays adequately with no style sheet applied. View your site with as many handhelds or handheld simulators as you can *(see page 201)*.

XHTML and CSS for Handhelds

Creating Style Sheets for Handhelds

You can create an entirely independent style sheet that will only be used for your Web page when it is viewed in a telephone, PDA or other handheld device.

To create a style sheet for handhelds:

1. In the head section of your XHTML document, type **<link rel="stylesheet" type="text/css" href="url.css"**, where *url.css* is the location of the handheld style sheet on the server.

2. Next, type **media="handheld"** to indicate that this style sheet be used only for small screen devices.

3. Close the link tag with **/>**.

4. If desired, in the link tag for your main style sheet, type **media="screen"** so that the styles you've set up for regular screens are not used for handheld browsers.

✔ Tips

■ The default value for media is all. So, unless you limit your main CSS document to the screen, it will be used *in addition to* your handheld CSS rules. (In this case, the style sheet that is called later over-rules any earlier ones.) For more details, see page 133 in Chapter 8, *Working with Style Sheet Files*.

■ In the examples for the rest of this chapter, we'll be creating a separate and independent style sheet that does not use or depend on the main style sheet.

■ Not all handheld browsers respect the media attribute, and will erroneously read screen style sheets. Some do better with @import rules *(see page 132)*.

```
<head>
<title>photobarcelona - Liz Castro's photographs
and blog about Barcelona </title>

<meta http-equiv="Content-Type"
content="text/html; charset=UTF-8" />
<link rel="stylesheet" type="text/css"
href="handheld.css" media="handheld" />
<link rel="stylesheet" type="text/css"
href="allformatting.css"  media="screen" />
<link rel="stylesheet" type="text/css"
href="text.css" media="screen" />

</head>
```

Figure 13.6 *Add the* screen *value to your regular style sheets so that their properties are not applied to your handheld style sheet.*

Image courtesy of Openwave Systems Inc.

Figure 13.7 *Here's what our example looks like when pointed to a blank handheld style sheet. This document produced an error when it overloaded on the image files at the end of the document. We'll hide them on the next page.*

```
.description {display: none;}
.miniphotos {display: none;}
```

Figure 13.8 *If people care enough about our site to come here on a telephone or PDA, we'll spare them reading through the description. We'll also hide the photo bar on the bottom of the page.*

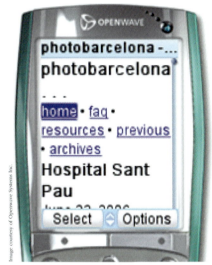

Figure 13.9 *Now after the navigation bar we go directly to the first article.*

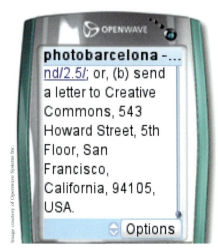

Figure 13.10 *Here is the bottom of the Web page, with the mini photos duly hidden.*

Hiding Extraneous Elements

Sometimes the easiest way to get rid of a problem element on your Web page that just doesn't look right on the small screen is to hide it all together.

To hide elements:

1. Type the selector that identifies the elements you want to hide.

2. Type **{display: none}** to completely remove them from the flow of the document.

✔ Tips

■ For more details about the display property, consult *Displaying and Hiding Elements* on page 190.

■ I have found the display property to be well supported by the handheld browsers that support CSS at all. I did have one problem with a browser that didn't like contextual selectors: h1 {display: none} worked fine, #header h1 {display:none} did not.

■ Note that just because you hide an element doesn't mean that the handheld browser won't download it. So, while you may indeed be improving what the page looks like, you might not necessarily be making it faster or cheaper. The only way to guarantee that a handheld browser won't download big images, scripts, or extra text is to serve it specialized pages without those elements.

■ If you create special items for your handheld pages, you may need to hide these on your regular screen style sheets.

■ The display property is often used to create interactive effects (see Chapter 12, *Dynamic Effects with Styles*).

Creating and Using an Image Header

The one place where it probably makes sense to use an image for a handheld page is as a title for the entire page, to give your page its own identity in that very small screen.

To create and use an image header:

1. Create a new image or reduce an existing one to only 100 pixels wide **(Figure 13.11)**.

2. Add the image to your header `div` in the usual way **(Figure 13.12)**.

3. Use the name of your Web site for the alternate text *(see page 91)*.

4. If this XHTML page will also be used for your regular screen site, add **#header img {display:none}** to hide the image in your header div for regular screen browsers **(Figure 13.13)**. (You may have to adjust this according to the contents of your own header `div`.)

5. If desired, hide the regular header **(Figure 13.14)**.

✔ Tip

■ If the image is bigger than 100 pixels it will be scaled proportionally to fit smaller screens, like on telephones, and may become too short to be legible. If it is larger, there will be room leftover, a much more palatable outcome.

Figure 13.11 *Here's our little 100-pixel wide header image.*

```
<div id="header">
    <img src="logo.jpg" alt="photoBCN"
height="30" width="100" />
    <h1>photobarcelona . . .</h1>
        <p id="navbuttons">
```

Figure 13.12 *Since this logo shows the name of the Web site, we should repeat this name in the* alt *attribute just in case the image is not displayed.*

```
#header img {display: none;}
```

Figure 13.13 *We don't want the logo to appear on our site when it's viewed with regular computer screens, so we'll add this line to our screen style sheet.*

```
h1 {display: none;}
```

Figure 13.14 *The logo conflicts with the text header, so we'll hide the* h1 *element on handhelds only.*

Figure 13.15 *Now the first thing our visitors see is our logo and the text header is hidden. (It will continue to be displayed on larger computer screens.)*

```
</div><!-- end .photo_text -->
      <p class="continued"><a
href="">continued</a><span class="totop"> -
</span><a class="totop" href="#header">to
top</a></p>

      </div> <!-- end .entry -->
```

Figure 13.16 *Add links back to the top (or back to the navigation bar) to make it easy for your visitors to move around your page.*

```
.totop {display: none;}
```

Figure 13.17 *We don't want the logo to appear on our site when it's viewed with regular computer screens, so we'll add this line to our screen style sheet.*

Figure 13.18 *We'll place a "to top" button at the end of every article so that our visitors can quickly return to the navigation bar if desired.*

Creating Extra Links to the Top

If your page has a lot of text, you may want to add some extra "to the top" buttons that make it easier for visitors to navigate around your page. Remember, they have no mouse!

To create extra links to the top:

1. Add the new links in the XHTML document, giving them the `totop` class **(Figure 13.16)**.

2. In the style sheet for big screens, add **.totop {display:none}** to hide the extra links from your visitors on computers **(Figure 13.17)**.

3. In the handheld CSS, style the `totop` class as desired.

✔ Tips

■ While you could just create a navigation bar and then repeat *it* throughout your document, that will create a lot of links to scroll through and may make your document even harder to browse. It's better to link to the navigation bar from places where it'll be useful.

■ Another option if you have a large navigation bar is to offer a Skip Navigation button at the top of your site so that visitors can go directly to the content.

■ Because the `div` already has an `id` of `header`, there is no need to create an anchor manually. For more details about linking to a particular part of a page, see see *Linking to a Specific Anchor* on page 107.

■ Note that I've added a dash (-) between the continued and to top links. To keep it from being shown on big screens, I've styled the dash with the `totop` class.

Adjusting for the Small Screen

There are a number of additional adjustments that you can make that will help your page be more readable on the small screen. Read through the tips on pages 202–203. Here are the adjustments I've made to the *photobarcelona* site.

Adjust margins and padding

Add some space above your headers or below your paragraphs to keep sections cleanly separated *(see pages 176–177)*.

Add borders

Add a border between divisions as a visual organization aid *(see page 184)*.

Reduce text size of minor elements

You might consider reducing the size of navigation bar links, continued and totop links, and others to keep the focus on the content. *(see page 156)*. Use percentages and ems, not pixels.

Center content

Centering content in a small screen makes it feel like you're maximizing space, since the extra space is divided between the left and right margins equally *(see page 165)*.

Remove image borders

If you have images that are links, consider removing the border from them so they are more attractive *(see page 184)*.

```
body {text-align: center;}

.description {display :none;}
.miniphotos {display: none;}

h1 {font-weight: normal;}
h1 {display: none;}

#navbuttons {font-size: 75%;}

.date, .continued {font-size: 75%;}
.continued {margin-bottom: 2em;}

h1, h2, h3 {margin:.5em 0 0 0; padding: 2px;
font-size: 90%; color: #193D79;
border-top: 4px solid #193D79;}

p {padding: 0; margin: 0;}

img {border: none;}
```

Figure 13.19 *Focus on improvements that divide the page from top to bottom, not left to right.*

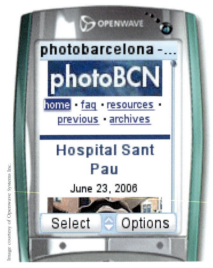

Figure 13.20 *There's not a lot you can do on a screen that measures 120 pixels wide, so keep it simple, clean, readable, and easy to navigate.*

STYLE SHEETS
FOR PRINTING

CSS lets you create specialized style sheets that control how Web pages are printed. These need not be anything like the screen version of the style sheets for that page. For example, you might want to remove extraneous sidebars or advertisements from a print version.

Creating a Style Sheet for Print

You can designate a style sheet to be used only when printing, only on screen, or for both print and screen. This allows you to hide those elements that don't need to be printed, as well as set special formatting that works well on paper for the elements you do want to print.

To create a style sheet for print:

Add **media="print"** to the opening `link` or `style` tags **(Figure 14.1)**.

Or, in an `@import` rule, add **print** after the style sheet's URL **(Figure 14.2)**.

✔ Tips

■ For more details on media-specific style sheets, see page 133 in Chapter 8, *Working with Style Sheet Files*.

■ You can make a style sheet that will be applied for more than one kind of output by adding additional values for the `media` attribute, separated by commas.

■ The default value for the `media` attribute is `all`. That means, that if you have one style sheet with no `media` attribute and one style sheet specifically for print, the styles in the `media`-less style sheet will also be applied to your printed output. To limit a style sheet to computer browser output, use **media="screen"**.

■ There is also an `@media` rule, though it is less well supported than the options described above.

```
<head>

    <meta http-equiv="content-type"
content="text/html; charset=utf-8" />

    <title>Red and Louis</title>

    <link rel="stylesheet" media="screen"
type="text/css" href="screen.css" />

    <link rel="stylesheet" media="print"
type="text/css" href="print.css" />

</head>

<body>

<div id="story">

<h1>Red and Louis</h1>
```

Figure 14.1 *In this (X)HTML document I've linked to the* screen.css *style sheet for the styles that will be used when displaying the page onscreen and the* print.css *style sheet for the styles that should be used when printing.*

```
<head>

    <meta http-equiv="content-type"
content="text/html; charset=utf-8" />

    <title>Red and Louis</title>

    <link rel="stylesheet" media="screen"
type="text/css" href="screen.css" />

    <style type="text/css">

@import "print.css" print;

</style>

</head>

<body>

<div id="story">

<h1>Red and Louis</h1>
```

Figure 14.2 *In this example, which should have the same effect in current browsers, I've linked to the* screen.css *style sheet but imported the* print.css *style sheet.*

Figure 14.3 *In a screen version, you might have a table of contents sidebar, some ads, and sans-serif fonts (which tend to be easier to read on screen).*

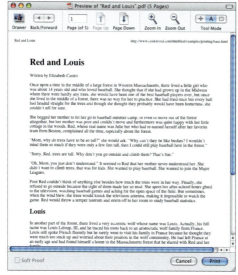

Figure 14.4 *When the document is printed, you can get rid of the sidebar and the ads, and use a serif font for added legibility. Note that the exact same (X)HTML code was used in both cases. The browser automatically selects the appropriate style sheet.*

How Print Style Sheets Differ

Depending on the complexity of your page, the print version might be very similar or indeed very different than the screen version.

Suggestions for print style sheets:

- Use appropriate fonts and font sizes, using points rather than pixels, since the former work best for printing. For more details, consult *A Property's Value* on page 124 as well as pages 152–159.

- Hide sections like sidebars or ads that need not be printed (using the `display` property described on page 190).

- Remove background colors and images and use colors that print reasonably in black and white *(see pages 160 and 172).*

- Adjust margins, if necessary *(see page 176).*

- Control page breaks and other print-specific properties *(see pages 212–214).*

- Explain to your visitors how and why the print version will be different from what they see on screen.

✔ Tips

- The page break and other print-specific CSS properties suffer from average to middling support. However, there are still many things that are worth changing that all browsers will understand.

- As you test style sheets for printed output, be sure to take advantage of your browser or system's Print Preview option, if it has one. Print Preview (typically in the File menu and sometimes in the Print dialog box itself) lets you see how the page will be printed without having to waste paper.

Controlling Page Breaks

Browsers can show very long pages in a single window thanks to the scroll bar. When visitors go to print a page, the contents of particularly long pages must be divided to fit on a given paper size. CSS lets you control where those page breaks should occur.

To control page breaks before elements:

In the style rule, type **page-break-before: when** or **page-break-after:when**, where *when* is one of `always` (so that page breaks always occur before/after the selected elements), `avoid` (so that page breaks only occur before/after the selected elements when absolutely necessary), or `auto` (to let the browser decide).

To keep elements from being divided between two pages:

In the style rule, type **page-break-inside: avoid**.

✔ Tips

- The `page-break-before` and `page-break-after` properties theoretically accept values of `left` and `right` (to make pages start on the left or right side, respectively), but those values are currently not supported on any browser.

- The default value for all of the page break properties is `auto`. Only `page-break-inside` is inherited.

- Currently, `page-break-before` and `-after` elements are supported by IE, Firefox, and Opera, though Explorer and Firefox don't understand the `avoid` value. Only Opera understands `page-break-inside`.

```
#toc {display: none;}
body {margin: .7in;}
p {font: 14pt serif; page-break-inside: avoid;}
h2 {page-break-before: always;}
```

Figure 14.5 *I don't want paragraphs to be divided between pages so I use* `page-break-inside:avoid`. *So that each second level header starts on its own page, I add* `page-break-before:always` *to the* `h2` *tags.*

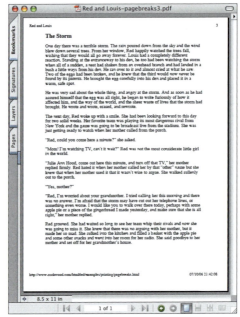

Figure 14.6 *By putting a page break before each* `h2` *element (like* The Storm*), I ensure that they start on a a fresh page. Notice also the extra space at the bottom of the page since the paragraph that followed was too big to fit in its entirety (and "inside page breaks" were to be avoided). Instead the entire next paragraph will be printed in full on the following page.*

```
#toc {display: none;}

body {margin: .7in;}

p {font: 14pt serif; page-break-inside: avoid;}

h2 {page-break-before: always;}


a {text-decoration: none; color: black;}

a:after {content: " (" attr(href) ")"; font-style: italic;}
```

Figure 14.7 *First I remove the typical coloring and underlining that on-screen links get. Then I take the* href *attribute of the selected element and add parentheses and finally italic formatting to it.*

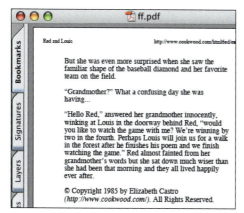

Figure 14.8 *The value of the link's* href *attribute, which is the URL that we want, is printed after the "click-me" part of the link (in this case, my name), enclosed in parentheses and styled with italics (on the very last line shown).*

Printing Link URLs

Since link URLs are not shown on a Web page, they are not usually printed with the page either. The CSS content property can reveal those URLs in the printed edition of your page. Too bad Internet Explorer (up to and including version 7) still doesn't get it.

To print link URLs:

1. If desired, remove the styling from your links by typing **a {text-decoration: none; color: black}**.

2. Add a new pseudo-selector for adding content after links by typing **a:after**.

3. Type the beginning **{** for the declaration.

4. Type **content:** to specify which content should appear after links.

5. To precede the link URL with a space and parentheses, type **" ("**.

6. To add the URL itself, that is the value of the href attribute of the a element, type **attr(href)**.

7. To add the final parentheses, type **")"**.

8. Type **;** to complete the rule.

9. Add additional formatting for the link URL, if desired. I used **font-style: italic;**.

10. Finish the declaration with a **}**.

✔ Tips

- The content property is supported by Firefox, Opera, and Safari, but not Internet Explorer. Sigh.

- You can keep internal links—that is links to other parts of the same page—from printing out with a:not([href^='#']):after as the selector in step 2. It's ugly but it works in Firefox and Safari.

Printing Link URLs

Controlling Widows and Orphans

CSS offers a number of other features that help control how Web pages are printed. Unfortunately, only widows and orphans are supported, and only by Opera. I'll give you a quick synopsis, nonetheless.

To control widows and orphans:

- If desired, in the style rule, type **orphans: n;**, where *n* is the minimum number of lines that should appear at the *bottom* of a page.

- If desired, in the style rule, type **widows: n;**, where *n* is the minimum number of lines in the element that should appear at the top of a page.

✔ Tips

- Only Opera supports the `orphans` and `widows` properties.

- It's a shame that these features are not better supported by other browsers. However, things move so quickly that perhaps by the time you read this, things will have improved.

- Note that the `page-break-inside` property can also help avoid stranded lines. See page 212.

- There were a few additional interesting properties for controlling the printed page, including `page`, `size`, and `marks`. These have all been removed from CSS 2.1.

Figure 14.9 *Before the* `widows` *property was applied, there were one and a quarter lines stranded at the top of page 3.*

```
toc {display: none;}

body {margin: 2in; font-family: "Times", serif;}

h2 {page-break-after: avoid;}

p {font: 12pt serif; orphans: 4; widows: 4;}
```

Figure 14.10 *The* `orphans` *property controls how many lines can be alone at the bottom of the page;* `widows` *determines the minimum number that will be required at the top of a page.*

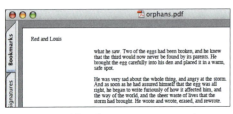

Figure 14.11 *After the* `widows` *property is applied, the page break is inserted two lines earlier and the result is four lines at the top of page 3.*

LISTS

The (X)HTML specifications contain special codes for creating lists of items. You can create plain, numbered, or bulleted lists, as well as lists of definitions. You can also nest one kind of list inside another. In the sometimes sketchy shorthand of the Internet, lists come in very handy.

All lists are formed by a principal code to specify what sort of list you want to create (ol for ordered list, dl for definition list, etc.) and a secondary code to specify what sort of items you want to create (li for list item, dt for definition term, etc.).

Lists

Creating Ordered and Unordered Lists

The ordered list is perfect for providing step-by-step instructions on how to complete a particular task or for creating an outline (complete with links to corresponding sections, if desired) of a larger document. You may create an ordered list anywhere in the body section of your HTML document.

Unordered lists are probably the most widely used lists on the Web. Use them to list any series of items that have no particular order, such as interesting Web sites or names.

To create lists:

1. Type **<ol>** for an ordered list or **<ul>** to begin an unordered list.

2. Type **<li>** (that's the first two letters of the word *list*) to begin the first list item.

3. Type the text to be included in the list item.

4. Type **</li>** to complete each list item.

5. Repeat steps 2–4 for each new list item.

6. Type **</ol>** or **</ul>**, to match the opening tag (from step 1) to complete the list.

```
<h1>Changing a light bulb</h1>

<ol>

<li>Make sure you have unplugged the lamp from
the wall socket.</li>

<li>Unscrew the old bulb.</li>

<li>Get the new bulb out of the package.</li>

<li>Check the wattage to make sure it's
correct.</li>

<li>Screw in the new bulb.</li>

<li>Plug in the lamp and turn it on!</li>

</ol>

</body>

</html>
```

Figure 15.1 *There is no official way to format a list's title. You can use a regular header (see page 61).*

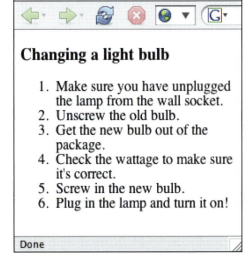

Figure 15.2 *This list uses the default Arabic numerals to create a numbered list.*

```
<body>

Unordered lists are probably the most widely used
lists on the Web. Use them to list any series of items
that have no particular order, such as hot Web sites
or names.

<h1>PageWhacker, version 12.0--Features</h1>

<ul>

<li>New or improved features marked with a solid
bullet.</li>

<li>One click page layout</li>

<li>Spell checker for 327 major languages</li>

<li>Image retouching plug-in</li>

<li>Special HTML filters</li>

<li>Unlimited Undo's and Redo's</li>

<li>Automatic book writing</li>

</ul>
```

Figure 15.3 *The list items of unordered lists are identical to those for ordered lists. Only the* ul *tag is different.*

Figure 15.4 *Unordered lists have round, solid bullets by default.*

✔ Tips

- Unless you specify otherwise *(see page 218)*, items in ordered lists will be numbered with Arabic numerals (1, 2, 3, etc.) **(Figure 15.2)**.

- Items in unordered lists have solid round bullets by default **(Figure 15.4)**. You can choose different bullets *(see page 218)* or even create your own *(see page 220)*.

- Keep the text in your list items short. If you have more than a few lines of text in each item, you may have better luck using headers (h1, h2, etc.) and paragraphs (p).

- Inserting a line break (br) in a list item breaks the text to the next line, but maintains the same indenting.

- No text is permitted between the opening ol or ul tag and the first li tag. Nevertheless, browsers will display such text with the same indentation as the first item in the list, but without a bullet.

- The ul tag is often used for indentation, though this is considered a hack from the pre-standards era.

- You may create one list inside another, even mixing and matching ordered and unordered lists. Be sure to nest each list properly, using all the required opening and closing tags.

- Lists are automatically indented from the left margin (40 pixels is typical for the default 16 pixel size text). If you use CSS to style your lists, changing or reducing the left margin may make your bullets disappear beyond the left edge of the window.

Choosing Your Markers (Bullets)

When you create a list, be it ordered or unordered, you can also choose what sort of markers (bullets or numbers) should appear to the left of each list item.

To choose your markers:

In the style sheet rule, type **list-style-type: marker**, where *marker* is one of the following values: disc (●), circle (○), square(■), decimal (1, 2, 3, ...), upper-alpha (A, B, C, ...), lower-alpha (a, b, c, ...), upper-roman (I, II, III, IV, ...), or lower-roman (i, ii, iii, iv, ...) **(Figure 15.6)**.

To display lists without markers:

In the style sheet rule, type **list-style-type: none**.

✔ Tips

■ By default, unordered lists use discs for the first level, circles for the first nested level, and squares for the third and subsequent level lists.

■ The disc, circle, and square bullets vary slightly in size and appearance from one browser to another.

■ You can also use the deprecated type attribute in the ul or ol tag and in individual li items to specify a marker style for the entire list or for individual list items, respectively. In unordered lists, the acceptable values are disc (for a solid round bullet), circle (for an empty round bullet), or square. In ordered lists, the acceptable values are A, a, I, i, and 1, which indicate the kind of numeration to be used.

■ A type attribute in an li tag overrides one in an ol or ul tag.

```
<body>
<h1>The Great American Novel</h1>
<ol>
<li>Introduction</li>
<li>Development</li>
<li>Climax</li>
<li>Denouement</li>
<li>Epilogue</li>
</ol>
</body>
```

Figure 15.5 *Here is our simple ordered list, to which we will apply capital Roman numerals (*upper-roman*).*

```
li {list-style-type: upper-roman;}
```

Figure 15.6 *You can apply the* list-style-type *property to any list item. If you had two lists on this page, one of which was unordered, you could apply capital Roman letters to just the ordered one by changing the selector in this example to* ol li.

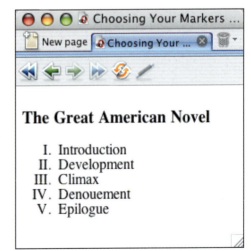

Figure 15.7 *Now the ordered list has capital Roman numerals. Note that most browsers align numeric markers to the right.*

```
<body>
<h1>Changing a light bulb</h1>
<ol start="2">
<li>Unscrew the old bulb.
<p>some omitted steps here</p></li>
<li value="5">Screw in the new bulb.</li>
<li>Plug in the lamp and turn it on!</li>
</ol>
</body>
```

Figure 15.8 *In this example, I've omitted some steps but want to maintain the original numbering. So I start the whole list at 2 (with* start="2"*) and then set the value of the third item to 5 (with* value="5"*).*

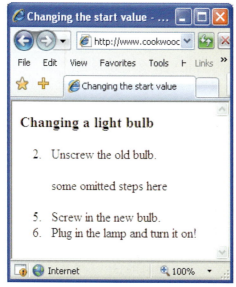

Figure 15.9 *Notice that not only are the first and third items numbered as we've specified, but the third item ("Plug in the lamp") is also affected.*

Choosing Where to Start List Numbering

You might want to start a particular ordered list's numbering somewhere other than 1 (which is the default).

To determine the initial value of an entire list's numbering scheme:

Within the ol tag, type **start="n"**, where *n* represents the initial value for the list.

To change the numbering of a given list item:

In the desired li item, type **value="n"**, where *n* represents the value for this list item. The value is always specified numerically and is converted automatically by the browser to the type of marker specified with CSS or with the type attribute *(see page 218)*.

✔ Tips

- By default, all lists start at 1.

- The value attribute overrides the start value.

- When you change a given list item's number with the value attribute, the subsequent list items are also renumbered accordingly.

- Unfortunately, the W3C has deprecated both the start and value attributes without offering a CSS alternative. If you need them, just be sure to use the proper (transitional) DOCTYPE *(see pages 40 and 56)*.

- The start value is always numeric regardless of the numbering scheme. For more on choosing number styles for markers, see page 218.

Using Custom Markers

If you get tired of circles, squares and discs, or even Roman numerals, you can create your own custom marker with an image.

To use custom markers:

In the style sheet rule for the desired list or list item, type **list-style-image: url(image.gif)**, where *image.gif* is the image you'd like to use for the list item's markers **(Figure 15.11)**.

To remove custom markers:

Type **list-style-image: none**.

✔ Tips

■ By default, you've got about a 15 by 15 pixel square space for the marker.

■ If your image is larger than the line height of the list items, some browsers overlap them. You can adjust a list-item's margins *(see page 176)* if necessary.

■ There should be no space between *url* and the opening parentheses. Quotes around the URL are optional.

■ Note that relative URLs are relative to the location of the style sheet, not the Web page.

■ Most browsers align custom markers to the right. IE for Windows (all versions) is the notable and annoying exception.

■ The list-style-image property overrides list-style-type. But, if for some reason the image can not be loaded, the marker specified with list-style-type is used.

■ The custom markers are inherited.

```
<ul>
<li>New or improved features marked with a solid
bullet.</li>
<li class="new">One click page layout</li>
<li>Spell checker for 327 major languages</li>
<li>Image retouching plug-in</li>
<li>Special HTML filters</li>
<li>Unlimited Undo's and Redo's</li>
<li class="new">Automatic book writing</li>
</ul>
```

Figure 15.10 *I want to add a special marker for the new features in my list.*

```
li.new {
    list-style-image: url(http://www.cookwood.com/
    html6ed/examples/lists/rightarrow.gif);
}
```

Figure 15.11 *To avoid confusion, you can specify the marker image's location with an absolute URL (see page 35).*

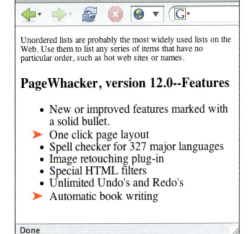

Figure 15.12 *It can be tricky mixing custom markers with default ones. You have to make sure the custom markers aren't too big.*

```
<ul>

<li>New or improved features marked with a solid
bullet.</li>

<li class="new">One click page layout. This is
particularly useful when you're under a heavy
deadline. You just select whether you want the end
product to be a book or a Web site, and poof, it's
done. </li>

<li>Spell checker for 327 major languages</li>

<li>Image retouching plug-in</li>
```

Figure 15.13 *I've added a bit more text to the first "new" feature so that the effect of hanging markers inside is more obvious.*

```
li.new {
    list-style-image: url(http://www.cookwood.com/
    html6ed/examples/lists/rightarrow.gif);
    list-style-position: inside;
    }
```

Figure 15.14 *I've added the inside list-style position to the style sheet rule shown in Figure 15.11 on page 220.*

Figure 15.15 *The markers for the "new" features begin at the left margin of the list item, instead of outside it to the left.*

Controlling Where Markers Hang

By default, lists are indented from the left margin (of their parent). Your markers can either begin halfway to the right of that starting point, which is the default, or flush with the rest of the text (called *inside*).

To control where markers hang:

1. In the style sheet rule for the desired list or list item, type **list-style-position:**.

2. Then type **inside** to display the markers flush with the list item text **(Figure 15.14)**, or **outside** to display the markers to the left of the list item text.

✔ Tips

■ Markers are hung outside the list paragraph, by default.

■ The list-style-position property is inherited.

Setting All List-Style Properties at Once

CSS has a shortcut property for the list-style features.

To set all the list-style properties at once:

1. Type **list-style:**

2. If desired, specify the kind of markers that should appear next to the list items, if any (as described on page 218).

3. If desired, specify the custom marker that should be used for list items (as described on page 220).

4. If desired, specify whether markers should be hung outside the list paragraphs or flush with the text (as described on page 221).

✔ Tips

■ You may specify any or all of the three list-style properties.

■ You might think that by omitting one of the three properties, you won't be affecting it, but that's not always the case. Any properties not explicitly set are returned to their defaults (disc for list-style-type, none for list-style-image, and outside for list-style-position).

■ The properties may be specified in any order.

■ The list-style property is inherited.

```
li.new {
   list-style: url(http://www.cookwood.com/
   html5ed/examples/lists/rightarrow.gif) inside
   square;}
```

Figure 15.16 *This style rule is equivalent to setting the* list-style-image *to the right-arrow.gif file, the* list-style-position *to* inside *and the* list-style-type *to* square. *It's just shorter.*

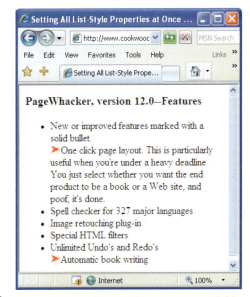

Figure 15.17 *As long as the image is available, the result is the same as in Figure 15.15 on page 221.*

Figure 15.18 *If the image is not available, the square is used.*

```
<h1>Classical Greek Verb Tenses</h1>

<dl>

<dt>Present</dt>

<dd><span class="example">e.g. .luo,
luomai</span>. The present usually shows the pure
verb stem in verbs with strong stems. [snip]</dd>

<dt>Future</dt>

<dd><span class="example">e.g. luso, lusomai,
luthesomai</span>. The future has the[snip]</dd>

<dt>Aorist</dt>

<dd><span class="example">e.g. .elusa, eluthen,
elusamen</span>. The aorist (from [snip]</dd>

</dl>
```

Figure 15.19 *Each entry word is labeled with the* dt *tag, while the definition itself is labeled with a* dd *tag.*

```
dt {font-weight: bold;}

.example {font-style: italic;}
```

Figure 15.20 *You may want to add formatting to your definition term to help it stand out.*

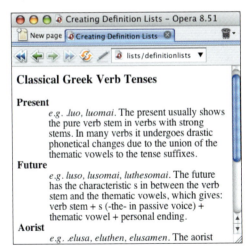

Figure 15.21 *By default, the defined word (the* dt*) is aligned to the left and the definition (*dd*) is indented.*

Creating Definition Lists

(X)HTML provides a special tag for creating definition lists. This type of list is particularly suited to glossaries, but works well with any list that pairs a word or phrase with a longer description. Imagine, for example, a list of Classical Greek verb tenses, each followed by an explanation of proper usage.

To create definition lists:

1. Type the introductory text for the definition list.

2. Type **<dl>**.

3. Type **<dt>**.

4. Type the word or short phrase that will be defined or explained, including any logical or physical formatting desired.

5. Type **</dt>** to complete the definition term.

6. Type **<dd>**.

7. Type the definition of the term that was entered in step 4.

8. Type **</dd>** to complete the definition.

9. Repeat steps 3–8 for each pair of terms and definitions.

10. Type **</dl>** to complete the list of definitions.

✔ Tips

■ Browsers generally indent definitions on a new line below the definition term.

■ You can create more than one dl line or more than one dt line to accommodate multiple words or multiple definitions.

Creating Definition Lists

Styling Nested Lists

You may insert one type of list in another. This is particularly useful with an outline rendered with ordered lists, where you may want several levels of items. While you can style nested lists using classes or ids, there's an easier way.

To style nested lists:

1. For styling the outermost list, type **toplevel li {style_rules}**, where *toplevel* is the list type of the outermost list (e.g., ol, ul, dt) and *style_rules* are the styles that should be applied.

2. For the second level list, type **toplevel 2ndlevel li {style_rules}**, where *toplevel* matches the *toplevel* in step 1 and *2ndlevel* is the list type of the second level list.

3. For the third level list, type **toplevel 2ndlevel 3rdlevel li {style_rules}**, where *toplevel* and *2ndlevel* match the values used in steps 1–2 and *3rdlevel* is the kind of list used for the third nested list.

4. Continue in this fashion for each nested list that you wish to style.

```
<h1>The Great American Novel</h1>
<ol>
    <li>Introduction
      <ol>
      <li>Boy's childhood</li>
      <li>Girl's childhood</li>
      </ol>
    </li>
<li>Development
    <ol>
      <li>Boy meets Girl</li>
      <li>Boy and Girl fall in love</li>
      <li>Boy and Girl have fight</li>
    </ol>
</li>
<li>Climax
    <ol>
      <li>Boy gives Girl ultimatum
        <ol>
          <li>Girl can't believe her ears</li>
          <li>Boy is indignant at Girl's
              indignance</li>
        </ol>
      </li>
      <li>Girl tells Boy to get lost</li>
    </ol>
</li>
<li>Denouement</li>
<li>Epilogue</li>
</ol>
```

Figure 15.22 *There are four nested lists here, one in the* Introduction *list item, one in the* Development *item, one in the* Climax *item and one, highlighted and in bold face, inside the* Boy gives Girl ultimatum *item (which is inside the* Climax *item).*

```
ol li {list-style-type: upper-roman; font-size: 75%;}

ol ol li {list-style-type: upper-alpha;}

ol ol ol li {list-style-type: decimal;}

li li {font-size: 100%;}
```

Figure 15.23 *You can format each level of a nested list separately. If you use percentages for list text, be sure to add the* li li {font-size:100%} *so that it doesn't disappear on you (see last tip).*

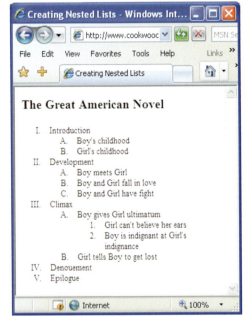

Figure 15.24 *The first level lists (*ol li*) have capital Roman numerals. The second level lists (*ol ol li*) have capital letters, and the third level lists (*ol ol ol li*) have Arabic numerals.*

✔ Tips

■ Your selectors should reflect the types of nested lists in your document, that is, you might need something like **ul ul ol li**.

■ Ordered lists always use Arabic numerals (1, 2, 3) by default, regardless of their nesting position. Use list-style-type to specify other numbering schemes *(see page 218)*. According to *The Chicago Manual of Style*, the correct nesting order for lists is *I, A, 1, a* (and then the *1* and *a* levels are repeated from then on).

■ By default, the first level of an unordered list will have solid round bullets, the next will have empty round bullets and the third and subsequent levels will have square bullets. Again, use list-style-type to specify the type of bullets you want *(see page 218)*.

■ Since list items (li elements) can be nested within other list items, you have to be a bit careful with font sizes specified in relative values. If you use something like li {font-size: 75%}, the font size of the outermost list item will be 75% of its parent element, which, if the parent is a default 16 pixels high, will be 12 pixels, and not a problem. However, the font size of the first nested list item will be 75% of *its* parent (the first list item, which is 12 pixels), and thus will be only 9 pixels high. Each level gets quickly worse. One solution is to add li li {font-size:100%}. Now nested list items will always be the same size as top level ones. (Thanks to Eric Meyer.)

Styling Nested Lists

TABLES

Figure 16.1 *Tables let you create fancy professional-looking layouts that will wow your visitors and be compatible with most older browsers.*

Tables have a storied history on the Web. While originally conceived just to hold tabular data, they were quickly appropriated for a much bigger task: serving as the foundation for complicated layouts, with multiple columns, sidebars and many other features that were simply impossible before the advent of CSS. The problem is that layouts with tables tend to be so complex that they are difficult to set up and cumbersome to update.

Now that CSS is here and well supported, you can create beautiful layouts without tables *(see page 169)*. However, some designers continue to do layout with tables due to the fact that they work almost exactly the same across all browsers.

And there's a middle road. As this chapter will illustrate, you can use tables for the basic structure of your page, but use CSS for all the text formatting, and much of the layout formatting (beyond the table itself). It will be that much easier to make the leap to full CSS when you (and your visitors) are ready.

One of the nice things about tables is that you can use them to create liquid design—design that expands and contracts proportionally to your visitor's browser window. The key is to use percentages instead of pixel-based widths and learn to let go of the need to control every last space.

Finally, if you want to use tables for tabular data, you still can. And CSS will help you make those tables shine.

Mapping Out Your Page

Before you create a complicated table, it's really important to have a vision of what you're about to construct. You should know how many rows and columns you need, how big these should be, and where each of the items on your page should go.

To map out your page:

1. Design your page on a piece of paper—with a pen!

2. Figure out how many rows and columns you will need. Identify any rows or columns that will span more than one space.

3. If necessary, you can nest one table inside another. However, you should keep nesting to a minimum as it tends to slow browsers down—and sometimes causes them to break down altogether.

4. If you're going to make a static, fixed design, measure how wide your table should be (the standard is around 600 pixels) and then decide how many pixels wide each column should be. For liquid designs, use percentages.

5. Create the skeleton of your page with just the table tags but little or no content.

6. Finally, create or insert the content.

✔ Tip

- One good way to get ideas for table structure is to look at how others do it *(see page 53)*. However, there are some very complicated setups out there. One way to get a handle on what's going on in someone else's page is to download the source code and then change the background color of each nested table *(see page 240)* so you can better see which parts of the layout belong to which table.

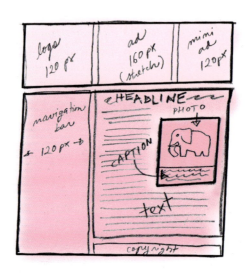

Figure 16.2 *Here's a map of the main example used in this chapter. I use one table for the top set of ads and logo and one table for the lower navigational bar and content area section. Note that there is a third table floating in the content text.*

```
<table>

<tr><td><img src="elephant.jpg" width="200"
height="150" alt="Elephant Baby"></td></tr>

<tr><td class="caption">A baby elephant hanging
out with its mom, aunts and great-aunts, and
maybe even its grandmother</td></tr>

</table>
```

Figure 16.3 *This very simple table has two rows, each of which has only one cell.*

```
body {font-family: "Trebuchet MS", Verdana,
sans-serif;}

.caption {font-size: .8em; font-style: italic;}
```

Figure 16.4 *The style sheet contains only pure text formatting; nothing that would affect the table per se.*

Figure 16.5 *By default, the table extends almost as far as the edge of the browser window.*

Figure 16.6 *Here's the exact same table in a narrower browser window. The table simply contracts to fit better in the window.*

Creating a Simple Table

Tables are made up of rows of cells. The number of cells in each row determines the table's shape.

To create a simple table:

1. Type **\<table>**.

2. If desired, press Return and Tab to visually distinguish the row elements. These won't affect display in the browser.

3. Type **\<tr>** to define the beginning of the first row.

4. Type **\<td>** to define the beginning of the cell.

5. Type the contents of the cell.

6. Type **\</td>** to complete the cell.

7. Repeat steps 4–6 for each cell in the row.

8. Type **\</tr>** to complete the row.

9. Repeat steps 2–7 for each row.

10. To finish the table, type **\</table>**.

✔ Tips

■ The `</table>` tag is *not* optional. Some browsers won't display tables without it.

■ There is also a `th` tag for creating *header* cells. Its default formatting is generally centered and boldface, but you can easily apply CSS to it to create special header styles. In addition, if you're organizing tabular data, header cells can help describe your table and make it more accessible.

■ You can create a title for the table with the `caption` element. Use **align= "direction"**, where *direction* is `top`, `bottom`, `left`, or `right` to align the caption. It's ugly and not well supported.

Adding a Border

A border helps distinguish your table from the rest of the page. However, if you're laying out your page with tables, you may not want to call so much attention to the border.

To create a border with (X)HTML:

1. Inside the initial `table` tag, type **border**.

2. If desired, type **="n"**, where *n* is the thickness in pixels of the border.

To create a border with styles:

1. In your style sheet, type **table** or **td**, or whichever selector denotes the part of the table that you want to apply a border to.

2. Type **{border: value}**, where *border* is the `border` property that you wish to apply and *value* is the type of border you want. For more details on the `border` property, consult *Setting the Border* on page 184.

✔ Tips

- The CSS `border` property is discussed in detail (and there are a lot of details) on page 184. This page focuses on how the `border` property interacts with the (non-deprecated) (X)HTML `border` attribute.

- The `border` attribute applies to both the table and the cells it contains. The CSS `border` property, in contrast, is not inherited. So, if you omit the (X)HTML `border` attribute but apply a CSS `border` to the table, the cells will have no borders. Conversely, if you use the `border` attribute but use `table {border: none}`, the cells will have borders, but the table won't.

- If you use the (X)HTML `border` attribute with no value (`border` alone, or `border="border"` to be XHTML compliant) and no CSS `border`, you get a black 1 pixel outset border, by default.

```
<table border="10">

<tr><td><img src="elephant.jpg" width="200" height="150" alt="Elephant Baby"></td></tr>

<tr><td class="caption">A baby elephant hanging out with its mom, aunts and great-aunts, and maybe even its grandmother</td></tr>

</table>
```

Figure 16.7 *In this example, we set a 10 pixel wide border for the outside of the table. When you set the* `border` *attribute, regardless of its value, the cell borders are always 1 pixel wide.*

A baby elephant hanging out with its mom, aunts and great-aunts, and maybe even its grandmother

Figure 16.8 *Although borders are not usually shown in tables used for layout, they are often temporarily useful for showing exactly what's happening with a table. Here we can see we've got two rows and each row contains a single cell. The (X)HTML* `border` *attribute turns on borders around tables and cells indiscriminately.*

```
body {font-family: "Trebuchet MS", Verdana, sans-serif}

table {border: 8px double red;}

.caption {font-size: .8em; font-style: italic;}
```

Figure 16.9 *You can specify the width, color, and style with the single shortcut* `border` *property.*

A baby elephant hanging out with its mom, aunts and great-aunts, and maybe even its grandmother

Figure 16.10 *This page is the result of the (X)HTML shown in Figure 16.7 and the CSS in Figure 16.9. Because we've applied the CSS* border *property only to the* table *element, the borders around cells are not affected at all.*

A baby elephant hanging out with its mom, aunts and great-aunts, and maybe even its grandmother

Figure 16.11 *This page uses the same CSS as the previous illustration (Figure 16.10), but no* border *attribute in the (X)HTML. Notice that there are no borders around the cells.*

```
body {font-family: "Trebuchet MS", Verdana,
sans-serif;}

table, td {border: none;}

.caption {font-size: .8em; font-style: italic;}
```

Figure 16.12 *Here is the CSS that we'll use with respect to borders in the rest of our example. So there!*

- The default CSS border style is `none`. So `border: 2px red` actually means `border: 2px none red` and will result in no border at all! The CSS `border` property overrides the (X)HTML's `border` attribute (except in IE, see below).

- The default CSS border width is `medium`, which Firefox and Opera interpret as 3 pixels, and IE interprets as 4 pixels. So `border:red groove` also implies a width of `medium`. The CSS `border` property overrides the (X)HTML `border` attribute (except in IE, see below).

- IE (up to and including 7) gets a number of things wrong about borders in tables. First, it cannot display very dark two-tone border styles, like `groove`, `ridge`, `inset`, and `outset` and displays them solidly. Second, it does not let the default values for the shortcut `border` property override the (X)HTML `border` attribute, as it should. So, if you use the (X)HTML `border` and CSS `border:red`, IE gives you a 1 pixel border instead of a `medium` one, which is implied with `border:red`. If you set the `border-style` or `border-width` properties explicitly: `border-width:2px`, then Internet Explorer properly lets the value override the (X)HTML `border` attribute.

- A border's default color is the color of the element itself (as specified with the CSS `color` property). Only IE for Mac and Firefox get that right.

- Tables naturally expand to the edge of the elements they contain or to the edge of the browser window, whichever comes first. That's sometimes hard to see unless you view the border.

- You can create a border while you're constructing your table and then banish it once you have everything in place.

Setting the Width

By default, a browser will automatically determine the width of your cells by looking at the elements and text they contain. It will then expand each cell to the edge of its contents or to the edge of the browser window, whichever comes first. With images, that's pretty clear cut; the edge of the image will be the edge of the cell. Text, however, is stretched out until the first line break, or until the end of the paragraph, which can be very long indeed.

Instead of relying on the browser's sometimes unusual algorithms for determining table width, you can specify the width of the table or of individual cells manually, either in pixels or as a percentage of window size. For example, when designing liquid layouts with tables, it's very common to specify a table width of 100% in order to force the table to expand to the size of the browser window, no matter what size the visitor makes it. It's also quite common to specify the width of the navigational column in pixels so that it is not affected by the ebb and flow of browser size.

It's important to note that no browser will let you make a table or cell narrower than its images. It will simply stretch the cell or table as necessary to make the image fit, adjusting the rest of your table as best it can.

To set the width of a cell or table:

In the `td` or `table` tag, type **width="n"**, where *n* is the desired width of the cell or of the entire table, in pixels.

Or type **width="n%"**, where *n* is the percentage of the browser window that the table should occupy.

To set the width with styles:

In the style sheet, type **width: value** where *value* is the desired width *(for more details, see page 174)*.

```
<table border=0 width="200"
class="rightsidebar">

<tr><td><img src="elephant.jpg" width="200"
height="150" alt="Elephant Baby"></td></tr>

<tr><td class="caption">A baby elephant hanging
out with its mom, aunts and great-aunts, and
maybe even its grandmother</td></tr>

</table>
```

Figure 16.13 *This table has a 200 pixel wide image with no borders. We set the width of the table to 200 pixels to keep the text from stretching out.*

```
table, td {border: none;}

.rightsidebar {width: 200px;}

.caption {font-size: .8em; font-style: italic;}
```

Figure 16.14 *You can use either the CSS, the (X)HTML or both. The CSS overrides the (X)HTML (though in this example, they're the same, so it doesn't matter.)*

Figure 16.15 *The CSS* width *property is well supported. You can feel comfortable using it instead of the* width *attribute in the (X)HTML.*

```
.rightsidebar {width: 100px;}
```

Figure 16.16 *In this case, the table is made narrower than the image it contains.*

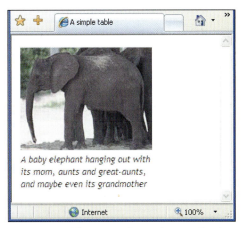

Figure 16.17 *The image (200px) overrides the* width *property and/or attribute (set to 100px) and ends up looking just like Figure 16.5 on page 229. You can't make a table or cell too small for its images!*

```
.rightsidebar {width: 300px;}
```

Figure 16.18 *In this case, the table is made wider than the image it contains.*

Figure 16.19 *Of course, you can make a table bigger than its contents. In that case, the text (and border if any) extends to fill the space.*

✔ Tips

- The CSS width property is described in detail on page 174. This page focuses on how the CSS width property interacts with the (X)HTML width attribute (which has *not* been deprecated).

- A table sized with percentages will adjust as the browser window is resized. Tables sized with pixels will not.

- Sometimes table cells with a specified width that contain only text will collapse to narrower widths in very small browser windows. An old-fashioned technique for keeping a cell open to a certain width is to put a transparent pixel spacer inside it and then set the width of the pixel spacer.

- You can't make the table too small for its contents; the browser will just ignore you.

- If you make the table too wide, visitors who don't use the entire screen for their browser (or who have smaller monitors) may have to scroll to see some parts of your table. If you must use a non-flexible layout, I don't recommend making tables any wider than 600 pixels.

- The widest cell in the column determines the width of the entire column.

- You don't necessarily have to specify a width for every column.

- In IE 5.x for Windows the value of width was the sum of the content, cellspacing, cellpadding and borders. In browsers that properly follow the specifications (like IE 6 and up, Firefox, Safari, and Opera), the value of the width property (or attribute) does not include padding or borders.

- There is also a height attribute but it is non-standard, and not well supported.

Centering a Table

You can draw attention to a table by centering it in the browser window.

To center a table with (X)HTML:

In the `table` tag, type **align= "center"** (**Figure 16.20**).

To center a table with CSS:

1. Make sure you've specified the width of the table *(see page 232)*.

2. Add **margin-right: auto** and **margin-left: auto** to the style rule for the table (**Figure 16.21**).

✔ Tips

■ You can also use the CSS `text-align` property in a surrounding `div` to center tables, but it seems a bit of a hack to me *(see page 165)*.

■ The `center` value for the `align` attribute has been deprecated by the W3C, though it continues to enjoy broad support.

■ You could also center the table by enclosing the entire table in opening and closing `center` tags, although they've also been deprecated.

■ You could conceivably center one table within another. For more information, consult *Combining Tables* on page 236.

■ You can also wrap text to the right or left of a table *(see page 235)*.

■ You can't align a table to the top or middle line of text as you can with images.

■ Centering the table with CSS by setting the right and left margins to `auto` does not work in very old browsers (like IE 5.5 or earlier).

```
<table border=0 width="200" class="rightsidebar"
align="center">
```

Figure 16.20 *The simplest way to center a table is to add the deprecated (but still well supported)* center *value to the* align *attribute.*

```
table, td {border: none;}
.rightsidebar {width: 200px; margin-right: auto;
margin-left: auto;}
.caption {font-size: .8em; font-style: italic;}
```

Figure 16.21 *Setting the right and left margins to* auto *makes them equal—which is the essence of centering.*

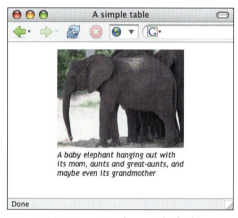

A baby elephant hanging out with its mom, aunts and great-aunts, and maybe even its grandmother

Figure 16.22 *No matter how wide the browser window is, the table is centered right in the middle.*

```
<h1>The Truth about Elephants</h1>

<table border=0 width="200" class="rightsidebar"
align="right">

<tr><td><img src="elephant.jpg" width="200"
height="150" alt="Elephant Baby"></td></tr>

<tr><td class="caption">A baby elephant hanging
out with its mom, aunts and great-aunts, and
maybe even its grandmother</td></tr>

</table>

<p>It's hard to tell what goes through a baby
elephant's mind when its mom is trying to put it to
```

Figure 16.23 *I've added some text that the table can float in. When you align a table to the right, the text flows to the left. Notice also that in the markup, the table comes before the text that flows around it.*

```
body {font-family: "Trebuchet MS", Verdana,
sans-serif; color: #006666;}

table, td {border: none;}

.rightsidebar {width: 200px; float: right;}

.caption {font-size: 8em; font-style: italic;
color: black;}
```

Figure 16.24 *You must specify a width when using the* float *property. Note that the new text is green and I colored the caption black.*

Figure 16.25 *Since the table is floated to the right, the text wraps around the left side.*

Wrapping Text around a Table

You can wrap text around a table in much the same way you can with images. While there are more sophisticated layout techniques, wrapping text around a table is helpful for keeping images together with captions in a long flow of text.

To wrap text around a table with (X)HTML:

1. In the table tag, either type **align="left"** to align the table to the left of the screen while the text flows to the right, or type **align="right"** to align the table to the right of the browser window while the text flows on the left side of the table **(Figure 16.23)**.

2. After the closing </table> tag, type the text that should flow around the table.

To wrap text around a table with CSS:

1. Make sure you've specified the width of the table.

2. Add **float: right** or **float: left** to the table's style rule **(Figure 16.24)**.

✔ Tips

■ For more details about floating elements, see pages 96 and 181. For more details on controlling where elements float, see pages 98 and 182.

■ The right and left values for the align attribute have been deprecated, though they continue to enjoy broad support.

Wrapping Text around a Table

Combining Tables

For more complex layouts, you may wish to combine tables. You can place combinations of tables and text in another table or you can use multiple tables.

To nest one table in another:

1. Create the inner table and any text or other elements that should accompany it.

2. Create the outer table. Determine which cell of the outer table will hold the inner table and type **placeholder** (or some other easily identifiable text) there as a placeholder.

3. Test both tables separately to make sure they look the way you want them to.

4. Replace the word *placeholder* with the inner table content by copying and pasting **(Figure 16.26)**.

The more complicated your tables become, the longer it will take for a browser to calculate their proper widths and display them. One way to simplify your code is to divide your layout into multiple tables that sit one on top of the next.

To use multiple tables:

1. Create the second table directly after the closing `</table>` of the first **(Figure 16.28)**

2. Use comments to identify the different parts of a layout.

3. Make sure the widths of the separate tables (and of the corresponding columns in each) match **(Figure 16.29)**.

```
<table width="100%" border="1">
<tr><td><!-- Left Navigation --></td>
<td><!-- Main Content -->
<h1>The Truth about Elephants</h1>
<table border=0 width="200" class="rightsidebar"
align="right">
<tr><td><img src="elephant.jpg" width="200"
height="150" alt="Elephant Baby"></td></tr>
<tr><td class="caption">A baby elephant hanging
out with its mom, aunts and great-aunts, and
maybe even its grandmother</td></tr>
</table>
<p>It's hard to tell what goes through a [snip]
</td>
</tr></table>
```

Figure 16.26 *Here I've created an outer table with a single row. The left column is devoted to a navigation bar and the right column contains the main content (what we've worked on so far in this chapter—which contains its own wrapped table).*

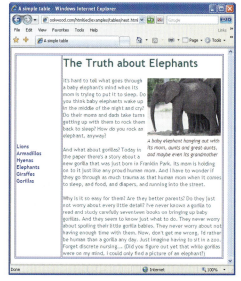

Figure 16.27 *Here I've combined the main content with the left navigation by placing them in a table in separate cells. I've added the border so you can see what's happening.*

```
<!-- Top Logo Bar -->

<table width="100%">

<tr><td ><img src="logo.jpg" width="120"
alt="Northampton Zoo Logo"></td>

...</td></tr></table>

<!--Left Nav and Main Content -->

<table width="100%">

<tr><!-- Left Navigation -->

<td class="toc">

<p><a href="lions.html">Lions</a>
```

Figure 16.28 *Instead of creating a new table to combine the logo bar and the table from Figure 16.27, the code will be cleaner, leaner, and faster if I create two independent tables.*

```
.caption {font-size: .8em; font-style: italic;
color: black;}

.toc {width: 120px;}

.toc a:link {text-decoration: none;
font-weight: bold;}
```

Figure 16.29 *I use CSS to match the width of the left column in the lower table with the width of the left column in the upper table.*

Figure 16.30 *The new table sits right above the old one. Since the first columns have the same width, they look like part of the same layout.*

✔ **Tips**

■ Creating the tables separately before combining them helps pinpoint where problems may lie, should they occur.

■ Only nest tables where it's absolutely necessary. They can slow down a browser considerably or even make it crash. Whenever possible, use multiple tables as an alternative.

■ Use ** ** in any cell that should remain empty. Otherwise, it may not display at all.

■ Use background colors *(see pages 172 and 240)* during testing to decipher which cells belong to which tables. You can use borders for this job as well, but the width of the borders can throw the columns out of alignment.

■ Make sure to close each table with its own closing `</table>` tag.

■ You can make a column wider than its contents by setting the CSS `width` property for that column. Otherwise, browsers will try to make the column as narrow as the contents will allow.

■ An old-fashioned way of making a column wider than its contents was to insert a transparent spacer GIF and set its width to the desired width of the column. It's frowned upon these days.

Combining Tables

Aligning a Cell's Contents

By default, a cell's contents are aligned two ways: horizontally to the left and vertically in the middle. When you're designing a liquid layout, in which cells should stretch out over an extended browser window, it's particularly important to specify where things should be aligned.

To align the contents of cells with (X)HTML:

1. Place the cursor in the initial tag for the cell, row, or section, after the name of the tag but before the final >.

2. If desired, type **align="direction"**, where *direction* is left, center, right or justify.

3. Type **valign="direction"**, where *direction* is either top, middle, bottom, or baseline.

To align the contents of cells with CSS:

1. In the desired rule, add **text-align: direction**, where *direction* is left, right, center, or justify.

2. And/or add **vertical-align: position**, where *position* is baseline, top, bottom, or middle.

✔ Tips

■ The default value for align is *left*. The default for valign is *middle*.

■ Although the align attribute has been deprecated for other properties, it is still valid for all table elements (except table itself). The valign attribute is also still valid. Both are well supported.

■ CSS properties text-align and vertical-align are also very well supported.

```
<table width="100%" border="0">

<tr><td ><img src="logo.jpg" width="120"
alt="Northampton Zoo Logo"></td>

<td align="center"><img src="ad2.gif"
width="320" alt="main ad" ></td>

<td align="right"><img src="miniad.jpg"
width="160" height="100" alt="mini ad"
></td></tr></table>

<table width="100%">

<tr>

<!-- Left Navigation -->

<td class="toc" valign="top"><img
src="spacer.gif" alt="" width="120" height="1">

<p><a href="lions.html">Lions</a>

<br /><a href="armadillos.html">Armadillos</a>
```

Figure 16.31 *We need the middle image in the logo bar to stay centered and the right image to stay to the right regardless of the browser window size. The left navigation items should be at the top of their cell, not the middle, which is the default.*

```
body {font-family: "Trebuchet MS", Verdana,
sans-serif; color:#006666;}

table, td {border:none;}

h1 {font-size: 1.8em; white-space: nowrap;}

p {font-size: .9em;}

.rightsidebar {width: 200px; float: right;
border: none;}

.caption {font-size: .8em; font-style: italic;
color: black; text-align: center;}

.toc {vertical-align: top; width: 120px;}

.center {text-align: center;}

.right {text-align: right;}

.main {vertical-align: top;}
```

Figure 16.32 *For the caption to the elephant photograph and the left navigation bar, I just added the alignment properties to the existing classes. For the other cells, I had to create special classes to do the alignment (which frankly, seems like a bit of trouble).*

Figure 16.34 *Notice how the middle cell in the top row stays centered even though the window is wider. Perhaps more important, the right-hand cell (with the lion) stays aligned to the right, flush with the elephant picture and the rest of the text.*

Aligning a Cell's Contents

- You can align all of the cells in a row by applying the `text-align` or `vertical-align` property to (or inserting the `align` or `valign` attribute in) the `tr` tag.

- Theoretically, you can align the contents with respect to any character you choose, for example to align monetary amounts with respect to the decimal point. In the (X)HTML, you'd use `align="char" char="x"`, where *x* is the character around which to align. In CSS, use `text-align:x`, again, where *x* is the desired alignment character. Unfortunately, no browser I've seen supports either method.

- The `baseline` value aligns the contents of each cell with the baseline of the first line of text that it contains. *Baseline* is the same as *top* when there are several lines of text and no images. *Baseline* is the same as *bottom* when the cells contain both images and text.

- The `vertical-align` property accepts a few other values (like `text-top`, `text-bottom`, `sub`, and `sup`) but these don't make sense with table cells, and so `baseline` is used in their place.

- For more information about `text-align`, see page 165. For more on `vertical-align`, see page 188.

Changing the Background

Changing the background color of one or more cells is a great way to add visual clarity and structure to your table.

To change a cell's background color with (X)HTML:

Within the desired tag, type **bgcolor= "color"**, where *color* is either a name or a hex color *(see page 126 and inside back cover).*

To change a cell's background image or color with CSS:

In the desired rule, type **background: value**, where *value* is described in detail on pages pages 172–173.

✔ Tips

■ The CSS background property is described in detail on pages 172–173. This section is devoted to explaining its peculiarities *with respect to tables.*

■ The CSS background property with a color value is well supported, all the way back to IE and Netscape 3. Background images are supported back to version 4 of both browsers.

■ The (X)HTML bgcolor attribute has been deprecated. The W3C would prefer you use the CSS background property. Nevertheless, bgcolor continues to be well supported.

■ You can add the bgcolor attribute to any table tag (table, tr, thead, etc.) to change the color of the cells in one or more rows or columns at once.

```
<body bgcolor= "white">

<table width= "100%" border= "0" class= "logobar" bgcolor= "#ffff66">

<tr><td ><img src="logo.jpg" width="120" alt="Northampton Zoo Logo"></td>

<td class="center"><img src="ad2.gif" width="320" alt="main ad" ></td>

<td class="right"><img src="miniad.jpg" width="160" height="100" alt="mini ad" ></td></tr></table>

<table width="100%">

<tr>

<!-- Left Navigation -->

<td class="toc" bgcolor="#339966"><img src="spacer.gif" alt="" width="120" height="1">
```

Figure 16.35 *You can add the* bgcolor *attribute to any part of the table. Here I've matched the background of the logo bar to the color of the middle image so that it looks like it stretches with the browser window. And I've added a dark green background to the left navigation bar.*

A baby elephant hanging out with its mom, aunts and great-aunts, and maybe even its grandmother

Figure 16.36 *At left, you can see the yellow background around and between the images in the logo bar. Notice (above) that the green background also surrounds the nested table and serves as the background for its text (that I've made white).*

```
body {font-family: "Trebuchet MS", Verdana,
sans-serif; color: #006666;}

table, td {border: none;}

h1 {font-size: 1.8em; white-space: nowrap;}

p {font-size: .9em;}

.rightsidebar {width: 200px; float: right;
border:none; background: #006666; color: white;}

.caption {font-size: .8em; font-style: italic;
text-align: center; color: white;}

.toc {vertical-align: top; width:120px;
background: #339966 url(longerfish.jpg);}

.center {text-align: center;}

.right {text-align: right;}

.main {vertical-align: top;}

.logobar {background: #ffff66;}
```

Figure 16.37 *In this example, I've created all the background colors with CSS instead of (X)HTML. In addition, I've added a background image for the left navigation bar.*

Figure 16.38 *Is the space around the cells bugging you yet? We're getting there next!*

- The `bgcolor` attribute in an individual cell (`th` or `td`) overrides the color specified in a row (in a `tr` tag), which in turn overrides the color specified for a group of rows or columns (in `thead`, `colgroup`, etc.), which, as you might expect, overrides the color specified for the entire table (in the `table` tag).

- Consult *CSS Colors* on page 126 and the inside back cover for help choosing colors.

- You can add both a background image and a background color to a cell. The background color will display before the image and then continue to shine through the transparent parts of the image, if there are any.

- You can also set the color of the contents of a cell. For details, see *Setting the Color* on page 160. For information about changing the color of the borders, consult *Adding a Border* on page 230.

- Make sure that your background images do not distract from the content that is placed on top of them. I am continually amazed at how many sites use bizarrely busy backgrounds with text that is for all intents and purposes illegible.

Controlling the Space

(X)HTML has long had two attributes for the table tag that allow it to control spacing between the contents of a cell and its border (`cellpadding`) and between one border and the next (`cellspacing`). And while they're well supported and perfectly reasonable, they're not very flexible. You can't, for example, affect the cell spacing on a single side, or add cell padding just to a few cells in a table.

CSS on the other hand lets you use the now familiar `padding` property *(see page 177)* to control space on every side of a cell, as well as between paragraphs and other elements. It is a welcome substitute for `cellpadding`.

Unfortunately, although the CSS property for controlling cellspacing (`border-spacing`), continues to be supported by almost all major browsers, Internet Explorer (up to and including version 7) remains the notable exception, rendering the property virtually unusable.

To control cell padding with (X)HTML:

In the `table` tag, type **cellpadding="n"**, where *n* is the number of pixels that should appear between the contents of a cell and its border.

To control cell spacing with (X)HTML:

In the `table` tag, type **cellspacing="n"**, where *n* is the number of pixels that should appear between one cell border and the next.

To control cell padding with CSS:

In the desired rule, type **padding: value**, where *value* is a length in pixels or a percentage of the parent element.

To control cell spacing with CSS:

In the desired rule, type **border-spacing: value**, where *value* is a length in pixels or a percentage of the parent element.

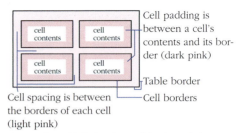

Cell padding is between a cell's contents and its border (dark pink)

Table border

Cell borders

Cell spacing is between the borders of each cell (light pink)

Figure 16.39 *Cell spacing adds space between cells. Cell padding adds space between a cell's contents and its border.*

```
<table width="100%" cellspacing="0"
cellpadding="0" border="0" class="logobar"
bgcolor="#ffff66">

<tr><td ><img src="logo.jpg" width="120"
alt="Northampton Zoo Logo"></td>
```

Figure 16.40 *I have set both the* `cellpadding` *and* `cellspacing` *to zero so that there is no extra space around or between the cells of my logo bar (and other elements).*

Figure 16.41 *The extra spaces between the cells disappear (especially in the logo bar and between the logobar and the fish bar). The table appears seamless (if a little squished). In Explorer, there is no margin or padding above the* p *and* h1 *elements in cells.*

Figure 16.42 *In many browsers, the margin and padding for the* h1 *and* p *elements leave extra space at the top of the cells' interior.*

Controlling the Space

```
h1 {font-size: 1.8em; white-space: nowrap;
margin: 10px 0 5px;}

p {font-size: .9em; margin: 0 0 10px 0;}

.rightsidebar {width: 200px; float: right;
border: none; background: #006666; color: white;
margin: 0 0 5px 10px;}

.caption {font-size: .8em; font-style: italic;
text-align: center; padding: 5px; margin: 0;
color: white;}

.toc {vertical-align: top; width: 110px;
background: #339966 url(longerfish.jpg);
padding: 25px 0 0 10px;}

.center {text-align: center;}
.right {text-align: right;}
.main {vertical-align: top; padding-left:10px;}
```

Figure 16.43 *To finish adjusting the spacing in the table, we need to adjust the* margin *and* padding *properties. I've reduced the width of the* toc *to 110 to accommodate the 10 pixels of left padding.*

✔ Tips

■ The default value for cell padding is 1. The default value for cell spacing is 2.

■ When using tables for layout, it's perhaps easiest to set both the `cellpadding` and `cellspacing` to zero and then selectively add padding and margins with CSS.

■ Both cellpadding and cellspacing must be applied to the entire table as a whole. To control spacing in and around individual cells, use the CSS properties.

■ You can use the CSS `margin` property *(see page 176)* to control the spacing between h1 and p elements that may be contained in cells, or the space around a table.

■ Remember that the CSS alternative to `cellpadding` is called `padding`, while the CSS alternative to `cellspacing` is called `border-spacing`. The `padding` property can be used on any element; `border-spacing` is just for table cells.

■ The `border-spacing` property is inherited but `padding` is not.

■ Netscape 6 is so scrupulous with standards that it adds a bit of space under inline images in table cells—for descenders, one must presume. As long as you only have one image per cell, you can get rid of the space by making the images block level *(see page 30)*. Or you can trigger quirks mode *(see page 41)*.

Figure 16.44 *Now we've got the spacing under control.*

Controlling the Space

Spanning a Cell across Columns

With a table, it's often useful to straddle or *span* one cell across a few columns. For example, with multicolumn text, you could span a headline across the columns of text.

To span a cell across two columns:

1. When you get to the point in which you need to define the cell that spans more than one column, type **<td**.

2. Type **colspan="n">**, where *n* equals the number of columns the cell should span.

3. Type the cell's contents.

4. Type **</td>**.

5. Complete the rest of the table. If you create a cell that spans 2 columns, you will need to define one less cell in that row. If you create a cell that spans 3 columns, you will define two less cells for the row. And so on.

✔ Tips

■ Each row in a table must have the same number of cells defined. Cells that span across columns count for as many cells as the value of their `colspan` attribute.

■ Writing the (X)HTML code for a table from scratch is, uh, challenging—especially when you start spanning columns and rows. It helps to sketch it out on paper first, as described on page 228, to get a handle on which information goes in which row and column. Or you can cheat and use a Web page authoring program like Dreamweaver to get started. You can always open the file and edit the (X)HTML by hand later.

■ There is no CSS alternative for `colspan`.

```
<table width="100%" cellspacing="0"
cellpadding="0" border="0">

<tr><!-- Left Navigation -->

<td class="toc"><img src="spacer.gif" alt=""
width="100" height="1">[snip]</td>

<td>     </td>

<td class="top">

<h1>The Truth about Elephants</h1>

[snip]

mind, I could only find a picture of an
elephant?)</p>

</td></tr>

<tr><td colspan="2" class="copyright">
Copyright &copy; 2002 by Northampton
Zoological Society, Inc.</td></tr>

</table>
```

Figure 16.45 *The lower table now has two rows. The first row contains the left navigation cell and the main content cell. The second row contains a single cell with copyright information that spans both columns.*

Figure 16.46 *The copyright row at the bottom spans both columns.*

```
<table width="100%" cellspacing="0"
cellpadding="0" border="0">

<tr><!-- Left Navigation -->

<td class="toc" rowspan="2"><img
src="spacer.gif" alt="" width="100"
height="1">[snip]</td>

<td>     </td>

<td class="top">

<h1>The Truth about Elephants</h1>

[snip]

mind, I could only find a picture of an
elephant?)</p>

</td></tr>

<tr><td class="copyright"> Copyright &copy;
2002 by Northampton Zoological Society,
Inc.</td></tr>
```

Figure 16.47 *I can make the left navigational bar span both rows, and then I have to adjust the second row's cell so that it no longer tries to span two columns.*

Figure 16.48 *Now the left navigational bar spans both rows and the copyright row is a simple cell.*

Spanning a Cell across Rows

Creating a cell that spans more than one row is essentially the same as spanning cells over more than one column—just from another direction.

To span a cell across two or more rows:

1. When you get to the point in which you need to define the cell that spans more than one row, type **<td**.

2. Type **rowspan="n">**, where *n* equals the number of rows the cell should span.

3. Type the cell's contents.

4. Type **</td>**.

5. Complete the rest of the table. If you define a cell with a rowspan of 2, you will not need to define the corresponding cell in the next row. If you define a cell with a rowspan of 3, you will not need to define the corresponding cells in the next two rows.

✔ Tips

- Each column in a table must have the same number of cells defined. Cells that span across rows count for as many cells as the value of their rowspan attribute.

- There is no CSS alternative for rowspan.

Dividing Your Table into Column Groups

When using tables for displaying tabular data (their classic purpose), you can divide your table into two kinds of column groups: structural and non-structural. The former control where dividing lines, or rules, are drawn *(see page 250)*. The latter do not. Both let you apply formatting to an entire column (or groups of columns) of cells all at once.

To divide a table into structural column groups:

1. After the `table` (and `caption`) tags, type **<colgroup**.

2. If the column group has more than one column, type **span="n"**, where *n* is the number of columns in the group.

3. If desired, define the attributes for the column group.

4. Type the final **>**.

5. If desired, define individual columns as specified below with `col`.

6. Type **</colgroup>**.

To divide a table into non-structural column groups:

1. After the `table` (and `caption`) tags, type **<col**.

2. If the column group has more than one column, type **span="n"**, where *n* is the number of columns in the group.

3. If desired, define the attributes for the column group.

4. Type the final **/>**.

5. Repeat steps 1–4 for each column group that you wish to define.

```
<table cellspacing="0">
<caption align=top>Fox sightings in Western
Massachusetts</caption>
<colgroup class="cities" />
<colgroup span="3" class="data" />
<tr>
    <td> </td>
    <td>Kits</td>
    <td>Adults</td>
```

Figure 16.49 *The first* `colgroup` *contains the city names, the second is for the table data.*

```
body {font-family: "Trebuchet MS", "Verdana",
sans-serif;}
td {padding: 4px 10px;}
caption {font-weight: bold; color: #9A6016;
padding-bottom: 5px;}
.cities {background: #D1A367;}
.data {background: #F0E7DB;}
```

Figure 16.50 *Apart from basic CSS formatting that we've discussed earlier, I also apply background colors to the* cities *and* data *classes. You can only apply* background, border, width, *and* visible *properties to* colgroup *elements.*

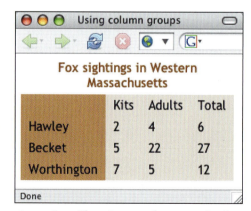

Figure 16.51 *The* colgroup *element makes it easy to select all of the cells in a column and apply formatting to them in one fell swoop. Here we've applied a background color to each* colgroup *element.*

```
<table cellspacing="0">
<caption align=top>Fox sightings in Western
Massachusetts</caption>
<colgroup class="cities" />
<colgroup span="3" class="data" >
    <col span="2" />
    <col class="totals" />
</colgroup>
<tr>
    <td> </td>
    <td>Kits</td>
    <td>Adults</td>
```

Figure 16.52 *Now I divide the second column group into two separate non-structural column groups (with* col*) so that I can format an entire column at a time without affecting how rules are drawn (see page 249).*

```
body {font-family: "Trebuchet MS", "Verdana",
sans-serif}
td {padding: 4px 10px;}
caption {font-weight: bold; color: #9A6016;
padding-bottom: 5px;}
.cities {background: #D1A367;}
.data {background: #F0E7DB;}
.totals {background: #F3D9B7;}
```

Figure 16.53 *We'll add a background color to the new* col *element.*

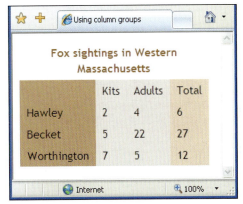

Figure 16.54 *Now the* Total *column has its own background color.*

✔ Tips

■ You can only legally apply `background`, `border`, `width` and `visibility` properties to `colgroup` and `col` elements, though IE accepts other formatting as well. The `border` property is only applied if you set the table's `border-collapse` property to `collapse`.

■ Use `colgroup` when you want to determine where dividing lines (rules) should go. Use `col` for *everything but* deciding where dividing lines go. For more information on drawing dividing lines, consult page 250.

■ You can divide column groups (`colgroup`) into columns (`col`) in order to add non-structural information (like size, alignment, or whatever) to individual columns within structural column groups. Simply type the `col` tag *after* the parent `colgroup` tag **(Figure 16.52)**. Note that `col` tags' attributes override the attributes in the `colgroup` tag.

■ If a column group is not divided into individual columns, you may combine the opening and closing tags: `<colgroup span="3" />`. In HTML, the closing tag for `colgroup` is optional.

■ The `col` element is always empty. In HTML you may omit the `/`.

■ If the column group only contains one column, you don't need to use the `span` attribute. Its default is 1.

■ Header cells—those marked with the `th` tag—are not affected by the alignment specified in a column group. For more information on aligning cells, consult *Aligning a Cell's Contents* on page 238.

Dividing Your Table into Column Groups

Dividing the Table into Horizontal Sections

You can also mark a horizontal section of your table—one or more rows—and then format it all at once. You'll also be able to draw dividing lines between sections, instead of between individual rows *(see page 249)*.

To divide the table into horizontal sections:

1. Before the first **tr** tag of the section you want to create, type **<thead**, **<tbody**, or **<tfoot**.

2. If desired, define the desired attributes for the section.

3. Type **>**.

4. If necessary, create the section's contents.

5. Close the section with **</thead>**, **</tbody>**, or **</tfoot>**.

✔ Tips

■ You can apply CSS (or indeed, formatting attributes) to horizontal sections of cells.

■ Horizontal section tags go *after* column group tags *(see page 246)*.

■ At least one **tbody** tag is required in every table. Both XHTML, as long as it is served as an HTML file (e.g., with the .html extension) and HTML will create an *implicit* **tbody** if you omit it. XHTML served as XML (with the .xml extension) *requires* an explicit **tbody** element.

■ You can only have one **thead** and one **tfoot** per table.

■ In HTML, but not XHTML, the closing tags are optional. A section is automatically closed when you begin the next.

```
  </colgroup>
<thead class="titles">
<tr>
    <td> </td>
    <td>Kits</td>
    <td>Adults</td>
    <td>Total</td></tr>
</thead>
<tbody>
<tr>
    <td>Hawley</td>
    <td>2</td>
...
    <td>12</td></tr>
</tbody>
```

Figure 16.55 *Once the first row is in a* thead *section, I can define a class of styles for it which will be applied to each cell in the* thead*.*

```
.data {background: #F0E7DB;}
.totals {background: #F3D9B7;}
.titles {text-align: center; background: #d1a367;}
tbody {text-align: center;}
```

Figure 16.56 *In the CSS, I'll give the* thead *element the same background as the left column and will center both the* thead *and the* tbody*.*

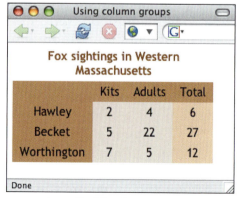

Figure 16.57 *All of the elements in the* thead *section are formatted and they will be considered a unit when the interior borders are drawn.*

```
<body>
<table cellspacing="0" border="4" frame="hsides"
rules="none">
<caption align=top>Fox sightings in Western
Massachusetts</caption>
<colgroup class="cities" />
<colgroup span="3" class="data" >
    <col span="2" />
    <col class="totals" />
    </colgroup>
<thead class="titles">
```

Figure 16.58 *Add the* frame *attribute within the* table *tag. I've added a thick border so that it's easier to see the effect. If you leave* border *out and the* frame *attribute is not* void, *you'll get a 1 pixel border by default.*

```
body {font-family: "Trebuchet MS", "Verdana",
sans-serif;}

table {border-color: #754F1D;}
td {padding: 4px 10px;}
```

Figure 16.59 *I've added a color to the border so that it's prettier. You could conceivably set the* border-width *here as well. However, if you set the* border-style *here, Internet Explorer decides you must want the border everywhere and ignores the* frame *attribute.*

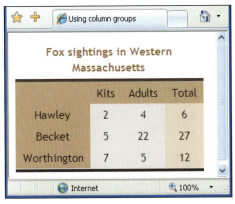

Figure 16.60 *Only the horizontal exterior borders are displayed.*

Choosing Which Borders to Display

When you use the border attribute *(see page 230),* a border appears between each cell and also around the table itself. (X)HTML lets you choose which external sides of the table should have a border as well as which internal borders should be displayed.

To choose which external sides should have a border:

In the table tag, type **frame="location"**, where *location* is one of the values listed below:

- void, for no external borders (default)

- above, for a single border on top

- below, for a single border on bottom

- hsides, for a border on both the top and bottom sides

- vsides, for a border on both the right and left sides

- rhs, for a single border on the right side

- lhs, for a single border on the left side

- box or border, for a border on all sides

continued

Choosing Which Borders to Display

To choose which internal borders should be displayed:

In the `table` tag, type **rules="area"**, where *area* is one of the following values:

- `none`, for no internal rules (default)

- `rows`, for horizontal rules between each row in the table

- `cols`, for vertical rules between each column in the table **(Figures 16.61 and 16.62)**

- `groups`, for rules between column groups (created with the `colgroup` element described on pages 246–247) and horizontal sections as defined by the tags described on pages 246–248 **(Figures 16.63 and 16.64)**

- `all`, for rules between each row and column in the table

✔ Tips

- It is the `groups` value for `rules` that illustrates the difference between `colgroup` and `col`. The `colgroup` element defines what is considered a column group and therefore where lines are drawn with the groups value. The `col` element does not.

- It is also the `groups` value which makes this whole technique worthwhile **(Figure 16.64)**. Otherwise, you can use the CSS `border` property to get much more control over borders *(see page 230)*.

```
<table cellspacing="0" border="4" frame="void"
rules="cols">

<caption align="top">Fox sightings in Western
Massachusetts</caption>

<colgroup class="cities" >
```

Figure 16.61 *The* rules *attribute determines which internal borders should be displayed, in this case, the vertical ones. I haven't changed anything in the CSS file.*

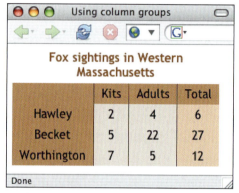

Figure 16.62 *With* rules *set to* cols *(and* frame *set to* void*), only the interior divisions between columns are drawn. Note their skinny width.*

```
<table cellspacing="0" border="4" frame="void"
rules="groups">
```

Figure 16.63 *I set the* rules *attribute to* groups *but keep hiding the external border.*

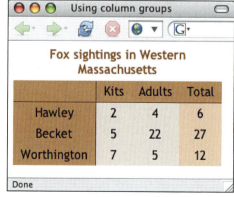

Figure 16.64 *Now the interior lines are drawn between groups, creating an interesting effect.*

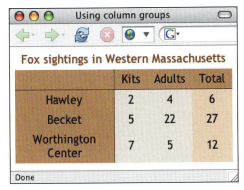

Figure 16.65 *If one of your cells has a two word entry just a little bit bigger than the others, you may want to avoid the text wrap so the numerical data looks more uniform.*

```
<tr>

    <td nowrap="nowrap">Worthington
Center</td>

    <td>7</td>

    <td>5</td>
```

Figure 16.66 *Just add the* nowrap *attribute to the* td *cell that should not be broken into multiple lines.*

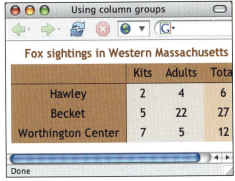

Figure 16.67 *No matter how narrow the window and the table get, the cell's contents will stay on a single line, even if it means some of the table extends beyond the window.*

Controlling Line Breaks in a Cell

Unless you specify otherwise, a browser will divide the lines of text in a cell as it decides on the height and width of each column and row. The nowrap attribute forces the browser to keep all the text in a cell on one line.

To keep text in a cell on one single line:

In a td or th cell, type **nowrap= "nowrap"**.

✔ Tips

- In HTML, but not XHTML, you can just type **nowrap** by itself.

- Browsers will make the cell (and the table that contains it) as wide as it needs to accommodate the single line of text—even if it looks really ugly. I don't recommend using the nowrap tag with tables used for layout. It overrides the width attribute.

- You can use regular line breaks (br) between words to mark where you *do* want the text to break.

- You can also type ** ** instead of a regular space to connect pairs of words or other elements with non-breaking spaces.

- For more information on line breaks, consult *Creating a Line Break* on page 66 and *Setting White Space Properties* on page 164.

Speeding up Table Display

Although tables are extremely powerful, they can be very slow to appear in your visitor's browser. The major factor is that the browser must calculate the width and height of the table before it can begin to display the cells. So, if you can keep the browser's calculations to a minimum, the table will appear more quickly and your visitors may actually wait to see it.

To speed up table display:

- Keep tables as small as possible. Where you can, divide large tables into smaller ones.

- Specify the width of the table in pixels *(see page 232)*.

- Use absolute values (in pixels) or percentages for determining cell width.

- Only specify proportional widths for cells, columns, and horizontal sections when you've already set a fixed width in pixels for the entire table.

- Divide your table into column groups.

- Add `table-layout:fixed` to your `table` element's style rule **(Figure 16.68)**. This instructs browsers to look only at the first row of a table in order to determine the widths of the columns, instead of worrying about every cell in every row. While the contents of some cells may not fit (their display is governed by the `over-flow` property—see page 187), the table renders more quickly.

```
table {table-layout: fixed;}
```

Figure 16.68 *The* `table-layout` *property with a value of* `fixed` *helps tables render more quickly. It is useful for tables whose cells are regular in size.*

FORMS

Up to now, all the (X)HTML you have learned has helped you communicate *your* ideas with your visitors. In this chapter, you'll learn how to create forms which enable your visitors to communicate with you.

There are two basic parts of a form: the collection of fields, labels, and buttons that the visitor sees on a page and hopefully fills out, and the processing script that takes that information and converts it into a format that you can read or tally.

Constructing a form's fields and buttons *(pages 254–276)* is straightforward and similar to creating any other part of the Web page. You can create text boxes, special password boxes, radio buttons, checkboxes, drop-down menus, larger text areas, and even clickable images. You will give each element a name that will serve as a label to identify the data once it is processed. I'll also show you how to format forms with CSS.

Processing the data from a form is only slightly more complicated. While in earlier editions I recommended using Perl to write CGI scripts, I now heartily recommend using PHP. It is easy and straightforward and perfectly suited to making Web pages interactive.

While both PHP and Perl are beyond the scope of this book, and even explaining how to use existing scripts stretches the limits a bit, I have provided some ready-made scripts to help you get started *(see pages 256 and 258)*.

Creating a Form

A form has three important parts: the `form` tag, which includes the URL of the script that will process the form; the form elements, like fields and menus; and the submit button which sends the data to the script on the server.

To create a form:

1. Type **<form method="post"**.

2. Type **action="script.url">** where *script.url* is the location on the server of the script that will run when the form is submitted *(see page 256)*.

3. Create the form's contents, as described on pages 262–280, including a submit button *(see page 272)* or active image *(see page 276)*.

4. Type **</form>** to complete the form.

```
<form method="post" action="showform.php">

<p class="legend">Personal information</p>

<fieldset id="personal">

<label>Name:</label><input type="text"
name="name" size="30" /> <br />

<label>Address:</label><input type="text"
name="address" size="30" /> <br />

<label>Town/City:</label><input type="text"
name="city" size="30" /> <br />

...

<p id="buttons"><input type="submit"
value="Order Bed" /><input type="reset"
value="Start Over" /></p>

</form>
```

Figure 17.1 *Every form has three parts: the* `form` *tag, the actual form elements where the visitor enters information, and the submit button (or active image) that sends the collected information to the server.*

```
#form {font-family: "Trebuchet MS", Verdana,
sans-serif; width: 25em;}

h2 {margin: 0 0 0 0; padding: 0;}

p {margin: 0 0 1em 0; padding: 0; font-size: 90%;}

fieldset {background: #C361D2; border: none;
margin-bottom: 1em; width: 24em;
padding-top: 1.5em;}

p.legend {background: #DED983; color: black;
padding: .2em .3em; font-size: 1.2em;
border: 2px outset #DED983; position: relative;
margin-bottom: -1em; width: 10em;
margin-left: 1em; margin-top: 1em;}

#personal {background: #F3B4F5;
border:outset #f3b4f5;}

#choices {background: #F5D9B4;
border: outset #f5d9b4;}
```

Figure 17.2 *Here is a portion of the style sheet used to format the form. You can find the full style sheet on the Web site (see page 26).*

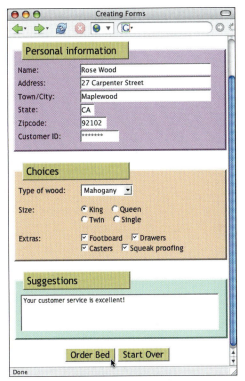

Figure 17.3 *Here is the complete form discussed in this chapter.*

✔ Tips

■ You can download the *showform.php* script from my Web site *(see page 26)* and use it in step 2 to test your forms as you go through this chapter. It is also shown in Figure 17.4 on page 256.

■ In order for your visitor to send you the data on the form, you'll need either a submit button or an active image. For more on submit buttons, consult *Creating the Submit Button* on page 272. For details on active images, consult *Using an Image to Submit Data* on page 276.

■ You can use CSS *(see page 169)* or tables *(see page 227)* to lay out your form elements. The example that I demonstrate with illustrations throughout this chapter and in Figure 17.3 was created using strict XHTML and CSS.

■ You can also use the get method to process information gathered with a form. However, since the get method limits the amount of data that you can collect at one time, I recommend using post.

Processing Forms

A form gathers the information from your visitor and the script processes that information. The script can log the information to a database on the server, send the information via email, or any number of other functions.

In this chapter, since the focus is on creating Web forms, we'll use a very simple PHP script to echo the data back to the visitor when they fill out and submit a form **(Figure 17.4)**. I'll also give you a script that you can use to submit a form's contents to your email address *(see page 258)*.

About PHP

PHP, which is a recursive abbreviation that stands for *PHP: Hypertext Preprocessor*, is an Open Source scripting language that was written specifically for making Web pages interactive. It is remarkably simple and straightforward. I wrote the scripts for this chapter after having worked with PHP for a very short time—though I was fortunate enough to have a copy of Larry Ullman's excellent *PHP for the World Wide Web: Visual QuickStart Guide, Second Edition*, which I highly recommend. While it's true that my scripts are not very complicated, that's sort of the point. I was able to get them to do what I needed without having to jump through a lot of hoops.

In addition to being easy to learn, PHP has a number of additional characteristics that make it ideal for processing (X)HTML forms. First of all, PHP is an *interpreted* or *scripting* language, which means that it does not need to be compiled first. You write it and off you go. In contrast with Perl scripts, you don't have to make PHP scripts executable or put them in any special place on your server. Indeed, although PHP scripts can be inde-

```
<!DOCTYPE html ... -transitional.dtd">
<html xmlns="http://www.w3.org/1999/xhtml">
<head>
    <title>Processing Form Data</title>
<style type="text/css">...</style>
</head><body>
<p>This is a very simple PHP script that outputs
...</p>
<table>
<tr><th>Field Name</th><th>Value(s)</th></tr>

<?php
if (empty($_POST)) {
    print "<p>No data was submitted.</p>";
} else {

foreach ($_POST as $key => $value) {
    if (get_magic_quotes_gpc()) $value=
stripslashes($value);
    if ($key=='extras') {
    if (is_array($_POST['extras']) ){
        print "<tr><td><code>$key</code>
</td><td>";
        foreach ($_POST['extras'] as $value) {
        print "<i>$value</i><br />";
        }
        print "</td></tr>";
    } else {
        print "<tr><td><code>$key</code>
</td><td> <i>$value</i></td></tr>\n";
        }
    } else {
    print "<tr><td><code>$key</code></td>
<td><i>$value</i></td></tr>\n";
    }
}
}
?>
</table>
</body>
</html>
```

Figure 17.4 *Here is the script used to process the forms in this chapter. Notice how the PHP script lives right in an (X)HTML page. (You can find a commented version of this script on my Web site.)*

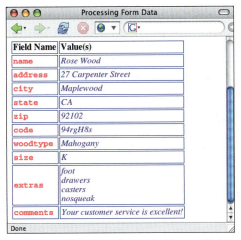

Figure 17.5 *The script shown in Figure 17.4 outputs the name and value(s) for each field in a table in the browser window. You can try it out on (and download it from) my Web site.*

Server side vs. Client side

PHP is a *server-side* language, which means that it is run on the computer that serves your Web pages (aptly called a *server*), not on your visitor's computer where the page is viewed. Indeed, it won't work at all if the script is not uploaded to a server. In addition, that server must have PHP installed for the script to be interpreted. Server-side languages are ideal for processing forms, sending email, and other functions that require a server.

Client-side languages, like JavaScript, work right inside the browser. They can do many tasks without interacting with the server at all. They are great for manipulating the browser window, checking that all the data has been entered before submitting a form, and other tasks that happen without the server (or before the server gets involved). You'll find more information on JavaScript in Chapters 19–20.

---

pendent text files, they are often written right inside the (X)HTML page itself, making PHP extremely convenient for Web designers.

Finally, because PHP was designed for the Web, it's good at the tasks that Web pages require and coordinates well with (X)HTML. There are hundreds of ready-made built-in functions that you can take advantage of. In this chapter we'll touch briefly on PHP's form processing tools. PHP's official site can be found at *http://www.php.net/*

Security

As always when you're sending information to the server, you need to be very careful with security. Never assume anything about your data. Just because you may have built safeguards into your form doesn't mean the bad guys won't create their own form that calls your script in order to send out millions of spam messages with it. Check your data explicitly and make sure that it is what it should be, with no extra bits lurking about.

Alternatives to PHP

There are many alternatives to PHP for processing forms. CGI scripts written in Perl are one common strategy, as are ASP, VisualBasic, and even AppleScript. You can find more information about Perl in my *Perl and CGI for the World Wide Web, Visual QuickStart Guide, Second Edition*, also published by Peachpit Press. A few of the examples in this chapter still rely on Perl scripts. You'll find the forms and accompanying scripts in the *Examples* section of my Web site *(see page 26)*.

Sending Form Data via Email

If you don't feel like messing with CGI scripts and can deal with not having your data perfectly formatted (or pre-processed by a script), you can have a visitor's data be sent to you via email.

To send form data via email:

1. Type **<form method="post"**.

2. Type **action="emailform.php"**, where *emailform.php* is the script that will send the form data to your email.

3. Type **>**.

4. Create the form's contents, as described on pages 262–280.

5. Type **</form>**.

```
...
<body>

<?php
//This is a very simple PHP script that ...

if (empty($_POST)) {
    print "<p>No data was submitted.</p>";
    print "</body></html>";
    exit();
}
function clear_user_input($value) {
    if (get_magic_quotes_gpc())
$value=stripslashes($value);
    $value= str_replace( "\n", '', trim($value));
    $value= str_replace( "\r", '', $value);
    return $value;
    }
```

Figure 17.6 *Here is a script used to send form data via email. You can find a commented version of this script on my Web site.*

```
if ($_POST['comments'] == 'Please share any
comments you have here') $_POST['comments'] =
'';
$body ="Here is the data that was submitted:\n";

foreach ($_POST as $key => $value) {
    $key = clear_user_input($key);
    $value = clear_user_input($value);
    if ($key=='extras') {

    if (is_array($_POST['extras']) ){
        $body .= "$key: ";
        $counter =1;
        foreach ($_POST['extras'] as $value) {
        //Add comma and space until last element
        if (sizeof($_POST['extras']) == $counter) {
            $body .= "$value\n";
            break;}
            else {
            $body .= "$value, ";
            $counter += 1;
            }}
            } else {
            $body .= "$key: $value\n";
            }
    } else {

        $body .= "$key: $value\n";
        }
}
extract($_POST);
$email = clear_user_input($email);
$name = clear_user_input($name);
$from='From: '. $email . "(" . $name . ")" . "\r\n"
. 'Bcc: alternate@yoursite.com' . "\r\n";

$subject = 'Bed Order from Web Site';

mail ('youremail@yoursite.com', $subject, $body,
$from);
?>
<p>Thanks for your order! We'll send your bed
right away.</p>
</body></html>
```

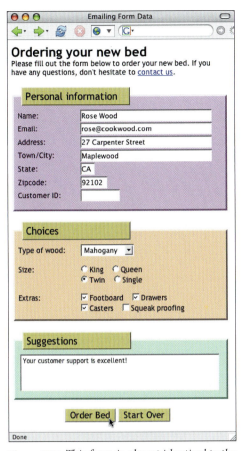

Figure 17.7 *This form is almost identical to the other except for an added email field.*

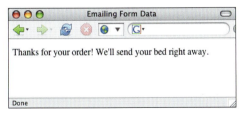

Figure 17.8 *It's always a good idea to give your visitor feedback about what just happened—since they can't see the email wending its way to you.*

✔ Tips

- You might want to ask for the email address to be entered twice, in order to prevent typos from keeping you from receiving the form data. Then have the script compare the two fields and return an error if they're not identical.

- You can find the code for this script on my Web site *(see page 26)*. You are welcome to use it on your own site.

- In earlier editions of this book, I offered a technique that used `enctype= "text/plain"` along with an `action` attribute set to an email address in order to receive form data via email. Unfortunately, it didn't work with some email programs (like Outlook) and so I substituted it for the PHP script shown here.

- If this script doesn't work on your server, it may be that your server doesn't have PHP installed. Contact your Web host and ask them (or check their Support pages).

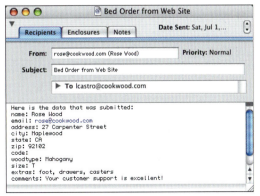

Figure 17.9 *Here is the email that was received after the form was submitted in Figure 17.7.*

Sending Form Data via Email

Organizing the Form Elements

If you have a lot of information to fill out on a form, you can group related elements together to make the form easier to follow. The easier it is for your visitors to understand the form, the more likely they are to fill it out correctly.

To organize the form elements:

1. Below the form tag but above any form elements that you wish to have contained in the first group, type **<fieldset>**.

2. If desired, type **<legend**.

3. If desired, type **align="direction"** where *direction* is left or right.

4. Type **>**.

5. Type the text for the legend.

6. Type **</legend>** to complete the legend.

7. Create the form elements that should belong in the first group. For more information, see pages 262–276.

8. Type **</fieldset>** to complete the first group of form elements.

9. Repeat steps 1–8 for each group of form elements.

```
<form method="post" action="showform.php">

<fieldset id="personal"><legend>Personal
Information</legend>

</fieldset>

<fieldset id="choices"><legend>Choices
</legend>

</fieldset>

<fieldset id="suggestions"><legend>Suggestions
</legend>

</fieldset>
```

Figure 17.10 *I have added an* id *attribute to each* fieldset *element to facilitate applying styles to each group of form elements.*

```
fieldset {margin-bottom:1em;
width: 24em; padding-top: 1.5em;}

#personal {background: #f3b4f5;
border:outset #f3b4f5;}
```

Figure 17.11 *I gave all the fieldset elements some margin, width, and padding, and then applied a separate background color and outset border to each one.*

Figure 17.12 *Internet Explorer does strange things to the* legend *element, pulling the background from the* fieldset *up and around it.*

```
<form method="post" action="showform.php">

<p class="legend">Personal information</p>

<fieldset id="personal">
```

Figure 17.13 *Because of Internet Explorer's lack of support of the* legend *element, I recommend using a regular* p *tag with a* class *of* legend.

```
p.legend {background:#DED983; color: black;
border: 2px outset #DED983; padding: .2em .3em;
font-size: 1.2em; position: relative;
margin: 1em 0 -1em 1em; width: 10em;}
```

Figure 17.14 *Next I style the legend paragraph with a background and outset border. Then I give it a negative bottom margin and relative positioning to pull it on top of the fieldset.*

Figure 17.15 *Now the legends look good even in the recalcitrant IE 6.*

✔ Tips

- I think fieldset elements look great formatted with an outset border. Use **background: color; border: outset color**, where *color* is the same in both instances and is what you want for the background of the fieldset. I formatted the legend elements the same way.

- The legend element is not at all well supported by Internet Explorer. If you create one and then give your fieldset a background, the background extends up and around the legend, looking really ugly **(Figure 17.12)**. I recommend recreating the legend effect with an aptly styled p element.

- Organizing your form into fieldsets is completely optional.

- While the align attribute for legend has been deprecated, it's still supported by Firefox and IE (from 4 on). It's default value is left. There were supposedly top and bottom values as well, but I've never seen a browser support them.

Organizing the Form Elements

Creating Text Boxes

Text boxes can contain one line of free-form text—that is, anything that the visitor wants to type—and are typically used for names, addresses, and the like.

To create a text box:

1. If desired, type the label that will identify the text box to your visitor (for example, **Name:**).

2. Type **<input type="text"**.

3. Type **name="label"**, where *label* is the text that will identify the input data to the server (and your script).

4. If desired, type **value="default"**, where *default* is the data that will initially be shown in the field and that will be sent to the server if the visitor doesn't type something else.

5. If desired, define the size of the box on your form by typing **size="n"**, replacing *n* with the desired width of the box, measured in characters.

6. If desired, type **maxlength="n"**, where *n* is the maximum number of characters that can be entered in the box.

7. Finish the text box by typing a final **/>**.

✔ Tips

- Even if your visitor skips the field (and you haven't set the default text with the `value` attribute), the `name` attribute is still sent to the server (with an undefined, empty `value`).

- The default for `size` is 20. However, visitors can type up to the limit imposed by the `maxlength` attribute. Still, for larger, multi-line entries, it's better to use text areas *(see page 269)*.

```
<form method="post" action="showform.php">

<p class="legend">Personal information</p>

<fieldset id="personal">

Name:<input type="text" name="name" size="30" /> <br />

Address:<input type="text" name="address" size="30" /> <br />

Town/City:<input type="text" name="city" size="30" /> <br />

State:<input type="text" name="state" size="2" maxlength="2" /><br />

Zipcode:<input type="text" name="zip" size="5" maxlength="5" /> <br />
```

Figure 17.16 *While it's essential to set the* name *attribute for each text box, you only have to set the* value *attribute when you want to add default values for a text box.*

Figure 17.17 *Text boxes can be different sizes to accommodate different types of fields. We'll straighten these up in just a moment (on page 264).*

Zipcode:<input type="text" name="zip" size="5" maxlength="5" />

Customer ID:<input type="password" name="code" size="8" />

Figure 17.18 *The* name *attribute identifies the password when you compile the data.*

Figure 17.19 *When the visitor enters a password in a form, the password is hidden with bullets or asterisks.*

Creating Password Boxes

The only difference between a password box and a text box is that whatever is typed in the former is hidden by bullets or asterisks. The information is *not* encrypted when sent to the server.

To create password boxes:

1. If desired, type the label that will identify the password box to your visitor (for example, **Enter password:**).

2. Type **<input type="password"**.

3. Type **name="label"**, where *label* is the text that will identify the input data to the server (and your script).

4. If desired, define the size of the box on your form by typing **size="n"**, replacing *n* with the desired width of the box, measured in characters.

5. If desired, type **maxlength="n"**, where *n* is the maximum number of characters that can be entered in the box.

6. Finish the text box by typing a final **/>**.

✔ Tips

- Even if nothing is entered in the password box, the name is still sent to the server (with an undefined value).

- You could set default text for value (as in step 4 on page 262), but that kind of defeats the purpose of a password.

- The only protection the password box offers is from folks peering over your visitor's shoulder as she types in her password. To really protect passwords you have to use them on a secure server.

Formally Labeling Form Parts

As you've seen, the explanatory information next to a form element is generally just plain text. For example, you might type "First name" before the text field where the visitor should type her name. (X)HTML provides a method for marking up labels so that you can formally link them to the associated element and use them for scripting or other purposes.

To formally label form parts:

1. Type **<label**.

2. If desired, type **for="idname">**, where *idname* is the value of the id attribute in the corresponding form element.

3. Type the contents of the label.

4. Type **</label>**.

✔ Tips

■ If you use the for attribute, you must also add the id attribute to the associated form element's opening tag in order to mark it with a label. (Otherwise, the document will not validate.) For more details about the id attribute, consult *Naming Elements* on page 63.

■ If you omit the for attribute, no id attribute is required in the element being labeled. The label and the element, in that case, are then associated by proximity, or perhaps by being placed in a common div element.

■ Another labeling technique is to use the title attribute. For more information, consult *Labeling Elements in a Web Page* on page 68.

■ You can use CSS to format your labels **(Figure 17.21)**.

```
<fieldset id="personal">

<label>Name:</label><input type="text"
name="name" size="30" /> <br />

<label>Address:</label><input type="text"
name="address" size="30" /> <br />

<label>Town/City:</label><input type="text"
name="city" size="30" /> <br />

<label>State:</label><input type="text"
name="state" size="2" maxlength="2" /><br />

<label>Zipcode:</label><input type="text"
name="zip" size="5" maxlength="5" /> <br />

<label>Customer ID:</label><input
type="password" name="code" size="8" />

</fieldset>
```

Figure 17.20 *Marking field labels in a formal way gives you an easy way to identify them in a CSS style sheet.*

```
#personal label {position: absolute; font-size: 90%;
padding-top: .2em; left: 20px;}

input {margin-left: 9em; margin-bottom:.2em;
line-height:1.4em; }
```

Figure 17.21 *Now I can sweep the labels out of the flow and align the text and password boxes to their right.*

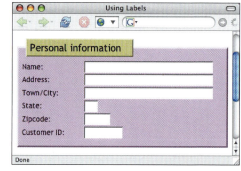

Figure 17.22 *The form is beginning to take shape.*

```
<fieldset id="choices">

<p id="size"><label>Size:</label><input
type="radio" name="size" value="K" />King

<input type="radio" name="size" value="Q"
/>Queen <br />

<input type="radio" name="size" value="T"
/>Twin

<input type="radio" name="size" value="S"
/>Single</p>
```

Figure 17.23 *The* name *attribute serves a dual purpose for radio buttons: it links the radio buttons in a given set and it identifies the value when it is sent to the script. The* value *attribute is crucial since the visitor has no way of typing a value.*

```
#choices label {position: absolute;
padding-top: .2em; left: 20px}

#size {font-size: 90%;}

input {margin-left: 9em;}

input+input {margin-left: 1em;}

br+input {margin-left: 9em;}
```

Figure 17.24 *This CSS positions the labels absolutely, just as in Figure 17.21. Then it gives the first radio button and any radio button after a* br *element a 9 em margin. The remaining radio buttons get 1 em margins.*

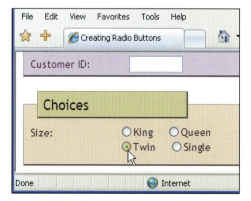

Figure 17.25 *The radio buttons themselves are created with the (X)HTML tags. The labels (King, Queen, etc.) are created with plain text alongside the (X)HTML tags.*

Creating Radio Buttons

Remember those old-time car radios with big black plastic buttons? Push one to listen to WFCR; push another for WRNX. You can never push two buttons at once. Radio buttons on forms work the same way (except you can't listen to the radio).

To create a radio button:

1. If desired, type the introductory text for your radio buttons. You might use something like **Select one of the following**.

2. Type **<input type="radio"**.

3. Type **name="radioset"**, where *radioset* both identifies the data sent to the script and also links the radio buttons together, ensuring that only one per set can be checked.

4. Type **value="data"**, where *data* is the text that will be sent to the server if the radio button is checked, either by you (in step 5) or by the visitor.

5. If desired, type **checked="checked"** to make the radio button active by default when the page is opened. You can only do this to one radio button in the set. (The **="checked"** is optional in HTML.)

6. Type the final **/>**.

7. Type the text that identifies the radio button to the visitor. This is often the same as value, but doesn't have to be.

8. Repeat steps 2–7 for each radio button in the set.

✔ Tip

■ If you don't set the value attribute, the word "on" is sent to the script. It's not particularly useful since you can't tell which button in the set was pressed.

Creating Menus

Menus are perfect for offering your visitors a choice from a given set of options.

To create menus:

1. If desired, type the text that will describe your menu.

2. Type **<select**.

3. Type **name="label"**, where *label* will identify the data collected from the menu when it is sent to the server.

4. If desired, type **size="n"**, where *n* represents the height (in lines) of the menu.

5. If desired, type **multiple="multiple"** to allow your visitor to select more than one menu option (with Ctrl or Command). (The **="multiple"** is optional in HTML.)

6. Type **>**.

7. Type **<option**.

8. If desired, type **selected="selected"** if you want the option to be selected by default. (The **="selected"** is optional in HTML.)

9. Type **value="label"**, where *label* identifies the data that will be sent to the server if the option is selected.

10. If desired, type **label="menu option"**, where *menu option* is the word that should appear in the menu.

11. Type **>**.

12. Type the option name as you wish it to appear in the menu.

13. Type **</option>**.

14. Repeat steps 7–13 for each option.

15. Type **</select>**.

```
<input type="radio" name="size" value="T" />Twin

<input type="radio" name="size" value="S" />Single</p>

<p id="woodtype"><label>Type of wood:</label><select name="woodtype" >

<option value="Mahogany">Mahogany</option>

<option value="Maplewood">Maplewood</option>

<option value="Pine">Pine</option>

<option value="Cherry">Cherry</option>

</select></p>

</fieldset>
```

Figure 17.26 *Menus are made up of two (X)HTML tags:* select *and* option. *You set the common* name *attribute in the* select *tag and the individual* value *attribute in each of the* option *tags.*

```
select {margin-left: 9em;}
```

Figure 17.27 *We'll use CSS again to push the menu over in line with the other fields.*

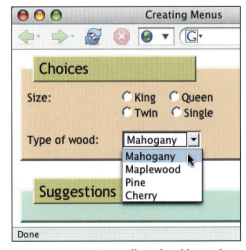

Figure 17.28 *A visitor will not be able to select nothing in a menu unless you set the* size *attribute. The default selection is either the first option in the menu or the one you've set as* selected *in step 8.*

```
<p id="woodtype"><label>Type of
wood:</label><select name="woodtype" >

<optgroup label="Hard woods">

<option value="Mahogany">Mahogany</option>

<option value="Maplewood">Maplewood
</option>

<option value="Cherry">Cherry</option>

</optgroup>

<optgroup label="Soft Woods">

<option value="Pine">Pine</option>

<option value="Fir">Fir</option>

</optgroup>

</select></p>
```

Figure 17.29 *Each submenu has a title, speci-fied in the* label *attribute of the* optgroup *tag, and a series of options (defined with* option *tags and regular text).*

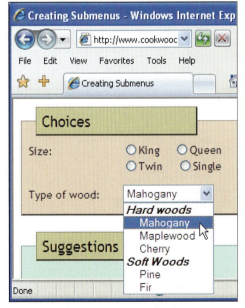

Figure 17.30 *Browsers generally don't create true submenus, but rather group the items in a single menu with subgroups.*

If you have a particularly large menu with many options, you may want to group the options into categories.

To group menu options:

1. Create a menu as described on page 266.

2. Before the first `option` tag in the first group that you wish to place together in a submenu, type **<optgroup**.

3. Type **label="submenutitle">**, where *sub-menutitle* is the header for the submenu.

4. After the last `option` tag in the group, type **</optgroup>**.

5. Repeat steps 2–4 for each submenu.

✔ Tips

- If you add the `size` attribute in step 4, the menu appears more like a list, and there is no automatically selected option (unless you use `selected`—see step 8).

- If `size` *(see step 4)* is bigger than the number of options, visitors can deselect all values by clicking in the empty space.

- The closing `option` tag in step 13 is optional in HTML 4 (but not in XHTML). You can also use the abbreviated `selected` and `multiple` in HTML, whereas XHTML requires `selected=` `"selected"` and `multiple="multiple"`.

Creating Menus

Creating Checkboxes

While radio buttons can accept only one answer per set, a visitor can check as many checkboxes in a set as they like. Like radio buttons, checkboxes are linked by the value of the name attribute.

To create checkboxes:

1. If desired, type the introductory text (something like **Select one or more of the following**) for your checkboxes.

2. Type **<input type="checkbox"**. (Notice there is no space in the word *checkbox*.)

3. Type **name="boxset"**, where *boxset* both identifies the data sent to the script and also links the checkboxes together.

4. Type **value="data"**, where *data* is the text that will be sent to the server if the checkbox is marked (either by the visitor, or by you as described in step 5).

5. Type **checked="checked"** to make the checkbox checked by default when the page is opened. You (or the visitor) may check as many checkboxes as desired. (The **="checked"** is optional in HTML.)

6. Type **/>** to complete the checkbox.

7. Type the text that identifies the checkbox to the user. This is often the same as the value, but doesn't have to be.

8. Repeat steps 2–7 for each checkbox in the set.

✔ Tip

- If you use PHP, you can automatically create an array (called $_POST['boxset']) out of the checkbox values by using **name="boxset[ ]"** in step 3, where *boxset* identifies the data sent to the script.

```
<p id="extras"><label>Extras:</label>

<input type="checkbox" name="extras[]"
value="foot" />Footboard

<input type="checkbox" name="extras[]"
value="drawers" checked="checked" />Drawers
<br />

<input type="checkbox" name="extras[]"
value="casters" />Casters

<input type="checkbox" name="extras[]"
value="nosqueak" />Squeak proofing <br /></p>

</fieldset>
```

Figure 17.31 *Notice how the label text (not highlighted) does not need to match the* value *attribute. That's because the label text identifies the checkboxes to the visitor in the browser while the* value *identifies the data to the script. The empty brackets are for PHP (see tip).*

```
#extras {font-size: 90%;}

input {margin-left: 9em;}

input+input {margin-left: 1em;}

br+input {margin-left: 9em;}
```

Figure 17.32 *The CSS is very similar to what we used for the radio buttons: give the first checkbox and any checkbox that follows a* br *element a 9 em margin. Remaining checkboxes get only 1 em.*

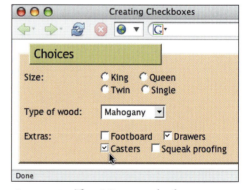

Figure 17.33 *The visitor can check as many boxes as necessary. Each corresponding value will be sent to the script, together with the checkbox set's name.*

```
<p class="legend">Suggestions</p>

<fieldset id="suggestions">

<textarea name="comments" rows="3"
cols="40">Please share any comments you have
here</textarea>

</fieldset>
```

Figure 17.34 *The* `value` *attribute is not used with the* `textarea` *tag. Default values are set by adding text between the opening and closing tags (as in "Please share..." shown here).*

```
textarea {font: .8em "Trebuchet MS", Verdana,
sans-serif; width: 29em; padding: .2em;}
```

Figure 17.35 *For some reason, I had to apply the* `font` *property directly to the* `textarea` *element to get it to take hold. It did not inherit from the* `body`.

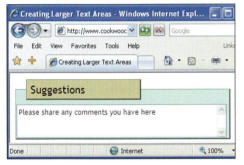

Figure 17.36 *The visitor can override the default text simply by typing over it.*

Creating Larger Text Areas

In some cases, you want to give the visitor more room to write. Unlike text boxes *(see page 262)*, text areas may be as large as your page, and will expand as needed if the person enters more text than can fit in the display area. They're perfect for eliciting questions and comments.

To create larger text areas:

1. If desired, type the explanatory text that will identify the text area.

2. Type **<textarea**.

3. Type **name="label"**, where *label* is the text that will identify the input data to the server (and your script).

4. Type **rows="n"**, where *n* is the height of the text area in rows.

5. Type **cols="n"**, where *n* is the width of the text area in characters.

6. Type **>**.

7. Type the default text, if any, for the text area. No formatting is allowed here.

8. Type **</textarea>** to complete the text area.

✔ Tips

- There is no use for the `value` attribute with text areas.

- Visitors can enter up to 32,700 characters in a text area. Scroll bars will appear when necessary.

- Both the `rows` and `cols` attributes are required.

Allowing Visitors to Upload Files

If the information you need from the folks filling out your form is complicated, you might want to have them upload an entire file to your server.

To allow visitors to upload files:

1. Type **<form method="post" enctype= "multipart/form-data"**. The enctype attribute ensures that the file is uploaded in the proper format.

2. Next, type **action= "upload.url">,** where *upload.url* is the URL of the script that processes incoming files. You'll need a special script for this.

3. Type the caption for the file upload area so your visitors know what to do. Something like **What file would you like to upload?** would work well.

4. Type **<input type="file"** to create a file upload box and a Browse button.

5. Type **name="title"**, where *title* identifies to the server the files being uploaded.

6. If desired, type **size="n"**, where *n* is the width, in characters, of the field in which the visitor will enter the path and file name.

7. Type the final **/>**.

8. Complete the form as usual, including the submit button and final </form> tag.

✔ Tips

- The size attribute is optional, but since most paths and file names are pretty long, it's a good idea to set it at 40 or 50. The default is 20.

- You can't use the get method for forms that allow uploading.

```
<form method="post" enctype="multipart/form-
data" action="http://www.cookwood.com/cgi-
bin/perl2e/uploading/uploading.cgi">

<h2>What files are you sending?</h2>

<p><input type="file" name="uploadfile"
size="30" />

</form>
```

Figure 17.37 *To allow visitors to upload files, you must make sure to set the proper* enctype *attribute, as well as create the* file *type* input *element.*

Figure 17.38 *When you create a file upload area, both a field where the visitor can type the path to the file and a Browse button (so the visitor can use an Open dialog box to choose the file) automatically appear on your page.*

Allowing Visitors to Upload Files

```
<form method=post action="whatever.php">
<input type="hidden" name="name"
value="$name" />
<input type=submit value="submit data" />
```

Figure 17.39 *When you create a hidden field, you use the variables from your script to set the value of the field to what the visitor originally entered.*

When to use a hidden field?

Imagine you've got a form and you want to be able to give your visitors a chance to review what they've entered before they submit it. Your processing script can show them the submitted data and at the same time create a form with hidden fields containing the same data. If the visitor wants to edit the data, they simply go back. But if they want to submit the data, the hidden fields will already be filled out, saving them the task of typing the data in again.

Creating Hidden Fields

Hidden fields are generated by the processing script to store information gathered from an earlier form so that it can be combined with the present form's data.

To create hidden fields:

1. Type **<input type="hidden"**.

2. Type **name="label"**, where *label* is a short description of the information to be stored.

3. Type **value="data"**, where *data* is the information itself that is to be stored. It is often a variable from the form processing script **(Figure 17.39)**.

4. Type **/>**.

✔ Tips

■ It doesn't matter where the hidden fields appear in your form since they won't appear in the browser anyway. As long as they are within the opening and closing `form` tags, you're OK.

■ To create an element that will be submitted with the rest of the data when the visitor clicks the submit button but that is also *visible* to the visitor, create a regular form element and use the `readonly` attribute *(see page 280)*.

Creating Hidden Fields

Creating the Submit Button

All the information that your visitors enter won't be any good to you unless they send it to the server. You should always create a submit button for your forms so that the visitor can deliver the information to you. (You can also use images to submit form data—see page 276.)

To create a submit button:

1. Type **<input type="submit"**.

2. If desired, type **value="submit message"** where *submit message* is the text that will appear in the button.

3. Type the final **/>**.

✔ Tips

■ If you leave out the value attribute, the submit button will be labeled *Submit Query*, by default.

■ The name-value pair for the submit button is only sent to the script if you set the name attribute. Therefore, if you omit the name attribute, you won't have to deal with the extra, usually superfluous submit data.

■ On the other hand, you can create multiple submit buttons (with both the name and value attributes) and then write your script to react according to which submit button the visitor presses.

```
<p id="buttons"><input type="submit"
value="Order Bed" /></p>
```

Figure 17.40 *If you leave out the* name *attribute, the name-value pair for the submit button will not be passed to the script. Since you usually don't need this information, that's a good thing.*

```
input {background: #DED983; font:1.2em
"Trebuchet MS", Verdana, sans-serif;}

#buttons {text-align: center;}
```

Figure 17.41 *I apply a background and font formatting to the submit button. For more information on selecting by attribute, see page 147.*

Figure 17.42 *The submit button activates the script that collects the data from the form. You can personalize the button's contents with the* value *attribute. (The phrase* Order Bed *is clearer for your visitors than the default text* Submit Query*).*

```
<input type="radio" name="cats" value="X"
accesskey="x" />Xixona<br />

<input type="radio" name="cats" value="L"
accesskey="l" />Llumeta<br />

<input type="radio" name="cats" value="A"
accesskey="a" />All of them (Don't

make me choose!)

<p id="buttons"><button type="submit"><img
src="check.gif" width="40" height="40" alt="Vote
button" /> Vote</button>
```

Figure 17.43 *You can create a submit button with an image by using the* button *tag.*

```
body {background: #FEFEE7;}

h2 {margin: 1em 0 0; padding: 0;}

button {font: 48px "Trebuchet MS", "Verdana",
sans-serif; background: #F9CC7D;
border: outset #F9CC7D;}


p#buttons {white-space: nowrap;}
```

Figure 17.44 *I gave the buttons more body by applying an outset border that is the same color as the background in the CSS.*

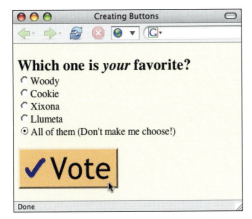

Figure 17.45 *The (X)HTML code for a submit button with an image is a little more complicated, but looks so good. (Of course, it would help if I could actually draw.)*

(X)HTML's `button` element lets you create prettier submit buttons. You can add an image, change the font, or even change the background color. That'll get them to submit that form!

To create a submit button with an image:

1. Type **<button type="submit">**.

2. Type the text, if any, that should appear on the left side of the image in the button.

3. Type **<img src="image.url"** where *image.url* is the name of the image that will appear on the button.

4. Type **alt="alternate text"**, where *alternate text* is what appears if the image doesn't.

5. If desired, add any other image attributes.

6. Type **/>** to complete the image.

7. Type the text, if any, that should appear on the right side of the image in the button.

8. Type **</button>**.

✔ Tips

- If you have multiple submit buttons, you can give a `name` and `value` attribute to each one so that your script can tell which one was pressed.

- You can also use the `button` tag to create a submit button without an image. Just skip steps 3–6.

- You can use CSS to style buttons.

- For information on creating buttons with scripts, consult *Creating a Button that Executes a Script* on page 316.

Creating the Submit Button

Resetting the Form

If humans could fill out forms perfectly on the first try, there would be no erasers on pencils and no backspace key on your computer keyboard. You can give your visitors a reset button so that they can start over with a fresh form (including all the default values you've set).

To create a reset button:

1. Type **<input type="reset"**.

2. If desired, type **value="reset message"** where *reset message* is the text that appears in the button. The default reset message is *Reset*.

3. Type **/>**.

✔ Tips

■ The name-value pair for the reset button is only sent to the script if you set the name attribute. Therefore, if you omit the name attribute, you won't have to deal with the completely superfluous reset data—which is usually something like "reset, Reset".

■ You could add the name attribute to a reset button for scripting purposes *(see page 316)*.

```
<input type="reset" value="Start Over" />
```

Figure 17.46 *You can use the* value *attribute to set any text you wish for the reset button.*

```
input {background: #DED983; font: 1.2em
"Trebuchet MS", Verdana, sans-serif;}
```

Figure 17.47 *The CSS from Figure 17.41 on page 272 already applies to the Reset button. No additions are necessary.*

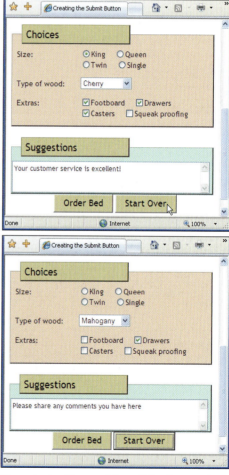

Figure 17.48 *If your visitor clicks the reset button, all the fields are set to their default values.*

```
<input type="radio" name="cats" value="X"
accesskey="x" />Xixona<br />

<input type="radio" name="cats" value="L"
accesskey="l" />Llumeta<br />

<input type="radio" name="cats" value="A"
accesskey="a" />All of them (Don't make me
choose!)

<p id="buttons"><button type="submit" name=
"submit" value="submit"><img src="check.gif"
width="40" height="40" alt="Vote button" />
Vote</button>

<button type="reset"> <img src="reset.gif"
width="40" height="40" alt="Reset button"
/>Reset</button></p>
```

Figure 17.49 *Make sure you set the* type *to* reset. *Otherwise, the button won't actually do anything at all.*

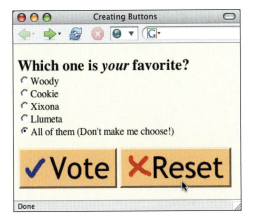

Figure 17.50 *Now both the submit and reset buttons really stand out. (It really works, by the way. Try it on my Web site—see page 26.)*

You can add images, font choices, and even a background color to your reset button.

To create a reset button with an image:

1. Type **<button type="reset">**.

2. Type the text, if any, that should appear on the left side of the image in the button.

3. Type **<img src="image.url"**, where *image.url* is the name of the image that will appear on the button.

4. Type **alt="alternate text"**, where *alternate text* is what appears if the image doesn't.

5. If desired, add any other image attributes.

6. Type **/>** to complete the image.

7. Type the text, if any, that should appear on the right side of the image in the button.

8. Type **</button>**.

✔ Tips

■ You can also use the button tag to create a reset button without an image. Just skip steps 3–6.

■ For information on creating buttons with scripts, consult *Creating a Button that Executes a Script* on page 316.

■ Current browsers support the button tag quite well. Older browsers do not, despite it being a standard part of (X)HTML.

■ I can't think of any good reason to add the value attribute to a reset button, but you might want to add a name attribute for scripting purposes.

Resetting the Form

Using an Image to Submit Data

You may use an image—called an *active image*—as a combination input element and submit button. In addition to submitting the data from the other fields in the form, a click on the image sends the current mouse coordinates to the server in two name-value pairs.

To use an image to submit data:

1. Create a GIF or JPEG image.

2. Type **<input type="image"**.

3. Type **src="image.url"**, where *image.url* is the location of the image on the server.

4. Type **name="label"**, where *label* will be appended by *x* and *y* and will identify the x and y coordinates sent to the server, when the visitor clicks the image.

5. Type **alt="description"**, where *description* will appear if the image does not.

6. Type the final **/>** to finish the active image definition for the form.

✔ Tips

■ Setting the value attribute has no effect. The values are set to the mouse coordinates automatically.

■ In a Perl script, the names are set to *label.x* and *label.y* for the x and y coordinates respectively, where *label* matches what you used in step 4 above, *x* is the horizontal distance in pixels from the image's left edge, and *y* is the vertical distance in pixels from the image's top edge. In a PHP script, the names are changed to *label_x* and *label_y* instead since PHP doesn't accept periods in variable names.

■ You can find the PHP script used in this example on my Web site (*see page 26*).

```
<input type="radio" name="infotype"
value="directions" />Directions

<input type="radio" name="infotype"
value="statistics" />City statistics <br /></small>

<input type="image" src="zonemap.gif"
name="coord" alt="US Map, Click to submit data"
/>

</form>
```

Figure 17.51 *If you use an active image, you don't need a submit button.*

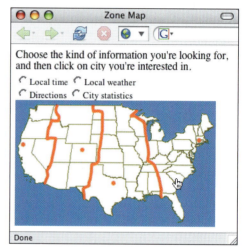

Figure 17.52 *The same form can have both regular fields (like the radio buttons) and an image map. When the visitor clicks the map, all of the data is sent to the script.*

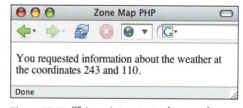

Figure 17.53 *This script outputs the coordinates from the mouse click in the image along with the radio button value.*

```
<body>

<a href="moreinfo.html" tabindex="4">About our
company</a>

<h2>Please tell us more about yourself:</h2>

<form method="post" action="showform.php">

<p>Name: <input type="text" name="firstname"
size="20" tabindex="1" /></p>

<p>Email address: <input type="text"
name="email" tabindex="2" /></p>

<p>Hobbies: <input type="text" name="hobbies"
tabindex="3" size="25" /></p>

<p><input type="submit" value="Tell us" /></p>

</form>

</body>
```

Figure 17.54 *By setting the* tabindex, *you control the order in which your visitor can tab through the fields.*

Figure 17.55 *With forms on a page that begins with a link, you may want to change the tab order so that the first tab takes you to the first field, not the first link.*

Setting the Tab Order in a Form

By pressing the Tab key, visitors can move the focus through the fields in your form from top to bottom (and then select the desired one by pressing Return). Depending on your form's layout, you may prefer to set the tab order yourself so that the visitor fills out all the fields in a particular group before going on to the next group.

To set the tab order:

In the form element's tag, type **tabindex="n"**, where *n* is the number that indicates the tab order.

✔ Tips

- *Getting the focus* means the form element is selected but not activated. Activation requires pressing the Return key (or a keyboard shortcut—see page 278).

- The value for tabindex can be any number between 0 and 32767.

- By default, the tab order depends on the order of the elements in the (X)HTML code. When you change the tab order, the lower numbered elements get the focus first, followed by higher numbered elements.

- In a form, you can assign tab order to text fields, password fields, checkboxes, radio buttons, text areas, menus, and buttons.

- You can also assign tab order to links *(see page 113)* and client-side image maps *(see page 117).*

- OK, I cannot tell a lie. Where the first Tab keystroke lands you depends on your browser and how it's configured. On IE 7 it took me 9 tabs to get to the *first* one.

Adding Keyboard Shortcuts

Keyboard shortcuts let your visitors select and activate links without using a mouse.

To add a keyboard shortcut to a form element:

1. Inside the form element's tag, type **accesskey="**.

2. Type the keyboard shortcut (any letter or number).

3. Type the final **"**.

4. If desired, add information about the keyboard shortcut to the text so that the visitor knows that it exists.

✔ Tips

■ Keyboard shortcuts are case-insensitive.

■ On Windows systems, to invoke the keyboard shortcut, visitors use the Alt key plus the letter you've assigned. On Macs, visitors use the Control key.

■ Explorer for Windows has supported keyboard shortcuts since version 4. Firefox and other Gecko browsers support them as well. Opera has its own keyboard navigation system and will ignore yours.

■ When a visitor uses a keyboard shortcut it not only gives the element the focus, but actually activates it. In the case of radio buttons and checkboxes, this means the item is selected. If it's a text box, the cursor is placed inside (after any existing text). If it's a button, the button is activated.

```
<p>Choose any option from the keyboard by
pressing Alt (Ctrl for Macintosh) plus its first letter.
So Alt-W/Ctrl-W would choose
<em>Woody</em> (he's awful cute). (Use "T" for
the comments box.)</p><hr />

<form action="http://www.cookwood.com/cgi-
bin/vote.cgi" method="post">

<input type="radio" name="cats" value="W"
accesskey="w" />Woody<br />

<input type="radio" name="cats" value="C"
accesskey="c" />Cookie<br />

<input type="radio" name="cats" value="X"
accesskey="x" />Xixona<br />

<input type="radio" name="cats" value="L"
accesskey="l" />Llumeta<br />

<input type="radio" name="cats" value="A"
accesskey="a" />All of them (Don't make me
choose!)

<p><textarea name="comments" cols="40"
rows="3" accesskey="t">Any special
comments?</textarea></p>

<p><input type="submit" value="Vote!"
accesskey="v" />
```

Figure 17.56 *Keyboard shortcuts can be especially helpful on mobile devices.*

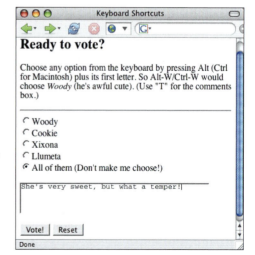

Figure 17.57 *Pressing Ctrl-T (Alt-T on Windows) puts the cursor in the comments box.*

```
<input type="radio" name="cats" value="L"
accesskey="l" onclick=
"document.vote.submit.disabled=false" />Llumeta
<br />

<input type="radio" name="cats" value="A"
accesskey="a" onclick=
"document.vote.submit.disabled=false" />All of
them (Don't make me choose!)

<p><input name="submit" type="submit"
value="Vote!" accesskey="v" disabled="disabled"
/>

<input type="reset" value="Reset" accesskey="r"
onclick="document.vote.submit.disabled=true"
/></p>
```

Figure 17.58 *Here, I use JavaScript and the* disabled *attribute to make the submit button inaccessible until other options are selected.*

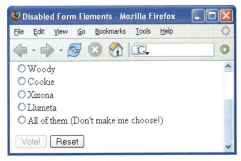

Figure 17.59 *When the visitor first views the form, nothing is selected and the submit button is disabled.*

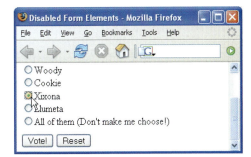

Figure 17.60 *When the visitor chooses an item, the submit button is no longer disabled (thanks to the JavaScript in Figure 17.58).*

Disabling Form Elements

In some cases, you may not want visitors to use certain parts of your form. For example, you might want to disable a submit button until all the required fields have been filled out.

To disable a form element:

In the form element's tag, type **disabled="disabled"**.

✔ Tips

- In HTML, you can just use `disabled` by itself. XHTML requires the redundant value.

- You can change the contents of a disabled form element with a script. For more information on scripting, consult Chapter 19, *Scripts*. You'll also need some JavaScript expertise. The very simple way I've added here is to add **onclick= "document.vote.submit.disabled=false"** to each radio button (where *vote* is the value of the form's `name` attribute, *submit* is the value of the disabled button's `name` attribute, and *disabled* is the attribute in that button whose value I want to change to *false*). So when one of the radio buttons is clicked, the Vote button will be enabled.

- If you disable a form element, its keyboard shortcut is also disabled. For more information on keyboard shortcuts, consult *Adding Keyboard Shortcuts* on page 278.

Keeping Elements from Being Changed

Sometimes it may be necessary to automatically set the contents of a form element and keep the visitor from changing it. For example, you could have the visitor confirm information, or you could show a past history of transactions and then submit that information again with the new data collected. You can do this by making the element "read-only".

To keep elements from being changed:

Type **readonly="readonly"** in the form element's tag.

✔ Tips

■ In HTML, you can just use readonly by itself. XHTML requires the redundant value.

■ You can use the readonly attribute in text boxes, password boxes, checkboxes, radio buttons, and text areas.

■ Setting the readonly attribute is something like using a hidden field without making it hidden. For more information on hidden fields, consult *Creating Hidden Fields* on page 271.

<p><textarea name="votehistory" cols="40" rows="3" readonly="readonly">Woody on Monday, Cookie on Tuesday, Xixona on Thursday, and Llumeta on Wednesday</textarea></p>

Figure 17.61 *Add the* readonly *attribute to any form element that you want to show to your visitors but that you don't want them to change.*

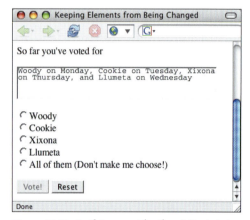

Figure 17.62 *In this example, the visitor's prior votes are displayed in the read-only area. They can be viewed—but not changed—by the visitor and then submitted with the new vote.*

VIDEO, AUDIO, AND OTHER MULTIMEDIA

One of the things that has made the Web so popular is the fact that you can add graphics, sound, animations, and movies to your Web pages. While in the past the prohibitive size of such files limited their effectiveness, newer technologies, like streaming audio and video, along with broadband Internet connections have opened the door for multimedia Web pages.

Some of those multimedia Web pages may serve as a base for an audio or video *podcast*, others may be advertisements or interactive displays. Still other Web pages may take advantage of occasional multimedia files in order to provide a richer experience to their visitors. This chapter will show you how to add multimedia to your Web pages for all these purposes and more.

Because the Web population is so diverse, it can sometimes be tricky ensuring that the files you provide can be viewed and heard by your visitors (or the largest number of them possible). You need to think about the files' format as well as the application—or player—necessary for viewing or listening. The fact that the developers of multimedia technologies can't seem to agree on standards makes it a bit more complicated.

Please note that this chapter is meant to be an introduction to multimedia Web files, with a strong emphasis on the (X)HTML code you need. It does not teach you how to create Flash animations or QuickTime movies, only how to make them available to your visitors.

Of Plugins and Players

A browser application is only capable of showing text and a few kind of images. But there are a lot of different kinds of files out on the Web, including video, audio, PDFs, Flash animations, Scorch sheet music, and even PowerPoint presentations and Excel spreadsheets. In order to play or display these other kinds of files, a browser needs the aid of applications called *players*. There are both external stand-alone players that function as separate programs on your visitor's computer as well as *plugin* players that work right inside the Web page in the browser window.

You determine the kind of player that will be used when you write the (X)HTML code. When you *link* to a multimedia file, as described on page 285, that file is opened in an *external* player. When you *embed* a multimedia file, as described on pages 286–309, the file is opened in the *plugin* within the browser window itself.

The most common plugins are the Flash and Shockwave players from Macromedia (part of Adobe), the QuickTime Player from Apple, the Windows Media Player from Microsoft, and Acrobat from Adobe. However, even these popular players are not installed on every computer—though Flash comes pretty close according to Macromedia. In addition, they are updated so often that visitors may not always have the particular version that your files require.

Object vs. Embed

There are two principal elements used to embed multimedia on a Web page: `object` and `embed`. The `embed` element started out as a Netscape extension and is not and has never been part of the (X)HTML specifications. Any page that contains it is not considered valid. Despite that fact, it continues to be universally supported.

In the other corner, we have the W3C's `object` element, an official component of both HTML 4.01 and XHTML 1.0. Unfortunately, Internet Explorer implements the `object` element in a way that makes other browsers ignore it—in order to use its proprietary ActiveX controls. And if that weren't enough, IE doesn't completely support the `object` element itself, failing—as the (X)HTML specifications require—to look for nested objects that it *can* support when the outer object proves too difficult.

The solution historically has been to offer IE an `object` element in the non-standard way that it requires for its ActiveX controls while at the same time nesting a non-standard `embed` element within the `object` element that the rest of the browser population can handle. Frankly, I think we can do better. In this chapter, I'll show you how to embed without `embed`.

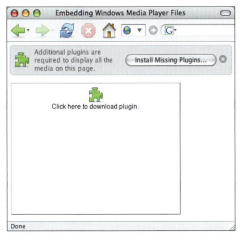

Figure 18.1 *If your visitor tries to view something for which they don't have a compatible plugin, they will generally see a puzzle icon or a broken image. They will also be invited to install the appropriate plugin.*

Figure 18.2 *In Internet Explorer 7 (and later versions of IE 6), the program will ask your visitors each time you want to run an ActiveX control. You can avoid this alert with JavaScript (see page 292).*

Figure 18.3 *When a Web page in IE 7 needs a plugin that's not already installed, IE will generally offer to help to install it. In my experience, though, it is not very good at facilitating the installation of QuickTime, taking a very long time and asking repeatedly if that's really what you want to do. You might want to advise visitors of this issue and offer alternative installation procedures if you have QuickTime movies on your site.*

Getting Players for Your Visitors

When a browser encounters a file it can't open on its own, it goes looking for a player or plugin on the visitor's computer. It doesn't always find one. While browsers often come bundled with one or more players, software developers, always competing for market share, continually come out with new versions. Depending on the file format and extension of your multimedia file, the visitor may have to download a *new* player with which to view it.

On Explorer for Windows, the ActiveX control can automatically install the appropriate plugin without making the visitor close and restart their browser. This is perhaps its major positive feature, although in my experience it's much better at installing Microsoft components than components from other companies. Other browsers will alert your visitor that a new player is required and will direct them to the proper page where the necessary plugin or player can be found, downloaded and installed.

So, to ensure that your visitors can access your multimedia files, you can:

- use standard formats (and perhaps not the very latest version) for which your visitors will likely already have an appropriate plugin or player installed,

- give information about the formats you're using and provide links to the download page for the corresponding players, and, as a last resort,

- offer multiple versions of your files in various formats.

Getting Multimedia Files

The most common multimedia files embedded on Web pages are sounds and videos. You can create sounds with a microphone and digitizing software (like SoundRecorder for Windows and Amadeus for Macintosh). And there are many programs that create MP3s from CDs.

With the advent of digital camcorders, getting video on the Web has gotten easier and easier. On the Mac you have the unbeatable iMovie (preinstalled free on new Macs) which lets you input digital video via the incorporated FireWire port, add special effects and transitions, and then automatically convert it to QuickTime format which is easily embedded on a Web page *(see page 286)*. Folks with Windows XP can use Windows Movie Maker. One good resource for information is *Secrets of Podcasting*, Second Edition, by Bart G. Farkas.

You can also find sounds and movies on the Web, although you should read the corresponding license agreements carefully. I'll show you how to embed videos from Google Video and YouTube on page 306.

But don't limit yourself to sounds and video. You can also embed Flash animations (with Macromedia Flash), PDF files (created with Adobe Acrobat), playable sheet music (with Sibelius Scorch), Java applets (with Sun's Java), and much more.

```
<a href="http://www.sarahsnotecards.com/
catalunyalive/segadors.mov"><img src="http://
www.sarahsnotecards.com/catalunyalive/
segadors.jpg" alt="Els Segadors, the singing of the
Catalan National Anthem" width="319"
height="241"></a>
```

Figure 18.4 *The link to the movie encloses a still image.*

Figure 18.5 *When the visitor clicks the image...*

Figure 18.6 *...the video opens, loads, and plays automatically in a separate browser window (notice the gray background) in an embedded player (as long as one is available).*

Linking to Multimedia Files

The easiest and fastest way to give your visitors access to multimedia files is by creating a link to the file. Links have several advantages. First, your visitor gets to choose whether to load a potentially large file or not. Second, the file will open in any compatible player the visitor has available, not just the one you chose, making it more likely the visitor won't have to download any special software.

To link to multimedia files:

1. Create a multimedia file and upload it to your server.

2. Type **<a href="multimedia.ext">**, where *multimedia.ext* is the location, name, and extension of the multimedia file.

3. Type the text or insert an image that the visitor will click on to activate the link.

4. Type **</a>** to complete the link.

✔ Tips

- You may wish to also include information about players with which they can view the file and a link to the download page.

- On most browsers, if the visitor has an appropriate plugin installed, the multimedia file will be opened in a new window with an embedded player. If the visitor does not have an appropriate plugin but does have a player, the linked file is opened in the external player. And, if there is neither a plugin nor a player available, most browsers will let visitors download the file and/or choose another program with which to open it.

- You can create links to songs in iTunes Music Store. Go to *http://www.apple.com/ itunes/linkmaker* and the program will generate the link for you.

Linking to Multimedia Files

Embedding QuickTime Movies for Windows

QuickTime is Apple's high-quality video format. There are free QuickTime players available for both Macintosh and Windows. Many movie studios use QuickTime for uploading their movie trailers to the Internet.

In this section, I'll teach you how to insert a QuickTime movie that will play in Internet Explorer for Windows. We'll get to the rest of the browsers on page 288.

To embed a QuickTime movie on your Web page for Internet Explorer:

1. Create a movie and save it in QuickTime format with the .mov extension.

2. In your Web page, where you want the movie to appear, begin the `object` element for IE for Windows by typing **<object classid= "clsid:02bf25d5-8c17-4b23-bc80-d3488abddc6b" codebase= "http://www.apple.com/qtactivex/qtplugin.cab"**.

3. Next, without closing the initial `object` tag yet, type **width="w" height="h"**, where *w* and *h* are the desired width and height, in pixels, of the box that will hold the movie.

4. Type **>** to complete the initial `object` tag.

5. Next, type **<param name="src" value="filename.mov">**, where *filename.mov* is the URL of your movie file.

6. Type **<param name="autoplay" value="false">**, to keep the movie from starting automatically when the visitor jumps to this page (IE 7 doesn't properly autoplay QuickTime movies—unless you use JavaScript, see page 292—and it looks better if you don't even let it try.)

```
<body>

 <object classid="clsid:02bf25d5-8c17-4b23-
 bc80-d3488abddc6b"
 codebase="http://www.apple.com/qtactivex/
 qtplugin.cab" width="320" height="256">

   <param name="src" value="http://
 www.sarahsnotecards.com/catalunyalive/
 diables.mov">

   <param name="controller" value="true" >

   <param name="autoplay" value="false">

   </object>

</body>
```

Figure 18.7 *This is the way Internet Explorer requires the* `object` *element to be used. Unfortunately, the use of a long (awful) number for the* `classid` *attribute (which calls Internet Explorer's proprietary ActiveX technology) is completely non-standard and causes standards-loving browsers to ignore the* `object` *element.*

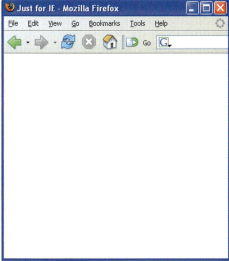

Figure 18.8 *The movie works fine for Internet Explorer (top) but doesn't appear at all in standards-loving browsers like Firefox for Windows (below).*

7. If you want control buttons to appear under the movie, type **<param name= "controller" value="true"**. Or use a value of `false` to hide the controls (in which case you better use `true` in step 6).

8. Insert more parameters as desired as described on pages 294–299.

9. Complete the `object` element by typing **</object>**.

✔ Tips

■ Apple recommends using JavaScript to call QuickTime movies for Internet Explorer. For more details and instructions, see page 292.

■ Create a template file site in order to save yourself from typing that incredible classid. What were they thinking?

■ You can find the size of the movie in the QuickTime player by choosing Window > Show Movie Info (and clicking the triangle, if necessary).

■ The height and width determine the size of the box that contains the movie. If the box is too small, the movie will be cropped (or scaled if you've set a scale factor—page 294). If the box is too big, there will be empty space around it.

■ You should include an additional 16 pixels in the `height` to allow for the play, rewind, and other buttons.

■ The default value for `autoplay` is defined by visitors in their QuickTime settings. The default value for `controller` is true.

■ Many QuickTime parameters are discussed on the following pages for adjusting the playback of your movies. For a complete list, see *HTML Scripting Guide for QuickTime* on Apple's site.

Embedding QuickTime Movies for Windows

Embedding QuickTime Movies for Everyone besides IE

All major browsers except Internet Explorer (from version 5.5 and up) use the standard object tag in a standard way. I'll describe it here. On page 290 we'll see how to combine this method with the IE method discussed earlier so that *all* browsers can see your video.

To embed QuickTime movies for everyone besides IE:

1. Create your QuickTime movie, save it in .mov format, and upload it to your server.

2. Begin the object for standards loving browsers by typing **<object**.

3. Indicate what kind of file the movie is by typing **type="video/quicktime"**.

4. Specify the movie's location on the Internet by typing **data="filename.mov"**.

5. Still without closing the initial object tag, type **width="w" height="h"**, where *w* and *h* are the desired width and height, respectively, in pixels, of the box that will hold the movie.

6. To give the location of the QuickTime player to visitors who don't yet have it installed, type **codebase="http://www.apple.com/quicktime/download"**

7. Finally, close the initial object tag by typing **>** (the right angle bracket).

8. Next type **<param name="autoplay" value="false" />** to keep QuickTime from starting until the visitor clicks the play button.

9. Type **<param name="controller" value="true" />** to have the controls appear below the movie.

10. Type **</object>** to complete the object.

```
<body>

<object type="video/quicktime"
data="http://www.sarahsnotecards.com/
catalunyalive/diables.mov" width="320"
height="256">

    <param name="autoplay" value="false" />

    <param name="controller" value="true" />

</object>

</body>
```

Figure 18.9 *The standard implementation of the* object *element includes a* type *that indicates the MIME type of the multimedia file, a* data *attribute with the URL of the file, the* width *and* height, *and one or more parameters.*

Figure 18.10 *Now we've got a movie showing in standards-loving browsers like Firefox.*

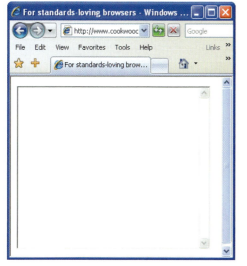

Figure 18.11 *But Internet Explorer does not support the standard implementation of the* object *element.*

✔ Tips

■ It really gets my goat that IE's non-standard use of the object tag used to force standards-loving browsers that did support object to give it up in favor of the non-standard embed tag. The embed element has never been part of the HTML standards. Pages containing it will not validate. That said, almost all pages with multimedia files, until now, have been forced to use it. No more.

■ On the next page, we will see how to combine the two methods so that all browsers can see your movies.

■ You can find the dimensions of the movie in the QuickTime player by choosing Window > Show Movie Info (and clicking the triangle, if necessary).

■ The height and width determine the size of the box that contains the movie. If the box is too small, the movie will be cropped (or scaled if you've set a scale factor—page 294). If the box is too big, there will be empty space around it.

■ You should include an additional 16 pixels in the height to allow for the controllers.

■ The default value for autoplay is defined by the visitor in their QuickTime settings. The default value for controller is true.

■ If you use true for the autoplay parameter, your video will start loading and playing when your visitor opens your page. You might want to make sure the video isn't too loud (or too big).

■ Many QuickTime parameters are discussed on the following pages for adjusting the playback of your movies. For a complete list, see *HTML Scripting Guide for QuickTime* on Apple's site.

Embedding QuickTime Movies for Everyone

Embedding QuickTime Movies for All

Here's the problem: Internet Explorer (from version 5.5 up) uses the standard object element in way that is so non-standard, it makes all standards-loving browsers ignore it. Luckily the object element is designed to be nested. If the outer layer doesn't work in a particular browser, the browser is supposed to try the second layer. If the second layer doesn't work, the browser should try the third layer, and so on.

So we should be able to use the outer object for IE and an inner one for other browsers. But Internet Explorer gets this wrong too. Even if you serve it the object element that it likes, it will continue to try (and fail in an obvious and annoying way) with the nested object elements. The solution is to hide the nested elements from IE. I recommend using Internet Explorer's *conditional comments* for this step.

To embed QuickTime movies for all major browsers:

1. First we'll follow the instructions for inserting QuickTime movies for Internet Explorer, as described on page 286.

2. Just before the final </object> element, use Internet Explorer's conditional commenting to hide the rest of your code from IE for Windows so that it doesn't erroneously display two object elements, by typing **<!--[if !IE]>-->**.

3. Next, follow the instructions for inserting QuickTime movies for standards-loving browsers (as described on page 288.).

4. Type **<!--<![endif]-->** to stop hiding content from Internet Explorer. That's it!
(Figure 18.14)

```
<body>
 <object classid="clsid:02bf25d5-8c17-4b23-
bc80-d3488abddc6b"  codebase=
"http://www.apple.com/qtactivex/qtplugin.cab"
width="320" height="256">
    <param name="src" value= "http://
www.sarahsnotecards.com/catalunyalive/
diables.mov" />
    <param name="controller" value="true" />
    <param name="autoplay" value="false" />

<object type="video/quicktime" data= "http://
www.sarahsnotecards.com/catalunyalive/
diables.mov" width="320" height="256">
    <param name="autoplay" value="false" />
    <param name="controller" value="true" />
</object>

</object>
</body>
```

Figure 18.12 *The* object *element is designed to be nested. If a browser doesn't support the outer element, it should look at the inner ones until it finds one it likes.*

Figure 18.13 *Internet Explorer shows the first movie and instead of ignoring the second object element, tries (and fails miserably) to display it as well. The result is that ghost movie at the bottom of the screen.*

```
<body>
 <object classid="clsid:02bf25d5-8c17-4b23-
bc80-d3488abddc6b" codebase=
"http://www.apple.com/qtactivex/qtplugin.cab"
width="320" height="256">
    <param name="src" value= "http://
www.sarahsnotecards.com/catalunyalive/
diables.mov" />
    <param name="controller" value="true" />
    <param name="autoplay" value="false" />
<!--[if !IE]>-->
<object type="video/quicktime" data= "http://
www.sarahsnotecards.com/catalunyalive/
diables.mov" width="320" height="256">
    <param name="autoplay" value="false" />
    <param name="controller" value="true" />
</object>
<!--<![endif]-->
</object>
</body>
```

Figure 18.14 *I recommend using IE's conditional comments (adapted as shown here so that they validate) to hide the second* object *element from IE.*

✔ Tips

■ The typical method for serving Quick-Time movies (and any other multimedia file) to both IE and the rest of the world has usually involved the embed element, as described on page 302 with respect to Windows Media Player. You can still do that with QuickTime too, but it won't validate.

■ You can find more information about IE's conditional comments on Microsoft's site: *http://msdn.microsoft.com/workshop/ author/dhtml/overview/ccomment_ovw.asp*

■ Microsoft's conditional comments actually don't validate (surprise) when used as they were originally designed. Thankfully, a guy named Lachlan Hunt figured out a way to write IE conditional comments in a way that makes them validate (as used in this technique).

Figure 18.15 *Once we hide the second* object *from IE (left), no ghostly apparitions appear. Standards-loving browsers like Firefox on the right continue properly ignoring the first* object *and properly displaying the second* object *as usual.*

Embedding QuickTime Movies for All

Using JavaScript to Call a Movie

Apple currently recommends using JavaScript to call movies. It all started because a company called Eolas sued Microsoft for making ActiveX components automatic. In January of 2006, Microsoft changed IE so that users had to click to activate ActiveX controls (like the QuickTime plugin). Although QuickTime movies should play in the background even without clicking (like Windows Media Player files do), they don't. Apple found that you can get QuickTime movies to play without user activation if you call the movie with JavaScript as shown here.

To use JavaScript to call a QuickTime movie:

1. Create a new text file for your JavaScript script.

2. In the JavaScript text file, type **function InsertSampleMovie() {** to begin the script.

3. Next, type **document.write('html');**, where *html* is the code for your movie (e.g., the `object` elements as described on pages 286–291) with absolutely no carriage returns **(Figure 18.16)**.

4. Finally, type **}** to complete the script.

5. Save the file in text-only format with the .js extension.

6. In the head section of your Web page, type **<script src="movie.js" type= "text/javascript"></script>**, where *movie.js* is the location on the server of the script that you created in steps 1–5.

7. In the place on your Web page where you want the movie to be embedded, type **<script language= "JavaScript" type= "text/javascript" > InsertSampleMovie( ); </script>**.

```
function InsertSampleMovie() {

document.write('<object classid="clsid:02bf25d5-
8c17-4b23-bc80-d3488abddc6b"
codebase="http://www.apple.com/qtactivex/
qtplugin.cab" width="320" height="256">
<param name="src"
value="http://www.sarahsnotecards.com/
catalunyalive/diables.mov" /> <param
name="controller" value="true" /> <param
name="autoplay" value="true" /> <!--[if !IE]>-->
<object type="video/quicktime"
data="http://www.sarahsnotecards.com/
catalunyalive/diables.mov"  width="320"
height="256"> <param name="autoplay"
value="true" /> <param name="controller"
value="true" /> </object> <!--<![endif]-->
</object> ');

}
```

Figure 18.16 *Here is the minimalist JavaScript: define the function, write out all the (X)HTML code for the movie, including any nested objects and conditional comments, being sure to omit all carriage returns and single quotes, and then close the function with a }.*

```
function InsertSampleMovie() {

document.write('<object classid="clsid:02bf25d5-
8c17-4b23-bc80-d3488abddc6b"
codebase="http://www.apple.com/qtactivex/
qtplugin.cab" width="320" height="256"> ');

document.write('<param name="src"
value="http://www.sarahsnotecards.com/
catalunyalive/diables.mov" /> ');

document.write('<param name="controller"
value="true" /> ');

document.write('<param name="autoplay"
value="true" /> ');

...

}
```

Figure 18.17 *If you like, you can create multiple* `document.write` *lines for each (X)HTML element. Be careful with your punctuation (see tip 3).*

```
<head>

    <title>Calling a QuickTime movie with
JavaScript</title>

<script src="http://www.cookwood.com/
html6ed/examples/multimedia/jsmovie.js"
type="text/javascript"></script>

</head>

<body>

<p>Watch out, this one uses
<code>autoplay</code>...</p>

<script language="JavaScript" type=
"text/javascript" >InsertSampleMovie();</script>

</body>

</html>
```

Figure 18.18 *In the Web page, you have to load the script in the head section and then call the function where you want the movie to appear.*

Figure 18.19 *The movie will open in all browsers with JavaScript activated and will autoplay even in Internet Explorer for Windows.*

✔ Tips

■ The method for inserting QuickTime movies that I give earlier in this chapter works fine for QuickTime movies except if you want them to autoload in IE 7 for Windows. In that case, I recommend going the JavaScript way. The JavaScript method also saves visitors from having to click to activate the ActiveX control.

■ About 6% of Internet users currently surf without JavaScript (see *http://www.the-counter.com/stats/*). Those folks won't be able to view movies called with this method.

■ If you'd rather not make one long endless line in step 3, you can divide the (X)HTML code up into various lines of JavaScript code. Each line of JavaScript code must start on its own line, begin with **document.write('** (no space, left parenthesis, single quote), followed by any amount of (X)HTML code, including white space but absolutely no returns or single quotation marks, followed by the **');** (single quote, right parenthesis, semi-colon) and a return **(Figure 18.17)**.

■ According to Microsoft, multimedia in ActiveX controls that requires no interaction should continue to function. That is, QuickTime movies should be able to load in the background and autoplay— with no clicking required. Unfortunately, that does not happen in Internet Explorer for Windows (I'm getting tired of typing "surprise!") even though it does work like that for Windows Media Player files. Seems like a conspiracy to me.

■ For inserting multiple movies, see *http://developer.apple.com/internet/ ieembedprep.html*. Or even better, Geoff Stearns' SWFObject: *http:// blog.deconcept.com/swfobject/*

Scaling a QuickTime Movie

You can adjust the size of a QuickTime movie in the (X)HTML code.

To scale a QuickTime movie:

Within each `object` element, type **<param name="scale" value="factor" />**, where *factor* is:

> **to fit**, if you want the movie to be reduced or expanded to fit its box.

> Or **aspect**, if you want the movie to be reduced or expanded to fit its box while maintaining its original proportions.

> Or **n**, where *n* is the number with which the original height and width of the movie will be multiplied to get the final height and width.

✔ Tips

■ You may wish to also adjust the height and width of the movie's box *(see page 286)*.

■ The `scale` parameter changes the size of the movie, not the size of the movie's box, which you specified with the `height` and `width` attributes. If you use a numerical scale factor and the box is too small or too big, the movie will be cropped, or empty space will appear around the movie **(Figure 18.21)**.

■ If you make the box smaller than the movie, the scale parameter gives you control over how the movie should be adjusted to fit. If you don't specify the scale parameter, the movie is simply cropped.

■ If you're using two `object` elements (as I recommend), remember to add the `param` elements to both.

```
<object classid="clsid:02bf25d5-8c17-4b23-
bc80-d3488abddc6b" codebase=
"http://www.apple.com/qtactivex/qtplugin.cab"
width="320" height="256">
    <param name="src" value=
"http://www.sarahsnotecards.com/catalunyalive/
segadors.mov" />
    <param name="controller" value="true" />
    <param name="autoplay" value="false" />
    <param name="scale" value=".7" />

<!--[if !IE]>-->
<object type="video/quicktime" data=
"http://www.sarahsnotecards.com/catalunyalive/
segadors.mov" width="320" height="256">
    <param name="autoplay" value="false" />
    <param name="controller" value="true" />
    <param name="scale" value=".7" />
</object>
```

Figure 18.20 *I've made the movie smaller by a scale of .7.*

Figure 18.21 *The movie is reduced to 70% of its original size, but notice how the movie's box is still controlled by the* `width` *and* `height` *attributes which I haven't changed.*

```
<object classid="clsid:02bf25d5-8c17-4b23-
bc80-d3488abddc6b" codebase=
"http://www.apple.com/qtactivex/qtplugin.cab"
width="320" height="256">
    <param name="src" value=
"http://www.sarahsnotecards.com/catalunyalive/
segadors.mov" />
    <param name="controller" value="true" />
    <param name="autoplay" value="false" />
    <param name="scale" value=".7" />
    <param name="bgcolor" value="yellow" />

<!--[if !IE]>-->
<object type="video/quicktime" data=
"http://www.sarahsnotecards.com/catalunyalive/
segadors.mov" width="320" height="256">
    <param name="autoplay" value="false" />
    <param name="controller" value="true" />
    <param name="scale" value=".7" />
    <param name="bgcolor" value="yellow" />
```

Figure 18.22 *The* bgcolor *attribute is only used if the movie is smaller than the height and width you've specified.*

Figure 18.23 *Now the background is bright yellow instead of dull gray. I think it's an improvement.*

Changing the Movie's Background Color

When we reduced the size of the movie on the previous page, its background became visible (and ugly). You can change the background color to make it more attractive (or to make it disappear).

To change the movie's background color:

Within each object element, type **<param name="bgcolor" value="color" />**, where *color* is one of the sixteen predefined values or a hexadecimal representation of a color *(see page 126 and the inside back cover).*

✔ Tips

- To get rid of the background altogether, either adjust the height and width so they match the size of the movie or match the background to the page's background color.

- If you make the frame just slightly larger than the movie, the bgcolor can look like an attractive border.

- If you're using two object elements (as I recommend), remember to add the param elements to both.

Changing the Movie's Background Color

Looping a QuickTime Movie

You can make a QuickTime Movie play over and over again.

To loop a QuickTime movie:

Within each `object` element, type **<param name="loop" value="option">**, where *option* is `true` if you want the movie to loop continuously, `false` if you want the movie to play just once and `palindrome` if you want the movie to play forwards and then backwards, continuously.

✔ Tips

- The default value for the `loop` parameter is `false`.

- If you're using two `object` elements (as I recommend), remember to add the `param` elements to both.

```
<object classid="clsid:02bf25d5-8c17-4b23-
bc80-d3488abddc6b"  codebase=
"http://www.apple.com/qtactivex/qtplugin.cab"
width="320" height="256">
    <param name="src" value=
"http://www.sarahsnotecards.com/catalunyalive/
segadors.mov" />
    <param name="controller" value="true" />
    <param name="autoplay" value="false" />
    <param name="loop" value="true" />

<!--[if !IE]>-->
<object type="video/quicktime" data=
"http://www.sarahsnotecards.com/catalunyalive/
segadors.mov" width="320" height="256">
    <param name="autoplay" value="false" />
    <param name="controller" value="true" />
    <param name="loop" value="true" />
</object>
```

Figure 18.24 *Don't forget to add the* `param` *element within both* `object` *elements.*

Figure 18.25 *With a* `loop` *value of* `true`, *the movie automatically starts over when it reaches the end. Notice that I returned the movie to its original size.*

```
<object classid="clsid:02bf25d5-8c17-4b23-
bc80-d3488abddc6b"
codebase="http://www.apple.com/qtactivex/
qtplugin.cab" width="320" height="256">
  <param name="src" value="http://
www.sarahsnotecards.com/catalunyalive/
segadors-preview.mov" />
    <param name="controller" value="false" />
    <param name="autoplay" value="true" />
    <param name="loop" value="true" />
    <param name="href" value=
"http://www.sarahsnotecards.com/catalunyalive/
segadors.mov" />
      <param name="target" value="myself" />
      <param name="bgcolor" value="white" />

<!--[if !IE]>-->
```

Figure 18.26 *Since the preview has no controls, I've added the* `bgcolor param` *element to hide the extra space until the main movie needs it.*

Figure 18.27 *The preview movie will loop until the visitor clicks. Then the regular movie will play.*

Offering a Preview Movie

One of the nice features of QuickTime is that you can offer a preview movie (also called a *poster movie*). This can be a single JPEG image or just a shortened version of your movie. Your full-length version will be played when the visitor clicks on the preview movie.

To offer a preview movie:

1. Create a single frame or shortened version of your movie. Save it in QuickTime format with the .mov extension and upload it to your server.

2. Insert the *preview.mov* file on your page in the usual fashion.

3. Use **<param name="controller" value="false" />** to hide the controller.

4. Type **<param name="href" value="fullmovie.mov" />**, where *fullmovie.mov* is the full-length version of your movie.

5. Type **<param name="target" value="myself" />** so that the full movie plays in the same space as the preview.

6. Type **<param name="autohref" value="true" />** if you want the full-length movie to load even before the visitor clicks the preview (so that it's ready to play when they do click on it).

✔ Tips

■ If you're using two `object` elements, be sure to add the parameters for each one separately.

■ Preview or poster movies are like thumbnail images—they give a taste of what the visitor will find in the full length version but don't take as long to download. Keep your previews short, small, and perhaps silent.

Offering a Preview Movie

Adding Attributes to Secondary Movies

When you set a `param` element, it always affects the movie specified by the `src` or `data` elements. Sometimes, however, you may want to control the attributes for a movie specified with the `href` parameter that we saw on the previous page, or with the `qtnext` parameter that we'll see on the next page. You do this with a rather convoluted system called *URL extensions*.

To add attributes to secondary movies:

1. Insert **<** (the code for the less than sign) before the URL for the secondary movie.

2. Add **>** (the code for the greater than sign) after the URL for the secondary movie.

3. Then, after the > code, type **T<place>**, where *place* specifies where the movie should be targeted.

4. After the target, type **E<name=value**, where *name* is the name of the parameter and *value* is the desired value for the secondary movie.

5. Separate each additional parameter pair with a space.

6. Type **>** to complete the set of parameter pairs.

✔ Tip

■ You can use regular less than and greater than signs instead of the corresponding escaped codes, but your page won't validate.

```
<object classid="clsid:02bf25d5-8c17-4b23-
bc80-d3488abddc6b"
codebase="http://www.apple.com/qtactivex/
qtplugin.cab" width="320" height="256">
    <param name="src" value="http://
www.sarahsnotecards.com/catalunyalive/
segadors-preview.mov" />
    <param name="controller" value="false" />
    <param name="autoplay" value="true" />
    <param name="loop" value="true" />
    <param name="href" value=
"&lt;http://www.sarahsnotecards.com/
catalunyalive/segadors.mov&gt; T&lt;myself&gt;
E&lt;loop=true&gt;" />
    <param name="target" value="myself" />
    <param name="bgcolor" value="white" />

<!--[if !IE]-->
```

Figure 18.28 *It's pretty ugly. Just remember to surround the URL with escaped less than and greater than signs, followed by the letter T and the target name surrounded by those escapes, and then finally the letter E and the parameters also duly enclosed.*

Figure 18.29 *Now the main movie will loop after it finishes playing.*

```
<object classid="clsid:02bf25d5-8c17-4b23-
bc80-d3488abddc6b"
codebase="http://www.apple.com/qtactivex/
qtplugin.cab" width="320" height="256">
   <param name="src" value="http://
www.sarahsnotecards.com/catalunyalive/
segadors.mov" />
   <param name="controller" value="true" />
   <param name="autoplay" value="false" />
   <param name="qtnext1"
value="&lt;http://www.sarahsnotecards.com/
catalunyalive/littledevil.mov&gt; T&lt;myself&gt;
E&lt;autoplay=true autohref=true&gt;" />
   <param name="target" value="myself" />

<!--[if !IE]>-->
```

Figure 18.30 *Those hideously ugly URL extensions in the* qtnext1 *value (described in more detail on the previous page) ensure that the sequel will appear in the same window as the main movie and that it will start playing and loading automatically.*

Figure 18.31 *Now the sequel will play after the main movie finishes.*

Offering a Sequel

You can specify a second, third, and subsequent movies that should play once the first movie is finished.

To offer a sequel:

1. Insert the movie as described earlier.

2. Within both `object` elements for the movie, type **<param name="qtnext1" value="sequel1.mov" />**, where *sequel1.mov* is the first movie that should play after the base movie (along with any URL extensions as described on the previous page).

3. Repeat step 2, changing the number of the `qtnext` parameter for each sequel.

✔ Tips

■ You can also use a *goto* number for the value of the `qtnext` parameter. The base movie (specified by the `src` and `data` attributes) is `goto0` (`goto` followed by the number 0). Any movie specified with a `qtnext` parameter is `goto` plus that number. For example, if you want to play the main movie again after the first sequel, use **<param name="qtnext2" value= "goto0" />**. And then if you want the sequel to play again after that, use **<param name="qtnext3" value= "goto1" />**. And so on.

■ Since the sequel has to load in order to play, it can sometimes seem like nothing is happening after the main movie is finished. One solution might be to serve a very short preview of the sequel, with a message that the sequel might take a moment to load.

Embedding MP3 Audio on a Page

The MP3 compression format is the de facto standard for audio files on the Web. One way to embed MP3 audio tracks right in your Web page is to use the QuickTime player for playback.

To embed MP3 audio on a page:

1. Save your audio tracks in MP3 format. You can use iTunes to convert AIFF files to MP3.

2. Follow the instructions for putting regular QuickTime movies on a page *(see pages 286–293)* using `audio/mpeg` for the `type` attribute in the second object.

3. Use a value of 16 for the height of your controller.

4. For the width, use:

   a value of 17 for just a play button **(Figure 18.34)**.

   a value of 33 to add a plug-in pop-up menu button to the play button **(Figure 18.35)**.

   a value of 49 to add a volume button to the other two **(Figure 18.37)**.

   a value higher than 74 to add a progress bar to the other three **(Figure 18.38)**.

   a value of 106 to add fast forward and rewind buttons to the other four **(Figure 18.40)**.

✔ Tips

- I recommend setting the `autoplay` parameters to false. But that's only because I hate it when I go to a site and it blares music at me. Especially when my husband is sleeping.

```
<object classid="clsid:02bf25d5-8c17-4b23-
bc80-d3488abddc6b"
codebase="http://www.apple.com/qtactivex/
qtplugin.cab" width="49" height="16">
    <param name="src"
value="http://www.sarahsnotecards.com/
catalunyalive/segadors.mp3" />
    <param name="controller" value="true" />
    <param name="autoplay" value="false" />

<!--[if !IE]>-->
```

Figure 18.32 *To determine which buttons appear on your page, adjust the* `width` *attribute of the* `object` *elements.*

Figure 18.33 *I've got two MP3 files on this page with just the first three buttons. As with other QuickTime files, Internet Explorer for Windows (top) reads the first* `object` *element while standards-loving browsers like Firefox (below) use the second.*

Figure 18.34 *The play button appears alone when you use width values between 17 (shown) and 32.*

Figure 18.35 *The plugin pop-up menu button is added to the play button when you set the width to 33 (shown here) or more.*

Figure 18.36 *If you use an intermediate value, like a width of 40 (shown here), you get extra space between the buttons.*

Figure 18.37 *When you use a width of 49 (shown here) or more, you get a volume button.*

Figure 18.38 *From 74 pixels on (shown here), you get a progress bar.*

Figure 18.39 *If you use a value between 74 and 105, the progress bar grows accordingly. (Here, the width is 90.)*

Figure 18.40 *At a width of 106 pixels, the fast forward and reverse buttons appear.*

Figure 18.41 *You can make the controller as wide as you wish. Any extra pixels after 106 are added to the progress bar. (This controller is 150 pixels wide.)*

■ You can hide the plug-in pop-up menu by adding **<param name="kioskmode" value="true" />** to the object elements, thereby making it a bit harder (but not impossible) for people to copy your MP3s. In that case, you'll have to adjust the widths accordingly.

■ If you use intermediate values other than the ones I've specified, you'll get more space between the buttons **(Figure 18.36)**.

■ Widths higher than 74 will make the progress bar wider, except when the fast forward and rewind buttons appear at width 106 **(Figures 18.39, 18.40, and 18.41)**.

■ You can hide the controller altogether by using **<param name="hidden" value="true" />**. While you might think you could just set the controller parameter itself to false, that option is really intended for hiding the controller under video. If you try to set an audio controller parameter to false, you'll get an empty gray box with the dimensions you specified for height and width. Apple does not recommend setting those to 0.

■ If you do hide your controller, say, to create background sound, remember to set the autoplay parameter to true. Otherwise, there won't be any way for your visitors to hear your MP3s.

■ Explorer will hide the controller if you use the hidden parameter, but it leaves an empty space for it. (Thanks a lot!) Since Apple cautions against using a height less than 2 pixels due to problems in some browsers, my recommendation would be to either use a value of 3 pixels (!) or put the hidden sound at the end of your (X)HTML page where it won't mess up your layout.

Embedding MP3 Audio on a Page

Embedding Windows Media, Part 1

Microsoft's suggested way of embedding Windows format movies and sounds on your Web page still requires the use of the old non-standard embed tag—if you want it to work in anything besides Internet Explorer for Windows. I'll show you how to embed it in a standards-compliant way on page 304.

To embed Windows Media Player files:

1. Create the desired movie or sound.

2. In your (X)HTML document, type **<object classid="clsid:6bf52a52-394a-11d3-b153-00c04f79faa6" id="player"**.

3. Next type **width="w" height="h"**, where *w* and *h* are the size in pixels of the media player that you'd like to embed.

4. Type **>** to complete the initial object tag.

5. To tell the player where the media file is, type **<param name="url" value= "movie.wmv">**, where *movie.wmv* is the name and extension of the movie file.

6. If desired, you can type **<param name= "autostart" value="false">** in order to keep the file from playing automatically. The default is true.

7. If desired, you can type **<param name="showcontrols" value="false">** to hide the play, rewind and other control buttons. The default value is true.

8. For browsers besides Internet Explorer, type **<embed type="application/x-mplayer2" id="MediaPlayer"** to tell them what to expect.

9. Next type **src="http://movie.wmv"**, where *movie.wmv* is the location, name, and extension of the movie file.

```
<p>Listen to Barcelona street sounds:</p>

<body>

<object classid="clsid:6bf52a52-394a-11d3-
b153-00c04f79faa6" id="player"  width="320"
height="260" >

   <param name="url" value="http://
www.sarahsnotecards.com/catalunyalive/
fishstore.wmv" />

      <param name="showcontrols" value="true" />

      <param name="autostart" value="true" />

<embed type="application/x-mplayer2" id=
"MediaPlayer" src="http://www.sarahsnotecards.
com/catalunyalive/fishstore.wmv" width=320
height=240 autostart="true" showcontrols="false"
/>

</object>
```

Figure 18.42 *Microsoft recommends using the* object *element in a non-standard way and the non-standard* embed *element.*

Figure 18.43 *The Windows Media Player is embedded in the page.*

Figure 18.44 *If your visitor does not already have Windows Media Player on their computer, they will be invited to install it.*

Figure 18.45 *Once the plugin is installed, the movie is displayed properly.*

10. Type **width="w" height="h">**, where w and h are the dimensions in pixels of your movie file.

11. If you want the movie to start playing automatically, type **autostart="true"**.

12. If you want to hide the control buttons, type **showcontrols="false"**.

13. Type **/>** to complete the embed element.

✔ Tips

■ The default format for movies for the Windows Media Player is *wmv*.

■ The classid is hideous but not case sensitive.

■ The embed tag is non-standard but very well supported by most major browsers. It's the only way I've found to embed a Windows Media Player in the Microsoft-sanctioned way (e.g., with the classid attribute) into non-Explorer browsers. (But I still hate it.) I'll show you another way to embed Windows Media Player files on page 304.

■ You can personalize the Windows Media Player with custom skins and scripting. See Microsoft's site for details.

■ Another alternative to using the embed element would be to use a second object element to set up a QuickTime version of the movie in QuickTime format for standards-loving browsers.

■ QuickTime can't view WMV files on its own, though it can view them with Flip4Mac (*http://www.flip4mac.com*).

Embedding Windows Media, Part 1

Embedding Windows Media, Part 2

Microsoft would like you to embed Windows Media with the `classid` attribute that calls the ActiveX control. That `classid` attribute, because it is non-standard, causes other browser to ignore the `object`. While I was researching this chapter, I discovered a new, standards-compliant way of embedding Window Media files that works on all major browsers, except Safari 2.

To embed Windows Media in a standards-compliant way:

1. Begin the movie by typing **<object**.

2. Specify the MIME type for Windows Media File movies by entering **type="video/x-ms-wmv"**.

3. Indicate the name and location of the movie on your server with **data="filename.wmv"**.

4. Specify the dimensions of your movie in pixels with **width="w" height="h"**.

5. Complete the opening `object` tag with **>**.

6. Help IE and Safari 1 find the movie by reiterating its URL by typing **<param name="src" value= "filename.wmv" />**, where *filename.wmv* matches what you used in step 3.

7. Add other `param` elements as desired.

8. Complete the `object` element with **</object>**.

✔ Tip

- This technique works in Internet Explorer, Firefox, Opera and Safari 1 (but unfortunately not Safari 2).

```
<body>

<object type="video/x-ms-wmv" data=
"http://www.sarahsnotecards.com/catalunyalive/
fishstore.wmv" width="320" height="260" >

<param name="src" value="http://
www.sarahsnotecards.com/catalunyalive/
fishstore.wmv" />

<param name="autostart" value="true" />

<param name="controller" value="true" />

<param name="qtsrcdontusebrowser"
value="true" />

<param name="enablejavascript" value="true" />

<a href="http://www.sarahsnotecards.com/
catalunyalive/fishstore.wmv">Movie of a Fish Store
in Barcelona</a>

</object>
```

Figure 18.46 *If you omit the Microsoft-specific* `classid` *attribute, and add the proper MIME type, you can use just the standard* `object` *element to embed Windows Media Files.*

Figure 18.47 *The Windows Media Player is embedded in the page.*

```
<head>
<title>Embed Flash Movie</title>
</head>
<body>
<object type="application/x-shockwave-flash"
data="http://www.sarahsnotecards.com/
catalunyalive/minipalau.swf" width="300"
height="240">

<param name="movie" value="http://
www.sarahsnotecards.com/catalunyalive/
minipalau.swf" />

</object>
</body>
```

Figure 18.48 *To embed Flash, set the MIME type to* `application/x-shockwave-flash`.

Figure 18.49 *The Flash animation is embedded on the page—without the nonstandard* `embed`.

Embedding Flash

Flash is an animated image format from Macromedia (now part of Adobe) that is widely used on the Web.

To embed Flash:

1. Begin the `object` element with **<object**.

2. Use **type="application/x-shockwave-flash"** to indicate the MIME type for Flash animations.

3. Type **data="filename.swf"**, where *filename.swf* is the name and location of the Flash animation on your server.

4. Specify the dimensions of your animation with **width="w" height="h"**, where *w* and *h* are both values in pixels.

5. Finish the opening `object` tag by typing **>**.

6. Add **<param name="movie" value="filename.swf" />**, where *filename.swf* matches what you used in step 3.

7. Type **</object>** to complete the object.

✔ Tips

- This technique is based on the article *Flash Satay* by Drew McLellan in *A List Apart (www.alistapart.com/articles/flashsatay)*.

- Drew figured out a way to use small reference movies to help Flash animations stream properly with this technique. See his article for details.

- Many people use a combination of `object` and the non-standard `embed` tag to insert Flash on a Web page. For more details, search for *embed Flash* on Adobe's site *(http://www.adobe.com/)*.

Embedding Flash

Embedding Google and YouTube Video

Google and YouTube (and others) now offer a server where you can upload your video files (which tend to be of considerable size) and make them available to your visitors.

To embed Google Video:

1. Go to Google Video and display the video you want to embed *(http://video.google.com/)*.

2. Copy the document id number from the Address bar. It comes right after `docid=-` and continues until the ampersand (&).

3. Follow the steps for embedding Flash given on the previous page. In the two instances where you must insert the URL for the Flash animation, type **http://video.google.com/googleplayer.swf?docId=-n**, where *n* is the document id you copied in step 2. Note there are no spaces and after `docId` (with a capital I) comes an equals sign (=) and then a dash (-), before the number itself.

To embed YouTube Video:

1. Go to YouTube and view the video you want to use *(http://www.youtube.com)*.

2. Copy the movie code from the Address bar. It comes right after the `v=` and continues until the first ampersand (&).

3. Follow the instructions for embedding Flash given on the previous page. In the two places where you must insert the URL for the Flash animation, type **http://www.youtube.com/v/moviecode**, where *moviecode* is what you copied in step 2.

Figure 18.50 *Search for the desired video on Google Video. Copy its document id from the Address bar, starting after* `docid=-` *and continuing until the first ampersand (&).*

Figure 18.51 *Use the Google video's document id to construct the URL in the regular Flash embedding code from page 305.*

Figure 18.52 *The video will now play from within your Web page.*

Figure 18.53 *Search for the desired video on YouTube. Copy its movie code from the Address bar, starting after v= and continuing until the first ampersand (&).*

```
<body>

<object type="application/x-shockwave-flash"

data=
"http://www.youtube.com/v/FoLWpm6gtMl"
width="400" height="326">

<param name="movie" value=
"http://www.youtube.com/v/FoLWpm6gtMl" />

</object>
```

Figure 18.54 *Use the YouTube video's movie code to construct the URL in the regular Flash embedding code from page 305.*

Figure 18.55 *The YouTube video plays from inside the Web page. (This is the YouTube version of the same movie that we embedded from Google Video on the previous page.)*

✔ Tips

■ Note that Google uses docid (with a small *i*) to reference the movie, but you must use **docId** (with a capital *I*) in your URL in step 3. Like it wasn't hard enough.

■ Similarly, when you grab the movie code for a YouTube movie, it comes after v=. But when you construct your URL for referencing the movie, you use **v/**.

■ Both Google and YouTube offer code for embedding their videos on Web pages. Unfortunately, the code they suggest is non-standard and does not validate because it needlessly uses the embed tag.

■ In my tests using this technique, both Google Video and YouTube movies stream correctly with no extra reference files.

■ Currently, when you upload video to Google Video you can decide (in the Advanced Options section of the Video Information) whether or not other people have the right to embed your video on their pages. Video can either be embedded everywhere or nowhere. In other words, if you can embed it on your site, someone else can embed it on theirs.

■ Google Video also lets you decide whether or not viewers can download your video.

■ You can embed interactive Google Maps, too. See *http://www.google.com/apis/maps/*.

Inserting Java Applets

Java applets are little applications (hence the term *applets*) that can run in your browser to create special effects on your page, like clocks, calculators, and interactive events. There are whole books devoted to Java; here we'll restrict the topic to how to insert applets on your page once you've written or copied them from another source.

To insert an applet:

1. Type **<object codetype="application/ java" classid="java:file.class"**, where *file.class* is the name of the applet you want to embed.

2. Then type **width="w" height="h"**, where *w* and *h* are the applet's size in pixels.

3. Close the opening `object` tag with **>**.

4. Include any parameters, with **<param name="parameter" value="value_of_ parameter" />**.

5. Finally, type **</object>** to finish.

✔ Tips

- You can get more information about Java applets at: *http://java.sun.com/applets/.*

- You don't need to know Java to be able to use applets on your page.

- You can also use the deprecated, but still supported `applet` element to embed Java applets on a page: **<applet code="applet.class" width="w" height= "h"><param name="param_name" value="param_value" /></applet>**, where *applet.class* is the name of the applet to be embedded and the other values are the same as described above.

```
<body>

Does anybody really know what time it is?

<object codetype="application/java"

classid="java:Clock2.class" width="170"
height="150">

</object>
```

Figure 18.56 *This applet doesn't have any parameters to adjust. Everything is in the opening* object *tag.*

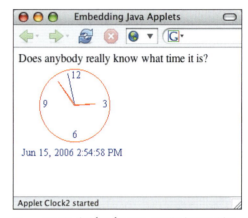

Figure 18.57 *Applets let you create interactive, multimedia effects on your page without having to know how to program or script.*

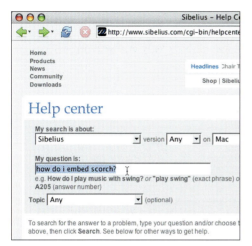

Figure 18.58 *Go to the player manufacturer's home page and search for "embed". (Scorch is a plugin for displaying sheet music on a Web page.)*

Embedding Other Multimedia Files

Other common types of multimedia files that you might want to embed on a page include Flash animations, Acrobat PDFs, Real audio and video, Scorch sheet music, and more.

To embed other multimedia files:

1. Go to the Web site of the company that develops the player for the multimedia files you want to embed. For example, for Scorch, go to Sibelius' site *(http://www.sibelius.com)*.

2. Look for developer information on the Web site or search for "embed". Most plugin developers provide information on their use.

✔ Tips

- If you can't find details on the site, try looking at the source code of a page that contains an embedded player.

- Almost all plugin developers offer the common but hardly standard `object`/`embed` combination in order to satisfy both Internet Explorer and its non-standard `classid` attribute as well as the rest of the browsers that can't handle it. If you want to avoid using the `embed` tag, try experimenting with the `data` and `type` attributes in the `object` element and a `src` or `url param` element with the URL of the desired file. And let me know what you find out *(http://www.cook-wood.com/html/contact.html)*.

Creating an Automatic Slide Show

And now for something completely different! You can use a special feature of the `meta` attribute, within the `head` section, to automatically move the reader from one page to another. If you set up a series of pages in this way, you create a Web slide show.

To create an automatic slide show:

1. In the first page, within the `head` section, type **<meta http-equiv="refresh"**. (That's a regular hyphen between `http` and `equiv`.)

2. Type **content="n;** where *n* is the number of seconds the current page should display on the screen.

3. Type **url=nextpage.html" />** where *nextpage.html* is the URL of the next page that you want the visitor to jump to automatically.

4. Repeat these steps for each page in the series.

✔ Tips

■ Omit the `meta` tag in the last page of the series if you don't want to cycle around again to the beginning.

■ Make sure you use a display time long enough for all of your images to load in each page.

■ This is a great way to show a portfolio or other series of images without having to create a lot of links and buttons.

■ Be careful with the quotation marks. Notice that the opening set comes before `content` and the closing set goes after the URL.

```
<head>

    <meta http-equiv="refresh" content="5;
url=page2.html" />

    <style> p {width:200px}</style>

<title>Slide Show Page 1</title>

</head>

<body>

<p><img src="tree1.jpg" alt="Tree in September"
width="200" height="293" /></p>

<p>I love autumn in New England. Last year,
```

Figure 18.59 *The* `meta` *tag must be in the* `head` *section. It won't work if you place it anywhere else.*

Figure 18.60 *The first page on the left, loads as usual. But wait five seconds, and then the second page (on the right) loads in its place.*

19

SCRIPTS

Scripts are little programs that add interactivity to your page. You can write simple scripts to add an alert box or a bit of text to your page, or more complicated scripts that create rollovers or load particular pages according to your visitor's browser. Because scripts are perfect for moving elements around on a page, they are the backbone of dynamic HTML, also known as DHTML.

Most scripts are written in JavaScript, since JavaScript is the scripting language that is supported by most browsers, including Firefox and Explorer.

Of course, there are entire books written about JavaScript—and some very fine ones indeed, including *JavaScript for the Web: Visual QuickStart Guide* by Dori Smith and Tom Negrino. In this chapter, rather than talking about how to write scripts, I'll stick to explaining how to insert those scripts, once created, into your (X)HTML documents.

For a look at a few little scripts that you can use in your pages, consult Chapter 20, *A Taste of JavaScript.*

Adding an "Automatic" Script

There are two kinds of scripts—those that are executed without the visitor having to do anything and those that react to something the visitor has done. The first group might be called "automatic scripts" and are executed by the browser when the page is loaded. You can have as many automatic scripts as you like on a page. They will run in the order they appear. (The second group, "triggered scripts", is discussed on page 314.)

To add an automatic script:

1. In your (X)HTML document, type **<script**.

2. Type **type="text/language-name"**, where *language-name* identifies the scripting language you're using: *javascript*, *vbscript*, etc.

3. Type **language="script"**, where *script* is the name of the scripting language you'll be using: *JavaScript*, *VBScript*, etc.

4. Type **>**.

5. Type the content of the script.

6. Type **</script>**.

✔ Tips

- The language attribute is deprecated and thus only valid in (X)HTML transitional *(see page 40)*. Nevertheless it is often used to maintain compatibility with older browsers.

- The location of the script on the (X)HTML page determines when it will load. Scripts are loaded in the order in which they appear in the (X)HTML file. If you want your script to load before anything else, be sure to place it in the head section.

- For hiding scripts in XHTML pages from XML parsers, see page 319.

```
<head>
<meta http-equiv="content-type"
content="text/html; charset=iso-8859-1" />
<title>Simple Scripts</title>
</head>
<body>
<script type="text/javascript"
language="JavaScript">

document.write("Visca Catalunya!")

</script>

<p>Here's the rest of the page.</p>
</body>
</html>
```

Figure 19.1 *A script may appear anywhere in your (X)HTML document. However, where it appears determines when it will be executed.*

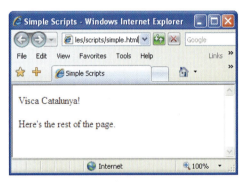

Figure 19.2 *This simple JavaScript script is output to the browser window itself. Other scripts send their results elsewhere.*

```
document.write("Visca Catalunya!")
```

Figure 19.3 *Here I've created an independent text file with the same script as in Figure 19.1. I can reference this external script from inside any (X)HTML file.*

```
<head>
<meta http-equiv="content-type"
content="text/html; charset=iso-8859-1" />
<title>Accessing external scripts</title>
</head>
<body>
<script type="text/javascript"
language="JavaScript" src="extscript.txt">

</script>

<p>Here's the rest of the page.</p>
</body>
</html>
```

Figure 19.4 *The* src *attribute not only references the script, it also automatically hides it from browsers that don't recognize the* script *tag.*

Figure 19.5 *The effect in the browser is the same as if it had been an internal script.*

Calling an External Automatic Script

If you use a script in several different Web pages, you'll save time and avoid typos by creating an external script (in text-only format) and then calling the script from each page where it is used.

To call an external automatic script:

1. Type **<script**.

2. Type **type="text/language-name"**, where *language-name* identifies the scripting language you're using: *javascript, vbscript,* etc.

3. Type **language="script"**, where *script* is the name of the scripting language you'll be using: *JavaScript, VBScript,* etc.

4. Type **src="script.url"**, where *script.url* is the location on the server of the external script.

5. If desired, type **charset="code"**, where *code* is the official name for the set of characters used in the external script.

6. Type **>**.

7. Type **</script>**.

✔ Tips

■ Using external scripts is a great way to keep older browsers from displaying your scripts as text. Since they don't understand the script tag, they ignore it (and the src attribute) completely. Use noscript to give those visitors using the older browsers an idea of what they're missing *(see page 317)*.

■ The language attribute is deprecated. Nevertheless it is often used to maintain compatibility with older browsers.

Triggering a Script

Sometimes you won't want a script to run until the visitor does something to trigger it. For example, perhaps you want to run a script when the visitor mouses over a particular picture or link, or when a page is loaded. These actions—mousing over or loading a page—are called *intrinsic events*. There are currently 18 predefined intrinsic events. You can use them as triggers to determine when a script will run.

To trigger a script:

1. Create the (X)HTML tag that the intrinsic event depends on **(Figure 19.6)**.

2. Within the tag created in step 1, type **event**, where *event* is an intrinsic event as defined below **(Figure 19.7)**. Unless otherwise noted, most events can be used with most (X)HTML tags.

onload occurs when a browser loads a page or frameset. **onunload** occurs when it unloads. They can be used in the `body` or `frameset` tags.

onclick occurs when the visitor clicks an element. **ondblclick** occurs when they double click it.

onmousedown occurs when the visitor points at an (X)HTML element and presses the mouse button down. **onmouseup** occurs when they let go.

onmouseover occurs when the visitor points at an element. **onmousemove** occurs when the visitor moves the pointer that is already over an element. **onmouseout** occurs when the visitor moves the pointer away from the element.

onselect occurs when the visitor selects some text in a form element.

```
<head>
<meta http-equiv="content-type"
content="text/html; charset=iso-8859-1" />
<title>Triggering scripts</title>
</head>
<body>
<p>What <a href="time.html">time</a> is it?
</p>

<p>Here's the rest of the page.</p>
</body>
</html>
```

Figure 19.6 *First, create the (X)HTML tag that the intrinsic event depends on. In this case, I want the script to occur when a visitor clicks the link. Therefore, I have to start with the link tag.*

```
<head>
<meta http-equiv="content-type"
content="text/html; charset=iso-8859-1" />
<title>Triggering scripts</title>
</head>
<body>
<p>What <a href="time.html"
onclick="alert('Today is '+ Date())">time</a> is it?
</p>

<p>Here's the rest of the page.</p>
</body>
</html>
```

Figure 19.7 *The event name and the script itself go right inside the (X)HTML tag. Make sure to enclose the script in double quotation marks.*

Figure 19.8 *A triggered script doesn't run until the visitor completes the required action. In this case, they have to click the link.*

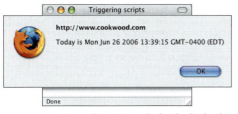

Figure 19.9 *Once the visitor clicks the link, the script runs. In this case, an alert appears, giving the current date and time.*

onfocus occurs when the visitor selects or tabs to an element. **onblur** occurs when the visitor leaves an element that was "in focus".

onkeypress occurs when the visitor types any character in a form element. **onkeydown** occurs even before the visitor lets go of the key and **onkeyup** waits until the visitor lets go of the key. As you might imagine, these only work with form elements that you can type in.

onsubmit occurs when the visitor clicks the submit button in a form *(see page 272)*. **onreset** occurs when the visitor resets the form *(see page 274)*.

onchange occurs when the visitor has changed the form element's value and has left that element (by tabbing out or selecting another).

3. Next, type **="script"**, where *script* is the actual script that should run when the event occurs.

✔ Tips

- If your script requires quotation marks, use single quotation marks so that they're not confused with the quotation marks that enclose the entire script (in step 3).

- If you need to use quotes within text that is already enclosed in single quotation marks, you can backslash them. So, you could use **onclick="alert('Here is today\'s date:' + Date())"**. Without the backslash, the apostrophe in *today's* would mess up the script.

- For a complete listing of which intrinsic events work with which (X)HTML tags, consult the table on page 418.

- Also see *Setting the Default Scripting Language* on page 320.

Triggering a Script

Creating a Button that Executes a Script

You can associate a button with a script to give your visitor full control over when the script should be executed.

To create a button that executes a script:

1. Type **<button type="button"**.

2. Type **name="name"**, where *name* is the identifier for the button.

3. Type **onclick="script"**, where *script* is the code (usually JavaScript) that will run when the visitor clicks the button.

4. If desired, type **style="font: 1.5em Helvetica, Arial, sans-serif; background: yellow; color: red; padding: .3em"** (or whatever) to change the appearance of the text on the button.

5. Type **>**.

6. If desired, type the text that should appear on the button.

7. Type **</button>**.

✔ Tips

- You can use other intrinsic events with buttons, but `onclick` makes the most sense.

- You can also add images to buttons. Simply insert the image between the opening and closing `button` tags (that is, after step 5 or 6).

- You can also use buttons with forms (*see pages 273 and 275*).

```
<!DOCTYPE html PUBLIC "-//W3C//DTD XHTML
1.0 Transitional//EN"
    "http://www.w3.org/TR/xhtml1/DTD/xhtml1-
transitional.dtd">
<html xmlns="http://www.w3.org/1999/xhtml">
<head>
<meta http-equiv="content-type"
content="text/html; charset=utf-8" />
<title>Associating scripts with a button</title>
</head>
<body>
<button type="button" name="time"
onclick="alert('Today is '+ Date())" style="font:
1.5em Helvetica, Arial, sans-serif; background:
yellow; color :red; padding: .3em">What time is
it?</button>
</body>
</html>
```

Figure 19.10 *Notice that the script is the same as the one used in the example in Figure 19.7. The style information here is optional, but it does make the button stand out. I also could have added an image.*

Figure 19.11 *The button element is more thoroughly explained in* Chapter 17, *Forms.*

Figure 19.12 *A click on the button executes the script, as shown here.*

```
<title>Llumi's big cat dreams</title>
<script type="text/javascript"
language="javascript">
   <!--
      littlecat = new Image(143,83)
      littlecat.src = "real.jpg"
      bigcat = new Image(143,83)
      bigcat.src = "dream.jpg"
   // -->

</script>
</head>
<body>
<noscript>Your browser isn't running scripts, so you
can't see what Llumi's thinking.</noscript>
<p>Point at Llumi to see what she's thinking. <a
href="llumipage.html"
onmouseover="document.catpic.src = bigcat.src"
```

Figure 19.13 *The* `noscript` *tag helps you take care of visitors who use a really old browser or one with scripting turned off.*

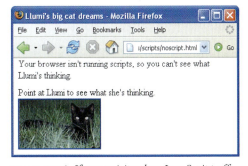

Figure 19.14 *If your visitor has JavaScript off, the* noscript *element will show a message informing them of what they're missing.*

Figure 19.15 *If JavaScript is on, the contents of the* noscript *element will be hidden.*

Adding Alternate Information

If you give your visitors access to information through scripts, you may want to provide an alternate method of getting that data if your visitor uses a browser—for example, on a mobile phone—that can't run the scripts.

To add alternate information:

1. Type **<noscript>**.

2. Type the alternate information.

3. Type **</noscript>**.

✔ Tips

■ If a browser doesn't understand the `script` tag, what hope is there that it will understand `noscript`? Actually it won't. It will completely ignore it and treat its contents as regular text—which, curiously, is exactly what you want. Only the browsers that understand `script` (and thus can run the script) will understand `noscript` as well. And as long as they've got JavaScript on, they'll *ignore* the contents of the `noscript` tag—which is also what you want. Clever, indeed.

■ Current browsers (and some older ones) allow your visitors to disable JavaScript. The `noscript` tag is perfect for telling those visitors what they're missing **(Figure 19.14)**.

■ Mobile devices don't always support JavaScript (though this will probably change in years to come).

■ The `noscript` tag will not help if the browser doesn't support the scripting language or if there is a problem with the script.

Hiding Scripts from Older Browsers

Older browsers don't always understand the `script` tag. If they don't, they'll just ignore it and display your script as if it were part of the body of the (X)HTML document. To keep that from happening, it's a good idea to use commenting to hide scripts from older browsers.

To hide scripts from older browsers:

1. After the initial `script` tag, type **<!--**.

2. Write the script as usual.

3. Right before the final `script` tag, type your scripting language's comments symbol. For JavaScript, type **//**. For VBScript, type **'** (a single quotation mark). For TCL, type **#**.

4. If desired, add text to remind yourself why you're typing all these funny characters. Something like **end comments to hide scripts** will work just fine.

5. Type **-->**.

✔ Tips

- The code in step 1 and in step 5 is for hiding the script from the browsers. The code in step 3 is for keeping the final **-->** from being processed as part of the script, and thus must be specific to the particular scripting language you're using.

- I have to admit I had a very hard time finding a browser old enough not to understand scripts. Hiding scripts from browsers was once a good idea, but I'm not sure it's essential any more.

- External scripts *(see page 313)* are automatically hidden from old browsers. They simply don't follow the URL.

Figure 19.16 *This is Mosaic 1. Because it doesn't understand the* `script` *tag, it ignores it and prints out the script as if it were regular text. Ugly!*

```
<title>Llumi's big cat dreams</title>
<script type="text/javascript"
language="javascript">
    <!--
        littlecat = new Image(143,83)
        littlecat.src = "real.jpg"
        bigcat = new Image(143,83)
        bigcat.src = "dream.jpg"
    // -->

</script>
</head>
<body>
Point at Llumi to see what she's thinking. <a
href="llumipage.html" onmouseover=
"document.catpic.src =bigcat.src"
onmouseout="document.catpic.src=littlecat.src"><i
mg src="real.jpg" name="catpic" width="143"
height="83" alt="The Real Llumi" /></a>
```

Figure 19.17 *This JavaScript script comes from Figure 20.11 on page 326. It preloads the images into cache to ensure speedy rollovers.*

Figure 19.18 *By commenting out the script, it is hidden from old browsers like this one. (Hey, it may not handle scripts, but this old version of Mosaic displays normal pages without trouble and runs on less than 1Mb of RAM.)*

```
<body>
<script type="text/javascript"
language="javascript">

<![CDATA[
   document.write("<p
align='right'><i>"+Date()+"<\/i><\/p>")
   ]]>

</script>

<h1>The Big Ben Home Page</h1>
```

Figure 19.19 *This JavaScript script is adapted from Figure 20.1 on page 322. The* CDATA *section removes the special meaning from the characters in the script, essentially hiding them from the XML parser.*

Hiding Scripts from XML Parsers

Scripts sometimes contain symbols that have special meaning in XHTML documents, namely the & and the >. If you use these symbols in a script, you should enclose them in a CDATA section to hide them from *XML parsers* (the programs that ensure that the XML, or XHTML in this case, is properly written).

To hide internal scripts from XML parsers:

1. Type **<script>** to begin your script as usual.

2. Type **<![CDATA[** to hide the script from the XML parser.

3. Insert the script itself.

4. Type **]]>** to complete the CDATA section.

5. And then type **</script>** to complete the script element.

✔ Tips

■ This is only necessary for XHTML documents with internal scripts. External scripts are automatically hidden from XML parsers.

■ It is also only necessary if you are serving your XHTML documents as XML. If you are serving them as HTML (which is true for the vast majority of Web pages), you don't have to enclose scripts in CDATA sections.

■ You can also hide internal style sheets in a CDATA section *(see page 131)*.

Setting the Default Scripting Language

According to the (X)HTML specifications, if you don't say what language you're using for the scripts on a page, your Web page is "incorrect". While you can use the `type` attribute to set the scripting language for internal and external scripts, the only mechanism for declaring the language of triggered scripts *(see page 314)* is with a `meta` tag.

To set the default scripting language:

1. In the `head` section of your (X)HTML document, type **<meta http-equiv= "Content-Script-Type"** (with both hyphens).

2. Then type **content="type"**, where *type* indicates the default format and language for your scripts. Use **text/javascript** for JavaScript, **text/vbscript** for VBScript, and **text/tcl** for TCL.

3. Type **/>**.

✔ Tips

■ The `Content-Script-Type` value sets the default scripting language for all of the scripts in a page, including the intrinsic events, internal scripts, and external scripts.

■ The scripting language indicated with the `type` attribute in the `script` tag *(see page 312)* overrides the `meta` tag specification. That means you can set the default scripting language, but still use scripts written in other languages, if desired.

■ While this `meta` tag is theoretically required for pages that contain intrinsic events, its absence generates no validation errors nor problems in browsers.

```
<!DOCTYPE html
    PUBLIC "-//W3C//DTD XHTML 1.0 Strict//EN"
    "http://www.w3.org/TR/xhtml1/DTD/xhtml1-strict.dtd">
<html xmlns="http://www.w3.org/1999/xhtml">
<head>
<meta http-equiv="content-type"
content="text/html; charset=utf-8" />
<title>Triggering scripts</title>
<meta http-equiv="Content-Script-Type"
content="text/javascript" />
</head>
<body>
<p>What <a href="time.html"
onclick="alert('Today is '+ Date())">time</a> is it?
</p>
<p>Here's the rest of the page.</p>
</body>
</html>
```

Figure 19.20 *The* `meta` *tag is always placed in the* `head` *section of your (X)HTML document. It specifies the default scripting language for all of the scripts on a page.*

Figure 19.21 *The result of the script itself is not changed.*

20

A Taste of JavaScript

Many of the most popular effects created on Web pages these days have little or nothing to do with (X)HTML and everything to do with *JavaScript*, a scripting language originally developed by Netscape Communications and now supported by all major browsers. There are entire books—and lots of them!—that go into JavaScript in full detail. This is not one of them.

Instead, I hope to whet your appetite with a tiny sampler of very simple scripts. Hopefully, they will give you the beginning of an idea of what you can do with JavaScript. Please note that there are probably much more elegant methods of achieving these effects that make the script more flexible and more powerful. But that would require a level of JavaScript that would not fit in a book about (X)HTML. If you'd like to find out more about what you can do with JavaScript, you might try the latest edition of *JavaScript for the Web: Visual QuickStart Guide*, by Tom Negrino and Dori Smith or the excellent online magazine *A List Apart (http://www.alistapart.com)*.

There are a couple of things to keep in mind while writing JavaScript. You should be very careful with spaces, returns, and all the funny punctuation. If you have trouble typing the scripts in yourself, feel free to download these examples from my Web site *(see page 26)*. I've personally tested these scripts—and they work fine—on current major browsers.

Adding the Current Date and Time

Nothing makes your page seem more current than adding the date and the time. While they're a bit more complicated to format in a particular way, just adding them is not difficult at all.

To add the current date and time to your page:

4. In a separate text document, on the first line, type **document.write(**

5. If desired, type **"<tag>"+**, where *tag* is the (X)HTML structure you'd like to apply to the date.

6. Next type **Date()** to call JavaScript's internal date function.

7. If you've added an element in step 5, type **+"<\/tag>"**, where *tag* is the corresponding closing tag. Notice the extra backslash that hides (X)HTML's forward slash / from JavaScript.

8. Type **)** to finish the *document.write* function **(Figure 20.1)**.

9. Save the document as in text-only format, using the file name *time.js*.

10. In your (X)HTML document, place the cursor where the time should appear.

11. Type **<script type="text/javascript" language="javascript" src="time.js"> </script>** to call the script from that location **(Figure 20.2)**.

✔ Tip

■ When you know more JavaScript, you can format the date, add the full name of the week and month, and change the order of the elements to better suit the situation at hand.

```
document.write("<p align='right'><i>"+
Date()+"<\/i><\/p>")
```

Figure 20.1 *I recommend creating your Java-Script scripts in independent, external documents. They should be saved in text-only format with the .js extension. For example, this file is called time.js. Notice that there is no return; it wraps here in order to fit in this narrow width column.*

```
<body>

<script type="text/javascript"
language="javascript" src="time.js"></script>

<h1>The Big Ben Home Page</h1>

<img src="bigben.gif" alt="A very rudimentary
picture of Big Ben" width="75" height="133"
align="left" /> <br />
```

Figure 20.2 *Put the* script *element in the place in your (X)HTML document where you'd like the time to appear. Note that the* language *attribute is deprecated and thus only valid in (X)HTML transitional (see page 313).*

Figure 20.3 *A time stamp on your page makes it appear more current. You just have to make sure the content is up to date as well.*

Nathaniel Hawthorne was one of the most important writers of 19th century America. His most famous character is <a href="javascript:location='hawthorne.html'; window.open('hester.html', 'characters', 'height=150, width=150, scrollbars=yes')"> Hester Prynne</a>, a woman living in Puritan New England. Another famous object of Hawthorne's

Figure 20.4 *The file name of the document shown here is* hawthorne.html. *The first part of the JavaScript statement says "keep displaying the* hawthorne.html *document right where it is". The second part of the JavaScript code says "and then open a window labeled* characters *that's 150 pixels by 150 pixels, with scrollbars, and display the* hester.html *file in it".*

Figure 20.5 *When the visitor clicks a link...*

Figure 20.6 *...the link is displayed in the new window. Contrast this example with the one shown in Figure 6.13 on page 108.*

Setting a New Window's Size

In Chapter 6, you learned how to open a link in a new window. JavaScript lets you control how big that window should be.

To set the size of a new window:

1. Type **<a href="javascript:location= 'current.html';**, where *current.html* is the URL of the page that contains the link.

2. Type **window.open('nextpage.html',**, where *nextpage.html* is the URL of the page to be opened in the new window.

3. Type **'label',**, where *label* is the name of the new window.

4. Type **'height=h,width=w**, where *h* and *w* are the desired height and width for the new window. (No spaces!)

5. If desired, type **,chrome=yes**, where *chrome* is scrollbars, toolbar, status, menubar, location, or resizable.

6. If desired, type a **,** (comma) and repeat step 5 as desired. Each window part should be separated from the previous one with a comma but no spaces.

7. Type **'** (a straight apostrophe)—whether or not you've set the window parts.

8. Type **)"** to finish the JavaScript code.

9. Type **>clickable text</a>**.

✔ Tip

■ To open a new window automatically as the main page loads (with no link at all), type **onload="javascript:** and then follow steps 2–8 above within the body tag of your main page's (X)HTML code. Then open other links in the new window by using **target="label"**, where *label* matches step 3. For details, see page 108.

Changing an Image When a Visitor Points

You can make an image change when the visitor points at it. This is commonly called a "rollover".

To change an image when the visitor points at it:

1. Type **<a href="page.html"**, where *page.html* is the page that will be displayed if the visitor actually clicks the link (as opposed to just pointing at it).

2. Type **onmouseover="document. imgname.src=**, where *imgname* is the value of the img tag's name attribute (see step 11, below). Note that there are no spaces before or after the periods.

3. Type **'image-in.jpg'**, where *image-in.jpg* is the name and extension of the image file that should be displayed when the visitor *points at* the image.

4. Type **"** to complete the attribute.

5. Type **onmouseout="document. imgname.src=**, where *imgname* is the value of the img tag's name attribute (see step 11, below). Note that there are no spaces before or after the periods.

6. Type **'image-out.jpg'**, where *image-out.jpg* is the name and extension of the image file that should be displayed when the visitor points *away from* the image.

7. Type **"** to complete the attribute.

8. Add other link attributes as desired *(see Chapter 6, Links)*.

9. Type **>** to finish the link.

```
<!DOCTYPE html PUBLIC "-//W3C//DTD XHTML
1.0 Transitional//EN"

"http://www.w3.org/TR/xhtml1/DTD/xhtml1-
transitional.dtd">

<html xmlns="http://www.w3.org/1999/xhtml">

<head>

<meta http-equiv="content-type"
content="text/html; charset=iso-8859-1" />

<meta http-equiv="Content-Script-Type"
content="text/javascript" />

<title>Llumi's big cat dreams</title>

</head>

<body>

Point at Llumi to see what she's thinking. <a
href="llumipage.html" onmouseover=
"document.catpic.src='dream.jpg'"
onmouseout="document.catpic.src='real.jpg'">
<img src="real.jpg" name="catpic" width="143"
height="83" alt="Llumi"/></a>

</body>

</html>
```

Figure 20.7 *Notice that the file names of the two images are enclosed in single quotes, since the script itself is contained in double quotes.*

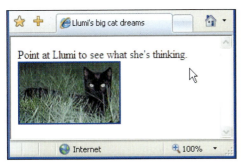

Figure 20.8 *The image that appears initially is the one specified by the* img *tag.*

Figure 20.9 *When the visitor passes the mouse over the image, the image referenced by the* onmouseover *attribute is revealed.*

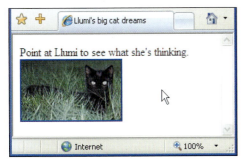

Figure 20.10 *When the visitor points the mouse away from the image, the image referenced by the* onmouseout *attribute is displayed (in this case, it's the same as the original image specified by the* img *tag).*

10. Type **<img src="initialimage.jpg"**, where *initialimage.jpg* is the file name for the image that should appear before the visitor even picks up their mouse.

11. Type **name="imgname"**, where *imgname* identifies the space for the images that will be loaded.

12. Type **width="w" height="h"**, where *w* and *h* represent the width and height of the images, respectively.

13. Type **alt="alternate text"**, where the *alternate text* describes the initial image.

14. Add other attributes to the img tag as desired. (For more details, consult *Chapter 5, Images*.)

15. Type **/>** to complete the img tag.

16. Type **</a>** to complete the link tag.

✔ Tips

■ The images should be the same size. If they're not, the second one will be shoe-horned in to fit.

■ Note that the img element's name attribute is used in both step 2 and step 5. That's because the name attribute identifies the space (the particular img element) that will be replaced with both of the other images. The name must match exactly, including case.

■ If you don't want the image to be part of the link, after step 9, type some clickable text, then do step 16 before completing steps 10–15.

■ You can preload the images involved in a rollover so that the effect is immediate. For more details, consult *Loading Images into Cache* on page 326.

Loading Images into Cache

You can use JavaScript to load all of the images into your browser's cache as the page is initially displayed on the screen. One benefit is that rollovers *(see page 324)* are instantaneous.

To load images into cache:

1. In a separate text document, on the first line, type **label=**, where *label* is a word that identifies the image.

2. Type **new Image(h,w)**, where *h* and *w* are the image's height and width, in pixels.

3. On the next line, type **label**, where *label* matches the label used in step 1.

4. Directly following the name in step 3 (i.e., with no extra spaces), type **.src="image.url"**, where *image.url* is the location of the image on the server.

5. Repeat steps 1–4 for each image you wish to load into cache **(Figure 20.11)**.

6. Save the script in text-only format and call it *loadimages.js*.

7. In the head section of the (X)HTML document that uses the images, type **<script type="text/javascript" language="javascript" src="loadimages.js"> </script>**, where *loadimages.js* is the name of the file you saved in step 6.

8. When you refer to the images in other scripts, use **label.src** (without quotes), where *label* is the word you used to describe the images in step 1 **(Figure 20.12)**.

```
littlecat = new Image(143,83)
littlecat.src = "real.jpg"
bigcat = new Image(143,83)
bigcat.src = "dream.jpg"
```

Figure 20.11 *Here's the* loadimages.js *file that I use to load the cat images into cache in order to make the rollover effect appear more fluidly. You can preload as many images as you'd like. There should be two lines for each image—one to create the image space and one to fill it with the corresponding URL.*

```
<!DOCTYPE html PUBLIC "-//W3C//DTD XHTML
1.0 Transitional//EN"
   "http://www.w3.org/TR/xhtml1/DTD/xhtml1-
transitional.dtd">
<html xmlns="http://www.w3.org/1999/xhtml">
<head>
<meta http-equiv="content-type"
content="text/html; charset=iso-8859-1" />
<meta http-equiv="Content-Script-Type"
content="text/javascript" />
<title>Llumi's big cat dreams</title>
<script type="text/javascript" language=
"javascript" src="loadimages.js"></script>
</head>
<body>
Point at Llumi to see what she's thinking. <a
href="llumipage.html"
onmouseover="document.catpic.src=bigcat.src"
onmouseout="document.catpic.src=littlecat.src"><i
mg src="real.jpg"
name="catpic" width="143" height="83"
alt="Llumi"/></a>
</body>
</html>
```

Figure 20.12 *Notice that the scripts in the body of the page (explained on page 324) now reference the* bigcat.src *and* littlecat.src *objects. You don't need to enclose these labels in quotes, as you do with the actual file names (step 3 on page 324).*

21

SYMBOLS AND NON-ENGLISH CHARACTERS

Global Reach *(http://www.glreach.com/ globstats/)* estimates that only 35% of the Web surfing public speaks English. That means that roughly 65% hopes that your Web page is written in some other language. And while many languages (particularly in Western Europe and the United States) are written with the same alphabet, many are written with scripts of their own: Cyrillic, Greek, and Chinese, just to mention a few. In addition, there are many useful symbols—common to English as well as other languages—that are not available in the current default system, known as ASCII.

Fortunately, (X)HTML is designed to support every symbol and character in every language in the world. When creating a Web page that will contain symbols and non-English characters, it's important to take into account the file's encoding (that is, the system used to convert the characters on the screen into the computer's internal system), the browser's support for such encodings (generally good in current browsers from versions 4 on) and the fonts that your visitors will have available.

Special thanks to Alan Wood for his help understanding how multilingual Web pages work. His site *(http://www.alanwood.net/ unicode/)* is an excellent resource. More thanks to Richard Ishida at the W3C who provided valuable feedback for this chapter. He has written a number of useful tutorials for creating multilingual Web pages which you can find at *http://www.w3.org/International/*

About Character Encodings

When you type, a computer translates each character into bits. The system it uses for doing this is called a *character encoding*. The most basic character encoding is called ASCII and has 128 characters: the letters of the English alphabet, the numbers, and some common symbols.

In non-English speaking countries, ASCII is clearly insufficient. Instead, they use slightly larger encodings sometimes encompassing more than one language. In order to maintain compatibility with English, these encodings treat the first 128 characters in the same way as ASCII and assign 128 new characters to positions 129–256. The only problem is that each regional encoding does it in a different way. So, for example, if you want to write in Spanish, you might use the ISO-8859-1 encoding but if you want to write in Cyrillic, you need the ISO-8859-5 encoding. And if you want to write Spanish and Cyrillic together, or send a Spanish document to a Russian computer, it's a big problem.

One rather cumbersome solution is to use *character references* to include characters in a document whose encoding otherwise wouldn't allow such characters. While this system continues to be used today *(see page 336)*, it is perhaps most useful for largely English documents that contain a few foreign letters or unusual symbols, whose writers don't want to worry about the encoding.

A more definitive solution is *Unicode*. Unicode is designed to be a universal system for encoding all of the characters in all of the world's languages. By assigning each character in each language a unique code, Unicode lets you include in a document any character from any language, and indeed multiple characters from multiple languages, without fear that it (or they) will be misinterpreted.

δ E4 is the Greek *sigma* in the ISO-8859-7 encoding.

ה E4 is the Hebrew *hay* in the ISO-8859-8 encoding.

ä E4 is the Germanic *umlaut a* in the ISO-8859-1 encoding.

Ф E4 is the Cyrillic *small letter ef* in the ISO-8859-5 encoding.

Figure 21.1 *Each of these characters has the same code (E4) in its respective local encoding, which makes it impossible, for example, to have both a Greek sigma and a Hebrew hay.*

δ The Greek *sigma* is character 03B4 in Unicode.

ה The Hebrew *hay* is character 05D4 in Unicode.

ä The Germanic *umlaut a* is character 00E4 in Unicode.

Ф The Cyrillic *small letter ef* is character 0424 in Unicode.

Figure 21.2 *In Unicode, each character has a unique code, and thus they may all appear in the same document without confusion (as long as that document is encoded with a Unicode encoding such as UTF-8).*

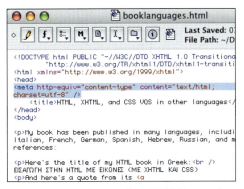

Figure 21.3 *Here's part of an XHTML page that contains English, Greek, and Japanese. Since I'm going to save it in the* utf-8 *encoding, I declare that encoding with the* meta *tag (details on page 330).*

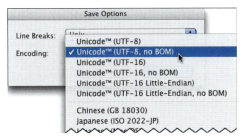

Figure 21.4 *When I save the document, I am careful to choose the same encoding:* utf-8, *in this case. BBEdit as of version 7 automatically chooses the same encoding that you've declared. What a great feature!*

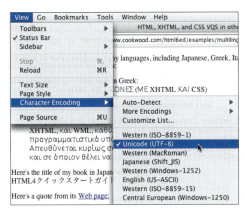

Figure 21.5 *When the visitor goes to this page, the browser sees the* meta *tag and automatically views the page with the proper encoding (*utf-8*).*

The form of Unicode most commonly used in HTML and XHTML is called UTF-8, which has the added advantage of encoding ASCII characters in the same way that ASCII does. This means that older browsers that may not recognize UTF-8 will still understand the English portion of the page, and indeed any character numbered 1–128. Its principal disadvantage is that pages written in double-byte languages (like Chinese, Japanese, and Korean) take up about 1.5 times as much file space as they would with a local, more limited encoding.

As a Web page designer, you must choose a proper encoding that encompasses all of the characters in your document, declare that encoding in the (X)HTML code **(Figure 21.3)**, and specify the encoding when you save your file **(Figure 21.4)**. If you've never specified an encoding before, your text editor selected one for you—probably the default encoding for your operating system. For example, most text editors on Windows in the U.S. will save "text-only" files in the Western ANSI encoding, whose official name is windows-1252.

Once you've done your part, your visitors still need a browser that recognizes the encoding you've used as well as a font that includes the characters in your page **(Figure 21.5)**. Most current browsers, including IE and Netscape/Firefox for both Mac and Windows from version 4 on, support UTF-8, as well as many regional encodings, although they sometimes require the installation of an additional *language kit* of some sort.

You may want to suggest that your visitors go to Alan Wood's excellent Unicode Resources site (*http://www.alanwood.net/unicode/*) which includes information about getting the appropriate language kits and fonts, as well as the W3C's International section, which has a wealth of helpful information about writing multilingual Web sites (*http://www.w3.org/International*).

About Character Encodings

Declaring Your Page's Character Encoding

Once you've decided which character encoding you're going to use, you should declare that encoding at the beginning of your Web page.

To declare your page's character encoding:

1. At the top of the head section of your page, type **<meta http-equiv="content-type" content="text/html;** (including the dash).

2. Then type **charset=code"**, where *code* is the name of the encoding with which you saved your page.

3. Type **/>** to complete the meta tag.

✔ Tips

■ Which encoding should you choose? My first choice would be UTF-8. It's more flexible than regional encodings, which are my second choice.

■ The encoding you declare *must* match the encoding with which your page was saved. Otherwise, characters that differ between the encodings will display incorrectly.

■ If you don't explicitly choose an encoding when saving your files, your text editor probably uses the default encoding for your system. You must still declare that encoding using the meta tag as described above. On Windows in the U.S. and Western Europe, the default encoding is windows-1252. On Macintosh in the U.S. and Western Europe, it's x-mac-roman.

■ If you don't specify your page's encoding, the browser (and search engines) will guess, based on the visitor's preferences, information from the server (see next tip),

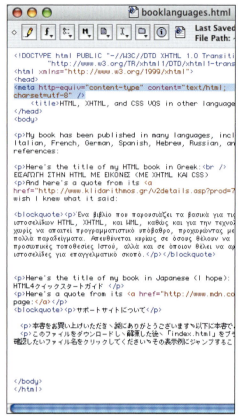

Figure 21.6 *In the* head *section of your Web page, create a* meta *tag that describes the encoding you used to save the file.*

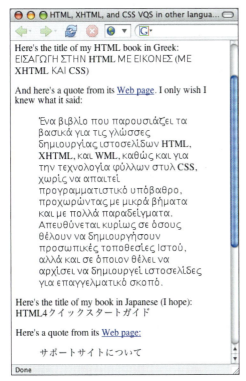

Figure 21.7 *When you tell the browser what encoding to expect, and as long as it supports that encoding and the visitor's system has an appropriate font, the characters display properly.*

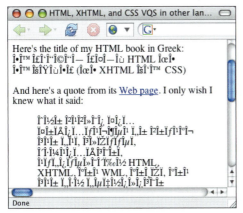

Figure 21.8 *If you don't tell the browser what to expect, it makes an attempt, but often doesn't know how to display the characters properly.*

the `charset` attribute (see last tip), or by examining the document. You have a better chance of the browser getting it right if you just make its life easy and tell it.

- Apache server users can add a line to their *.htaccess* file to declare the encoding of all files with a particular extension. The line should look like **AddType 'text/html;charset=code' .html**, where *code* is the character encoding. The .htaccess file overrides what you set with the `meta` tag. If you're having trouble, it may be that the server administrator has *already* adjusted the .htaccess file. For more details, see *http://www.w3.org/International/questions/qa-htaccess-charset* (including both dashes).

- To write a page in a different language from that of your operating system, you may also need keyboard layouts (or perhaps an IME, *input method editor*) that let you input the characters, and a text editor that supports the desired languages and that can save the page in the proper encoding. If the text editor can at least save the file in Unicode, you can use IE for Windows to convert the file to any of the encodings that it recognizes (by opening the file and choosing File > Save As).

- IE 6 for Windows, when browsing a page with an encoding it's not set up for, will automatically ask the visitor if they'd like to download the appropriate resources. This is an important reason to include the proper encoding.

- You can theoretically add the `charset` attribute to a link or script to describe the associated files' encodings. However, this feature is not yet widely supported.

Declaring a Style Sheet's Encoding

Because style sheets are mostly made up of CSS properties and enumerated values, they don't often contain anything but ASCII text. However, there's no reason why the classes, ids, or even content couldn't contain non-ASCII characters. Especially in those cases, it's important to declare the style sheet's encoding (and save it properly as well, as described on page 333).

To declare a style sheet's encoding:

On the very first line of your style sheet, type **@charset "code";**, where *code* is the name of the encoding with which you saved the style sheet.

✔ Tips

- The encoding declaration must be the very first line of your CSS document.

- Be sure to save your style sheet with the same encoding as the one you declare.

- If your style sheet contains only ASCII characters, which is the norm for most English-language style sheets, declaring the encoding is not crucial.

- Some font names include non-ASCII characters. In that case, it's a good idea to declare the style sheet's encoding.

- You can include individual escaped non-ASCII characters in a style sheet without worrying too much about the encoding. Use **\hex** , where *hex* is the hexadecimal number that refers to the desired character and there is a space at the end. This is analogous to using character references in (X)HTML documents as described in more detail on page 336.

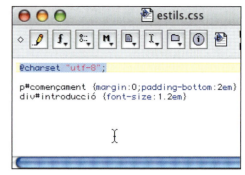

Figure 21.9 *Because this style sheet includes* id *names with non-ASCII characters, you should declare its encoding in the very first line.*

Figure 21.10 *In BBEdit, a popular (X)HTML editor for Mac, click the Options button when you go to save your file.*

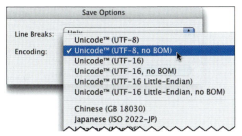

Figure 21.11 *Choose the desired encoding from the Encoding pop-up menu. I recommend choosing UTF-8, no BOM (Byte-Order Mark). You should only use an option with BOM if you're using UTF-16 (which needs it). Otherwise, it causes problems with some browsers.*

Saving Your Page with the Proper Encoding

At the beginning of this book, I said you had to save your Web pages as "text-only" documents, and made little mention of the encoding *(see page 46)*. That's because most of my readers create Web pages and style sheets in the same language as their operating system and because most text editors automatically save files with the default system encoding. You only need to manually choose the encoding as you save if your document contains characters that *don't belong* to your system's default character encoding.

To save your page with the proper encoding:

1. When you go to save your document, choose the option for selecting an encoding.

   In BBEdit, it's a button called Options.

   In Word, it's called Encoded Text, and you'll find it in the Save as type box.

2. Choose the desired encoding from the list or options that appear **(Figure 21.11)**.

3. Finish saving the document.

✔ Tips

■ Which is the proper encoding? My first choice would be UTF-8. My second choice would be the regional encoding for the main language used on your page. For a list of regional encodings, see *http://www.w3.org/International/O-charset-lang.html.*

■ When you declare the encoding *(see page 330)*, BBEdit, from version 7 on, automatically saves your file with that same encoding. I love that.

Editing a Page with the Proper Encoding

Once a file is encoded, it's not always easy to figure out which encoding was used. Some editors, like BBEdit, use the `meta` declaration, if present, to try to figure it out. Others are not so savvy. A good text editor will let you manually choose the proper encoding.

To edit a page with the proper encoding:

1. Choose File > Open in your text editor.

2. Select your file.

3. Choose the appropriate option for decoding an encoded file.

   In BBEdit, choose the proper encoding from the Read As pop-up menu (but see tip).

   In Word, choose Encoded Text from the Files of type box (and note tip) and then choose the encoding from the box that appears.

4. Click OK or Open.

Figure 21.12 *This document was saved without a* `charset` `meta` *declaration with the Latin 1 encoding. Since this file was not originally created in BBEdit, BBEdit couldn't tell what encoding it had and used the default, which was unfortunately not the right choice.*

Figure 21.13 *BBEdit lets you manually choose the encoding you think the file was saved with.*

```
<!DOCTYPE html PUBLIC "-//W3C//DTD XHTML 1.0
Transitional//EN"

"http://www.w3.org/TR/xhtml1/DTD/xhtml1-transitional.dtd">
<html xmlns="http://www.w3.org/1999/xhtml">
<head>
    <title>Encodings and such</title>
</head>
<body>
<p>Aquí hi ha un text en català, amb paraules com "Visca
Barça" i "pel·lícula". Si el guardo amb una codificació i
l'obro amb una altra, no hauria de funcionar, oi?</p></body>
</html>
```

Figure 21.14 *Once you've chosen the correct encoding, the characters beyond ASCII are displayed properly.*

✔ Tips

■ If you open the file and see garbage, close it without saving and try again with a different encoding.

■ Unless you tell it otherwise, BBEdit uses the encoding declared in the `meta` tag to open the file, or in its absence, the information it saved if you created the file in BBEdit, or as a last resort, the default encoding set in the Text Files: Opening preferences.

■ You have to make Word *ask* you for the proper encoding—choose Tools > Options, click the General tab, and check "Confirm Conversion at Open"—otherwise it uses your system's default encoding.

Editing a Page with the Proper Encoding

Adding Characters from Outside the Encoding

If most of the characters on your page belong to one encoding and you just want to add a few characters from another, you can set the main encoding for the document (*see page 330*) and then use *character references* for characters outside of the main encoding.

A character reference can represent any character in Unicode by giving the character's unique code within that set. A character's code can be represented as either a regular (base 10) number or as a hexadecimal number. Some characters also have associated *entities*, that is, unique identifying words, that you can use instead of the number.

You can find a character's code, in hexadecimal form (which is the most common), at the Unicode site: *http://www.unicode.org/charts/*. You can find the complete list of characters that have associated entities in Appendix D or at my site: *www.cookwood.com/entities/*

To add characters from outside the encoding:

1. Type **&** (an ampersand).

2. Next, type **#xn**, where *n* is the hexadecimal number that represents the desired character **(Figure 21.15)**.

   Or type **#n**, where *n* is the base 10 number for your character **(Figure 21.16)**.

   Or type **entity**, where *entity* is the name of the entity that corresponds to your character **(Figure 21.17)**.

3. Finally, type **;** (a semicolon).

✔ Tips

■ In general, you only *need* to use character references for characters that are *not* part of the document's character encoding.

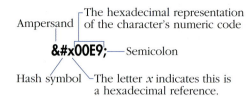

Figure 21.15 *A hexadecimal reference is comprised of an ampersand, a hash symbol (#), the letter* x, *the hexadecimal representation of the numeric code for the character, and a semicolon. You can use hexadecimal references to insert any character from the Universal Character Set. This particular character is an* é.

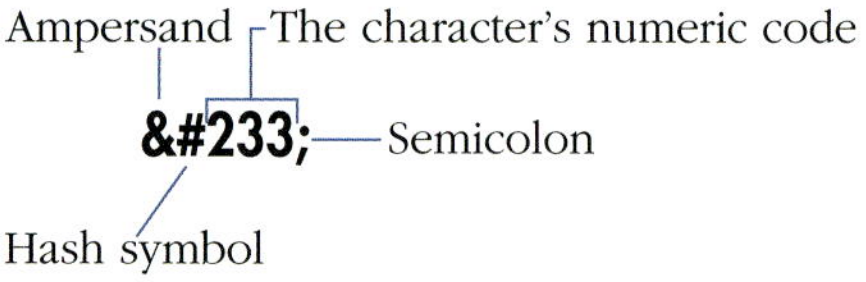

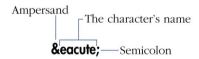

Figure 21.16 *A numeric reference is comprised of an ampersand, a hash symbol (#), the numeric code for the character, and a semicolon. You can use numeric references to insert any character from the Universal Character Set. This reference is also for an* é.

Figure 21.17 *An entity reference, also known as a character entity reference or named reference, is made up of an ampersand, the character's name, and a semicolon. There are 252 named references that you can use in your (X)HTML pages. They are case-sensitive. This reference is also for an* é.

```
<!DOCTYPE html PUBLIC "-//W3C//DTD XHTML
1.0 Transitional//EN" "http://www.w3.org/TR/
xhtml1/DTD/xhtml1-transitional.dtd">

<html xmlns="http://www.w3.org/1999/xhtml">

<head>

<meta http-equiv="content-type"
content="text/html; charset=windows-1252" />

    <title>Character References</title>

    <style>p {font-size:24px}</style>

</head>

<body>

<p>&ldquo;Parla vost&eacute;
angl&egrave;s?&rdquo; he asked.</p>

<p>&ldquo;Yes, a little,&rdquo; she said.</p>

<p>&ldquo;How much is that in euros?&#8221; he
asked.</p>

<p>&#x201C;&euro;25,&#x201d; she
replied.</p>
```

Figure 21.18 *You can use any combination of named, numeric, or hexadecimal references in your document. It doesn't matter which encoding the document is in. Of course, it's better just to use an encoding like UTF-8 that supports the characters you need.*

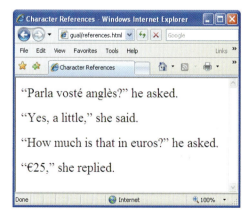

Figure 21.19 *The characters display properly. Note that the visitor's browser must have an appropriate font for the characters.*

- The principal exception to the first tip is the & symbol. In XHTML documents, when used as text (as in *AT&T*), you *must* use its character reference (`&amp;`).

- The greater than, less than, and double quotation mark symbols also have special meaning in (X)HTML. You should use their character references—`&gt;`, `&lt;`, and `&quot;`, respectively—when not using them in the markup code itself.

- While using references for characters like *é* and *£* is valid, using the proper encoding (e.g., `utf-8`) is much faster for large chunks of text.

- The most common default encodings, including `windows-1252` and `x-mac-roman` lack several useful symbols. You can use character references to create these symbols without touching the default encoding.

- If you're using a hexadecimal or numeric reference, don't forget the **#** between the ampersand and the number. And if you're using a hexadecimal, don't forget the lowercase letter **x**, that indicates that the hexadecimal is coming.

- While there are hex and numeric references for *every* character in Unicode, there are named entity references for only 252 of them. They are case-sensitive. See Appendix D for a complete listing.

- Your visitors will only be able to view the characters for which they have adequate fonts installed. While you can specify a particular font *(see page 152)*, it's not required; in its absence browsers should search the available fonts for one that includes the characters in question.

- You may also insert small quantities of special characters by using GIF images *(see page 90)*.

Specifying A Page's Language

While saving with the proper encoding and declaring that encoding is essential, it can also be useful to specify the main language in which your page is written. This information may be used by search engines to determine which pages satisfy a language-limited match, or perhaps by a server so that it can serve the appropriate version of a document.

To specify a page's language:

In XHTML, within the opening `html` tag, type **xml:lang= "code" lang="code"**, where *code* is the abbreviation for your page's main language, as well as any subtags you may want to specify.

✔ Tips

■ The value of `xml:lang` overrides the value for `lang`.

■ For HTML, use only the `lang` attribute. For XHTML served as XHTML, use only the `xml:lang` attribute.

■ You may add the `xml:lang` and `lang` attributes to almost any element to define the language for that element and override the language noted in the `html` tag.

■ Browsers may use this information to determine hyphenation, assist spell checkers and speech synthesizers, etc.

■ Search engines *may* use this information, but they also use proprietary algorithms to determine which language a page is in.

■ Note that since encodings often encompass more than one language, this tag lets you be more explicit about which language you've actually used.

■ You can find more information about language codes at: *http://www.w3.org/ International/articles/language-tags/*

```
<!DOCTYPE html PUBLIC "-//W3C//DTD XHTML
1.0 Transitional//EN"

    "http://www.w3.org/TR/2000/REC-xhtml1-
20000126/DTD/xhtml1-transitional.dtd">

<html xmlns="http://www.w3.org/1999/xhtml"
xml:lang="en" lang="en">

<head>

    <meta http-equiv="content-type"
content="text/html; charset=utf-8" />

    <title>Quotes in French</title>

<style type="text/css">p {font-size:24px}</style>

</head>

<body>

<p xml:lang="fr" lang="fr">Alceste dit <q>Mais
enfin, vos soins sont superflus.</q> </p>

<p>Alceste says <q>But in the end, what you want
is superfluous.</q></p>

</body></html>
```

Figure 21.20 *Specify the principal language in the* html *tag. Here I've used* fr *for French. You can override that value in individual elements, as I've done for the English paragraph at the bottom of this Web page.*

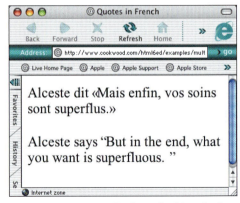

Figure 21.21 *Internet Explorer for Mac displays guillemet quotes when the language specified is French but curly quotes if the language is English.*

Testing and Debugging Web Pages

22

So, you've written up a brand new page and you fire up your browser only to find that it doesn't look anything like you expected. Or it doesn't display at all. Or maybe it looks great in your default browser but when you call your client she says it looks, well, kind of funny on her computer.

Between HTML, XHTML, CSS and the multitude of browsers and platforms on which you can view them, it's easy to have a bit of trouble. This chapter will alert you to some common errors, and will also help you weed out your own homegrown variety.

Some of the debugging techniques may seem pretty basic. The thing is that most problems with Web pages are pretty basic, too. Before you go looking for a big problem, make sure you don't have any little ones. I'll show you how in the first section.

Once your code is correct, you should then thoroughly test your site on one or more browsers, in one or more platforms, to see if each page works the way you want it to.

Some Debugging Techniques

Here are my tried and true techniques for getting the kinks out of a Web page.

- Check the easy stuff first *(see pages 341–344)*.

- Imagine you're a scientist. Be observant and methodical.

- Work incrementally. Make small changes and test after each change. This way you'll be able to pinpoint the source of a problem if one occurs.

- In the same vein, when you're debugging, start with what you know works. Only then should you add the hard parts chunk by chunk—testing the page in a browser after each addition—until you find the source of the problem.

- Conversely, use the process of elimination to figure out which chunks of your code are giving you trouble. For example, you can comment out half of the code to see if the problem is in the other half. Then comment out a smaller portion of the offending half, and so on, until you find the problem *(see pages 67 and 121)*.

- Be really careful about typos. Many of my most perplexing problems have ended up being simple spelling mistakes.

- In CSS, if you're not sure if the problem is with the property or with the selector, try adding a very simple declaration to your selector, like `color:red`. If the element turns red, the problem is with your property, if it doesn't, the problem is with your selector.

- Take a break. Time isn't linear. Sometimes you can get much more done in the fifteen minutes after an hour long walk to clear your head than you ever could have gotten done during that hour otherwise.

Figure 22.1 *I've commented out the middle section (displayed in gray) to see if it's the culprit. Note that many (X)HTML editors, like BBEdit shown, offer automatic color-coding that can be a huge aid to your debugging. If you mistype the name of a CSS property, for example, BBEdit won't show it in blue.*

Check the Easy Stuff First!

While the difference you see between browsers *might* be due to some obscure browser bug or some new technique you're using, nine times out of ten, it's just something simple. It's easy to blame a problem on a new technique and spend hours debugging it, only to find that you're changing one file but uploading and viewing a different one.

The general easy stuff:

- Make sure you've uploaded the actual file you want to test *(see page 353)*.

- Make sure you've uploaded the file in the location that you think you have.

- Make sure you've typed the URL that corresponds to the file you want to test.

- Make sure you've saved the file—including the very latest changes—before you upload it.

- Make sure you've uploaded any auxiliary files—CSS, images, music, videos, etc.

- Make sure the upper- and lowercase letters in your URL match the upper- and lowercase letters in your filenames—*exactly*. And make sure you haven't used spaces or other punctuation in filenames at all.

- Make sure the problem is not the browser's fault. The easiest way to do that is to test it in another browser.

On the following three pages, I'll give you some ideas of how to check the easy stuff in HTML, XHTML, and CSS.

Checking the Easy Stuff: HTML

Here are some common problems with HTML code. Many of these also apply to XHTML.

To check the easy stuff with HTML:

■ Make sure you've spelled everything right. I can't tell you how many times I write scr instead of src (which stands for *source*, by the way).

■ Be careful about nesting. If you open <p> and then use <b> make sure the closing </b> comes before the final </p>.

■ The final / in empty XHTML tags is not part of the HTML specification. If you want the file to validate as HTML, you'll have to get rid of it. (Better yet, switch to XHTML.)

■ Make sure the DOCTYPE matches the HTML you're actually using. For example, if you want to use deprecated tags, don't use HTML strict, use HTML transitional *(see pages 40 and 56)*.

■ Avoid non-standard tags. Their support across browsers is notoriously spotty.

■ Be aware that most valid DOCTYPE declarations will make IE and Firefox go into standards mode. If you're relying on old quirky behavior, you may be disappointed *(see page 41)*.

■ If accented characters or special symbols are not displaying properly, see Chapter 21, *Symbols and Non-English Characters*.

```
<img scr="image.gif" alt="Woody the cat" />
```

Figure 22.2 *Can you see where the problem is? I've misspelled* src. *I can't tell you how many times I've torn apart a table or some other complicated construction only to find a miserable little typo like this.*

```
<img src="image.gif" alt="Woody the cat">
```

Figure 22.3 *The corrected version shows the* src *attribute spelled correctly, plus I've removed the final* / *that is used only in XHTML, not HTML.*

```
<img src="jungle.jpg" alt="Llumi's jungle" />
```

Figure 22.4 *If an attribute's value contains a single quote, you can just enclose it in double quotes as usual.*

```
<img src="cookie.jpg" alt="Cookie's saying
&quot;Enough!&quot;" />

<img src="tough_llumi.jpg" alt='Llumi replies, "This
is _my_ jungle."' />
```

Figure 22.5 *If an attribute's value contains double quotes, either use references (top), or enclose the attribute value in single quotes (bottom).*

```
<p />

<img src="jungle.jpg" alt="Llumi's jungle" >
</img>
```

Figure 22.6 *Here are two examples of valid XHTML that will give most browsers a headache.*

```
<p></p>

<img src="jungle.jpg" alt="Llumi's jungle" />
```

Figure 22.7 *Instead, don't combine the opening and closing tags of elements that aren't usually empty (like p) and don't use individual opening and closing tags for elements that are usually empty (like img).*

Checking the Easy Stuff: XHTML

If you're making the jump to XHTML, it's easy to miss a few of its syntax rules. Make sure you check them first.

To check the easy stuff with XHTML:

- Be sure all attribute values are enclosed in straight, not curly, quotes. If the value itself contains quotes, use references *(see page 336)*. Also note that a value can contain single quotes if the value is enclosed in double quotes, or double quotes if the value is enclosed in single quotes **(Figures 22.4** and **22.5)**.

- Make sure all elements have opening and closing tags, or one combination tag (with a final /). Always put a space before the / to ensure compatibility with older browsers.

- Don't combine opening and closing tags for elements that usually have content. For example, while `<p />` is technically correct in XHTML, browsers won't always know what to do with it. In the same vein, don't use separate opening and closing tags for empty elements as in `<img src="woody.gif" alt="cat"> </img>`. Again, while this is perfectly valid XHTML, browsers will be confused **(Figures 22.6** and **22.7)**.

- Be careful about case. All elements, attributes, and predefined values should be in lowercase letters.

- Don't leave out the # when specifying hexadecimal colors.

- If symbols or accented characters are not displaying properly, see Chapter 21, *Symbols and Non-English Characters.*

Checking the Easy Stuff: CSS

While CSS syntax is pretty straightforward, it has some common pitfalls, especially if you've gotten used to writing HTML or XHTML.

To check the easy stuff with CSS:

■ Make sure you separate your properties from their values with a colon (:) not an equals sign, like you do in (X)HTML **(Figures 22.8 and 22.9)**.

■ Be sure to complete each property-value pair with a semicolon (;). Make sure there are no extra semicolons **(Figures 22.10 and 22.11)**.

■ Don't add spaces between numbers and their units **(Figures 22.12 and 22.13)**.

■ Don't forget to close your brackets.

■ Don't quote values—as you do in (X)HTML. The only values that have quotes in CSS are multiword font names.

■ Make sure you're using an accepted value. Something like `font-style: none` isn't going to work since the "none" value is called `normal`. You can find a complete list of CSS properties and values in Appendix B, *CSS Properties and Values*.

■ Don't forget the closing `</style>` tag with internal style sheets *(see page 131)*.

■ Make sure you've linked the (X)HTML document to the proper CSS file, and that the URL points to the desired file. URLs are relative to the CSS file, not to the (X)HTML file *(see page 129)*.

■ Watch the spaces and punctuation between the selectors.

■ Make sure the browser supports what you're trying to do *(see page 350)*. Support for CSS varies.

```
p {font-size=24px}
```

Figure 22.8 *Bad! It's hard to break the habit of separating properties and values with the equals sign. But you must.*

```
p {font-size: 24px}
```

Figure 22.9 *Much better. Always use a colon between the property and the value. Note that it doesn't matter if you add extra spaces before and after the colon.*

```
p {font-size:24px font-weight:bold;; font-style:italic}
```

Figure 22.10 *Bad! You must put one and only one semicolon between each property-value pair. Here there's one missing and one extra.*

```
p {
    font-size: 24px;
    font-weight: bold;
    font-style: italic;
}
```

Figure 22.11 *One way to make sure that each property-value pair is separated by the next with a semicolon is to give each one its own line. It's easier to see the semicolons when they're not in a sea of properties, values, and colons.*

```
p {font-size: 2 em}
```

Figure 22.12 *Bad! Never put spaces between the number and the unit.*

```
p {font-style: 2em}
```

Figure 22.13 *This will work. Note that the spaces between the colon and the value are optional.*

Figure 22.14 *That text to the right of the image isn't supposed to be so big. What's the problem?*

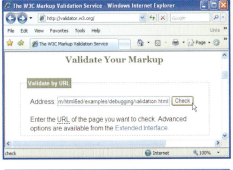

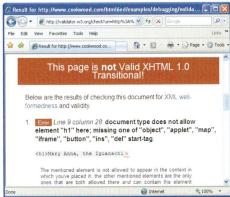

Figure 22.15 *The error found on Line 9 seems to be the problem—instead of a closing </h1> tag, I've put in another opening <h1> tag by mistake. Notice how the description doesn't really have to do with our mistake. The validator often misinterprets typos.*

Validating Your Code

One good tool for finding errors on a page is to run it through a validator. An (X)HTML validator will look at the `DOCTYPE` to see which version of HTML or XHTML you say you're using *(see pages 40 and 56)*, compare your code against the actual specifications of that version, and then display any inconsistencies it finds. A CSS validator works similarly.

To validate your code:

1. First check your (X)HTML with the W3C's *http://validator.w3.org/*

2. Once your (X)HTML validates, you can make sure your CSS is free of errors with *http://jigsaw.w3.org/css-validator/*

✔ Tips

- Validators have a hard time getting the big picture. While they're good at noticing missing closing tags or missing quotes, they're not always so smart about what that means in the rest of the file. For example, a missing closing tag can trigger lots of error messages throughout your document. Fix the closing tag, and all of those subsequent "errors" go away. The trick, then, is to fix a few errors at a time, starting at the top of the file, and then immediately revalidate the file to see if other problems are also resolved **(Figure 22.15)**.

- Many text editors, like BBEdit, have incorporated syntax checkers. They are great for catching errors before you get to the official validator.

- Use the `DOCTYPE` to tell the validator which specifications to judge your HTML and XHTML with *(see page 56)*.

- There are other validators out there. I think the ones from the W3C are the best.

Testing Your Page

Even if your code validates, your page still may not work the way you want it to. Or it may work properly in one browser, but not in the next. It's important to test your page in as many browsers as possible, on as many platforms as possible. At the very least, test your page on current versions of both Explorer and Netscape on both Windows and Macintosh.

To test your (X)HTML pages:

1. Validate your (X)HTML and CSS *(see page 345)*. Make any necessary changes.

2. Open a browser, and choose File > Open File.

3. Find the Web page on your hard disk that you want to test and click Open. The page appears in the browser.

4. Go through the whole page and make sure it looks exactly the way you want it. For example:

   • Is the formatting like you wanted?

   • Does each of your URLs point to the proper document? (You can check the URLs by clicking them if the destination files are located in the same relative position on the local computer.)

   • Is your CSS file referenced properly?

   • Do all of your images appear? Are they placed and aligned properly?

   • Have you included your name and email address so that your users can contact you with comments and suggestions? (Or, to avoid spambots, have you included a form that people can use to submit comments?)

Figure 22.16 *This page validates but it doesn't look anything like it's supposed to. What's the problem?*

```
<!DOCTYPE html PUBLIC "-//W3C//DTD XHTML
1.0 Transitional//EN" "http://www.w3.org/TR/
xhtml1/DTD/xhtml1-transitional.dtd">

<html xmlns="http://www.w3.org/1999/xhtml">

<head>

<title>Mary Anna, the Iguana</title>

<link rel="stylesheet" type="text/css"
href="testerpage.css" /></head>

<body>

<img src="iguana.jpg" alt="Iguana" width="220"
height="165" />

<h1>Mary Anna, the Iguana</h1>

<p>There once was an iguana

whose name was <em>Mary Anna</em>

her skin was so dry

that she'd have to cry

Here's some cream: would you please put it
onna?</p>

</body></html>
```

Figure 22.17 *The problem is the link to the CSS file—the file is named* testpage.css *and here I'm linking to* testerpage.css. *It should be no surprise that the browser can't find the CSS and thus displays the page wrong.*

Figure 22.18 *Now that the link to the CSS is corrected, the page is displayed properly.*

5. Without closing the page in the browser, open the appropriate (X)HTML or CSS document and make any necessary changes.

6. Save the changes.

7. Switch back to the browser and press Refresh or Reload to see the changes.

8. Repeat steps 1–7 until you are satisfied with your Web page. Don't get discouraged if it takes several tries.

9. Revalidate the code to make sure you haven't introduced any new errors.

10. Upload the files to the server *(see page 353)*.

11. Return to the browser and type your page's URL in the Address bar and hit Return. The page will appear in the browser.

12. With your page on the server, go through your page again to make sure everything is all right.

✔ **Tips**

■ Again, if you can, test your (X)HTML documents in several browsers on various platforms. You never know what browser (or computer) your visitors will use. The major browsers are discussed on pages 15–16.

■ The rest of this chapter deals with common problems that can occur in validated code as well as their solutions.

■ Sometimes it's not your fault—especially with styles. Make sure a browser supports the feature you're having trouble with before assuming the problem is with your code.

When the Browser Displays the Code

Although you may be proud of your (X)HTML code, when you view your file with a browser, you want that code converted into a beautiful Web page, not displayed for all to see.

When the browser displays the code instead of the page:

■ Have you saved the file in text-only format (sometimes called "Text Document" or "Plain Text")? Sometimes, if you've saved the file previously as a, say, Word document, saving it as text-only isn't enough. You have to create a brand new document, copy and paste the code to that new document, and then save it as text-only.

■ Have you saved the file with an .htm or .html extension? You must *(see page 46).*

■ Have you begun the page with the proper DOCTYPE? *(see page 56).*

■ Do you shun Word's (or some other word processor's) "Save as Web Page" or "Save as HTML" command and the Web page format for saving files? That command, in all its incarnations, is only for converting regular text into Word's idea of a Web page **(Figures 22.19** and **22.20)**. If you're writing your own code, this command will "code your code" *(see page 48).* Instead, choose Save As and then save the file in Text Document format with the .htm or .html extension.

■ Is Windows adding .txt extensions to the files you save as "page.html", creating something like "page.html.txt"? Find out by viewing file extensions in the folder. To avoid it, enclose the file name in double quotation marks in the Save As dialog box.

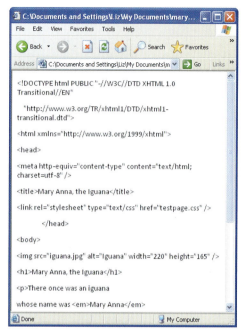

Figure 22.19 *This page, shown here in Internet Explorer, was created in Word by choosing Web Page as the format in which to save the file. Word "coded the code", making a Web page that shows the code instead of using it. I would bet it's not what you expected.*

Figure 22.20 *If you select View Source, you can see how Word coded the code, changing the angle brackets (< and >) to < and >, converting quotation marks to " and adding an incredible amount of superfluous junk.*

```
<body>

<img src="Iguana.jpg" alt="Iguana" width="220"
height="165" />

<h1>Mary Anna, the Iguana</h1>

<p>There once was an iguana
```

Figure 22.21 *The file name for the image is* iguana.jpg *but here it is incorrectly referenced as* Iguana.jpg, *with a capital* I.

Figure 22.22 *On your computer, the page looks fine because your computer isn't picky about upper- and lowercase letters.*

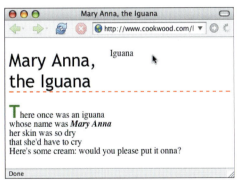

Figure 22.23 *When the page is published to the server, which is case sensitive, the image cannot be found and the* alt *text is shown instead.*

When Images Don't Appear

Little red x's, broken icons, alternate text, or nothing at all. Regardless, it's a drag if what you really wanted was a picture of an iguana.

When images don't appear:

■ First, check that the file name of the image on the server matches the name you've referenced in the img tag *exactly*, including upper- and lowercase letters, and the extension **(Figure 22.21)**.

■ Don't use spaces in file names. While they may work locally (on your personal computer), servers can't handle them. For more information, consult *File Names* on page 34.

■ Next, make sure the image's location is specified correctly in the URL in the img tag. One easy test is to put an image in the same directory as the (X)HTML page. That means you'll just need the proper file name and extension in the img tag, but no path information. If the image shows up, you can be pretty sure that the problem was in the path. For more information on URLs, see pages 35–37.

■ If the image shows up when you view your page on your computer but not when you upload the page to the server, make sure you've uploaded the image to the server *(see page 353)*, and that its location on the server is reflected in the img tag's URL.

■ Have you saved the image as GIF or JPG? I've seen Windows users create images in BMP format (which Internet Explorer for Windows has no trouble with) and then not understand when a non-Microsoft browser (on Windows *or* Mac) displays a broken image icon instead of the graphic. For more information, see Chapter 5, *Images*.

Differences from Browser to Browser

This one's probably not your fault. Unfortunately, no browser supports the standard specifications 100 percent. While most support virtually all of (X)HTML, their support of CSS varies. Firefox and Opera currently have the best support, followed by IE 7 and IE 6.

When your page looks different from one browser to the next:

- Test your page on as many browsers and platforms as you can. Read your server logs to see which browsers your visitors use and which browsers they don't so that you can make informed choices about which browsers to focus on.

- Be aware of which CSS properties are supported by current browsers and which are the most problematic. There are a number of good resources. For example, you might try the css-discuss Wiki (*http://css-discuss.incutio.com/*)

- Design your page so that even if something you use is not supported, your page still functions. This is called "degrading gracefully".

- Cater your page to your desired audience. Web designers can be expected to have all the latest plug-ins, members of the American Iguana Club might not.

✔ Tip

- Check out The Web Standards Project page (*www.webstandards.org*) for more information on what you can do to promote the adoption of standards by the major Web browser manufacturers (as well as by any newcomers to the game).

```
#choices label {position:absolute;padding-
top:.2em;left:20px}

select {margin-left:9em;margin-bottom:0}

#size {font-size:90%}
#size input {margin-left:9em}
#size input + input {margin-left:1em}
#size br+ input {margin-left:9em}

#extras {font-size:90%}
#extras input {margin-left:9em}
#extras input +input {margin-left:1em}
#extras br+input {margin-left:9em}
```

Figure 22.24 *Here is the CSS from the main example in the Forms chapter.*

Figure 22.25 *Firefox (shown) and other standards-loving browsers get it right.*

Figure 22.26 *Internet Explorer 6 doesn't support adjacent sibling selectors (see page 143) and so completely misses the highlighted code in Figure 22.24 above, resulting in 9em margins for all the* input *elements instead of just the first ones.*

Figure 22.27 *If you get stuck, try posting a question to my Question and Answer Forum (http://www.cookwood.com/html/qanda/). At press time, the Forum was not yet updated to reflect this Sixth Edition, but the URL will be the same.*

Still Stuck?

If you've gotten to this page, you're probably frustrated. Don't think I'm being patronizing when I suggest you go take a break. Sometimes the best thing you can do for a problem is leave it alone for a minute. When you come back, the answer may be staring you in the face. If it's not, let me offer you these additional suggestions.

1. Check again for typos. Revalidate your code *(see page 345)*.

2. Check the easy pieces first. So many times I've spent hours fiddling with an exciting new tag that just wouldn't work only to find that the problem was a typo in some tag that I'd used a thousand times before. Familiarity breeds contempt—check the stuff you think you know really well before you harass the newcomers.

3. Simplify the problem. Go back to the most recent version of your page that worked properly (which might be a blank page in some cases). Then test the page after adding each new element.

4. Read through this chapter again.

5. Check one final time for typos.

6. Post the piece of code that doesn't work on my Question and Answer Forum *(www.cookwood.com/html/qanda/)*. Be sure to include the relevant code (or a URL), a description of what is happening, and a description of what you think *should* be happening. People are very helpful there.

23

PUBLISHING YOUR PAGES ON THE WEB

Once you've finished your masterpiece and are ready to present it to the public, you have to transfer your pages to your Web host server so that people can get to them.

You may also want to contact your Web host (or Internet Service Provider) to ask them about the best way to upload your files.

Be sure to thoroughly test your pages before publishing them. For more details, consult Chapter 22, *Testing and Debugging Web Pages*.

Finding a Host for Your Site

Unless you have your own server, you'll probably have to pay someone to host your site. There are hundreds, maybe thousands of companies that provide Web site hosting. Most charge a monthly fee that depends on the services they offer. Some offer free Web hosting in exchange for advertising from your site. Although you can search on the Internet for a Web host, I recommend talking to friends or looking in your local yellow pages.

When considering a host, there are a number of things—besides price—to keep in mind.

- How much disk space will they let you have for your Web site? Don't pay for more than you need. Remember that (X)HTML files take up very little space while images, sounds, and videos take up successively larger quantities.

- Do they offer technical support? If so, is it by telephone or by email? How long will it take them to get back to you?

- Will they register a domain name *(see page 355)* for you? How much will they charge?

- How fast is their connection to the Internet? This will determine how fast your pages are served to your visitors. Do they have multiple connections in case one of them should become inoperable?

- Do they include dial-up access to the Internet? (They don't usually.) Will they if you need it?

- Will they let you run custom CGI scripts, Server Side Includes, FrontPage extensions, RealAudio, Telnet/SSh, PHP, MySQL, and other advanced features?

- Do they offer a Web hit statistics service to let you know how many people have been visiting your site?

Your ISP as Web host

If you have Internet access, you probably already have a small amount of Web space through your Internet Service Provider (ISP). For example, AOL offers its members 20Mb for each screenname (up to a total of 7 screen names or 140Mb). EarthLink gives its members 10Mb per screenname (up to a total of 8 screen names or 80Mb). Comcast gives its subscribers 25Mb and Verizon offers a rather stingy 10Mb. It might not be enough for your entire Web site but it's certainly enough to get started. Ask your ISP for details.

Figure 23.1 *Go Daddy is one of the accredited registrars of domain names. You can use their site to see if a desired domain name is available.*

Figure 23.2 *If the name is available, you can either register it through Go Daddy or call your Web host and get them to do it for you. (Now you know: the very useful* www. catalancats.com *domain can be yours!)*

Getting Your Own Domain Name

Generally a Web page's address or URL is made up of the name of the server along with the path to the file on that server. When you use a Web host, they rent you a piece of their server and your Web pages take the name of that Web host, by default. For example, in my case, my Web host's server name is *www.crocker.com* and thus the URL for my pages might look something like *www.crocker.com/~lizcastro/.*

However, if you don't want your Web host's server name to appear in your Web page's URL, you can register your own domain name (for around $10 a year) and then ask your Web host to create a *virtual domain* on their server with your domain name. In my case, while my pages are still on Crocker's server, they *look like* they're on my own server: *www.cookwood.com.* Even if your visitors don't know about servers and where the files actually reside, having your own domain name makes your URLs simpler and easier to type, and thus easier to visit.

They also have one very important advantage. If you ever decide to change your Web host (or if they go out of business), you can move your domain to another server and all of your URLs will stay exactly the same.

To get your own domain name:

1. Point your browser at a domain registrar (see *http://www.internic.net/alpha.html* for a list) and check to see if the domain you want is available.

2. Once you've found a domain name, either register it yourself or ask your Web host to set it up for you. Charges vary from host to host, but less than $10 a year is not uncommon. Some Web hosts offer domain registration as part of a discounted hosting fee.

Transferring Files to the Server

In order for other people on the Internet to see your pages, you have to upload them to your Web host's server. One easy way to do that is with an FTP program, like WS_FTP for Windows *(see below)*, or Fetch for Macintosh *(see page 358)*. Many Web page editors offer publishing features as well. (AOL members can either use AOL's rather awkward FTP tools, or an FTP program like those described here.)

To define a new FTP site's properties:

1. In the Connect to Remote Host window (which appears upon launching WS_FTP Pro), click Create Site, or click the Connection Wizard button in WS_FTP's toolbar **(Figure 23.3)**.

2. In the WS_FTP Connection Wizard boxes, name your connection so you can find it in the list, choose the type of connection **(Figure 23.4)**, specify the name of the FTP server (ask your Web host if you're not sure), and enter your user name and password. Click Next for each screen and click Finish when you're done.

To transfer files to the server with WS_FTP (for Windows):

1. Connect to the Internet and open WS_FTP.

2. Click Connect in the upper-left corner of WS_FTP's main window **(Figure 23.5)**.

3. Choose your site in the list and click Connect. The server is accessed.

4. On the right side of the window, navigate to the directory on the server to which you want to upload files.

5. On the left side of the window, navigate to the directory on your hard disk that has the files you want to upload.

Figure 23.3 *If you didn't enter information about your Web host's FTP server when you launched the program, or to enter information about a new server, click the Connection Wizard button in the main WS_FTP window.*

Figure 23.4 *Follow the instructions in the series of windows that appear. For example, in this window, you have to choose what sort of connection you want to create. If you have any doubts, contact your Web host.*

Figure 23.5 *To connect to your Web host's FTP server, click the Connect button in WS_FTP's main window. Then choose your site in the Site Manager window.*

Transferring Files to the Server

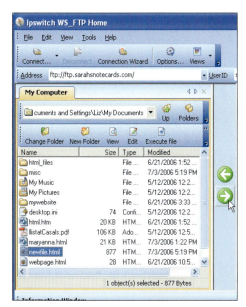

Figure 23.6 *In the left part of the window (shown), select the files from your hard disk that you want to upload. In the right part of the window (shown in Figure 23.7), select the destination directory on the server. Then click the right-pointing arrow in the middle to transfer the files.*

Figure 23.7 *The newly transferred file appears in the frame on the right side of the window.*

6. Select the desired files in the left frame and click the right-pointing arrow in the middle of the screen **(Figure 23.6)**. The files are transferred **(Figure 23.7)**.

7. Click Disconnect to close the connection to the server.

✔ Tips

- You can find WS_FTP's home page at *www.ipswitch.com/products/ws_ftp/*.

- (X)HTML, CSS, CGI, and JavaScript files should be transferred in ASCII mode. All other files, including images, sounds, and videos should be transferred in Binary mode. WS_FTP knows how to transfer most common Web files. You can define additional types in the ASCII Filenames tab that appears when you press the Options button in the toolbar.

- There are many other file transfer programs for Windows besides WS_FTP. Do a search at CNET's shareware site *(www.shareware.com)* if you'd prefer to use some other program. They all work pretty much the same way.

Fetch is the leading FTP client for Macintosh. It was recently upgraded to include native support for Mac OS X 10.4 (Tiger) but there are older versions that run on earlier systems.

To transfer files to the server with Fetch (for the Mac):

1. Open your Internet connection.

2. Open Fetch.

3. Choose File > New Connection.

4. In the New Connection window, enter the server name in the Hostname box, your user name in the Username box, the way you want to connect in the Connect using menu (ask your Web host if you're not sure), your password in the Password box, and, if desired, the path to the directory where you plan to save the Web pages in the Initial folder box **(Figure 23.9)**.

5. Click OK to open the connection. Fetch will make the connection to the server you requested and open the designated directory (or the top directory if you haven't specified one).

6. If necessary, navigate to the directory where you wish to place your Web files.

7. Click the Put button or press Command-U **(Figure 23.10)**.

8. In the dialog box that appears, choose the files that you wish to transfer to the server. Select multiple files holding down the Shift key. Select multiple non-contiguous files holding down the Command key. When you have selected all the files you wish to transfer, click the Put button **(Figure 23.11)**.

9. Click OK. The files are transferred to the server and maintain the hierarchy they had on the local system **(Figure 23.12)**.

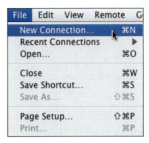

Figure 23.8 *Choose File > New Connection to give Fetch the information about your Web host's server.*

Figure 23.9 *Enter the name of your Web host's server, your account username and password, and the initial folder that you want to see. Click Connect (not shown).*

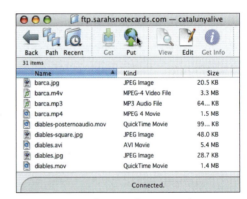

Figure 23.10 *Make sure the proper directory on the server (where you want to transfer the files) is showing in the window bar before transferring the files (here, catalunyalive). Click the Put button, or press Command-U.*

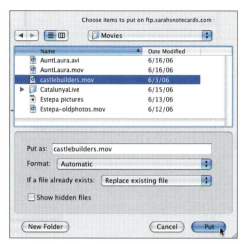

Figure 23.11 *Select the desired file from your computer. You can change the name that it will have on the server if you like (with the Put as box). Then click Put.*

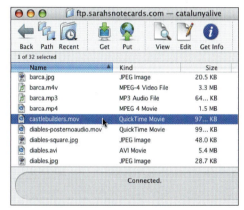

Figure 23.12 *The chosen files are uploaded to the desired directory.*

✔ Tips

■ Fetch used to belong to Dartmouth University but was bought back by its principal engineer, Jim Matthews (thanks to winnings from a stint on the television show, *Who Wants to Be a Millionaire?*). You can find Fetch's Web site, complete with upgrades, documentation, and support at *http://fetchsoftworks.com*.

■ (X)HTML, CSS, CGI, and JavaScript files should always be transferred as Text (in ASCII mode). Any other file, including images, sound, and video, should be transferred as Raw Data. Fetch's Automatic option in the Format menu will automatically upload these typical kinds of Web files in the proper format.

■ You can use Fetch for secure FTP by choosing SFTP in the Connect using box in Figure 23.9.

■ You can resize the main window so that it shows more files at one time. Just click and drag the bottom-right corner.

■ Relative URLs *(see page 37)* are maintained when you transfer a folder to the server. Absolute URLs *(see page 36)*, must be updated to reflect the files' new locations.

■ In version 4.0.3 of Fetch, the program would convert characters from the default MacRoman character set to ISO-8859-1. If you use Fetch 4 and save your document as anything other than MacRoman *(see pages 46 and 333)*, it's better to turn this feature off (Customize > Preferences > Misc and then uncheck Translate ISO Characters). If you *do* use this feature, your files' `meta` tags should specify the ISO 8859-1 character set, *not* MacRoman *(see page 330)*. Fetch 5 does not have this feature.

24

Getting People to Visit

With billions of Web pages in existence and thousands more being created every day, you may have to shout a little to get your page noticed. This chapter explains the (X)HTML tags you can use to identify your page to search engines like Google and Yahoo as well as a few strategies you can use to get noticed by these portals to the Web.

There are a number of good resources on the Web for improving one's ranking in search engines. For this chapter, I am indebted to two excellent WebMonkey articles written by Paul Boutin *(hotwired.lycos.com/webmonkey/ 01/23/index1a.html* and *www.hotwired.com/ webmonkey/99/31/index1a.html)* and to the site put together at *searchenginewatch.com* by Danny Sullivan.

There are several *search engine optimization* companies who would like to charge you for completing the steps I outline in this chapter —while making big promises about search engine results. Unfortunately, some of them go too far and spend much too much energy (not to mention your money) trying to trick visitors into coming to your site (or trying to trick search engines into listing your site). Their slimy techniques, apart from annoying potential visitors, can even get you removed from some search engines. If you have real (non-pornographic, non-gambling) content on your site, you can do just as good or better without them.

About Keywords

When prospective visitors go to a search engine to find information, they type a few identifying *keywords* that describe what they're looking for. The more those words are honestly reflected on your page, the better your chances are that your page will appear in a search engine's results. So, it's a good idea to think about what your page is about, decide on some keywords that describe your page (and that might be used to find it), and then use your keywords consistently.

Do

- Use keywords in your title *(see page 60)*.

- Use keywords in headers *(see page 61)*.

- Keep the content of your page as specific and focused on your topic as possible, and be sure to include your keywords.

- Specify keywords in a `meta` tag *(see page 363)*.

- Use keywords in an image's `alt` tag, where applicable *(see page 91)*.

But...

- Don't create headers out of GIF images if they contain keywords since search engines cannot understand the text in an image. At the very least, add keywords to such an image's `alt` tag *(see page 91)*.

- Don't use keywords where they don't make sense. It is their *natural* and consistent use which is rewarded.

- Don't repeat keywords endlessly and meaninglessly, perhaps in a small font or with the same color as the background. This is called *spamming* and can get you banned from a search engine's results.

```
<head>
    <title>Barcelona's Market</title>
    ...
</head>
<body>
<h1>Barcelona's Market</h1>
<img src="barcelonamarket.jpg" alt="Barcelona's
Market" width="160" height="204" />
<p>This first picture shows the entranceway to the
Mercat de la Boquería, Barcelona's central market
that is just off the Rambles. It's an incredible place,
full of every kind of fruit, meat, fish, or whatever you
might happen to need. It took me a long time to get
up the nerve to actually take a picture there. You
might say I'm kind of a chicken, but since I lived
there, it was just sort of strange. Do you take
pictures of your supermarket?</p>
</body>
```

Figure 24.1 *In this document, I've used the keywords* Barcelona *and* market *in the title, headers, alternate text for images, and in the first paragraph. Try searching for* Barcelona market *on Google.*

Figure 24.2 *Use keywords as consistently and naturally as you can. If you do it right, there's no reason to cheat.*

```
<head>

<title>Barcelona's Market</title>

<meta name="keywords" content="Barcelona,
market" />

   ...

</head>

<body>

<h1>Barcelona's Market</h1>

<img src="barcelonamarket.jpg" alt="Barcelona's
Market" width="160" height="204" />

<p>This first picture shows the entranceway to the
Mercat de la Boquería, Barcelona's central market
that is just off the Rambles. It's an incredible place,
full of every kind of fruit, meat, fish, or whatever you
might happen to need. It took me a long time to get
up the nerve to actually take a picture there. You
might say I'm kind of a chicken, but since I lived
there, it was just sort of strange. Do you take
pictures of your supermarket?</p>

</body>
```

Figure 24.3 *If you want to emphasize to a search engine what your page is about, you can specify the keywords with a* meta *tag.*

Explicitly Listing Keywords

You can explicitly tell search engines exactly what your page is about by specifying a list of relevant keywords.

To explicitly list keywords:

1. In the head section of your page, type **<meta name="keywords" content="**.

2. Type a few words or phrases that concisely describe the topic discussed on your page. Separate each word or phrase with a comma and a space.

3. Type **" />** to complete the meta tag.

✔ Tips

- Google ignores keywords specified with a meta tag. It's more interested in keywords that appear in the page's content.

- Use a combination of unique and more general words to describe the contents of your page. *Chihuahua* is unique, but *dog* may also net you some visitors who didn't realize they were interested in Chihuahuas (or couldn't spell it).

- Actually, adding misspelled keywords (in *addition* to correctly spelled ones) is not such a bad idea. You might offer several alternative spellings for foreign words.

- More words is not necessarily better. According to Paul Boutin *(see page 361)*, the closer you match what a prospective visitor types (with no extra words), the higher up you'll get listed in the results.

- If you're using frames, include keywords in each frame and in the frameset itself.

Explicitly Listing Keywords

Providing a Description of Your Page

Search engines try to help visitors distinguish between results by adding information about the individual pages next to their URLs. Some search engines let you specify the description that should appear next to your page.

To control your page's summary:

1. In the head section of your page, type **<meta name="description" content="**.

2. Type a concise sentence or two that describes your page and hopefully persuades folks to click through.

3. Type **" />** to complete the meta tag.

✔ Tips

■ When a visitor sees a list of links that match their keywords, the description of your page may help it outshine the competition. Be careful to describe your page succinctly and descriptively. Avoid generic marketing hype in favor of specific features that set your site apart from the rest.

■ If your page is set up with frames, be sure to include a description in every frame page, as well as the frameset itself.

■ Google does not pay any attention to the description you include with the meta tag. Instead, it shows visitors the specified keywords in the context of the matching pages.

```
<head>

<meta http-equiv="content-type"
content="text/html; charset=utf-8" />

<meta name="keywords" content="Barcelona,
market" />

<meta name="description" content="An insider's
view of the Barcelona market, complete with
photos." />

<title>Barcelona's Market</title>

</head>

<body>

<h1>Barcelona's Market</h1>
```

Figure 24.4 *You can offer search engines a concise description of your site.*

Figure 24.5 *Yahoo begins the listing description with what you've put in the description* meta *tag and then adds the initial content of the page itself.*

```
<head>

<meta http-equiv="content-type"
content="text/html; charset=utf-8" />

<meta name="keywords" content="Barcelona,
market" />

<meta name="description" content="An insider's
view of the Barcelona market, complete with
photos." />

<meta name="generator" content="BBEdit 8.2.6"
/>

<meta name="author" content="Liz Castro" />

<meta name="copyright" content="&copy; 2002-
2006 Liz Castro" />

<title>Barcelona's Market</title>

</head>

<body>

<h1>Barcelona's Market</h1>
```

Figure 24.6 *You can use as many* meta *tags as you need.*

Figure 24.7 *The* meta *information is always invisible in the browser.*

Controlling Other Information

You can also add information to your page about who wrote it, what program was used (if any) to generate the (X)HTML code, and if it is copyrighted. Note, however, that search engines do not currently use this information (though they may some day), and browsers don't display it.

To control other information about your page:

1. In the head section of your Web page, type **<meta name="author" content= "name" />**, where *name* is the person who wrote the (X)HTML page.

2. In the head section of your Web page, type **<meta name="generator" content= "program" />**, where *program* is the name of the software that created (or edited) the (X)HTML page.

3. In the head section of your Web page, type **<meta name="copyright" content= "© year holder" />**, where *year* is the calendar year of the copyright, and *holder* is the name of the person or entity who holds the copyright to the page.

✔ Tips

■ The generator is created automatically by most Web page editors. You can delete it if you prefer not to give them credit.

■ When you saved pages with Internet Explorer 5 for Windows, it actually had the chutzpah to add meta information to the pages, claiming to be its generator. (For more information on saving the source code from a page on the Web, consult *The Inspiration of Others* on page 53.) IE 6 and IE 7 are not so bold.

Keeping Visitors Away

Search engines employ little programs called *robots* or *spiders* to hang out on the Web and look for new pages to add to the engine's index. But sometimes, you don't want search engines to know your page exists. Perhaps it's a personal page designed only for your family or an internal page for your company. You can add information to the page so that most search engine robots will stay out.

To keep search engine robots out:

1. In the head section of your page, type **<meta name="robots" content="**.

2. If desired, type **noindex** to keep the robot from adding the page to its index.

3. If desired, type **nofollow** to keep the robot from following the links on the page and indexing those pages.

4. Type **" />** to complete the tag.

✔ Tips

■ Separate multiple values with a comma and a space.

■ With a couple billion Web pages in existence, the easiest (but not foolproof) way to keep people away from your page is to never create any link *to* that page from any other page on your or anyone else's site (and, obviously, don't submit it to a search engine).

■ If a page has already been indexed, you'll have to go to the search engine's Web site and use the Remove URL page.

■ You can use the values `all` and `index` to have robots add the current page (and its links) to the search engine's index. However, these are the default values and so leaving them out is the same as specifying them (but faster).

```
<head>
    <meta http-equiv="content-type"
content="text/html; charset=utf-8" />

<meta name="copyright" content="&copy; 2007
Liz Castro" />

<meta name="robots" content="noindex,
nofollow" />

    <title>Private thoughts</title>
</head>
<body>
This is my personal page! I don't want it to be
indexed by search engines.
</body>
</html>
```

Figure 24.8 *When a search engine's robot encounters this page, it will ignore both the page and the page's links.*

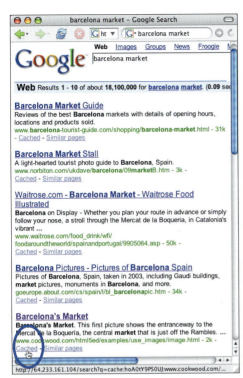

Figure 24.9 *Some search engines, like Google shown here, keep a copy of the pages that they index so that visitors can see what's on the page even if the page is not available.*

```
<head>

<meta name="copyright" content="&copy; 2002
Liz Castro" />

<meta name="robots" content="noarchive" />

    <title>Untitled</title>

</head>

<body>

<p>This is a page I update frequently (or perhaps
it's a temporary page). I don't want search engines
to keep a copy of it in their archives.</p>
```

Figure 24.10 *When a search engine's robot encounters this page, it will continue to index the page, but it won't archive it (and thus won't be able to offer a cached version should your page (or server) be unavailable).*

Keeping Pages From Being Archived

Some search engines save a copy of your Web page and offer it as an alternative if your site is down or otherwise inaccessible. However, there is no guarantee that this cached version is up to date. If you'd rather your page not be archived on a search engine's server, you can tell the robot not to archive it.

To keep search engines from archiving your pages:

In the head section of your page, type **<meta name="robots" content="noarchive" />**.

✔ Tip

■ Presently, Google is the most important search engine that archives Web pages. If you'd like to keep only Google from archiving your pages, you can specify googlebot instead of robots as the value of the name attribute above.

Creating a Site Map Manually

Search engines let you submit individual URLs and promise to follow all the links they find in order to index your site. To make it especially easy for them to find all the nooks and crannies on your site, you can create a site map with links to all of the most important sections of your site and then submit that map to the search engine, thus ensuring that the proper pages will be noticed and indexed.

To create a site map with your browser:

1. Create a new Bookmarks or Favorites Folder.

2. On the Web, navigate to the important pages on your site that you want to be sure the search engine finds.

3. Add those pages to your new folder.

4. Export your Bookmarks or Favorites into a file.

5. Open the file in your text editor and remove the bookmarks that don't belong to your site. The resulting file will be your site map.

6. Upload the file to your server *(see page 356)*.

7. Submit the site map to the desired search engines as described on page 370.

✔ Tips

- Other browsers, like Firefox and Opera, have similar tools for adding bookmarks and then exporting them to a file.

- Google's Sitemap Generator, described on the next page, is a more robust tool for creating a site map.

Figure 24.11 *In the Organize Favorites dialog box, click New Folder and give the new folder a name. Then click Done.*

Figure 24.12 *After choosing Add to Favorites, select the site map page folder in which the link should be added.*

Figure 24.13 *In the Import/Export Wizard, be sure to choose the Export Favorites option and then click the Next button where you can give the site map file a name.*

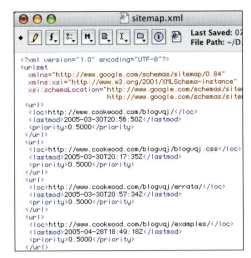

Figure 24.14 *Google's Sitemap Generator creates an XML file with the URL, last modification date and relative importance of each of the pages on your site. It can generate the file from a list of directories, your access logs, or even a text file you've written manually.*

Using Google Sitemaps

Google is working on some interesting tools for getting your site indexed as fully as possible. First, they have developed the *sitemap protocol*, which is an XML application that lists all the URLs on your site, as well as when they were last updated and how important they are with respect to the site as a whole.

Second, they have created the Sitemap Generator, an Open Source Python program that you can run on your site to create a site map in Google's sitemap format from a list of your site's directories, from your site's access logs, or even from a simple text-format listing of the URLs on your site.

Finally, Google offers some very helpful diagnostic and statistical tools called Google Sitemaps. They can tell you if they're having trouble analyzing your site, the average rank of your twenty highest ranked pages, and much more.

And it's all free.

✔ Tips

- You can find more information about Google Sitemaps, including the sitemap protocol and Sitemap Generator at *https://www.google.com/webmasters/ sitemaps/docs/en/about.html*

- There is a very helpful step-by-step instruction set for using the Sitemap Generator at *https://www.google.com/ webmasters/sitemaps/docs/en/sitemap- generator.html* (including the dash after *sitemap*).

- Because the program is still in beta, in the future, some of the offerings may differ from what is described here.

Submitting Your Site to a Search Engine

Once you have carefully used keywords and added `meta` tags to all of the desired pages on your site and perhaps created a site map (as described on page 368) that lists those pages, you'll want to invite a search engine to visit your site in order to add your pages to its database.

To submit your site to a search engine:

1. Connect to the search engine of your choice.

2. Find their Add URL page.

3. Google's is at *http://www.google.com/ addurl.html* **(Figure 24.15)**.

Yahoo's is at *http://docs.yahoo.com/ info/suggest/*

4. Type your (site map) page's URL in the appropriate text box and click the Submit button.

5. Go back to the search engine in two weeks and search for your site. If it doesn't appear, submit it again.

Figure 24.15 *Go to the search engine's Add URL page. This is Google. You can add comments about your page, though they are not used in the search results.*

✔ Tips

■ The most popular general search engines are Google and Yahoo. Also see *http:// www.useit.com/about/searchreferrals.html.*

■ You might also want to register your site with a search engine that specializes in a particular topic. For a list of such engines, see *http://searchenginewatch.com/links/ article.php/2156351*

Improving Your Ranking by Getting Linked

While matching a visitor's search criteria might get your page among the results, one of the key factors in bubbling your page to the top of those results is its *popularity*, as measured by the number and importance of similar pages (outside your site) that link to it. In short, if you get other sites to link to your site, your page will appear higher up in the rankings.

To improve your ranking by getting linked:

- Ask sites with similar content if they would link to your site.

- Join Web rings of sites with similar content.

- Offer to exchange links with sites of similar content.

- Make sure to submit your site to major as well as specific search engines.

✔ Tips

- Don't create bogus domains and then link to your page from there. Search engines can spot this scam from a mile away.

- Links from authoritative, high-traffic sites of the same topic are more valuable than links from less authoritative, less visited, or more generic sites.

- You can find out who links to you by typing **link:yourdomain.com** in Google.

- Note that the wording of the link and the keywords on the originating page can be almost as important in determining how and whether a page gets listed as the keywords on the page itself. (For more details, do a search for *googlebombing*.)

Writing Pages That Are Easy to Index

There are three major Web design practices that can sabotage your efforts to get noticed by search engines: frames, image maps, and dynamically generated pages.

Frames

While frames were useful for showing more than one page at a time, this flexibility can also kept them from getting indexed by search engines. Some search engines will ignore a frameset's frames in favor of its alternate content (as marked by the `noframe` tag). And if they do index an individual frame, search engines often give the individual frame as a result, which may or may not make sense without the enclosing frameset **(Figures 24.16**, **24.17**, and **24.18**). For more on frames, see my Web site *(see page 25)*.

Image maps

Some search engines don't know what to do with image maps and ignore them altogether. Any linked pages may thus not get indexed. It's always a good idea to repeat the links from an image map as text, both for search engines and for visitors who cannot use images.

Dynamically generated pages

While you can create fancy, customized effects by dynamically creating pages based on information you've collected from your visitors, these pages are hard for search engines to deal with. On the one hand, they may be suspicious that you're trying to serve different versions to search engines than you are to regular visitors (a big no-no that can also get your page removed from a search engine). On the other hand, the page is a moving target; there's no place to link to once a prospective visitor says they're interested in going back. At the very least, use URLs that search engines can digest, preferably without ? or & (as may appear in CGI instructions).

Figure 24.16 *So inspired by the endless Catalan examples in this book, you go searching for* Catalan *at Yahoo and find this page.*

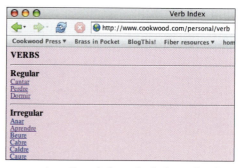

Figure 24.17 *You click on the link, and unbeknownst to you, see only an individual frame, instead of the entire frameset. You're missing a huge part of the site.*

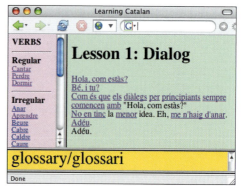

Figure 24.18 *You might never see the rest of the site. The person who designed this frame-based site (yes, it was me) should have given you a way to get to the frameset from the individual frame.*

Other Techniques for Publicizing Your Site

Although getting your site to appear at the top of the list when a prospective visitor looks for related topics at Google is a laudable goal, there are several additional ways to let people know your page exists.

- Add your URL to your signature so that it will be included in all outgoing email.

- Answer questions or post information on a related newsgroup and make sure your URL is prominently included in your signature. (On the other hand, it's also considered good form to keep your signature relatively brief and humble.)

- Create a blog and write frequent, substantive, interesting articles on the same or a similar topic as your Web site. Add a link to your Web site from your blog.

- Join a Web ring. A Web ring is a group of related Web sites that have links that go from one site to the next. Web rings encourage visitors from one site to explore related ones. You can search for pertinent Web rings at Yahoo.

- Even simpler than a Web ring is to exchange links with other sites that have similar content.

- Make sure your Web site's URL appears on your stationery, business cards, pamphlets and other promotional material, and advertisements.

- And of course, you can always pay someone to advertise your page for you.

Other Techniques for Publicizing Your Site

SYNDICATION AND PODCASTING

When you make changes to your site, it's nice to have people notice. Although mass emailings might do the trick, they also might alienate your visitors. Instead, you can publish a summary of recent changes or *feed* of your site, in a format that can be read by specialized programs called *aggregators*. If your visitors decide to subscribe to your feed, the aggregator automatically notifies them of any updates to your site. The visitors can then either view the change right in the aggregator window, or jump back to your site to read it *in situ*. This process is called *syndication*. One of its strong points is that it gives control to your visitors—they choose whether or not to subscribe—as it gives them access to your updated content.

In the early days, it was only text articles that were syndicated. Since 2004, however, with the advent of enclosures, you can create multimedia feeds called *podcasts*. Podcasts make audio, video, still image, or even PDF files available to your subscribers, sometimes with no affiliated Web site at all. They're not necessarily designed for iPods, despite their name, though iPods can make them mobile. Apple has helped make podcasts popular by making them freely available through its iTunes Music Store, which serves as a podcast aggregator, or *podcatcher*.

In this chapter, I'll show you how to decide what to include in a feed for your Web site, how to write the actual feed, how to publish the feed, and how to subscribe to the feed.

What a Feed Looks Like

There are two principal families of feeds: namely Atom and RSS (*Really Simple Syndication*). RSS in turn is divided into several more subgroups. Currently, however, the trend is towards *RSS 2.0* and so that's what I'll stick to in this chapter. The others are not that different though, so you should be able to use what you find here and then quickly Google the differences.

All feeds are XML files. RSS 2.0 feeds have two main parts: an *introductory section* and a *list of items*. The introductory section contains elements that describe the Web site, giving its name, URL, and a description, as well as information about when it was last updated, who the webmaster is, and much more.

The introductory section is followed by a list of items which describe the site's individual articles or sections. Sometimes items are summaries of larger articles found elsewhere with a link to the rest of the content. Sometimes, the entire article is found in the item itself, complete with (X)HTML formatting. Sometimes, the item is a multimedia enclosure, like an audio or video file. At the very least, an item must be comprised of a title or a description. Items can have much more though, including links to the full content, the name of the author, the category in which the item belongs, a unique identifier, and more.

Strictly speaking, an RSS feed doesn't have to be affiliated with a Web site. A podcast, for example, tends to be an independent stream of video or audio files. While their creators might have a support site, the podcast is more than an updatable summary of the site, it has a life of its own.

```xml
<?xml version="1.0" encoding="UTF-8"?>

<rss xmlns:itunes="http://www.itunes.com
/dtds/podcast-1.0.dtd" version="2.0">

<channel>

<itunes:owner>

    <itunes:name>Elizabeth Castro</itunes:name>

    <itunes:email>sarah@cookwood.com
</itunes:email></itunes:owner>


<title>Catalunya Live</title>

<link>http://catalunyalive.blogspot.com</link>

<description>This is what Catalunya looks like-- in
action!</description>

<language>en</language>

<copyright>Copyright 2006 Elizabeth Castro. All
Rights Reserved</copyright>

<managingEditor>sarah@cookwood.com
</managingEditor>

<lastBuildDate>Sat, 03 Jun 2006 09:00:00
EST</lastBuildDate>

<ttl>144</ttl>

<itunes:image href="http://
www.sarahsnotecards.com/catalunyalive/
segadors-square2.jpg" />

<itunes:author>Elizabeth Castro</itunes:author>

<itunes:summary>This is what Catalunya looks like-
- in action!</itunes:summary>

...

<item>

<title>What does Barcelona Look Like? (Part 1: The
Eixample)</title>

<link>http://catalunyalive.blogspot.com/2006/
07/what-does-barcelona-look-like-part-1_06.html
</link>
```

Figure 25.1 *An RSS feed is an XML document that describes (and sometimes contains) the latest additions to your Web page, blog, or podcast.*

Figure 25.2 *In an aggregator (like NetNews-Wire Lite, shown), the items in your feed appear as articles in the upper-right frame and the articles themselves, along with a link to your site, appear in the lower-right frame.*

Figure 25.3 *In iTunes, the same RSS feed is displayed slightly differently, with the items in a list below the description of the podcast and the first image of the video enclosure in the Now Playing box in the lower left.*

Of course, a feed looks a lot different in an aggregator (also called *readers*, *RSS readers*, *news aggregators,* and for multimedia podcasts, *podcatchers*). And it may look a lot different from one aggregator to the next.

Typical aggregators, like FeedDemon or its Mac counterpart NetNewsWire, have a two- or three-paned window with the feeds listed in one pane, the article names in the second, and the content of the article in a third **(Figure 25.2)**. You can see at a glance which feeds have new articles, and which articles you've already read. These aggregators are particularly good at text feeds but are increasingly able to handle podcasts as well.

Apple's iTunes (available free for both Mac and Windows) specializes in multimedia feeds, or podcasts. Podcast creators submit their podcasts to iTunes and then iTunes sorts them, makes them available, manages the subscriptions, and has one special feature: if desired, it can copy podcasts, complete with audio or video, to an iPod, which enables the subscriber to take the podcast with them. iTunes' special RSS tags for describing podcasts have become the de facto standard. We'll discuss them on pages 386–393.

You can also use most current browsers as aggregators. In Firefox, click the orange feed icon next to the URL. In Opera, click the RSS button next to the URL. In IE 7, click the orange feed menu in the toolbar. Of course, the icons will only appear if the browser detects an RSS feed for the site.

It's important to note that browsers show RSS feeds pretty differently. While Opera and IE have separate feed windows that look a lot like standalone aggregators, Firefox displays the items in an RSS feed as a submenu. Firefox's method lends itself to using the RSS feed as an expanded bookmark system—giving quick access to important parts of your site right from the bookmark menu.

What a Feed Looks Like

Getting Ready for Syndication

Whether you want to syndicate text, audio, or video, an RSS feed is most often used to distribute *new* content as opposed to changed content. Imagine a long running television series as opposed to an individual movie. Bloggers want their visitors to know when they've written a new entry; podcasters want their latest program to be available.

As you get ready to syndicate your own site, think about what will go in the feed. Does your site have features that are regularly updated? Does it have a blog? Does it have any other sort of regular column? These kinds of dynamic, timely articles are the ideal content for an RSS feed.

How many articles do you want to include? While there is no real limit on how many items can go in a feed, adding too many items may overwhelm your readers or make it difficult for them to find what they're looking for. Anywhere from ten to 50 items is about average. You can always make your older items available on your Web site.

Another decision that you have to make is whether to include entire articles, summaries or excerpts of articles, or just the first twenty or thirty words with a link to the full page. Since aggregators style content very simply, you have to choose whether you want visitors to have easy access to all your content, even if it means less control over what it looks like, or if you want to try and tease them over to your site by only offering summaries or excerpts. (Currently, there is no way to style content in the aggregator.)

Finally, think about what kind of descriptive information you want to add. There are many meta tags that help visitors find your feed. I'll discuss these in detail further along in the chapter.

```
<?xml version="1.0" encoding="UTF-8"?>

<rss version="2.0">

<channel>


</channel>

</rss>
```

Figure 25.4 *An RSS feed is an XML document. This means it must start with an XML declaration and then the* `<rss>` *root element. The syntax is persnickety but not particularly complex.*

RSS Feed Generators

There are tools that facilitate creating RSS feeds but it's a little bit like using an accountant to do your taxes. If you hire an accountant, her job is to ask you questions about your last year's earnings, but the task of assembling that information still stays with you. Feed writers (like Feeder—*http://reinventedsoftware.com/feeder/*), are similar. They provide dialog boxes where you enter the data and then they assemble the feed in the proper format for you. You have to weigh whether the cost and learning curve associated with such programs, as well as the loss of absolute control over the output is worth the automation that they provide.

And you can always do what I do: hire an accountant *and* tweak the results.

Starting an RSS Feed

An RSS feed is an XML document and as such must conform with XML syntax *(see page 38)*. Over the next few pages, I'll show you how to write the whole thing with just a text editor. While you can create syndication feeds in several formats, RSS 2.0 is perhaps the most widespread and the most versatile. It's what we'll use in this chapter.

To start an RSS feed:

1. Open a new text document with any text editor.

2. At the top, begin the XML declaration by typing: **<?xml version="1.0"**

3. Next, declare the character encoding as *utf-8* by typing **encoding="UTF-8"**.

4. Complete the xml declaration with **?>**.

5. Next, declare that you're using RSS 2.0 by typing **<rss version="2.0">**.

6. To begin the information about your site, type **<channel>**.

7. Leave a few spaces for the rest of the feed (which you'll complete in the rest of this chapter) and then close the `channel` and `rss` elements by typing **</channel> </rss>**.

8. Save the document as text only with the .xml extension. Make sure you encode it in UTF-8. (See page 333 for details.)

✔ Tips

■ While the UTF-8 encoding is not required for all aggregators, it is required for some (iTunes among them), and is the norm.

■ RSS is case sensitive. *<channel>* is not the same as *<Channel>*. Follow the examples closely.

Describing Your Site in the Feed

Once you've got the declarations done, you can work on the introductory section of your feed, the part that describes your Web site.

To describe your site:

1. After the opening `<channel>` tag that you created in step 6 on page 379, type **<title>Web Site</title>**, where *Web site* is the name of your site.

2. Next, type **<link>url</link>**, where *url* is the location of your Web site.

3. Type **<description>about site</description>**, where *about site* describes the Web site.

4. If desired, add additional descriptive elements. In each case, use the syntax **<tag>content</tag>**.

   Use `<language>` to advise prospective readers what language your content is in. Use the two-letter code listed in *http://www.rssboard.org/rss-language-codes*. English is *en*.

   Use `<copyright>` to declare the rights restrictions for your content.

   Use `<managingEditor>` to give the email of the person who is in charge of content.

   Use `<webMaster>` to give the email address of the person in charge of technical issues regarding your site.

   Use `<pubDate>` for the official publication date of your content, like the dateline on a newspaper article. The date must be in RFC-822 format (see the third tip).

   Use `<lastBuildDate>` to specify the actual date and time the content was last updated, in RFC-822 format (again, see the third tip).

```xml
<?xml version="1.0" encoding="UTF-8"?>

<rss version="2.0">

<channel>

<title>Catalunya Live</title>

<link>http://catalunyalive.blogspot.com</link>

<description>This is what Catalunya looks like-- in action!</description>

<language>en</language>

<copyright>Copyright 2006 Elizabeth Castro. All Rights Reserved</copyright>

<managingEditor>sarah@cookwood.com</managingEditor>

<webMaster>sarah@cookwood.com</webMaster>

<pubDate>Thu, 06 Jul 2006 09:00:00 EST</pubDate>

<lastBuildDate>Thu, 06 Jul 2006 09:00:00 EST</lastBuildDate>

<category>Catalunya</category>

<category>Barcelona</category>

<category>Travel</category>

<ttl>144</ttl>

<item>
```

Figure 25.5 *The elements that describe your RSS feed go between the opening* `<channel>` *element and the first* `<item>` *element (which we'll get to in the next section).*

Use `<category>` to help aggregators classify your feed and make it easier for folks to find you (but see sidebar).

Use `<ttl>` (which stands for *time to live*) to indicate how frequently you are most likely to update it and thus how often the aggregator should come back and refresh.

5. Create the `item` elements as described on pages 382–383.

✔ Tips

- Only the `title`, `link`, and `description` elements are absolutely required.

- Specifying the additional descriptive elements helps prospective visitors find you.

- The date in `pubDate` and `lastBuildDate` should be in the form *Mon, 23 Apr 2007 11:15:01 EST.* The day of the week is optional but if present, should be abbreviated to three letters and in English. The month is required and should also be in English and abbreviated to 3 letters. The seconds are optional. The time zone must be one of *UT, GMT, EST, EDT, CST, CDT, MST, MDT, PST, PDT,* or military abbreviations, or can be specified by a plus or minus sign plus the difference in hours and minutes from GMT: -0800. You can find the full specification by Googling RFC 822.

- There are several more elements that can go in your RSS feed (inside the `channel` element) but aren't widely used or supported. These are: `generator`, `docs`, `image`, `cloud`, `skipHours`, `skipDays`, `rating`, `textInput`. You can find more information about them, along with the full RSS 2.0 specification, at *http://www.rssboard.org/rss-specification.*

About RSS Categories

As far as I can tell, there's no "official" list of categories to choose from when describing your RSS feed with the `category` element. Indeed, the only aggregator that I have found that pays attention to categories at all is iTunes, but it uses a different syntax (that we'll discuss on pages 388–391).

Describing Your Site in the Feed

Adding Items to a Feed

The items are the individual articles that will show up in an aggregator. They can either be a teaser with a link to the full article, or they can include the entire story.

To add items to a feed:

1. After the final element in the introductory section, as described on pages 380–381, begin the first article by typing **<item>**.

2. Describe your item by using one or more of the following elements. Again, use the syntax **<tag>content</tag>**:

   Use the `<title>` element to identify each item in your feed.

   Use the `<link>` element to point your visitors toward the full version of the article on your site.

   Use the `<description>` element for either a summary, excerpt, or for the entire article. The description may contain (X)HTML (except for iTunes).

   Use `<guid>` (which stands for *globally unique identifier*) to enclose a permalink URL or other unique value so that aggregators can have some way of uniquely identifying your feed articles. If the link *is* a permalink, add `isPermaLink="true"` to the initial `guid` tag. In this case, the `guid` element must be a URL.

   Use `<pubDate>` to give the publication date for the item. The date must be formatted according to RFC 822 as described in the tips on page 381.

   Use `<author>` for the email address of the person who created the item.

   Use `<category>` to tag the article with a category so that it's easier for your prospective audience to find it.

```
<category>Barcelona</category>

<category>Travel</category>

<ttl>144</ttl>

<item>

<title>What does Barcelona Look Like? (Part 1: The
Eixample)</title>

<link>http://catalunyalive.blogspot.com/2006/
07/what-does-barcelona-look-like-part-1_06.html
</link>

<description>Here is some video of Barcelona's
lower Eixample district, around Carrer Casp north
(to the right) of Passeig de Gracia. You'll see the
typical six or seven story apartment building, with
ever-present balconies and other wonderful
architectural details. There are inlaid designs on the
building exteriors, wrought iron, stained glass,
textured concrete, and more.</description>

<guid isPermaLink="true">http://catalunyalive.
blogspot.com/2006/07/what-does-barcelona-
look-like-part-1_06.html</guid>

<pubDate>Wed, 05 Jul 2006 15:45:00
EST</pubDate>

</item>

<item>

<title>Barça, Barça, Barrrrrr-ça!</title>

<link>http://catalunyalive.blogspot.com/2006/0
6/bara-bara-barrrrrr.html</link>

<description>We went to our favorite bar one night
and the bar owner recognized us from other visits
and we started talking. He then offered us his
Barcelona Football Club Membership card and said
we should go see a game. I was flabbergasted but
we accepted.

We have a friend who thinks that the future of
Catalan Independence lies with the Barça...
perhaps he's right.</description>
```

Figure 25.6 *The* item *elements describe the individual articles in your RSS feed.*

Figure 25.7 *An RSS feed's items are listed in the articles frame of most aggregators, like Net-NewsWire, shown. Note how the first item in the RSS feed appears at the top of the list. The content of the* description *element is displayed in the content panel when the item is chosen. The content of the* link *element is used to create a link to the item's Web location out of the article's name. The link at the bottom of the content panel is created from the channel's* link *element.*

Use `<comments>` to point to the URL where comments are allowed for your item.

3. Type **</item>**.

4. Repeat steps 1–3 for each article in the feed.

✔ Tips

■ You can create as many items as you like. Add new `item` elements at the top of the XML document.

■ While no element is required, you must at least have either a `title` or a `description`.

■ You can add (X)HTML tags (though not for iTunes) either with a CDATA section *(see page 319)* or by substituting < and > for < and >.

■ You can also add an enclosure to an item, that can be downloaded with the article. This is the basic technique behind podcasts and is described on page 384.

■ I have not found a list of standardized category names, except for podcasts in iTunes as described on pages 388–389. For text-based feeds, you might try looking at the feeds of similarly themed sites to see what they're using.

■ There are additional sets of elements (namespaces) that let you add more information about your item. For example, Flickr's feeds use the RSS Media Module (*http://search.yahoo.com/mrss*).

■ There is also a `source` element that can be added to an item, but it should be automatically generated by the aggregator when the article is forwarded.

Add an Enclosure

If you want to add audio, video, or even still JPEG images to your feed, you'll need to create an enclosure for them in which you'll specify their URL, size, and MIME type.

To find the size of an enclosure:

1. Select the file that you want to add to your RSS feed.

2. In Windows, choose Properties, and on the Mac, select Get Info.

3. Jot down the number of bytes in the desired enclosure **(Figure 25.8)**.

To add an enclosure:

1. Within the article's i tem (that you created on page 382), type **<enclosure.**

2. Next, type **url="http://www. yourdomain.com/file.ext"**, to indicate the location of the multimedia file on your server.

3. Type a space followed by **length="n"**, where *n* is the number of bytes in your multimedia enclosure. You should use only digits—no commas or periods (e.g., *36699714*).

4. Add **type="type/subtype"**, where *type* and *subtype* make up the official MIME code for your enclosure (see tip).

5. Type **/>** to complete the enclosure.

Figure 25.8 *When you choose the item on the Desktop and then either choose Properties (on Windows) or Get Info (on a Mac, shown), you'll see the number of bytes in the enclosure (in this case, 36,699,714).*

```
<item>

<title>What does Barcelona Look Like? (Part 1: The
Eixample)</title>

<link>http://catalunyalive.blogspot.com/2006/
07/what-does-barcelona-look-like-part-
1_06.html</link>

<description>Here is some video of Barcelona's
lower Eixample district, around Carrer Casp north
(to the right) of Passeig de Gracia. You'll see the
typical six or seven story apartment building, with
ever-present balconies and other wonderful
architectural details. ...</description>

<guid isPermaLink="true">http://catalunyalive.
blogspot.com/2006/07/what-does-barcelona-
look-like-part-1_06.html</guid>

<enclosure url="http://
www.sarahsnotecards.com/catalunyalive/
BuildingsBarcelona.mov" length="36699714"
type="video/quicktime" />

<pubDate>Wed, 05 Jul 2006 15:45:00
EST</pubDate>

</item>
```

Figure 25.9 *The* enclosure *element goes inside the* item *element.*

Add an Enclosure

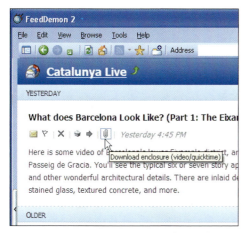

Figure 25.10 *Some aggregators, like Feed-Demon (shown), let you download enclosures by clicking on a special icon or choosing a menu item.*

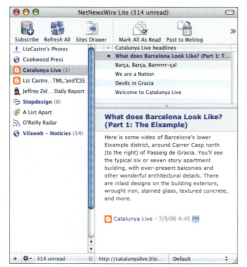

Figure 25.11 *Other browsers, like this "Lite" version of NetNewsWire, may not support the enclosure at all, and not even reveal its existence to your readers.*

✔ Tips

- Make sure you use a full URL, complete with the HTTP protocol. Other protocols are not permitted.

- Be sure to use the *bytes*, not the KB, MB, or GB when noting the size of the enclosure. Use only digits—and no place separators like commas or periods—for specifying the size (e.g., *36699714*).

- You can find a list of MIME types here: *http://www.iana.org/assignments/media-types/*.

- You can enclose any kind of file, it doesn't have to be audio or video. That doesn't mean that every aggregator will be able to handle it though. Some aggregators offer links to multimedia files that they cannot handle, while others ignore them completely.

- iTunes can not only see multimedia enclosures, but can download and play them automatically as well.

- Although this is technically all you need to create a podcast for iTunes, there are additional RSS tags developed by Apple that will help describe your podcast to prospective viewers and listeners, as described on the following pages.

Add an Enclosure

Creating Podcasts for iTunes

Apple's iTunes is the most popular audio and video podcast aggregator. If you want to add your feed to iTunes so that your content is available through the iTunes Music Store, you can adapt the RSS feed that you created with the instructions on pages 379–385 by including iTunes special elements to describe your data.

You'll first prepare your RSS feed for iTunes, and then add the individual iTunes elements (as described on the following pages).

To prepare your RSS feed for iTunes elements:

Within the r ss element, specify the iTunes namespace by adding **xmlns:itunes= "http://www.itunes.com/dtds/ podcast-1.0.dtd"**.

✔ Tips

■ Remember: a podcast is nothing more than an RSS feed with multimedia enclosures. The iTunes tags are optional, though they do describe your podcast more fully in iTunes itself.

■ Podcasts on iTunes are currently free.

■ Namespaces let you add extensions onto RSS without changing RSS itself. There are several different namespaces that are commonly used with RSS, including iTunes and the RSS Media Module (*http://search.yahoo.com/mrss*, which is used for Flickr's photo RSS feeds), among others.

■ For more information about namespaces, you might like to consult my book on XML: *XML for the World Wide Web: Visual QuickStart Guide*, published by Peachpit Press.

```
<?xml version="1.0" encoding="UTF-8"?>

<rss xmlns:itunes="http://www.itunes.com/
dtds/podcast-1.0.dtd" version="2.0">

<channel>

<title>Catalunya Live</title>

<link>http://catalunyalive.blogspot.com</link>
```

Figure 25.12 *By specifying the iTunes namespace, you enable the RSS feed to include the special iTunes elements—and still validate.*

```
<channel>

<itunes:owner>

    <itunes:name>Elizabeth Castro</itunes:name>

    <itunes:email>sarah@cookwood.com
</itunes:email>

</itunes:owner>

<title>Catalunya Live</title>
```

Figure 25.13 *Information in the* itunes:owner *element is used by Apple to get in touch with the creator of the podcast.*

Although RSS already has ways of specifying the owner and technical lead on a podcast, iTunes prefers you to use its own tags.

To add contact information about yourself for Apple:

1. After the initial channel element at the top of your RSS feed, type **<itunes:owner>**.

2. Next, type **<itunes:name>you </itunes:name>**, where *you* is your name.

3. Type **<itunes:email>your email </itunes:email>**, where *your email* is the address where you would like Apple to contact you if they have any trouble with your podcast or any news to relate.

4. Type **</itunes:owner>** to complete the contact information.

✔ Tips

■ For example, when you submit a podcast to iTunes, Apple will send you an email letting you know whether or not it was accepted.

■ In addition, if Apple changes the specifications for iTunes RSS elements, they will notify you at the address you give in the itunes:email element.

■ The information enclosed in the itunes:owner element is not visible in iTunes. However, it is not private, since anyone can look at the source code of the XML document if they wanted to.

Creating Podcasts for iTunes

The next section of iTunes elements are those that describe your podcast as a whole. They are used in podcast's main window on iTunes to tell what your podcast is about.

To add information about your podcast:

1. Add the following elements to the `channel` element to describe your podcast further in iTunes: (Use the **<tag> content</tag>** syntax except for `itunes:image` which is a single tag that ends in `/>`.)

Type **<itunes:image href="url" />** to specify the URL of a square image to be used as the cover art for your podcast in iTunes.

Use the `<itunes:author>` element to specify the name that should appear below your podcast's title.

Use the `<itunes:summary>` element to specify what should appear in the Podcast Description area.

Use `<itunes:keywords>` to specify up to 12 words that describe the content of your podcast and that prospective visitors might type when looking for you.

Use the `<itunes:category>` element to list up to three categories so that iTunes can group your podcast with others that are similar. Each category may contain an optional subcategory, also specified with the `<itunes:category>` element.

Use `<itunes:explicit>` to note whether the podcast has explicit language (use `yes` if so), is free of explicit language (use `clean`), or is not rated (use `no` or omit the `itunes:explicit` element altogether).

```
<title>Catalunya Live</title>

<link>http://catalunyalive.blogspot.com</link>

...[snip]

<itunes:image href="http://www.sarahsnotecards.
com/catalunyalive/segadors-square2.jpg" />

<itunes:author>Elizabeth Castro</itunes:author>

<itunes:summary>This is what Catalunya looks like-
- in action!</itunes:summary>

<itunes:category text="Society &amp; Culture">

    <itunes:category text="Places &amp; Travel" />

    </itunes:category>

<itunes:category text="Education" />

<itunes:category text="Arts">

    <itunes:category text="Performing Arts" />

    </itunes:category>


<itunes:keywords>Catalunya, Catalonia,
Barcelona, video, Elizabeth
Castro</itunes:keywords>

    <itunes:explicit>no</itunes:explicit>


<item>
```

Figure 25.14 *The order in which the individual iTunes elements appear does not matter as long as they come after the initial* `channel` *element and before the first* `item`.

Creating Podcasts for iTunes

Figure 25.15 *Here is how iTunes displays the podcast when it comes up in search results. Notice how it displays a reduced version of the cover art specified with the* itunes:image *element, and then on the right, the contents of the* title, itunes:author, *and first* itunes:category *elements.*

Figure 25.16 *When a prospective visitor clicks on your podcast's cover art, they see your podcast's description page. The cover art is shown full size, the* title, itunes:author, *first* itunes:category, *and* language *elements are shown to the right as before. Under Podcast Description you'll see the contents of the* itunes:summary *element. The URL in the* link *element is used for the Website arrow button. And the podcast's items will be shown in the list below.*

✔ Tips

- If you say your podcast has explicit language, a small explicit icon (EXPLICIT) will appear next to its name in the Name column as well as next to the cover artwork in the iTunes Music Store.

- Only use the official categories listed on Apple's site: *http://www.apple.com/ itunes/podcasts/techspecs.html*

- You can also add <itunes:block>yes </itunes:block> to completely block a podcast from appearing in the iTunes Music Store, although it probably makes more sense when used to block individual episodes *(see page 391).*

- Although none of the iTunes tags are required for the podcast to appear in the iTunes Music Store, they are required if you want to be featured on the iTunes Home Page.

- Note that iTunes uses the value of the regular RSS title, link, and language elements to advise prospective viewers of your podcast's title, URL, and language, respectively.

Creating Podcasts for iTunes

You can use iTunes' special RSS elements to give information about your podcast's individual episodes.

To describe individual episodes:

1. Within the `item` element of the episode in question (in **<tag>content</tag>** format):

   Use `<itunes:author>` to denote the person who created the particular episode. This name will appear in the Artist column.

   Use `<itunes:subtitle>` to give a short description for the episode. It will appear in the Description column.

   Use `<itunes:duration>` to specify how long the episode lasts, in one of the following formats: HH:MM:SS, H:MM:SS, MM:SS, or M:SS.

   Use `<itunes:keywords>` to specify up to 12 keywords that are specific to this particular episode, and not necessarily to the podcast as a whole.

✔ Tips

- New episodes appear in iTunes in order of their publication date (as specified in the `pubDate` element), not in the order in which they appear in the RSS feed.

- The contents of the `title` element for an item is used in the Podcast column in the iTunes list (**Figure 25.18**).

- The image in the `itunes:image` element applies to the entire podcast, not specific episodes. You can add images to individual MP3 podcast episodes (but not video ones). Select the podcast in iTunes, choose Get Info, click the Artwork tab and then click the Add button. Choose the desired JPEG image and then save the changes. Then make sure it is this MP3 file that you upload for your podcast.

```
<itunes:explicit>no</itunes:explicit>
<item>
<title>What does Barcelona Look Like? (Part 1: The Eixample)</title>
<itunes:author>Elizabeth Castro</itunes:author>
<itunes:subtitle>Barcelona's gorgeous everyday architecture</itunes:subtitle>
<link>http://catalunyalive.blogspot.com/2006/07/what-does-barcelona-look-like-part-1_06.html</link>
<description>Here is some video of Barcelona's lower Eixample district, around Carrer Casp north (to the right) of Passeig de Gracia. You'll see the typical six or seven story apartment building, with ever-present balconies and other wonderful architectural details. There are inlaid designs on the building exteriors, wrought iron, stained glass, textured concrete, and more.</description>
<guid isPermaLink="true">http://catalunyalive.blogspot.com/2006/07/what-does-barcelona-look-like-part-1_06.html</guid>
<enclosure url="http://www.sarahsnotecards.com/catalunyalive/BuildingsBarcelona.mov" length="36699714" type="video/quicktime" />
<pubDate>Wed, 05 Jul 2006 15:45:00 EST</pubDate>
<itunes:duration>01:53</itunes:duration>
<itunes:keywords>Catalunya, Catalonia, Barcelona, video, architecture, buildings, Eixample, Ensanche, architects, construction, balconies, stained glass, Elizabeth Castro</itunes:keywords>
</item>
```

Figure 25.17 *There are a few special tags for describing individual episodes of a podcast in iTunes.*

Figure 25.18 *The* itunes:subtitle *is used in the Description column. The* itunes:duration *element is used in the Time column, and the* pubDate *is used for the Release Date column. Although the Artist column is not shown by default for podcasts, the* itunes:author *element would appear there if the user chose to show it. The* itunes:author *element also appears under the* item*'s* title *element in the play box in the center top of the iTunes window (alternately with the podcast's title).*

Figure 25.19 *When a visitor clicks the circled i to the right of the* itunes:subtitle *content in the Description column, the Podcast Information box appears with the* channel *element's* title, *the* item*'s* title, *and the* item*'s* description *element.*

✔ **Tips continued**

■ The contents of the description element within an item element will appear when a visitor clicks the circled i (ⓘ) in the Description column (which rather confusingly contains what's in itunes: subtitle, not what's in description) in the iTunes list. You can also use <itunes:summary> for containing the circled-i information, but I prefer using the more standard description element which will also be understood by other aggregators.

■ The contents of the pubDate element is used in the Release Date column in the iTunes list.

■ You can add <itunes:block>yes </itunes:block> to keep an individual explicit episode from appearing in iTunes, perhaps to avoid getting your entire podcast removed.

■ You can add <itunes:explicit>yes </itunes:explicit> to individual episodes to alert potential viewers of their content.

Creating Podcasts for iTunes

Validating a Feed

You can use an online validator to check the syntax of your feed and make sure you haven't made any typographical or syntactic errors.

To validate a feed:

1. Upload your feed to your server.

2. Open your browser and point it at *http://feedvalidator.org/*

3. Type in your feed's URL.

4. Make any corrections necessary until your feed validates.

✔ Tips

■ I highly recommend using a validator to check that your feed is properly written before you make it public or submit it to iTunes.

■ You can also test a podcast to see if it works properly in iTunes by choosing Advanced > Subscribe to Podcast (in iTunes) and then entering the feed's URL. It is not necessary to submit the podcast to iTunes beforehand (as described on the next page). Indeed, it's a good idea to test if your podcast works with iTunes *before* submitting it for inclusion in the iTunes Music Store.

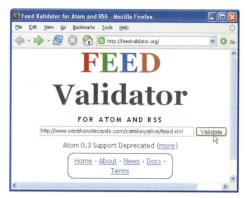

Figure 25.20 *The Open Source FEED Validator is a valuable tool for finding errors in your RSS (and Atom) feeds. Just type in your URL and click Validate.*

Figure 25.21 *The FEED Validator will notify you of any problems it finds. Fix them, upload the feed again, and then click Validate again.*

Figure 25.22 *Once you get the lovely "Congrat-ulations!" message that your feed is valid, you're ready to publicize your feed.*

Validating a Feed

Figure 25.23 *Click Podcasts in the Inside the Music Store list in iTunes.*

Figure 25.24 *Then click Submit a Podcast in the new menu that appears.*

Submitting a Podcast to iTunes

Once you have created your RSS feed for your podcast, you can submit it to iTunes for inclusion in the iTunes Music Store.

To submit a podcast to iTunes:

1. Go to the iTunes Music Store (by clicking Music Store in iTunes) and then choose Podcasts in the Inside the Music Store list **(Figure 25.23)**.

2. Select Submit a Podcast in the new Inside the Music Store list **(Figure 25.24)**.

3. Enter the URL of your RSS feed in the box that appears and click Submit.

4. You will have to log in to your Apple account, or create one if you don't have one. (It's free.)

5. Wait a few days for Apple to check your feed and decide whether or not to accept your podcast.

✔ Tips

■ You'll have better luck getting accepted at iTunes if you use the iTunes elements as described on the preceding pages.

■ Before you submit your feed, make sure it validates *(see page 392)*

■ Make sure your podcast episodes are uploaded to a public server and that they work properly when you type their URL directly in a browser or media player.

■ You can publish multimedia-rich podcasts to iTunes, but not text-only ones. Publish text-based RSS feeds on your own site *(see page 394)*.

■ To remove a podcast from the iTunes Music Store, click the Report a Concern link in the podcast's Description area.

Publishing your RSS Feed on Your Site

You can make your RSS feed available to pro-spective subscribers by providing a link to it on your Web site or blog.

To publish your RSS feed:

Create a link in your Web site or blog to the RSS feed on your server **(Figure 25.25)**.

✔ Tips

- Even if you have submitted your podcast to iTunes (and had it accepted) you can also make your feed available directly through your site.

- Lots of people use the RSS logo to identify their RSS feed. You can download the logo from just about anywhere and then create an image link with it **(Figure 25.25)**. See page 114 for more details on labeling links with images.

- When a visitor clicks a link to an RSS feed they see the XML file displayed as is in their browser. It's pretty ugly. Still, this very ugliness helps people realize that they're not supposed to read it right away, but rather subscribe to it. If you like, you can use XSLT to transform the XML file so that it displays like a regular Web page in the browser.

- Feedburner.com can transform a regular RSS feed (even one written by hand as described in this chapter) into one with more bells and whistles that you can use to monitor subscriptions, and more.

- You can also use **feed:http://www.your-domain.com/feed.xml** as the value of the `href` attribute in your link. This will open the visitor's default newsreader if and only if they already have one installed.

```
<h2 class="sidebar-title">Links</h2>
<ul>
<li><a href="http://lizcastrohtml.blogspot.com/">
Liz's HTML Blog</a></li>
<li><a href="http://www.sarahsnotecards.com/
catalunyalive/feed.xml"><img src="http://
www.sarahsnotecards.com/catalunyalive/
feedicon.jpg" /> Podcast Feed</a></li>
</ul>
```

Figure 25.25 *Here is the XHTML code from my blog where I created the link to the podcast's feed. Note that I've inserted the orange feed icon inside the link to quickly identify it as an RSS feed.*

Figure 25.26 *This is how the link to the RSS feed looks in the list of Links on my blog,* http://catalunyalive.blogspot.com.

Publishing your RSS Feed on Your Site

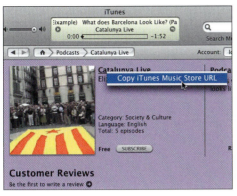

Figure 25.27 *Right-click or Control-click (on the Mac) the podcast title in iTunes and then choose Copy iTunes Music Store URL from the pop-up menu that appears.*

```
<ul>

<li><a href="http://lizcastrohtml.blogspot.com/">
Liz's HTML Blog</a></li>

<li><a href="http://phobos.apple.com/
WebObjects/MZStore.woa/wa/viewPodcast?
id=158521477"><img src="http://
www.sarahsnotecards.com/catalunyalive/
feedicon.jpg" /> Open in iTunes</a></li>

</ul>
```

Figure 25.28 *This time, I've inserted the URL that I copied in Figure 25.27 above. When a prospective subscriber clicks on this link, they will be transported to iTunes where they can subscribe to my podcast directly.*

```
<ul>

<li><a href="http://lizcastrohtml.blogspot.com/">
Liz's HTML Blog</a></li>

<li><a href="itpc://www.sarahsnotecards.com/
catalunyalive/feed.xml"><img src="http://
www.sarahsnotecards.com/catalunyalive/
feedicon.jpg" /> Subscribe in iTunes</a></li>

</ul>
```

Figure 25.29 *If you use the* itpc *protocol for your feed link, clicking the link will launch iTunes and not only show the podcast, but also automatically subscribe the visitor. You should label your links accordingly (see right).*

■ You can create a direct link to a podcast in the iTunes Music Store by right-clicking (or Control-clicking on the Mac), the podcast's link in iTunes and choosing Copy iTunes Music Store URL from the pop-up menu **(Figure 25.27)**. Then use this URL in the link on your Web site **(Figure 25.28)**. When a prospective subscriber clicks the link, iTunes will open on their computer and they will be automatically directed to subscribe to your podcast. If, however, they don't have iTunes installed, they will be forwarded to Apple's site in order to download iTunes.

■ The previous tip simply opens iTunes to your podcast's description page. The prospective subscriber still has to click the Subscribe button to actually sign up. If you want to subscribe them with a single click, use *itpc://www.yourdomain.com/feed.xml*. Make sure that the link is properly labeled so that your visitors know what they're getting into **(Figure 25.29)**. Nobody likes to be strong-armed.

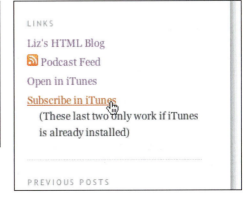

Subscribing to an RSS Feed

It's not a bad idea to subscribe to your own RSS feed so you can make sure it's working properly.

To subscribe to an RSS feed:

1. Right-click or Control-click the RSS feed link and choose Copy Link Location (or whatever your browser calls it) to copy the RSS feed's URL **(Figure 25.30)**.

2. Open your aggregator.

3. Choose the Subscribe command (however it is named) **(Figure 25.31)**.

4. Enter (by typing or pasting) the URL of the RSS feed to which you want to subscribe.

5. Click Subscribe **(Figure 25.32)**.

✔ Tips

- The illustrations shown are from NetNewsWire for Macintosh. Other aggregators (with the exception of iTunes, page 397) look and work in much the same way.

- Some aggregators automatically put the contents of the Clipboard (that is, whatever you just copied) in the URL box, saving you from typing or pasting.

- Once you are subscribed to an RSS feed, your aggregator will check the feed periodically for updates and download these automatically for your reading pleasure.

Figure 25.30 *Don't click the Feed link. Instead, right-click or Control-click it and choose Copy Link Location (or however it's called in your browser) to copy the RSS feed's URL.*

Figure 25.31 *Click the Subscribe button or choose the Subscribe command in your news aggregator.*

Figure 25.32 *Type or paste the feed's URL in the New Subscription box and click Subscribe.*

Figure 25.33 *Browse to the desired podcast in the iTunes Music Store. Click Subscribe.*

Figure 25.34 *Confirm that you want to subscribe to the podcast by clicking the Subscribe button.*

Figure 25.35 *Click Podcasts in the Source column to see the podcasts to which you are subscribed. Listen to or watch a podcast by double-clicking an episode's name. Note that when you (or your visitors) first subscribe, iTunes automatically downloads the most current episode and lets you (or your visitors) choose whether or not to download earlier episodes (by clicking the Get button).*

Subscribing to a Podcast with iTunes

Subscribing to a podcast with iTunes is not much different than in any other aggregator. It's just a little simpler.

To subscribe to a podcast with iTunes:

1. Browse to the desired podcast in the iTunes Music Store.

2. Click the Subscribe button **(Figure 25.33)**.

3. If necessary, confirm that you want to subscribe in the alert box that appears **(Figure 25.34)**.

4. Click the Podcasts item in the Source list in iTunes' left column to see the podcasts to which you've subscribed **(Figure 25.35)**.

✔ Tips

■ You can subscribe to a podcast through iTunes even if it has not been submitted to the iTunes Music Store, or if it has been submitted so recently that it doesn't show up when you search for it. To do so, choose Advanced > Subscribe to Podcast and then type in the URL of the desired podcast's feed. This is a great way to test that your feed works properly before submitting it to the iTunes Music Store.

■ iTunes does not currently support text-only RSS feeds. It does support podcasts with audio, video, and PDF files.

■ You can have iTunes download your podcasts automatically. You can have it upload podcasts to your iPod automatically as well.

(X)HTML Reference

On the following pages, you'll find a list of the (X)HTML elements and attributes described in this book (including the chapters that have been moved to the Web site—see page 25). Each element has a short description, an annotated list of its associated attributes, and the page number in the book where you'll find more information. If a particular attribute has no page reference, it means that it is discussed on the same page as the element with which it is listed.

Elements and attributes that the W3C would like to discourage you from using are marked with a D (for deprecated) or an F (for frameset). Deprecated items can only be used if you've specified the DOCTYPE for transitional or frameset (X)HTML. Frameset items can only be used in frameset (X)HTML. Thus, if your intention is to write strict (X)HTML, you should use only those elements and attributes with *nothing* in the Vers. column. For more information on choosing and then specifying an appropriate DOCTYPE, consult *Versions, flavors, and DOCTYPE* on page 40 and *Starting Your Web Page* on page 56.

The only non-standard element that I have included in this listing is `embed`. Although it is not and has never been part of the official (X)HTML specifications, its widespread use continues to warrant its inclusion, for reference, if nothing else.

(X)HTML Elements and Attributes

TAG/ATTRIBUTE(S)	DESCRIPTION	VERS.
--MOST TAGS--	The following attributes may be used with most (X)HTML tags	
class	For identifying a set of tags in order to apply styles to them (pp. 63, 64, 65)	
event	For triggering a script (p. 314). Also see *Intrinsic Events* on page 418	
id	For identifying particular tags so that they can be linked to, styled, or scripted with JavaScript (pp. 63, 64, 65, 106)	
lang	For specifying the language an element is written in (p. 338)	
style	For adding local style sheet information (p. 134)	
title	For labeling elements with tool tips (p. 68)	
!--	For inserting invisible comments (p. 67)	
!DOCTYPE	Theoretically required. For indicating the version of (X)HTML used (p. 56)	
a	For creating links and anchors (p. 104)	
accesskey	For adding a keyboard shortcut to a link (p. 112)	
event	For triggering a script (p. 314)	
href	For specifying the URL of a page or the name of an anchor that a link goes to	
name	For marking a specific area of a page that a link might jump to (p. 106)	
tabindex	For defining the order in which the Tab key takes the visitor through links and form elements (p. 113)	
target	For specifying the window or frame where a link should open (pp. 108, 109)	D
abbr	For explaining the meaning of abbreviations (p. 78)	
acronym	For explaining the meaning of acronyms (p. 78)	
address	For formatting the email address of the Web page designer (p. 70)	
applet	For inserting applets (p. 308)	D
code	For specifying the URL of the applet's code	D
width, height	For specifying the width and height of an applet	D
area	For specifying the coordinates of image maps (p. 117)	
accesskey	For adding a keyboard shortcut to a particular region of the map	
alt	For giving information about an area	
coords	For giving the coordinates of an area in an image map	
href	For specifying the destination URL of a link in an area in an image map	
nohref	For making a click in an image map have no effect	
shape	For specifying the shape of an area in an image map	
target	For specifying the window or frame where a link should open	D

Page numbers are omitted for those attributes discussed on the same page as the tag to which they belong.

TAG/ATTRIBUTE(S)	DESCRIPTION	VERS.
b	For displaying text in boldface (p. 70)	
base		
href	For specifying the URL to be used to generate relative URLs (p. 109)	
target	For specifying the default target for the links on the page (p. 109)	D
basefont	For specifying default font values for a page *(see Web site)*	D
color	For specifying the default color for text	D
face	For specifying the default font for text	D
size	For specifying the default size for text	D
big	For making text bigger than the surrounding text (p. 71)	
blockquote	For setting off a block of text on a page (p. 74)	
cite	For giving the URL of the source of the quote	
body	For enclosing the main content area of a page (p. 58)	
alink, link, vlink	For specifying the color of active links, new links, and visited links *(see Web site)*	D
background	For specifying a background image *(see Web site)*	D
bgcolor	For specifying the background color *(see Web site)*	D
text	For specifying the color of text *(see Web site)*	D
br	For creating a line break (p. 66)	
clear	For stopping text wrap (p. 98)	D
button	For creating buttons (pp. 273, 275, 316)	
accesskey	For adding a keyboard shortcut to a button	
disabled	For graying out a button until some other event occurs	
event	For associating the button with a script	
name	For identifying the data sent with a button, or for identifying the button itself (perhaps for a JavaScript function)	
type	For using the button as a form element	
value	For specifying the data that should be submitted when the button is clicked	
caption	For creating a caption for a table (p. 229)	
align	For positioning the caption above or below the table	D
center	For centering text, images, or other elements (p. 79)	D
cite	For marking text as a citation (p. 70)	
code	For marking text as computer code (p. 72)	
col	For joining columns in a table into a non-structural group (p. 246)	
align, valign	For specifying the alignment of columns in a column group	
span	For specifying the number of columns in a column group	
width	For specifying a column's width	

Page numbers are omitted for those attributes discussed on the same page as the tag to which they belong.

(X)HTML Elements and Attributes

TAG/ATTRIBUTE(S)	DESCRIPTION	VERS.
colgroup	For joining columns in a table into a structural column group (p. 246)	
align, valign	For specifying the alignment of columns in a column group	
span	For specifying the number of columns in a column group	
width	For specifying the default width for the enclosed col elements	
dd	For marking a definition in a list (p. 223)	
del	To mark deleted text by striking it out (p. 77)	
div	For dividing a page into block-level sections (pp. 64, 170)	
align	For aligning a given division to the left, right, or center	D
class	For identifying a group of divisions (so that you can apply styles to them all in one fell swoop)	
id	For identifying particular divisions (so they can be linked, styled, or scripted)	
dl	For creating a definition list (p. 223)	
dt	For marking a term to be defined in a list (p. 223)	
em	For emphasizing text, usually with italics (p. 70)	
embed	For adding multimedia (pp. 286, 302)	*
autostart	For making a multimedia event begin automatically	*
controls	For displaying the play, pause, rewind buttons	*
loop	For determining if the multimedia event should play more than once	*
src	For specifying the URL of a multimedia file	*
width, height	For specifying the size of the embedded multimedia player	*
fieldset	For grouping a set of form elements together (p. 260)	
font	For changing the size, face, and color of the text *(see Web site)*	D
color	For changing text color	D
face	For changing text font	D
size	For changing text size	D
form	For creating fill-in forms (p. 254)	
action	For giving the URL of the script that will process the form data	
enctype	For making sure files are sent to the server in the proper format (pp. 259, 270)	
method	For specifying how data should be sent to the server	

Page numbers are omitted for those attributes discussed on the same page as the tag to which they belong.
*The embed element, while non-standard, is universally supported.

TAG/ATTRIBUTE(S)	DESCRIPTION	VERS.
frame	For creating frames *(see Web site)*	F
frameborder	For displaying or hiding frame borders *(see Web site)*	F
longdesc	For linking to a document with more information *(see Web site)*	F
name	For naming a frame so it can be used as a target *(see Web site)*	F
noresize	For keeping users from resizing a frame *(see Web site)*	F
marginwidth, marginheight	For specifying a frame's left and right, and top and bottom margins *(see Web site)*	F
scrolling	For displaying or hiding a frame's scrollbars *(see Web site)*	F
src	For specifying the initial URL to be displayed in frame *(see Web site)*	F
target	For specifying which frame a link should be opened in *(see Web site)*	F
title	For indicating a frame's purpose *(see Web site)*	F
frameset	For defining a frameset *(see Web site)*	F
cols	For determining the number and size of frames *(see Web site)*	F
frameborder	For displaying or hiding frame borders *(see Web site)*	F
rows	For determining the number and size of frames *(see Web site)*	F
h1, h2, h3, h4, h5, h6	For creating headers (p. 61)	
align	For aligning headers	D
head	For creating the head section, which contains information *about* the page, including the title, author, keywords, style sheets, and scripts (p. 58)	
hr	For creating horizontal rules (p. 101)	
align	For aligning horizontal rules	D
noshade	For displaying horizontal rules without shading	D
size	For specifying the height of a horizontal rule	D
width	For specifying the width of a horizontal rule	D
html	For identifying a text document as an (X)HTML document (p. 56)	
xmlns	For specifying the xhtml namespace	
i	For displaying text in italics (p. 70)	
iframe	For creating floating frames *(see Web site)*	D
align	For aligning floating frames	D
frameborder	For displaying or hiding frame borders *(see Web site)*	D
height	For specifying the height of a floating frame	D
name	For specifying the name of the floating frame, to be used as a target	D
width, height	For specifying the size of a floating frame	D
scrolling	For displaying or hiding scrollbars *(see Web site)*	D
src	For specifying the URL of the initial page	D

Page numbers are omitted for those attributes discussed on the same page as the tag to which they belong.

(X)HTML Elements and Attributes

TAG/ATTRIBUTE(S)	DESCRIPTION	VERS.
img	For inserting images on a page (p. 90)	
align	For aligning images (p. 100) and for wrapping text around images (pp. 96, 97)	D
alt	For offering alternate text that is displayed if the image is not (p. 91)	
border	For specifying the thickness of the border, if any (pp. 90, 114)	D
hspace, vspace	For specifying the amount of space above and below, and to the sides of an image (p. 99)	D
src	For specifying the URL of an image (p. 90)	
usemap	For specifying the image map that should be used with the referenced image (pp. 117, 118)	
width, height	For specifying the size of an image so that the page is loaded more quickly, or for scaling (pp. 92, 93, 94)	
input	For creating form elements (pp. 262, 263, 265, 268, 270, 271, 272, 274)	
accesskey	For adding a keyboard shortcut to a form element (p. 278)	
align	For aligning form elements	D
checked	For marking a radio button or check box by default (pp. 265, 268)	
disabled	For graying out form elements until some other event occurs (p. 279)	
event	For triggering a script with an event like onfocus, onblur, etc.	
maxlength	For specifying the maximum number of characters that can be entered in a form element (pp. 262, 263)	
name	For identifying data collected by an element	
size	For specifying the length of a text or password box (pp. 262, 263)	
src	For specifying the URL of an active image (p. 276)	
readonly	For keeping visitors from changing certain form elements (p. 280)	
tabindex	For specifying the order in which the Tab key should take a visitor through the links and form elements (p. 277)	
type	For specifying if a form element is a text box, password box, radio button, checkbox, hidden field, submit button, reset button or active image	
value	For specifying the default data in a form element	
ins	For marking inserted text with an underline (p. 77)	
kbd	For marking keyboard text (p. 72)	
label	For labeling form elements (p. 264)	
for	For specifying which form element the label belongs to	
legend	For labeling fieldsets (p. 260)	
align	For aligning legends	D

Page numbers are omitted for those attributes discussed on the same page as the tag to which they belong.

TAG/ATTRIBUTE(S)	DESCRIPTION	VERS.
li	For creating a list item (p. 216)	
type	For determining which symbols or type of numerals should begin the list item	D
value	For determining the initial value of the first list item	D
link	For linking to an external style sheet (p. 129)	
href	For specifying the URL of the style sheet	
media	For noting a style sheet's purpose (pp. 133, 204, 210)	
title	For labeling alternate style sheets (p. 130)	
type	For noting a style sheet's MIME type	
rel	For indicating that a style sheet is preferred or alternate (pp. 129, 130)	
map	For creating a client-side image map (p. 117)	
name	For naming a map so it can be referenced later	
meta		
content	For adding extra information about the Web page itself (pp. 310, 320, 330, 363, 364, 365, 366)	
http-equiv	For creating automatic jumps to other pages (p. 310), setting the default scripting language (p. 320), and declaring the character encoding (p. 330)	
name	For identifying extra information about the Web page (pp. 363, 364, 365, 366)	
noframes	For providing alternatives to frames *(see Web site)*	F
noscript	For providing alternatives to scripts (p. 317)	
object	For embedding objects in Web pages (pp. 286, 288, 290, 302, 304, 305, 306, 308)	
align	For aligning objects	D
border	For creating (or hiding) a border around an object	D
classid	It is supposed to be a URL that specifies the location of an object's "implementation" but currently is incorrectly used by Microsoft to call its ActiveX controls	
codebase	It is supposed to be the base URL for resolving relative URLs in the other attributes, but in fact is mostly used to specify the location of the desired multimedia player	
data	For identifying the source of the multimedia file to be embedded	
hspace, vspace	For specifying the amount of space around an object	D
name	For identifying the object (e.g., so it can be scripted)	
standby	For displaying a message as the object is loading	
type	For noting the object's MIME type	
width, height	For specifying the dimensions of the object's box	

Page numbers are omitted for those attributes discussed on the same page as the tag to which they belong.

(X)HTML Elements and Attributes

TAG/ATTRIBUTE(S)	DESCRIPTION	VERS.
ol	For creating ordered lists (p. 216)	
type	For specifying the kind of numerals that should begin each list item	D
start	For specifying the initial value of the first list item	D
optgroup	For dividing a menu into submenus (p. 267)	
disabled	For graying out menu options until some other event occurs	
label	For specifying how the option should appear in the menu	
option	For creating the individual options in a form menu (p. 266)	
disabled	For graying out menu options until some other event occurs	
label	For specifying how the option should appear in the menu	
selected	For making a menu option be selected by default in a blank form	
value	For specifying the initial value of a menu option	
p	For creating new paragraphs (p. 62)	
align	For aligning paragraphs	D
param	For setting properties of an object (pp. 286, 288, 290, 302, 304, 305, 306, 308)	
name	For identifying the kind of property	
value	For setting the value of the named property	
pre	For maintaining the spaces and returns that were in the original text (p. 73)	
q	For quoting short passages of text (p. 74)	
cite	For giving the URL of the source of the quote	
s	(Same as strike) For displaying text with a line through it *(see Web site)*	D
samp	For displaying sample text—in a monospaced font (p. 72)	
script	For adding "automatic" scripts to a page (p. 312)	
charset	For specifying the character set an external script is written in (p. 313)	
language	For specifying the scripting language the script is written in	D
src	For referencing an external script (p. 313)	
type	For specifying the scripting language the script is written in	
select	For creating menus in forms (p. 266)	
disabled	For graying out menu options until some other event occurs	
name	For identifying the data collected by the menu	
multiple	For allowing users to choose more than one option in the menu	
size	For specifying the number of items initially visible in the menu (and for displaying the menu as a list)	
small	For decreasing the size of text (p. 71)	

Page numbers are omitted for those attributes discussed on the same page as the tag to which they belong.

TAG/ATTRIBUTE(S)	DESCRIPTION	VERS.
span	For creating custom character styles (p. 65)	
class	For naming custom styles	
id	For identifying particular (X)HTML elements so that they can be linked to, styled, or controlled with a script	
strike	(Same as the s element) For displaying text with a line through it *(see Web site)*	D
strong	For emphasizing text logically, usually in boldface (p. 70)	
style	For adding style sheet information to a page (p. 131)	
media	For indicating a style sheet's purpose (pp. 133, 204, 210)	
type	For indicating a style sheet's MIME type	
sub	For creating subscripts (p. 76)	
sup	For creating superscripts (p. 76)	
table	For creating tables (p. 229)	
align	For aligning an entire table with respect to the window (p. 234)	D
bgcolor	For specifying the background color of the table (p. 240)	D
border	For specifying the thickness, if any, of the border (p. 230)	
cellpadding	For setting the space between a cell's contents and its borders (p. 242)	
cellspacing	For setting the amount of space between cells (p. 242)	
frame	For displaying external borders (p. 249)	
rules	For displaying internal borders (p. 250)	
width	For specifying the size of the table (p. 232)	
tbody	For identifying the body of the table (in contrast with the header (thead) or footer (tfoot) (p. 248)	
align, valign	For aligning the contents of the body of the table	
bgcolor	For changing the color of an entire row (p. 240)	D
td, th	For creating regular and header cells, respectively, in a table (p. 229)	
align, valign	For aligning a cell's contents horizontally or vertically (p. 238)	
bgcolor	For changing the background color of a cell (p. 240)	D
char	For aligning the contents of a cell with respect to a character (p. 239)	
colspan	For spanning a cell across more than one column (p. 244)	
nowrap	For keeping a cell's contents on one line (p. 251)	D
rowspan	For spanning a cell across more than one row (p. 245)	
width, height	For specifying the size of the cell (p. 232)	D

Page numbers are omitted for those attributes discussed on the same page as the tag to which they belong.

(X)HTML Elements and Attributes

TAG/ATTRIBUTE(S)	DESCRIPTION	VERS.
textarea	For creating text block entry areas in a form (p. 269)	
accesskey	For adding a keyboard shortcut to a text area	
disabled	For graying out a text block until some other event occurs	
name	For identifying the data that is gathered with the text block	
readonly	For protecting a text area's contents (p. 280)	
rows, cols	For specifying the number of rows and columns in the text block	
tfoot, thead	For identifying the footer and header area of a table (p. 248)	
align, valign	For aligning the footer or header cells (p. 238)	
bgcolor	For changing the color of an entire row (p. 240)	D
title	Required. For creating the title of the page in the browser's title bar area (p. 60)	
tr	For creating rows in a table (p. 229)	
align, valign	For aligning the contents of a row horizontally or vertically (p. 238)	
bgcolor	For changing the color of an entire row (p. 240)	D
tt	For displaying text in a monospaced font (p. 72)	
u	For displaying text with a line underneath it *(see Web site)*	D
ul	For creating unordered lists (p. 216)	
type	For specifying the markers that should precede each list item	D

Page numbers are omitted for those attributes discussed on the same page as the tag to which they belong.

(X)HTML Elements and Attributes

CSS Properties and Values

This book does not cover every single property defined in the Cascading Style Sheets Level 1 and Level 2 specifications. Instead, I focus on those properties that are supported by at least one browser.

The table in this chapter is designed to be a quick reference to each of the properties and its allowed values. I have also indicated each property's default or initial value, the elements to which it may be applied, whether or not the property is inherited, and what percentages refer to if they may be used. Finally, I have referenced the page number in the book where the property or value is discussed.

The table is derived from the complete specifications at *http://www.w3.org/TR/CSS21/ propidx.html* and is copyright © World Wide Web Consortium, (Massachusetts Institute of Technology, Institut National de Recherche en Informatique et en Automatique, Keio University). All Rights Reserved.

Many of the properties accept a length, percentage, or color for values. For more details on entering values, see *A Property's Value* on page 124.

I hope you will find it useful.

CSS Properties and Values

PROPERTY/VALUES	DESCRIPTION AND NOTES
background any combination of the values for *background-attachment, background-color, background-image, background-repeat,* and/or *background-position,* or `inherit`	for changing the background color and image of elements (pp. 172, 240) initial value depends on individual properties; not inherited; percentages allowed for *background-position*
background-attachment either `scroll`, `fixed`, or `inherit`	for determining if and how background images should scroll (p. 172) initial value: `scroll`; not inherited
background-color either a color, `transparent`, or `inherit`	for setting just the background color of an element (pp. 172, 240) initial value: `transparent`; not inherited
background-image either a URL, `none`, or `inherit`	for setting just the background image of an element (pp. 172, 240) initial value: `none`; not inherited
background-position either one or two percentages or lengths (or one percentage and one length) or one of `top`, `center`, or `bottom` and/or one of `left`, `center`, or `right`. Or use `inherit`.	for setting the physical position of a specified background image (p. 172) initial value: `0% 0%`, if a single percentage is set, it is used for the horizontal position and the initial value of the vertical is set to 50%, if only one keyword is used, the initial value of the other is `center`; applies to block-level and replaced elements: not inherited; percentages refer to the size of the box itself
background-repeat one of `repeat`, `repeat-x`, `repeat-y`, `no-repeat`, or `inherit`	for determining how and if background images should be tiled (p. 172) initial value: `repeat`; not inherited
border any combination of the values of *border-width, border-style,* and/or a color, or `inherit`	for defining all aspects of a border on all sides of an element (pp. 184, 230) initial value depends on individual properties; not inherited
border-color from one to four colors, `transparent`, or `inherit`	for setting only the color of the border on one or more sides of an element (pp. 184, 230) initial value: the element's `color` property; not inherited
border-spacing either one or two lengths or `inherit`	for specifying the amount of space between borders in a table (p. 242) initial value: 0; may be applied only to table elements; inherited

CSS Properties and Values

PROPERTY/VALUES	DESCRIPTION AND NOTES
border-style one to four of the following values: `none`, `dotted`, `dashed`, `solid`, `double`, `groove`, `ridge`, `inset`, `outset`, `inherit`	for setting only the style of a border on one or more sides of an element (pp. 184, 230) initial value: `none`; not inherited
border-top, border-right, border-bottom, border-left any combination of a single value each for *border-width*, *border-style*, and/or a color, or use `inherit`.	for defining all three border properties at once on only one side of an element (pp. 184, 230) initial value depends on individual values; not inherited
border-top-color, border-right-color, border-bottom-color, border-left-color one color or `inherit`	for defining just the border's color on only one side of an element (pp. 184, 230) initial value: the value of the *color* property; not inherited
border-top-style, border-right-style, border-bottom-style, border-left-style one of `none`, `dotted`, `dashed`, `solid`, `double`, `groove`, `ridge`, `inset`, `outset`, or `inherit`	for defining just the border's style on only one side of an element (pp. 184, 230) initial value: `none`; not inherited
border-top-width, border-right-width, border-bottom-width, border-left-width one of `thin`, `medium`, `thick` or a length	for defining just the border's width on only one side of an element (pp. 184, 230) initial value: `medium`; not inherited
border-width one to four of the following values: `thin`, `medium`, `thick` or a length	for defining the border's width on one or more sides of an element (pp. 184, 230) initial value: `medium`; not inherited
bottom either a percentage, length, `auto`, or `inherit`	for setting the distance that an element should be offset from its parent element's bottom edge (pp. 179, 178, 180) initial value: `auto`; not inherited; percentages refer to height of containing block
clear one of `none`, `left`, `right`, `both`, or `inherit`	for keeping elements from floating on one or both sides of an element (p. 182) initial value: `none`; may only be applied to block-level elements; not inherited

CSS Properties and Values

PROPERTY/VALUES	DESCRIPTION AND NOTES
clip one of auto, rect, or inherit	for displaying only a portion of an element (p. 191) initial value: auto, applies only to absolutely positioned elements
color a color or inherit	for setting the foreground color of an element (p. 160) initial value: parent's color, some colors are set by browser; inherited
cursor one of auto, crosshair, default, pointer, progress, move, e-resize, ne-resize, nw-resize, n-resize, se-resize, sw-resize, s-resize, w-resize, text, wait, help, a URL, or inherit	for setting the cursor's shape (p. 186) initial value: auto; inherited
display one of inline, block, list-item, none, inherit	for determining how and if an element should be displayed (pp. 190, 193, 194, 196, 205) initial value: inline; not inherited
float one of left, right, none, inherit	for determining on which side of an element other elements are permitted to float (pp. 181, 235) initial value: none; may not be applied to positioned elements or generated content; not inherited
font if desired, any combination of the values for *font-style*, *font-variant* and *font-weight* followed by the required *font-size*, an optional value for *line-height* and the also required *font-family*, or use inherit	for setting at least the font family and size, and optionally the style, variant, weight, and line-height of text *(p. 159)* initial value depends on individual properties; inherited; percentages allowed for values of *font-size* and *line-height*
font-family one or more quotation mark-enclosed font names followed by an optional generic font name, or use inherit	for choosing the font family for text (p. 152) initial value: depends on browser; inherited
font-size an absolute size, a relative size, a length, a percentage, or inherit	for setting the size of text (p. 156) initial value: medium; the computed value is inherited; percentages refer to parent element's font size
font-style either normal, italic, oblique, or inherit	for making text italic (p. 154) initial value: normal; inherited

CSS Properties and Values

PROPERTY/VALUES	DESCRIPTION AND NOTES
font-variant either `normal`, `small-caps`, or `inherit`	for setting text in small caps (p. 167) initial value: `normal`; inherited
font-weight either `normal`, `bold`, `bolder`, `lighter`, `100`, `200`, `300`, `400`, `500`, `600`, `700`, `800`, `900`, or `inherit`	for applying, removing, and adjusting bold formatting (p. 155) initial value: `normal`; the numeric values are considered keywords and not integers (you can't choose 150, for example); inherited
height either a length, percentage, `auto`, or `inherit`	for setting the height of an element (p. 174) initial value: `auto`; may be applied to all elements except non-replaced inline elements, table columns, and column groups; not inherited
left either a length, percentage, `auto`, or `inherit`	for setting the distance that an element should be offset from its parent element's left edge (pp. 179, 180, 178) initial value: `auto`; may only be applied to positioned elements; not inherited; percentages refer to width of containing block
letter-spacing either `normal`, a length, or `inherit`	for setting the amount of space between letters (p. 162) initial value: `normal`; inherited
line-height either `normal`, a number, a length, a percentage, or `inherit`	for setting the amount of space between lines of text (p. 158) initial value: `normal`; inherited; percentages refer to the font size of the element itself
list-style any combination of the values for *list-style-type, list-style-position* and/or *list-style-image*, or use `inherit`	for setting a list's marker (regular or custom) and its position (p. 222) initial value depends on initial values of individual elements; may only be applied to list elements; inherited
list-style-image either a URL, `none`, or `inherit`	for designating a custom marker for a list (p. 220) initial value: `none`; may only be applied to list elements; overrides `list-style-type`; inherited
list-style-position either `inside`, `outside`, or `inherit`	for determining the position of a list's marker (p. 221) initial value: `outside`; may only be applied to list elements; inherited
list-style-type either `disc`, `circle`, `square`, `decimal`, `lower-roman`, `upper-roman`, `lower-alpha`, `upper-alpha`, `none`, or `inherit`	for setting a list's marker (p. 218) initial value: `disc`; may only be applied to list elements; not used if `list-style-type` is valid; inherited

CSS Properties and Values

PROPERTY/VALUES	DESCRIPTION AND NOTES
margin one to four of the following: `length`, `percentage`, or `auto`, or `inherit`	for setting the amount of space between one or more sides of an element's border and its parent element (pp. 176, 208, 211, 234) initial value depends on browser and on value of `width`; not inherited; percentages refer to width of containing block
margin-top, margin-right, margin-bottom, margin-left either a length, percentage, `auto`, or `inherit`	for setting the amount of space between only one side of an element's border and its parent element (p. 176) initial value: `0`; not inherited; percentages refer to width of containing block; the values for `margin-right` and `margin-left` may be overridden if sum of `width`, `margin-right`, and `margin-left` are larger than parent element's containing block
max-height, max-width either a length, percentage, `none`, or `inherit`	for setting the maximum height and/or width of an element, respectively (p. 174) initial value: `none`; may not be applied to non-replaced inline elements or table elements; not inherited; percentages refer to height/width of containing block
min-height, min-width either a length, percentage, or `inherit`	for setting the minimum height and/or width of an element, respectively (p. 174) initial value: `0`; may not be applied to non-replaced inline elements or table elements; not inherited; percentages refer to height/width of containing block
orphans either an integer or `inherit`	for specifying how many lines of an element may appear alone at the bottom of a page (p. 214) initial value: `2`; may only be applied to block-level elements; inherited
overflow either `visible`, `hidden`, `scroll`, `auto`, or `inherit`	for determining where extra content should go if it does not fit in the element's content area (p. 187) initial value: `visible`; may only be applied to block-level and replaced elements; not inherited
padding one to four lengths or percentages, or `inherit`	for specifying the distance between one or more sides of an element's content area and its border (p. 177) initial value depends on browser: not inherited; percentages refer to width of containing block
padding-top, padding-right, padding-bottom, padding-left either a length, percentage, or `inherit`	for specifying the distance between one side of an element's content area and its border (p. 177) initial value: `0`; not inherited; percentages refer to width of containing block

CSS Properties and Values

PROPERTY/VALUES	DESCRIPTION AND NOTES
page-break-after, page-break-before either `always`, `avoid`, `auto`, `right`, `left`, or `inherit`	for specifying when page breaks should or should not occur (p. 212) initial value: `auto`; may only be applied to block-level elements; not inherited
page-break-inside either `avoid`, `auto`, or `inherit`	for keeping page breaks from dividing an element across pages (p. 212) initial value: `auto`; may only be applied to block-level elements; inherited
position either `static`, `relative`, `absolute`, `fixed`, or `inherit`	for determining how an element should be positioned with respect to the document's flow (pp. 179, 178, 180) initial value: `static`; may not be applied to generated content; not inherited
right either a length, percentage, `auto`, or `inherit`	for setting the distance that an element should be offset from its parent element's right edge (pp. 179, 178, 180) initial value: `auto`; may only be applied to positioned elements; not inherited; percentages refer to width of containing block
table-layout one of `fixed`, `auto`, or `inherit`	for choosing the algorithm that should be used to determine the widths of cells (p. 252) initial value: `auto`; not inherited
text-align one of `left`, `right`, `center`, `justify`, a string, or `inherit`	for aligning text (p. 165) initial value depends on browser and writing direction; may only be applied to block-level elements; inherited
text-decoration any combination of `underline`, `overline`, `line-through`, and `blink`, or `none` or `inherit`	for decorating text (mostly with lines) (p. 168) initial value: `none`; not inherited
text-indent either a length, percentage, or `inherit`	for setting the amount of space the first line of a paragraph should be indented (p. 163) initial value: `0`; may only be applied to block-level elements; inherited; percentages refer to width of containing block
text-transform either `capitalize`, `uppercase`, `lowercase`, `none`, or `inherit`	for setting the capitalization of an element's text (p. 166) initial value: `none`; inherited

CSS Properties and Values

PROPERTY/VALUES	DESCRIPTION AND NOTES
top either a length, percentage, auto, or inherit	for setting the distance that an element should be offset from its parent element's top edge (pp. 179, 178, 180) initial value: auto; may only be applied to positioned elements; not inherited; percentages refer to height of containing block
vertical-align either baseline, sub, super, top, text-top, middle, bottom, text-bottom, a percentage, a length, or inherit	for aligning elements vertically (pp. 188, 238) initial value: baseline; may only be applied to inline-level and table cell elements; not inherited; percentages refer to the element's *line-height* property
visibility either visible, hidden, collapse, or inherit	for hiding elements without taking them out of the document's flow (p. 190) initial value: inherit, which rather makes the fact that it's not inherited a moot point
white-space either normal, pre, nowrap, pre-wrap, pre-lined, or inherit	for specifying how white space should be treated (p. 164) initial value: normal; may only be applied to block-level elements; inherited
widows either an integer or inherit	for specifying how many lines of an element may appear alone at the top of a page (p. 214) initial value: 2; may only be applied to block-level elements; inherited
width either a length, percentage, auto, or inherit	for setting the width of an element (pp. 174, 232) initial value: auto; may not be applied to non-replaced inline elements, table rows, or row groups; not inherited; percentages refer to width of containing block
word-spacing either normal, a length, or inherit	for setting the distance between words (p. 162) initial value: normal; inherited
z-index either auto, an integer, or inherit	for setting the depth of an element with respect to overlapping elements (p. 183) initial value: auto; may only be applied to positioned elements; not inherited

INTRINSIC EVENTS

An intrinsic event determines when an associated script will run. However, not every intrinsic event works with every (X)HTML element. This table illustrates which events and tags work together. For more information on associating a script with an intrinsic event, consult *Triggering a Script* on page 314.

Intrinsic Events

EVENT	WORKS WITH	WHEN
onblur	`a, area, button, input , label, select, textarea`	the visitor leaves an element that was previously in focus (see `onfocus` below)
onchange	`input, select, textarea`	the visitor modifies the value or contents of the element
onclick	All elements *except* `applet, base, basefont, br, font, frame, frameset, head, html, iframe, meta, param, script, style, title`	the visitor clicks on the specified area
ondblclick	Same as for `onclick`	the visitor double clicks the specified area
onfocus	`a, area, button, input , label, select, textarea`	the visitor selects, clicks, or tabs to the specified element
onkeydown	`input` (of type name or password), `textarea`	the visitor types something in the specified element
onkeypress	`input` (of type name or password), `textarea`	the visitor types something in the specified element
onkeyup	`input` (of type name or password), `textarea`	the visitor lets go of the key after typing in the specified element
onload	`body, frameset`	the page is loaded in the browser
onmousedown	Same as for `onclick`	the visitor presses the mouse button down over the element
onmousemove	Same as for `onclick`	the visitor moves the mouse over the specified element after having pointed at it
onmouseout	Same as for `onclick`	the visitor moves the mouse away from the specified element after having been over it
onmouseover	Same as for `onclick`	the visitor points the mouse at the element
onmouseup	Same as for `onclick`	the visitor lets the mouse button go after having clicked on the element
onreset	`form` (*not* input of type `reset`)	the visitor clicks the form's reset button
onselect	`input` (of type name or password), `textarea`	the visitor selects one or more characters or words in the element
onsubmit	`form` (*not* input of type `submit`)	the visitor clicks the form's submit button
onunload	`body, frameset`	the browser loads a different page after the specified page had been loaded

(X)HTML
SYMBOLS AND CHARACTERS

D

As you saw in Chapter 21, *Symbols and Non-English Characters*, you can add symbols and characters that don't belong to your page's encoding or that can't be typed (like invisible characters), by inserting a *character reference*, that is, the symbol's associated number, hexadecimal number, or name in Unicode.

Since there are more than 65,000 characters in Unicode, printing out each one's numeric or hexadecimal reference would require a book of its own, and be rather unwieldy to boot. Instead, you can consult Unicode's site, *(www.unicode.org)* where the characters are neatly divided by language and theme.

I can, however, provide you with a list of the 252 named references (officially called *character entity references*, but also known as *entity references* or *named entity references*) that can be used in (X)HTML. You'll find the complete tables in this appendix, as well as on my Web site: *www.cookwood.com/entities/*. I have included the equivalent numeric codes for your reference. They are divided into categories that I hope will help make them easier to find. (Perhaps the easiest way to find the desired symbol is to go to the Web page cited above and use the Find command.)

Instructions for inserting these symbols and characters on your Web pages can be found in *Adding Characters from Outside the Encoding* on page 336.

Note that the tables were generated with a browser, for authenticity's sake, and thus appear slightly more pixelated than regular text in this book.

Characters with special meaning in HTML and XHTML

Symbol	Entity	Number	Description
&	&	&	ampersand
>	>	>	greater-than sign
<	<	<	less-than sign
"	"	"	quotation mark = APL quote

Accented characters, accents, and other diacritics from Western European Languages

Symbol	Entity	Number	Description
´	´	´	acute accent = spacing acute
¸	¸	¸	cedilla = spacing cedilla
ˆ	ˆ	ˆ	modifier letter circumflex accent
¯	¯	¯	macron = spacing macron = overline
·	·	·	middle dot = Georgian comma = Greek middle dot
˜	˜	˜	small tilde
¨	¨	¨	diaeresis = spacing diaeresis
Á	Á	Á	latin capital letter A with acute
á	á	á	latin small letter a with acute
Â	Â	Â	latin capital letter A with circumflex
â	â	â	latin small letter a with circumflex
Æ	Æ	Æ	latin capital letter AE
æ	æ	æ	latin small letter ae
À	À	À	latin capital letter A with grave
à	à	à	latin small letter a with grave
Å	Å	Å	latin capital letter A with ring above
å	å	å	latin small letter a with ring above
Ã	Ã	Ã	latin capital letter A with tilde
ã	ã	ã	latin small letter a with tilde
Ä	Ä	Ä	latin capital letter A with diaeresis
ä	ä	ä	latin small letter a with diaeresis

Accented characters, accents, and other diacritics from Western European Languages (continued)

Symbol	Entity	Number	Description
Ç	Ç	Ç	latin capital letter C with cedilla
ç	ç	ç	latin small letter c with cedilla
É	É	É	latin capital letter E with acute
é	é	é	latin small letter e with acute
Ê	Ê	Ê	latin capital letter E with circumflex
ê	ê	ê	latin small letter e with circumflex
È	È	È	latin capital letter E with grave
è	è	è	latin small letter e with grave
Ð	Ð	Ð	latin capital letter ETH
ð	ð	ð	latin small letter eth
Ë	Ë	Ë	latin capital letter E with diaeresis
ë	ë	ë	latin small letter e with diaeresis
Í	Í	Í	latin capital letter I with acute
í	í	í	latin small letter i with acute
Î	Î	Î	latin capital letter I with circumflex
î	î	î	latin small letter i with circumflex
Ì	Ì	Ì	latin capital letter I with grave
ì	ì	ì	latin small letter i with grave
Ï	Ï	Ï	latin capital letter I with diaeresis
ï	ï	ï	latin small letter i with diaeresis
Ñ	Ñ	Ñ	latin capital letter N with tilde
ñ	ñ	ñ	latin small letter n with tilde
Ó	Ó	Ó	latin capital letter O with acute
ó	ó	ó	latin small letter o with acute
Ô	Ô	Ô	latin capital letter O with circumflex
ô	ô	ô	latin small letter o with circumflex
Œ	Œ	Œ	latin capital ligature OE
œ	œ	œ	latin small ligature oe

Accented characters, accents, and other diacritics from Western European Languages (continued)

Symbol	Entity	Number	Description
Ò	&Ograve;	&#210;	latin capital letter O with grave
ò	&ograve;	&#242;	latin small letter o with grave
Ø	&Oslash;	&#216;	latin capital letter O slash
ø	&oslash;	&#248;	latin small letter o slash
Õ	&Otilde;	&#213;	latin capital letter O with tilde
õ	&otilde;	&#245;	latin small letter o with tilde
Ö	&Ouml;	&#214;	latin capital letter O with diaeresis
ö	&ouml;	&#246;	latin small letter o with diaeresis
Š	&Scaron;	&#352;	latin capital letter S with caron
š	&scaron;	&#353;	latin small letter s with caron
ß	&szlig;	&#223;	latin small letter sharp s = ess-zed
Þ	&THORN;	&#222;	latin capital letter THORN
þ	&thorn;	&#254;	latin small letter thorn
Ú	&Uacute;	&#218;	latin capital letter U with acute
ú	&uacute;	&#250;	latin small letter u with acute
Û	&Ucirc;	&#219;	latin capital letter U with circumflex
û	&ucirc;	&#251;	latin small letter u with circumflex
Ù	&Ugrave;	&#217;	latin capital letter U with grave
ù	&ugrave;	&#249;	latin small letter u with grave
Ü	&Uuml;	&#220;	latin capital letter U with diaeresis
ü	&uuml;	&#252;	latin small letter u with diaeresis
Ý	&Yacute;	&#221;	latin capital letter Y with acute
ý	&yacute;	&#253;	latin small letter y with acute
ÿ	&yuml;	&#255;	latin small letter y with diaeresis
Ÿ	&Yuml;	&#376;	latin capital letter Y with diaeresis

Punctuation characters

Symbol	Entity	Number	Description
¢	¢	¢	cent sign
¤	¤	¤	currency sign
€	€	€	euro sign
£	£	£	pound sign
¥	¥	¥	yen sign = yuan sign
¦	¦	¦	broken bar = broken vertical bar
•	•	•	bullet = black small circle
©	©	©	copyright sign
†	†	†	dagger
‡	‡	‡	double dagger
/	⁄	⁄	fraction slash
…	…	…	horizontal ellipsis = three dot leader
¡	¡	¡	inverted exclamation mark
ℑ	ℑ	ℑ	blackletter capital I = imaginary part
¿	¿	¿	inverted question mark
	‎	‎	left-to-right mark
—	—	—	em dash
–	–	–	en dash
¬	¬	¬	not sign
‾	‾	‾	overline = spacing overscore
ª	ª	ª	feminine ordinal indicator
º	º	º	masculine ordinal indicator
¶	¶	¶	pilcrow sign = paragraph sign
‰	‰	‰	per mille sign
′	′	′	prime = minutes = feet
″	″	″	double prime = seconds = inches
ℜ	ℜ	ℜ	blackletter capital R = real part symbol
®	®	®	registered sign = registered trade mark sign

Punctuation characters, continued

Symbol	Entity	Number	Description
®	®	®	registered sign = registered trade mark sign
	‏	‏	right-to-left mark
§	§	§	section sign
	­	­	soft hyphen = discretionary hyphen
¹	¹	¹	superscript one = superscript digit one
™	™	™	trade mark sign
℘	℘	℘	script capital P = power set = Weierstrass p
„	„	„	double low-9 quotation mark
«	«	«	left-pointing double angle quotation mark = left pointing guillemet
"	“	“	left double quotation mark
‹	‹	‹	single left-pointing angle quotation mark
'	‘	‘	left single quotation mark
»	»	»	right-pointing double angle quotation mark = right pointing guillemet
"	”	”	right double quotation mark
›	›	›	single right-pointing angle quotation mark
'	’	’	right single quotation mark
‚	‚	‚	single low-9 quotation mark
			em space
			en space
			no-break space = non-breaking space
			thin space
	‍	‍	zero width joiner
	‌	‌	zero width non-joiner

Mathematical and technical characters, (including Greek)

Symbol	Entity	Number	Description
°	°	°	degree sign
÷	÷	÷	division sign
½	½	½	fraction one half
¼	¼	¼	fraction one quarter
¾	¾	¾	fraction three quarters
≥	≥	≥	greater-than or equal to
≤	≤	≤	less-than or equal to
−	−	−	minus sign
²	²	²	superscript two = squared
³	³	³	superscript three = cubed
×	×	×	multiplication sign
ℵ	ℵ	ℵ	alef symbol = first transfinite cardinal
∧	∧	∧	logical and = wedge
∠	∠	∠	angle
≈	≈	≈	almost equal to = asymptotic to
∩	∩	∩	intersection = cap
≅	≅	≅	approximately equal to
∪	∪	∪	union = cup
∅	∅	∅	empty set = null set = diameter
≡	≡	≡	identical to
∃	∃	∃	there exists
f	ƒ	ƒ	latin small f with hook = function = florin
∀	∀	∀	for all
∞	∞	∞	infinity
∫	∫	∫	integral
∈	∈	∈	element of
⟨	⟨	〈	left-pointing angle bracket = bra
⌈	⌈	⌈	left ceiling = apl upstile
⌊	⌊	⌊	left floor = apl downstile

Mathematical and technical characters (including Greek), continued

Symbol	Entity	Number	Description
∗	∗	∗	asterisk operator
µ	µ	µ	micro sign
∇	∇	∇	nabla = backward difference
≠	≠	≠	not equal to
∋	∋	∋	contains as member
∉	∉	∉	not an element of
⊄	⊄	⊄	not a subset of
⊕	⊕	⊕	circled plus = direct sum
∨	∨	∨	logical or = vee
⊗	⊗	⊗	circled times = vector product
∂	∂	∂	partial differential
⊥	⊥	⊥	up tack = orthogonal to = perpendicular
±	±	±	plus-minus sign = plus-or-minus sign
∏	∏	∏	n-ary product = product sign
∝	∝	∝	proportional to
√	√	√	square root = radical sign
〉	⟩	〉	right-pointing angle bracket = ket
⌉	⌉	⌉	right ceiling
⌋	⌋	⌋	right floor
·	⋅	⋅	dot operator
∼	∼	∼	tilde operator = varies with = similar to
⊂	⊂	⊂	subset of
⊆	⊆	⊆	subset of or equal to
∑	∑	∑	n-ary sumation
⊃	⊃	⊃	superset of
⊇	⊇	⊇	superset of or equal to
∴	∴	∴	therefore

Mathematical and technical characters (including Greek), continued

Symbol	Entity	Number	Description
Α	Α	Α	greek capital letter alpha
α	α	α	greek small letter alpha
Β	Β	Β	greek capital letter beta
β	β	β	greek small letter beta
Χ	Χ	Χ	greek capital letter chi
χ	χ	χ	greek small letter chi
Δ	Δ	Δ	greek capital letter delta
δ	δ	δ	greek small letter delta
Ε	Ε	Ε	greek capital letter epsilon
ε	ε	ε	greek small letter epsilon
Η	Η	Η	greek capital letter eta
η	η	η	greek small letter eta
Γ	Γ	Γ	greek capital letter gamma
γ	γ	γ	greek small letter gamma
Ι	Ι	Ι	greek capital letter iota
ι	ι	ι	greek small letter iota
Κ	Κ	Κ	greek capital letter kappa
κ	κ	κ	greek small letter kappa
Λ	Λ	Λ	greek capital letter lambda
λ	λ	λ	greek small letter lambda
Μ	Μ	Μ	greek capital letter mu
μ	μ	μ	greek small letter mu
Ν	Ν	Ν	greek capital letter nu
ν	ν	ν	greek small letter nu
Ω	Ω	Ω	greek capital letter omega
ω	ω	ω	greek small letter omega
Ο	Ο	Ο	greek capital letter omicron
ο	ο	ο	greek small letter omicron

Mathematical and technical characters (including Greek), continued

Symbol	Entity	Number	Description
Φ	Φ	Φ	greek capital letter phi
φ	φ	φ	greek small letter phi
Π	Π	Π	greek capital letter pi
π	π	π	greek small letter pi
ϖ	ϖ	ϖ	greek pi symbol
Ψ	Ψ	Ψ	greek capital letter psi
ψ	ψ	ψ	greek small letter psi
Ρ	Ρ	Ρ	greek capital letter rho
ρ	ρ	ρ	greek small letter rho
Σ	Σ	Σ	greek capital letter sigma
σ	σ	σ	greek small letter sigma
ς	ς	ς	greek small letter final sigma
Τ	Τ	Τ	greek capital letter tau
τ	τ	τ	greek small letter tau
Θ	Θ	Θ	greek capital letter theta
θ	θ	θ	greek small letter theta
ϑ	ϑ	ϑ	greek small letter theta symbol
ϒ	ϒ	ϒ	greek upsilon with hook symbol
Υ	Υ	Υ	greek capital letter upsilon
υ	υ	υ	greek small letter upsilon
Ξ	Ξ	Ξ	greek capital letter xi
ξ	ξ	ξ	greek small letter xi
Ζ	Ζ	Ζ	greek capital letter zeta
ζ	ζ	ζ	greek small letter zeta

Shapes and Arrows

Symbol	Entity	Number	Description
↵	↵	↵	downwards arrow with corner leftwards = carriage return
↓	↓	↓	downwards arrow
⇓	⇓	⇓	downwards double arrow
↔	↔	↔	left right arrow
⇔	⇔	⇔	left right double arrow
←	←	←	leftwards arrow
⇐	⇐	⇐	leftwards double arrow
→	→	→	rightwards arrow
⇒	⇒	⇒	rightwards double arrow
↑	↑	↑	upwards arrow
⇑	⇑	⇑	upwards double arrow
♣	♣	♣	black club suit = shamrock
♦	♦	♦	black diamond suit
♥	♥	♥	black heart suit = valentine
♠	♠	♠	black spade suit
◊	◊	◊	lozenge

The information in these tables is Copyright © 1994-2002 W3C ® (Massachusetts Institute of Technology, Institut National de Recherche en Informatique et en Automatique, Keio University), All Rights Reserved. *http://www.w3.org/Consortium/Legal/*

HEXADECIMALS

Hundreds
  Tens
    Ones

127

$$1 \times 100 = 100$$
$$2 \times 10 = 20$$
$$\underline{7 \times 1 = 7}$$
$$\text{Total} = 127$$

256's
  Sixteens
    Ones

7F

$$0 \times 256 = 0$$
$$7 \times 16 = 112$$
$$\underline{F\ (15) \times 1 = 15}$$
$$\text{Total} = 127$$

Figure E.1 *Hexadecimal numbers are base 16, that is the first digit (starting on the right) represents the ones, the second digit represents the 16's, the third digit represents the 256's, and so on.*

"Regular" numbers are based on the base 10 system, that is, there are ten symbols (what we call "numbers"): 0, 1, 2, 3, 4, 5, 6, 7, 8, and 9. To represent numbers greater than 9, we use a combination of these symbols where the first digit specifies how many *ones,* the second digit (to the left) specifies how many *tens,* and so on.

In the hexadecimal system, which is base 16, there are sixteen symbols: 0, 1, 2, 3, 4, 5, 6, 7, 8, 9, a, b, c, d, e, and f. To represent numbers greater than *f* (which in base 10 we understand as *15*), we again use a combination of symbols. This time the first digit specifies how many ones, but the second digit (again, to the left) specifies how many sixteens. Thus, 10 in the hexadecimal system means one *sixteen* and no *ones*. In the base 10 system, it'd be *16*.

In (X)HTML and CSS, hexadecimal numbers are used to define colors *(see page 126)* and to insert symbols *(see page 336)*. While you can convert hexadecimal numbers by hand, I've also included a table to help you quickly look up a number's hexadecimal equivalent.

Hexadecimal Equivalents

#	Hex.	#	Hex.	#	Hex.	#	Hex.	#	Hex.	#	Hex.	#	Hex.	#	Hex.
0	00	32	20	64	40	96	60	128	80	160	A0	192	C0	224	E0
1	01	33	21	65	41	97	61	129	81	161	A1	193	C1	225	E1
2	02	34	22	66	42	98	62	130	82	162	A2	194	C2	226	E2
3	03	35	23	67	43	99	63	131	83	163	A3	195	C3	227	E3
4	04	36	24	68	44	100	64	132	84	164	A4	196	C4	228	E4
5	05	37	25	69	45	101	65	133	85	165	A5	197	C5	229	E5
6	06	38	26	70	46	102	66	134	86	166	A6	198	C6	230	E6
7	07	39	27	71	47	103	67	135	87	167	A7	199	C7	231	E7
8	08	40	28	72	48	104	68	136	88	168	A8	200	C8	232	E8
9	09	41	29	73	49	105	69	137	89	169	A9	201	C9	233	E9
10	0A	42	2A	74	4A	106	6A	138	8A	170	AA	202	CA	234	EA
11	0B	43	2B	75	4B	107	6B	139	8B	171	AB	203	CB	235	EB
12	0C	44	2C	76	4C	108	6C	140	8C	172	AC	204	CC	236	EC
13	0D	45	2D	77	4D	109	6D	141	8D	173	AD	205	CD	237	ED
14	0E	46	2E	78	4E	110	6E	142	8E	174	AE	206	CE	238	EE
15	0F	47	2F	79	4F	111	6F	143	8F	175	AF	207	CF	239	EF
16	10	48	30	80	50	112	70	144	90	176	B0	208	D0	240	F0
17	11	49	31	81	51	113	71	145	91	177	B1	209	D1	241	F1
18	12	50	32	82	52	114	72	146	92	178	B2	210	D2	242	F2
19	13	51	33	83	53	115	73	147	93	179	B3	211	D3	243	F3
20	14	52	34	84	54	116	74	148	94	180	B4	212	D4	244	F4
21	15	53	35	85	55	117	75	149	95	181	B5	213	D5	245	F5
22	16	54	36	86	56	118	76	150	96	182	B6	214	D6	246	F6
23	17	55	37	87	57	119	77	151	97	183	B7	215	D7	247	F7
24	18	56	38	88	58	120	78	152	98	184	B8	216	D8	248	F8
25	19	57	39	89	59	121	79	153	99	185	B9	217	D9	249	F9
26	1A	58	3A	90	5A	122	7A	154	9A	186	BA	218	DA	250	FA
27	1B	59	3B	91	5B	123	7B	155	9B	187	BB	219	DB	251	FB
28	1C	60	3C	92	5C	124	7C	156	9C	188	BC	220	DC	252	FC
29	1D	61	3D	93	5D	125	7D	157	9D	189	BD	221	DD	253	FD
30	1E	62	3E	94	5E	126	7E	158	9E	190	BE	222	DE	254	FE
31	1F	63	3F	95	5F	127	7F	159	9F	191	BF	223	DF	255	FF

So, to use this chart, imagine you want to find the hex value for a color with 35% red, 0% green, and 50% blue. The percentages are relative to 255, so 35% x 255 = 89. Now, find the hexadecimal equivalent of 89, near the bottom of the third column above. So for red, we have 59. Green is easy; 0 = 00. For blue, we again have to multiply the percentage by 255 to get the numerical value. 50% x 255 is 127 (more or less). Then find the hex value for 127, at the very bottom of the fourth column. So, the blue is 7F. The final step is to write it all together: #59007F, which will get us a fine dark purple, precisely 35% red, 0% green, and 50% blue.

Hexadecimal Equivalents

(X)HTML Tools

The lists on the following pages are by no means exhaustive. There are literally hundreds of programs, some commercial, some shareware, and some Open Source, of varying quality, that you can use as you design and create your Web pages. If you don't find what you're looking for on these pages, jump to any search service on the Web (e.g., *www.google.com*) and look for *Web tools, Web graphics*, or whatever it is you need.

(X)HTML Editors

You can use *any* text editor to write (X)HTML, including TextEdit on the Mac, WordPad for Windows, or vi in Unix systems. However, you might find it useful to try a text editor that is specialized for writing (X)HTML. Some let you work right in a "browser-view" mode, dragging elements around the screen. These are called WYSIWYG. Others are purely text-based but offer powerful shortcut tools for writing and editing (X)HTML.

What (X)HTML editors offer	Disadvantages of (X)HTML editors
Dedicated (X)HTML editors offer the following advantages over simple text editors (of course, not every (X)HTML editor has every feature): • they insert opening and closing tags with a single click • they check and verify syntax in your (X)HTML and CSS • they allow you to add attributes by clicking buttons instead of typing words in a certain order in a certain place in the document • they offer varying degrees of WYSIWYG display of your Web page • they correct mistakes in existing (X)HTML pages • they make it easy to use special characters • they color code elements, attributes, and values, making them easy to edit and proofread	These extra features come at a price, however. Some things that may annoy you about (X)HTML editors is that • they don't always support the full (X)HTML or CSS specs 100% • they are more difficult to learn, and less intuitive than they promise • they cost money (all simple text editors are included free with their respective system software) • they use up more space on disk and more memory • some add proprietary information (like *their* name, for example), and tags to the (X)HTML document • some eliminate tags that they don't understand—even if the tags are part of the standard (X)HTML specifications • some suggest using non-standard or deprecated tags without explaining the implications of their use.

(X)HTML Editors

WYSIWYG		
Macromedia Dreamweaver	$400. Probably the most popular editor among Web professionals. Now belongs to Adobe. For Macintosh and Windows.	*http://www.adobe.com/ products/dreamweaver/* demo available
Adobe GoLive	$400. Purportedly more friendly than Dreamweaver. For Macintosh and Windows.	*http://www.adobe.com/ products/golive/* demo available
NetObjects Fusion	$200. NetObjects WYSIWYG editor for professional Web masters. Windows only.	*http://www.netobjects.com/* demo available
Text Based		
BBEdit	$200. Excellent HTML editor from Bare Bones Software. The most popular non-WYSIWYG (X)HTML editor. Macintosh only.	*http://www.barebones.com* demo available
HTML-Kit	Free. ("Registered" version is $55). Chami.com. Hundreds of plugins available for added features. Windows only.	*http://www.chami.com/ html-kit/*
jEdit	Free (Open Source). Many plugins available for added features. Java based and so runs on Mac, Windows, Linux, etc.	*http://www.jedit.org/*

Images and Graphics

Name	Description	URL
Yahoo	List of sites with graphics	*http://dir.yahoo.com/Arts/Design_Arts/Graphic_Design/Web_Page_Design_and_Layout/Graphics/*
Flickr	Searchable database of images (check rights)	*http://www.flickr.com/*
Google	Site that searches the Web for images that fit your criteria	*http://images.google.com* or go to *http://www.google.com* and click the Images button

Graphics Tools

Name	Description	URL
Adobe Photoshop (M, W)	$650. Excellent, all-purpose image editing program. Version CS2 includes Image-Ready, Adobe's Web graphics program	*http://www.adobe.com/products/photoshop/* demo available
Adobe Photoshop Elements (M, W)	$80. A remarkably robust, consumer-end version of the excellent Adobe Photoshop	Windows: *http://www.adobe.com/products/ photoshopel/* Mac: *http://www.adobe.com/products/photoshopelmac/*
Macromedia Fireworks	$300. A specialized graphics program for creating Web images	*http://www.macromedia.com/software/fireworks/* demo available
Macromedia Flash	Basic: $400; Professional: $700. For creating Web animations.	*http://www.macromedia.com/software/flash/* demo available
Paint Shop Pro (W)	$80. Corel. (Previously a software program from Jasc Software.) Image editing program for Windows.	*http://www.corel.com/* demo available
GraphicConverter (M)	$30. Thorsten Lemke's image editor for Macintosh. Reads and writes an incredible array of graphics formats, including Progressive JPEG, GIF89a (Animated), etc.	*http://www.lemkesoft.com/en/graphcon.htm* demo available
LView Pro (W)	$40. Popular shareware graphics program.	*http://www.lview.com*

INDEX

Symbols

& (ampersand) *32*
  and XHTML *337*
* (asterisk)
  comments in CSS *121*
  for wild card selector *139*
`@charset` rules *128*
`@import` rules *132*
  and image replacement *196*
  for handhelds *204*
  for print *210*
  media specific *133*
`@media` rules *133*, *210*
\ (backslash)
  for escaping characters in style sheets *332*
  in JavaScript *315*
[ ] (brackets), for selecting based on attributes *147*
, (comma), for grouping selectors *148*
-- (dashes), in comments *67*, *131*
!-- (exclamation point and dashes) *67*, *131*
/ (forward slash)
  comments in CSS *121*
  for (X)HTML *28*
  HTML vs. XHTML *38*
  in URL *35*
> (greater than symbol)
  character reference for *337*
  for child selector *142*
  (X)HTML elements *28*
< (less than symbol)
  character reference for *337*
  (X)HTML elements *28*
` ` (non-breaking space) *62*, *237*, *251*
  and empty cells in tables *237*
. (period), for class selector *140*
| (pipe symbol), in selectors *147*
+ (plus), for adjacent sibling selectors *143*
# (sharp)
  anchors *107*
  for id selector *140*
3D positioning *183*

A

a element *104–115*
  for multimedia files *285*
A List Apart, Web magazine *39*, *192*, *305*
  switching style sheets *130*
`abbr` element *78*
abbreviations
  describing *78*
  for languages *338*
  hexadecimal colors *126*
absolute positioning *179*
  See also page layout

absolute units *125*
absolute URLs *36*
  See also URLs
accented characters. *See* characters, special
accessibility *22*
  importance of *39*
`accesskey` attribute
  in a element *112*
  in `area` element *118*
  in form elements *278*
Acrobat *282*
`acronym` element *78*
acronyms, describing *78*
`action` attribute, in `form` element *254*
active images *276*
active links, color of *146*
`:active` pseudo-class *146*
ActiveX controls
  and background play *293*
  and `object` element *282*
Address bar, icon in *102*
`address` element *70*
Adobe GoLive *435*
Adobe Photoshop and Photoshop Elements *87*, *88–89*, *436*
  adding space around images *99*
  and image size *92*, *95*
  for examples *87*
Adobe Systems, membership in W3C *17*
aggregators
  description *375*, *377*
  subscribing to RSS feeds with *396*
Aladdin Systems. *See* Allume Systems
`align` attribute
  in `caption` element *229*
  in `div` element *79*
  in hn tag *61*
  in hr element *101*
  in `img` element
    for aligning *100*
    for floating images *96*
  in `legend` element *260*
  in p element *62*
  in `table` element
    for centering *234*
    for text wrap *235*
  in table elements *238–239*
aligning
  cells *238–239*
    with column groups *246–247*
  header cells *247*
  headers *61*
  images *100*
  paragraphs *62*
  text *61*, *62*, *165*
  vertically *188*

Index

Colophon:

I wrote and laid out this book entirely in Adobe FrameMaker 6 (on a G4 Mac running Classic!). Although I find Frame increasingly awkward, I could never have done all of the cross references, figure numbering, and especially the index without it.

I viewed the examples on all major browsers on both platforms. I used Parallels WorkStation to run Windows right in my MacBook. I took screen captures with Snapz Pro X and then cleaned them up with Adobe Photoshop CS. I used Adobe Illustrator to create the line drawings. The font faces in this book are various weights of Garamond and Futura.

Except for the ones in other people's Web sites (obviously), and the nice illustration in Figure 16.2 on page 228 by Andreu Cabré, the videos, photos, and drawings in this book are of my own creation, though I'm sometimes embarrassed to admit it. You can see more of my photographs at *http://www.flickr.com/photos/cookwood*